Brown Sugar

Donald Bogle

**Over One Hundred Years
of America's Black
Female Superstars**

New Expanded &
Updated Edition

continuum

NEW YORK • LONDON

2007

The Continuum International Publishing Group Inc
80 Maiden Lane, New York, NY 10038

The Continuum International Publishing Group Ltd
The Tower Building, 11 York Road, London SE1 7NX

Cover and text design by Tosh Thomas Hall

Printed in the United States of America

www.continuumbooks.com

791.43
B675b
2007

Library of Congress Cataloging-in-Publication Data

Bogle, Donald.
  Brown Sugar: over one hundred years of America's Black female superstars / Donald Bogle.
    p. cm.
  Includes bibliographical references and index.
  ISBN-13: 978-0-8264-1675-9 (pbk. : alk. paper)
  ISBN-10: 0-8264-1675-6 (pbk. : alk. paper)
  1. African American entertainers–Biography. 2. Women entertainers–United States–Biography. I. Title. II. Title: Over 100 years of America's Black female superstars.

PN2286.B6 2007
791.092'273–dc22
[B]
                                                          2007016738

Grateful acknowledgment is made to the following for the loan of photographs used in this book: Photofest, Lincoln Center (Library of the Performing Arts), and the author's personal collection.

Grateful acknowledgment is made to the following for permission to reprint excepts from previously published material: Atheneum Publishes, Black Manhattan, by James Welden Johnson copyright © 1930 by James Welden Johnson, copyright renewed in 1958 by Mrs. James Welden Johnson; Dodd, Mead and Co., Inc., Black and White Baby by Bobby Short, copyright © 1971 by Bobby Short; Little, Brown and Co. in association with The Atlantic Monthly Press, Celebrating the Duke & Louis, Bessie, Billie, Bird, Carmen, Miles, Dizzy & Other Heroes by Ralph J. Gleason, copyright © 1975 by the Estate of Ralph J. Gleason, Jane R. Gleason, executrix; The New York Times © 1940/77/78 by The New York Times; The New Yorker, a passage from "Tables for Two" by Douglas Watt in the October 30, 1948, issue; The Viking Press, My Lord, What a Morning, by Marian Anderson, copyright © 1956 by Marian Anderson; The Viking Press, Paris Was Yesterday by Janet Flanner, copyright 1925-1939 (inclusive) © 1972 by The New Yorker Magazine, Inc., copyright 1934, 1935, 1940, copyright © renewed 1962, 1963, 1969 by Janet Flanner.

Frontispiece: Billie Holiday

This book is dedicated to a number of very

special women in my life: to my mother,

to my sisters Jacqueline and Roslynne,

to Marie Kanalas Bogle, to Susan Peterson

and Carol Leonard, and to the one and only

Marie Dutton Brown, and to the

sensational Marian-Etoile Watson

Contents

Introduction   7

Acknowledgments   10

1900 – 1920 Beginnings   13

The 1920s Personas   27

The 1930s Pop Myths   59

The 1940s Social Symbols   91

The 1950s Sex Symbols   119

The 1960s Political Symbols   147

The 1970s Survivors   177

The 1980s Old School Goddesses
of Gliltz, New School Ingenues   211

The 1990s Million Dollar Babies   271

The 2000s Mavens of the New Millennium   339

Notes   366

Select Bibliography   370

Index of Names   373

Introduction

When I was a kid, I was fascinated by black entertainers and show business, but mainly by African Americans in the movies. I spent most of my Saturday afternoons at the local movie house, seeing as many movies as I could. Or I sat at home propped up in front of the television set watching old films with stars like Hattie McDaniel and Eddie "Rochester" Anderson. On those Saturdays when there wasn't anything good at the movies or on television, I settled for going with my father to his office. My father was the Vice President and Advertising Director of *The Philadelphia Tribune*, one of the oldest African American newspapers in the country. While he was busy working, I would prowl around, almost always finding my way to the newspaper's makeshift "library" where I leafed through back issues of two, three, and if I was lucky, sometimes five or ten years before. One day I came across a photograph of a woman with a gardenia in her hair. I had never seen a face like hers: open, lush, romantic. The caption referred to her as Lady Day, and the headline over the article read that she had died in New York. There were other photographs tracing a career that began in the 1930s. I was puzzled because, as someone addicted to movies, I didn't know very much about entertainers outside the world of film and television. Yet, I had a vague recollection of my mother having commented on Holiday at various times. When I asked my father who this woman was, he looked at me as if to say, "Where have you been all your life?" He said little that day. And I was not sure what the newspaper fuss was all about. But later when I heard a Billie Holiday record, I immediately knew that here indeed was an extraordinary woman. I still had many unanswered questions about exactly who she was and what she had done. Aside from her artistry, what intrigued me most was how a black woman could have become such a national heroine, whose every move was covered by the press. I had never read about such a figure before, and I knew I would learn more about her as time went on.

At *The Tribune* on other Saturdays, I discovered other black personalities: Paul Robeson, Fredi Washington, Ethel Waters, Marian Anderson, Duke Ellington, Mahalia Jackson, and, of course, Dorothy Dandridge, whom I had already heard much about at home and whose face had graced the covers of *Ebony*. I got caught up in the careers of all these personalities, the moments when they first became successful, the years they peaked as artists, and the periods afterward when some slipped into decline. The old personalities seemed to have such a great sense of style. Often they were decked out in extravagant, elegant clothes. And the smiles on their faces led me to believe they had found the secret for enjoying life. But I was troubled and haunted by many of their personal difficulties and tragedies. Many of the names and faces I read about were no longer spoken of. Except for scattered comments in jazz histories, there were no reference books that commented on their experiences, their careers, and mainly their images. Even then, I could not understand why, at that time, no books had then been written about the contributions Black Americans had made to popular culture. Perhaps more than any other aspect of American life, popular culture had consistently been invigorated by black achievements and innovations, not only in music but in dance, sports, and movies. I knew there were stories that had not yet been told. Billie Holiday's was only one of many.

Years later, when I wrote my first book, *Toms, Coons, Mulattoes, Mammies, and Bucks: An Interpretive History of Blacks in American Films*, I had a chance to tell some of the stories that interested me, those of black performers working in American motion pictures. Afterward, however, I still felt that there was more to say, additional comments to make on those artists. But I was not sure on what I wanted to focus.

More than anything else, what made me decide to write about black female entertainers was an extensive series of lecture tours that I did after the publication of my first book. At innumerable college campuses around the country, I spoke on black film history. I went to all types of schools: many, mainly white; others, all black; others, well-integrated. I traveled to some forty-two different states and every major American city, as well as towns and communities I had never heard of. What always impressed and sometimes surprised me most were the great number of questions asked about black female entertainers—in movies and out. The questions were endless. How did Josephine Baker's career begin? Why had Baker never been as great a sensation in the States as she was in Europe? Why and when had she first gone abroad? What did Ethel Waters do before she became the prototypical black matriarch in films? Had she ever really been a skinny, slinky vixen called Sweet Mama Stringbean? What was Marian Anderson's People's Concert all about? Why hadn't Dorothy Dandridge made more movies? Who were Bessie Smith and Ma Rainey?

I knew the answers to many questions, but there was much I did not know. I was certain of one thing however: that many Black American female entertainers were already legendary figures about whom there was great interest. I also knew that there was no book around that told their history and their contributions. Theirs was a complex story too, because it no only involved their careers but touched also on America's attitudes about gender and race.

The college groups' curiosity sparked my own. And I finally decided I wanted to write a book that answered not only their questions but some of my own—the very kind I had privately asked myself as a kid when I first saw Billie Holiday's picture.

It would be impossible to discuss the work of every black female performer, so I decided to concentrate on the important figures—those women who captured the imagination of millions and became bona fide legends. As I worked on the book I approached each woman individually. Often information on a woman's career was not enough. In some cases (as with Billie Holiday, Josephine Baker, Ethel Waters, Dorothy Dandridge, even Diana Ross and the Supremes, and later Tina Turner), it was important to comment on or examine their private lives and their personalities. In other cases (as with Marian Anderson and Lena Horne), it was important to comment on their public images and personal styles. With all the women, though, I wanted to show the effect they had on the periods in which they performed—and to show, too, how they dazzled audiences decade after decade. Most importantly, *Brown Sugar* is an examination of images and how audiences were moved or inspired often by a fusion of the public and private personas of these women.

For this new, expanded edition of *Brown Sugar*, I have added three new chapters. The original *Brown Sugar* ended at the start of the 1980s. Now the story continues with an examination of the careers and lives of such remarkable performers as Angela Bassett, Anna Deavere Smith, Janet Jackson, Halle Berry, Queen Latifah, Beyoncé, and, perhaps the greatest of the new era divas, Whitney Houston. I've made a few changes in the original text but not many. Rereading the book has been like revisiting an earlier time in my life. When *Brown Sugar* was first published, the word *diva* was not in widespread usage. I have vivid memories of an interview in Washington, during a promotion tour for the book. I was asked about the term *diva*. When I explained that the word *diva* had been around for quite some time and was mostly used to describe operatic prima donnas, the interviewer drew a total blank, as if unable to comprehend what I was saying. Today *diva* is a word so widely used that it has almost become a cliché. But I was using *dark diva* to describe women who lived by a certain code with a larger than life attitude and style that seemed very much tied to an African American cultural–show business tradition. In fact, I had first heard the term used by an African American female performer to describe black female stars of the past. For the most part, I have left the term *dark diva* in the first part of the book exactly as it was used originally.

What struck me most when writing the three new chapters for this edition was the way in which the themes of race and racism did not seem – on the surface – as much a part of traditional diva life narrative as it had in the past. Certainly, the new stars of the last part of 20th century and the early years of the 21st came of age with opportunities awaiting them that had been denied to the women who had preceded them. Generally, the new stars also did not have to deal with the blatant kind of racism that their predecessors endured and fought. Many past stars, like Ethel Waters and Josephine Baker, had grown up in abject poverty. Discrimination and racial boundaries were a part of their everyday lives. Even once they attained stardom, women like Waters or Billie Holiday had been forced to use back doors at their engagements and when traveling through the South, often stayed at colored boarding houses because there were no white hotels that would accept them. A performer like Baker had discovered in Europe the type of stardom that was denied her in her own country. She never let anyone forget that either. And stars such as Bessie Smith and Ma Rainey performed almost exclusively for African American audiences. For women of the past, it was always a struggle to break down barriers – to get to Broadway, to perform at the big nightclubs, and to play leading roles in movies – and clear the way not only for themselves but the women who followed. Their struggles and their achievements were all the more impressive because of the way they confronted and ultimately changed certain racial attitudes.

The life narratives of some stars of the latter part of the 20th century and the early part of the 21st – such women as Whitney Houston, Janet Jackson, Beyoncé, Lauryn Hill, and Alicia Keys – appear to be free of the debilitating effects of poverty. Many of the women grew up in middle-class families. That's true even of Janet Jackson, though her family would have to be described, at best, as an atypical middle-class unit. But there were others such as Mary J. Blige who grew up in tight, economically difficult circumstances. Though her childhood didn't have the horrors of those of Baker or Waters, Blige in all likelihood would be quick to say her childhood was hardly a bed or roses. Regardless, such stars as Blige and Queen Latifah as well as Whitney Houston understood that racism, in its less blatant form, still existed and had to be combated. One only has to see some of their public statements on the subject.

At the same time, where the entertainment world has remained most sharply tied to the past is that although there are African American women like the successful producer Debra Martin Chase and although African American men such as Sean Combs, Andre Harrell, Jay-Z, and Damon Dash have made great impacts in the music business, the entertainment industry is still dominated by white male executives. Those African American women coming to prominence have still had to battle attitudes about gender and race, and most still find themselves constantly in a struggle to define themselves on their own terms. Nowhere has this fact been more apparent than in Hollywood. Actresses like Whoopi Goldberg and Halle Berry have walked off with Oscars. But even they still discovered that significant roles in the film capital were limited for them, not as much so as had been the case with Dorothy Dandridge in the 1950s but still restricted nonetheless. That has clearly been most apparent in the film career of Angela Bassett. In fact, Bassett's struggles and the way a later generation viewed her artistic integrity helped create a distinct public persona for her, similar to that of the great Cicely Tyson in the 1970s and 1980s. Bassett, like Tyson, has been considered something of an incorruptible artist. Regardless in the early part of the 21st century, the experiences of African American women in Hollywood remained the most blatant example of the way in which some aspects of entertainment have not changed, at least not enough. Still, the great stars of the late 20th century and early 21st have managed, like their predecessors, to survive and endure and often to give audiences personal messages and personal visions of the way life is *and* the way it might be.

All in all, the original years of research and writing of the first edition of *Brown Sugar* and the new period of research and writing of this edition have been a hectic, invigorating, trying time, but also greatly challenging and satisfying. All the women covered in this book have been on a quest: to discover who they were through their work. They all had ups and downs. It's been exhilarating to be able to go along with them on that quest again – to see how some stumbled and fell, but how most were always able to pull themselves back up and continue on.

Acknowledgments

I would like to extend my gratitude to various people who helped me while I was writing this book. Foremost, I thank my first editor, Laura Dearborn, whose comments were always intelligent, sensitive, and encouraging. I would also like to thank my editor, Harriet Bell, as well as the following: David Jackson of the Studio Museum in Harlem; Jerald Silverhardt of Hush Productions; and, of course, the staffs of the Schomburg Center for Research in Black Culture and at the Library of Performing Arts at Lincoln Center. My gratitude is also extended to Bettina Glasgow Batchleor, Cheryll Greene, Ann Marie Cunningham, Lester Glassner, Alberta Hunter, Gloria Foster, Barney Josephson, Fredi Washington, Vivian Dandridge, Carol Scott Leonard, Susan Peterson, Bobby Short, Catherine Bogle Garcia, Jeanne Moutoussamy Ashe, Monty Arnold, Barbara Reynolds, Herma Ross, Anna Deveare Smith, Eric Poindexter, Ronald Mason, Linda Doll Tarrant, Zeffie Fowler, Robert Bogle, Brad Shiley, Frank Driggs, Cheryl Dare, and Elaine Markson. And final special thanks go to David Anthony Stewart, Marian Watson, Henry Ramdess, Arthur Rossi, and dear Sally, who one evening asked that I take her to see Josephine Baker on a return appearance in New York. I balked at first, but, God, did I glow afterward!

For this new expanded, updated edition of *Brown Sugar*, I would like to express my gratitude to a number of people who were of great assistance (and often great encouragement) as I brought this book to publication. Foremost, I have to thank my editor Evander Lomke. Not only has he been knowledgeable and sensitive to the material, but he has also been diligent in helping with all aspects of the book, from providing suggestions on the text and photographs to the design itself. Perhaps best of all, he's been patient! It seemed to take even longer to complete this new edition than it had been to do the original. I'd also like to thank the staff at Continuum International for their time and their skills as I worked on this edition, especially Gabriella Page-Fort, who helped during long sessions as we sorted through photographs and deftly handled the many details of production; Amy Wagner, who proofread the book; Thelma Frederick-Stewart, who always knew where everyone was; and Ed Suthon, Executive Vice President and North American Marketing Director. Also, thanks to Jennifer Glosser, of Momentum, for her unparalleled composition and design skills; Tosh Thomas Hall; and to Carol Darwin Deason for thoughtful indexing. Many of the photographs and other memorabilia in the book are from my own collection. But many are also from the collection of Photofest. And I am deeply indebted to Howard Mandelbaum and his staff at Photofest, including his brother Ron Mandelbaum and also Theresa Demick. My visits to Photofest were always an exciting adventure as I went through photo after photo, searching for the right picture. Howard's knowledge and enthusiasm have been (as always) greatly appreciated. Again I'd like to thank the staff at the Schomburg Center for Research in Black Culture, especially my friend Sharon Howard, who goes beyond the call of duty to be helpful. I'd also like to thank again the staff at the Library of Performing Arts at Lincoln Center. I also have to acknowledge my friends and associates at Turner Classic Movies. While I was working on this new edition, I co-hosted the series *Race and Hollywood* for TCM and was happy to have the opportunity to view again the films of some women included in the first edition of *Brown Sugar*. So my gratitude goes to Jeanne Franz, Dena Krupinsky, TCM host Robert Osborne, Darcy Hettrich, and especially to TCM's Vice President Charlie Tabesh, who originated the idea for the series, and also to Jennifer Dargan, now at CNN. My former students David Aglow and Zac Kline have also done fine jobs of research as did Kim Mason, who was excellent at navigating her way on the Internet to locate important information. Also helpful were Olga James (the extraordinary singer who played Cindy Lou in the film *Carmen Jones*) and the fantastic trumpeter Clora Bryant. Dorothy Nicholas Morrow and her late husband Byron Morrow, Rae Rossini, and Dorothy Hughes McConnell have proved to be more helpful and inspiring than they may have realized. My former researcher, now a director, Phil Bertelsen was exceptionally helpful as I wrote the new material and often tossed ideas around with him. And, of course, I have to thank my good friend and producer-extraordinaire, Debra Martin Chase, with whom it is always stimulating and enlightening to discuss American popular culture. I have to express again my gratitude to the late Geri Branton, whom I first met while writing my biography of Dorothy Dandridge and who understood the old Black Hollywood better than anyone else I have ever known. She was an extraordinary woman and an extraordinary friend. I also would like to extend my gratitude to Joerg Klebe, executive director of German Educational Television, who was the executive producer of the four-part PBS series based on *Brown Sugar* and who, despite the various headaches and hassles of the production, saw *Brown Sugar*, the series, through to its completion.

My gratitude is also extended to the great agent Marie Dutton Brown, to whom this book is dedicated; to my other editor, Elisabeth Dyssegaard, who has always been insightful and encouraging; to Jerald Silverhardt, the best Hollywood contact imaginable—he can track down information on such about anybody; to Janet Alhanti, one of the country's great acting teachers and coaches, with whom it is always a pleasure to discuss the performances of various actresses and actors; to Bruce Goldstein, of New York's Film Forum, once again a valuable source of information; to my colleagues in the Department of Dramatic Writing at New York University's Tisch School of the Arts, especially David Ranghelli, Janet Neipris, Mark Dickerman, and the department Chair, Richard Wesley; to my colleagues at the Center for Africana Studies at the University of Pennsylvania, especially Carol Davis.

No book is ever completed without the help and encouragement of family, friends, and associates. So it is a pleasure to express my gratitude to the following: Bob Silverstein, my first editor on my book *Toms, Coons, Mulattoes, Mammies, and Bucks* and now a great friend; Fred Charleston of E Entertainment; my good friends Sarah Orrick and Nels Johnson; Alan Sukoenig and Hiroko Hatanaka; dear Barbara Reynolds (I could not ask for a better friend); Herma Ross Shorty; Robert Katz and Jay Peterson of K2 Pictures; Dr. Harry Ford and Peg Henehan; Luellen Fletcher; Rigmor Newman Nicholas; Yemaya Bogle; Shaaron Bogle; my former teaching assistant and now good friend Josslyn Luckett; Ayana Charleston; Hassan Charleston; Martha Orrick and her husband, Jim Malcolm; Martin Radburd; Heidi Stack; Leah Hunter; Daniel Beer; John Dudley Bogle Jr.; the irrepressible Dr. Clisson Woods; Jeanne Bogle Charleston; Janet Bogle Schenck; Lori Stimpson Guile; Roger Bogle; Gerald Grant Bogle; Jay Bogle; Mechelle Mosley Palmer; Mariskia Bogle; Mark Mosley; Robert Bogle Jr.; Jerry Schenck; Grace and Jim Frankowsky; David Crosthwaite; Doug Rossini and Liza Kelly Rossini; Patricia Ferguson; Logan Johnson; Irene Mecchi; and the fantastic Jeanne Moutoussamy Ashe. My gratitude goes to my great friend Enrico Pellegrini and his lovely wife Kelly Brock Pellegrini, and their darling daughter Margherita. I still cherish memories of the way they opened their lavish home in Rome to me when I was busy at work and in need of a break. I could not have asked for better hosts in that magical city. Finally, I'd like to thank my former professor Emery Wimbish, who remains a source of inspiration.

— D.B.

Beginnings
1900-1920

I n 1900 in a tiny town in Georgia, a black girl, no more than fourteen, stepped onto a stage and in all likelihood looked straight ahead. Her audience must have quickly given her the once-over. She was short, heavy, and black with a mop of unruly hair. And no doubt she was scared since this was her very first public performance. And in an age that judged everything by appearances, she was not even considered attractive. But when she opened her mouth to sing, well, everything changed for her and her audience. The little girl grew up to be the woman and the legend that refused to die: Ma Rainey, the mother of the blues, and one of America's first black beauties of wit and style.

Ma Rainey heads a long line of talented and dynamic African American women—Bessie Smith, Josephine Baker, Ethel Waters, Fredi Washington, Billie Holiday, Ivie Anderson, Lena Horne, Katherine Dunham, Dorothy Dandridge, Aretha Franklin, Diana Ross, Cicely Tyson, Donna Summer, Whitney Houston, Halle Berry, and Queen Latifah.

Everyone has been fascinated by these women who stood before us with an array of attitudes. With a wink or a nod or a shake of their shoulders or hips, they acted out fantastic stories full of whispers and secrets.

Ada Overton Walker with George Walker and Bert Williams in the play *In Dahomey.*

Page 12: Bessie Smith.

They played with myths, created legends, turned the social order topsy-turvy. In black show-business circles, these women were sometimes known as *dark divas—black beauties* or *sepia sirens.* But call them what you will, one thing is certain: from the beginnings of popular culture in 20th-century America to the very present, an impressive lineup of striking African American women have dazzled and delighted us with their energy and style. They were incandescent women who lit up the Great White Way and movie screens, and turned nightclubs, cafés, concert halls, and even television sets aglow with their particular brand of black magic.

We have watched these women onstage and off. And in time, their images, their careers, their childhoods, their families, their marriages, their divorces, their tumultuous ups and downs, their private anxieties, and their public poses have seemed a part of our own lives. Often when the divas' troubles have overshadowed their careers, we have watched with an even greater fascination because their lives have told us something about America's attitudes on race and gender.

Most of the divas have started in the same way. They have risen from ghettoes around the nation. Early in life, they decided to hit the road, to entertain, and to grasp hold of the American Dream itself. No matter what they encountered in their professional or personal lives, they learned early how America viewed its black women.

In the eyes of the white world, the black woman of the early 20th century was rarely thought of as pretty, soft, or sweet. If she was young and attractive, at best, she was considered little more than a lusty sexual object, to be used, dumped, and forgotten. Or if she were older, then she was considered a sexless motherly figure, miraculously endowed with certain spiritual powers and the ability to heal all wounds. To paraphrase Zora Neale Hurston, *the black woman was the mule of the world.* All sorts fo misconceptions were loaded on her. Often, too, she represented Mystery, the Other Dark Side of Experience. But she was never accepted simply as herself.

A glamorous Billie Holiday in the mid-1930s: lush, sensual, romantic.

America's dark divas have seen all the misconceptions and eventually have laid those misconceptions to waste. All the divas from Josephine Baker to Beyoncé Knowles have been determined to prove that the black woman was to be taken seriously. But at the same time, the divas have exuded a cunning sense of self, which has made all of us aware that something else transpired beneath the smile and the glamorous gloss; that indeed, alluring as they were, they could not be taken cheaply.

Ethel Waters became famous for her blues and sexy bumps and grinds.

Right: Lena Horne, a Brooklyn–born beauty who began her career as a sixteen-year-old chorus girl at the Cotton Club.

Taking pride in themselves as black women, America's dark divas have demanded respect. And always what they have used to gain that respect—and to entertain so brilliantly and so distinctly—has been their sense of style.

Each diva has perfected a public personality uniquely hers. But as different as Josephine Baker, Ethel Waters, Bessie Smith, Diana Ross, and Whitney Houston have been, all have had uncanny similarities of style that have set them apart from conventional white goddesses.

Diva style has sometimes been part put-on, part come-on, part camp, and part a reflection of an authentic African American cultural tradition. Haughtiness, control, and energy seemed to govern the style. Extravagance, optimism, and humor were all part of it, too. They have always lived by three distinct rules: dazzle your audience, keep 'em hungry, and don't lose your cool, sister. Their costumes—the colors and fabrics—have sparkled, shimmered, and danced in the night. The repartee between songs has been spicy and naughty, yet used to keep the audience at a distance. The attitude underlying a line of dialogue has sometimes been used to give a movie character a whole other subtext, counter to what the film might have set out to say. And despite their backgrounds, not a one has ever projected the image of the poor, woebegone ghetto girl. Instead, they have been live wires.

In the black communities where they grew up, they hadn't been taught to be ashamed of their bodies or of movement. Never had they been taught to fear big emotions. Nor had they been taught to be embarrassed by extravagance and elegance. So they have strolled, strutted, stomped, and sashayed like crazy, attitudinizing all over the place. They have liked showing off, speaking up for their rights, shouting out to the world that they were women born for luxury and that they had no intention of holding back. Each diva has been a champion of rebelliousness and self-assertion. That in itself may be the essential characteristic defining their appeal and the basis of their style. Sometimes, a white goddess might wilt and wither on us

Josephine Baker, the poor girl from the ghetto who became an international star.

or sigh and cry. But we have always felt America's dark divas never had time for that.

Different divas have done different things with that basic style, but all have used it to examine life, sometimes politics, not through blatantly spelled-out dogma but through push and pizzazz. And with their style intact, the divas have made their way through various periods, saying different things to us all. In the 1920s, we saw the great diva personalities, such stars as Josephine Baker, Bessie Smith, and Ethel Waters, each of whom was genuinely larger than life. In the 1930s, we saw divas who were the embodiments of popular myths, such stars as Billie Holiday and Ivie Anderson, whose smooth, mellow styles comforted Americans during the hard years of the Great Depression. In the 1940s, such new stars as Lena Horne and Hazel Scott emerged as social symbols for a nation torn in two by war. In the 1950s, steamy stars such as Dorothy Dandridge and Eartha Kitt became sex symbols for a period hungry for sexy rebelliousness. In the 1960s, when politics was very much on the minds of all Americans, Aretha Franklin arose as a transcendent, soulful political symbol. In the relaxed atmosphere of the 1970s, America's

dark divas emerged as survivors — and also with the emergence of Diana Ross, Cicely Tyson, and Donna Summer as superstars. In the 1980s, survivor-divas like Tina Turner reached new heights of success whereas younger ingenue-divas such as Janet Jackson and Whitney Houston became heroines for an increasingly youth-oriented culture. Through the 1990s, hip-hop/rhythm-and-blues stars such as Mary J. Blige and Faith Evans also reached the young as did a naughty girl performer like Lil' Kim. Such serious dramatic actresses as Angela Bassett and Anna Deavere Smith also came to prominence. In that era Whitney Houston and Oprah Winfrey commanded huge salaries as the age saw the rise of Million Dollar Baby Stars. And into the new century, performers such as Halle Berry and Beyoncé Knowles proved that the old-style glamour and glitz was as appealing as ever.

No matter what the period, the divas were able to pick up on the temper of the times, to answer the specific needs of their age, and to use their style to make personal statements. That was certainly true during the earliest days of the 20th century, when America's first dark diva, a country woman named Ma Rainey, decided that she wanted to go on the road and sing.

Dorothy Dandridge, a life of groundbreaking triumphs and heart-breaking tragedies.

Beyoncé, a goddess of the new millennium.

Ma Rainey
Olympian Blues
Goddess

Audiences were suspicious of any woman who called herself an entertainer. Female entertainers were looked upon as not much better than streetwalkers.

Ma Rainey was the woman who popularized the blues in America. She represented the woman who had been everywhere, done everything, and seen everybody. She drank hard, lived hard, and fought hard too. She liked her men. And sometimes she liked her women. And she didn't give a good damn what anybody had to say! Life was tough. But she wasn't ready to call it quits. Even in her day, nobody knew what was really true and what wasn't about Ma Rainey. But it was more fun to believe that she was wild, tough, and unpredictable since that was the kind of woman about whom she sang.

Little is known about her early life. She was born Gertrude Pridgett in 1886, the second of five children of a couple who had recently migrated from Alabama to Columbus, Georgia. She was baptized at the First African Baptist Church, and at age fourteen debuted at the Springer Opera House in a talent show. Four years later, at age eighteen, she upped and married a minstrel showmanager, Will "Pa" Rainey. Afterward, she became the star of his road-show company, The Rabbit Foot Minstrels. Later, she worked in Silas Green's shows and Tolliver's Circus, and for a time she and Pa were billed as "Rainey and Rainey, Assassinators of the Blues."

In her day, black entertainers still made their living by traveling from one town to another, appearing in tent shows, theaters, circuses, or whatever was available. They lived out of their trunks and stayed in colored boardinghouses. There were countless road companies, all of which were fast moving and hotly competitive. Amid the hustle

and bustle, the singers and dancers had to compete not only with one another but with acrobats, jugglers, and sideshow acts. And there were signs on the roads in small southern towns that read *"Nigger! Read and Run! If You Don't Read, Then Run Anyway!"* And then there were the audiences: farmers, field hands, factory workers, day laborers, all ready for a raucous, lively down-home style show. The show was a communal experience, and they didn't hesitate to participate, to reveal their feelings, to shout to a friend, or even eat their dinner while watching a show. "They did what they pleased while you were killing yourself onstage," Ethel Waters once said of the black audiences that she encountered during the early days of her road career. But if they liked you, she added, "They were the most appreciative audiences in the world. They'd scream, stomp, and applaud until the building shook."

Usually, audiences were suspicious of any woman who called herself an entertainer since this still was, after all, a man's world. The church looked on female entertainers as not much better than streetwalkers. Most of the big stars of the minstrel or medicine shows and of early black vaudeville were men, such as Bert Williams and George Walker. Occasionally, some women had met with success. As far back as 1851, concert performer Elizabeth Taylor Greenfield had performed with the Buffalo Musical Association. Later this gifted singer, who was known as the Black Swan, gave concerts in New York and throughout New England. Eventually, she worked her way to

Europe where she was invited to sing at Buckingham Palace. Sissieretta Jones, known as Black Patti, also had made a name for herself and even had her own traveling show, Black Patti's Troubadours. Ada Overton Walker had become well known after she worked onstage with her husband George. But these African American women were exceptions to the general rule. Ma Rainey's success, however, proved that the world of black vaudeville had to make permanent room for a female headliner.

For most, Ma Rainey best represented the black woman out to glorify herself, dressing up and stepping high, the "average" black woman of color determined to live large. She would saunter onto the stage, loud and rowdy, flashing a wicked killer of a smile. Her very look announced that she was a queen, ready to flaunt her success in a world that had said no such thing was possible for a colored woman. She wore rhinestones and sequined gowns, elaborate headbands and horsehair wings. Then there were her gold bracelets, the gold fillings in her teeth, her string upon string of necklaces, and, most of all, there were her diamonds—in her hair, on her clothes, around her neck and arms. She strolled, strutted, posed, and postured, jammed and whammed, did the whole magnificent snap-crackle-and-pop bit. The diamonds and gowns, and the push and power of Rainey's personality—her *attitudinizing*—helped transform a plain Jane into a blues goddess.

Ma's blues, some of which she wrote, were usually classic in form (twelve-bar melody, three-line stanza), burning deeply into the consciousness of her audience. The songs were varied, relaying a range of feelings, gliding easily from hot to cold, heavy to light. Often, her talk was about men, the dirty critters, the lowdown no 'counts. She would caution her sisters to "Trust No Man" and set herself up as an example of what could go wrong, 'cause now here she was, she would sing, drunk as she could be just 'cause that no-good man was tryin' "to make a fool of me."

But she did not stop there. She talked to the men, too. In a sly, comic tune, "Sleep Talking Blues," Ma warned that when a papa talked in his sleep, he had better be sure his mama's not awake. Other times, she sang such songs as "Bo-Weevil Blues" or "Levee Camp Moan." Or she might turn playful with a number like "Prove It on Me Blues," in which she sang of a woman who dresses like a man and then goes out for some fun with the girls. Even today on recordings and CDs, you can almost hear the strut in her voice.

And finally, of course, there was the sad, somber Ma, who sang of the days and nights when nothing seemed to work out, when she was ready to call it quits. Take me to the basement, she sang, 'cause she was as low as she could be. And with a song like "Leavin' this Morning," her voice heavy and weary, she was a woman ready to clear out, fed up with the way life had treated her.

No matter what the mood or tone, Ma Rainey's blues always retained a folksy purity that her audience could always immediately respond to. Her songs had a religious fervor to them since her audience was made up of churchgoers out for some fun on the sly. Ma could pound out a number like a pious churchgoer testifying before her congregation. In the middle of a song she might cry out, "Lord, Lord, Lord"; other times, Ma hummed and ran one word into another or sometimes forgot the words. When the lyrics were brooding or melancholy, Ma would be quiet and reflective. As her recordings now reveal, her basic enthusiasm—her fundamental joy in being able to communicate—always took over during a performance. Her name, *Ma*, which she started using when she was eighteen, immediately set up a distinct one-on-one communication with the audience.

At the turn of the 20th century, America was connected only by the railroads, newspapers, a few telephones, and even fewer automobiles. The traveling black road shows soon became underground railroads of sorts in which information, news, and gossip were disseminated. The position of the African American entertainer took on an unexpected significance since she or he brought messages of hope or despair. Ma Rainey never spoke directly about politics

Concert singer Black Patti toured the country with her own troupe.

Ma Rainey found her earthy blues music replaced in popularity by jazz. By 1935 she gave up her career, ran two theaters in Rome, Georgia, and became a churchgoer.

nor did she comment on the Great War raging in Europe where black boys were sent to fight for other people's freedom. But those audiences listening to the songs such as "Leavin' this Morning," "Runaway Blues," and "Black Cat, Hoot Owl Blues," heard stories of a tight, oppressive world that offered nothing but bad luck. If one black cat did not cross her path, Ma sang, then another surely would. She had to run away, she announced; she had to leave this neighborhood. Armed with such material, black performers editorialized, satirized, sometimes prophesied too. Ma Rainey was aware that in this new world of popular entertainment, where performer might be prophet, she, as the first colored female blues singer anyone had ever heard of, was an oddity, a woman in a man's arena who would have to have a device that would automatically quiet the cynics, which would wipe away doubts and command prompt audience respect. The name *Ma* gave her a place in the scheme of things, setting up a clearly defined relationship between her and the audience.

Later, other divas would adopt similar maternal poses. Jackie Mabley became Moms Mabley. The young Ethel Waters was billed as Sweet Mama Stringbean. Even Sophie Tucker, influence by Waters and Alberta Hunter, was called The Last of the Red Hot Mamas. Other divas would be represented as royalty, female heads of state in the world of entertainment. Dinah Washington was known as the Queen. Aretha Franklin became the Queen of Soul. And New Jersey's Dana Owens changed

hip-hop gender dynamics when she arrived on the rap scene as Queen Latifah.

Ma Rainey entertained from the turn of the century to the Great Depression era. In time, she traveled with her own group, the Georgia Jazz Band. The stories about her were often racy, catty, and not always plausible. Ma was sometimes called the ugliest woman in show business—but never to her face and never when she was performing. Other entertainers watched her, studied her style, and marveled at her rapport with her audience. Mary Lou Williams, who would later become a fine jazz pianist, has never forgotten her childhood excitement upon seeing the great Ma at work. And surely, no one was more influenced by Rainey than Bessie Smith. For years, it was rumored that Bessie was just a plump, oversized gal up from Tennessee trying to find her way around in the tent shows and tiny theaters when Ma and Pa Rainey had been so taken with her talent that they kidnapped her.

Years after the two had met, when Bessie was a big star and when Ma's career was almost over, Bessie, arriving in a town where Ma was performing, slipped out to see the older woman's show. That was indeed a rarity since it was well known that Bessie Smith almost never went to see any other performer. But here was the first great link between two important African American female stars, each recognizing the other's position, each giving the other her due. Later some divas, such as Waters and Baker (or even Bessie and Waters, or Waters and Lena Horne), might be fiercely competitive or suspicious of each other. But Rainey and Smith's friendship reveals their mutual respect.

As the years passed, Ma Rainey found her earthy blues music replaced in popularity by jazz. By 1935 she gave up her career entirely, ran two theaters she owned in Rome, Georgia, and became a regular churchgoer. When she died in 1939, her death certificate stated that she had been a housekeeper. Ma Rainey had clearly been a phenomenon on the entertainment scene, not only an extraordinary artist but a presence and stylist who had altered the basic nature of the minstrel/vaudeville circuit. Now there was a place for other black women headliners. No road show would be complete without a Mama singing the blues. And in the long run, she set the tone for the fast and furious twenties.

Jammin': a glammed-up Ma Rainey and her band.

Personas
The 1920s

After Ma Rainey had cleared the way, she was jolted from her throne, when there was a mad rush and scramble to see who would be the next wearer of the crown. And there were countless contenders eager for the spotlight.

Suddenly in the 1920s, an array of black female entertainers emerged, almost all of whom sang or danced, romped or stomped, or cavorted like crazy in hopes for something that they now knew was attainable—stardom.

During the twenties, the great diva personas—Bessie Smith, Josephine Baker, Florence Mills, and Ethel Waters—emerged. "Up You Mighty Race," black leader Marcus Garvey announced to the Black Community of the time. And few seemed to understand his message as well as the divas. But they also understood something else—the basic mood of an age eager for the daring, the bizarre, and the new. And they made the most of it.

No other period has been quite as permissive and encouraging for the divas as the 1920s. The whole look and feel, tone and texture, of American popular entertainment was undergoing a dramatic transformation. Despite President Harding's proclamation that this new era would mark a return to "normalcy," in the twenties it seemed as if everyone—at least in the big urban centers—suddenly wanted to break loose, to pry himself or herself from the traditional middle-class moral order of the past, to forget the fake optimism that had characterized the turn of the century, to wipe out the pain and disillusionment of World War I. The twenties can now be seen as the dawning age of America's intense, often unfathomable, interest in the celebrity, be it Babe Ruth, Clara Bow, or Charles Lindbergh. Celebrities represented part of a golden dream of unlimited fun and adventure. Records, movies, and plays picked up on the new fun spirit. On dance floors around the country, the black bottom and the Charleston (both of which originated in the Black Community) caught hold of the mass imagination as no other popular dances ever had. Nightclubs and speakeasies sprouted up, overcrowded with dapper hotshot young men and a new kind of young woman, the pencil-thin, flat-chested, sexually liberated flapper. Not only had corsets and long skirts gone out the window, so too had many of the inhibitions of the past.

In this period, there were black flappers too. But generally, because the nature of her existence always demanded that she be resourceful, the black woman had long been more independent than her white counterpart. Many black women already worked outside the home. What the twenties did for her, if she chose to entertain, was simply to offer her new arenas in which to shine and dazzle. So caught up was consumer-oriented America in its own uninhibited frenzy that there was repeated demand for fresh products, new, different, offbeat items to be quickly snapped up, digested, and enjoyed. Anything was permissible as long as it was not boring. Nightclubs, theaters, movies, and in time Europe all made way for the black beauty of the twenties, so much so that there was indeed a cultural revolution going on in America. But all those fabulous twenties opportunities grew out of something old and something new: the blues and race records.

Page 26: The great Josephine Baker.

Alberta Hunter.

Blues Sisters

Perhaps more than any other art-entertainment form, the blues legitimized the black female entertainer. Even in the days before the scholars and the buffs moved in to explain the artistry of the early blues singers, African American audiences responded to the power and grace of the female blues singers. What added to their popularity was the coming of the race record, which arrived in the hands of a black woman.

In 1920, black composer Perry Bradford brashly marched into the offices of OKeh, an independent, ambitious phonograph company in New York City. Convinced that there was a black audience as eager as whites for music that could be taken home and played on the Victrola, Bradford persuaded one of the white executives of OKeh to record black singer Mamie Smith. When OKeh released Smith's version of "Crazy Blues," executives of the company thought it might make a little bit of money. To their surprise, "Crazy Blues" sold 75,000 copies within the first month-and-a-half, and over a half-million copies within the next half year in the Black Community. The music industry realized that there was a whole new market for records. Soon, the major companies were spinning out race records, music by black artists for black record buyers. Listed in special catalogs and sold in black areas, race records kept a number of music companies in business.

The success of race records created a wild search for blues talent. In New York, one of the few black-owned record companies, W. C. Handy and Harry Pace's Black Swan label, ambitiously and quickly signed up a singer who showed great promise: Ethel Waters. At the same time, Black Swan rejected another singer named Bessie Smith. Out of Chicago, Paramount released records by the very popular Ida Cox and a newcomer named Alberta Hunter, who also wrote blues songs, one of which, "Down Hearted Blues," became a hit for Bessie Smith. Paramount also launched a search for the most legendary of blues singers, Ma Rainey. (Louis Armstrong was sometimes one of her backup musicians.) Trixie Smith, Clara Smith, Edith Wilson, Rosa Henderson, Bertha "Chippie" Hill,

Victoria Spivey, Maggie Jones, Gertrude Saunders, Martha Copeland, Lucille Hegamin, and Sara Martin all recorded race records. Not all were blues singers in the classic sense. Some were vaudeville entertainers more at home with pop tunes.

With so many blues singers, many were eventually given nicknames to distinguish them from the other singers for the record buyers. Ma Rainey was billed as the "Mother of the Blues." Mamie Smith was known as "the first blues singer on records." Clara Smith, who did occasional duets with Bessie, was "Queen of the Moaners." Sippie Wallace was the "Texas Nightingale." Lucille Hegamin was called the "Chicago Cyclone." And Ida Cox was touted as the "Uncrowned Queen of the Blues."

With her blues and her nickname, each woman created a distinct persona. Alberta Hunter represented the vulnerable-but-tough little cookie who could take care of herself. Hunter was a small woman with a quick, mischievous smile. In 1907, at the age of twelve, she ran away from her home in Memphis and hopped a train to Chicago, She had heard that girls there were paid ten dollars a week to sing. Hunter performed and worked with such entertainers as Bricktop, Florence Mills, Cora Green, and the legendary King Oliver Band. She came to know many of the important music figures of her day: Louis Armstrong, Fletcher Henderson, Fats Waller, Lil Hardin, Sidney Bechet, and Bessie Smith. Eubie Blake said that when she sang, "You felt so sorry for her you would want to kill the guy she was singing about." Hunter and the other blues sisters used their material to act out dramas and to examine the "issues": money, heartache, and men. And occasionally, they were just dishing out sex—with the bawdiest of lyrics. In one song, a singer might announce that "if the fellow didn't like her ocean, then he better not fish in her sea." Or she might tell him to stay out of her valley and to let her mountain be.

In time, the blues brought black women from behind the shadows. Curiously, the sisters were far bolder than some of their male counterparts (and far more popular), perhaps because as mere women they were not considered as threatening, so it did not matter what they said; perhaps also because finally, through song, women had found an outlet for articulating the things affecting them most. Here again, though, the black woman presented herself as the embodiment of restless energy, intelligence, maturity, and drive. Many became pop heroines for the African American community. Ida Cox toured the United States with her own revue. She had sixteen chorus girls, comics, and backup singers. She also wrote her own material and selected the musicians who accompanied her. If all this were not enough to dazzle her audience, then surely the stories of her mansion in Tennessee and her luxuri-

sad, even tragic twists and turns. During her heyday, Mamie Smith made nearly a hundred records in seven years and later appeared in movie shorts. But when she died in 1946, her money and fame were gone. Some performers like Ida Cox continued singing long after the blues had gone out of vogue. Her last recordings were made in 1961 and she died in 1967. Victoria Spivey got a chance to work in the movie *Hallelujah* and in later years managed her own small record company. Edith Wilson returned to the musical theater and also posed as Aunt Jemima for the famous Quaker Oats pancake advertisements. Spunky Alberta Hunter used the blues as a

In time, the blues brought black women from behind the shadows.

ant lifestyle were certain to keep the fans in awe. By the mid-1920s, the blues sisters had had such an extraordinary effect on popular culture that even so mainstream a publication as *Vanity Fair* ran an article by Carl Van Vechten on blues performers Ethel Waters, Bessie Smith, and Clara Smith.

The styles created by the blues singers were eventually lifted and presented in far more acceptable form by white quasi-blues/torch singers Sophie Tucker, Helen Morgan, and Ruth Etting. No matter how successful the black blues singers were, not a one ever reaped the vast rewards and acclaim generated by the white singers—with the possible exception of Ethel Waters. Yet, her greatest fame came once she conquered Broadway. Some blues singers never knew what royalties were. Others took the few dollars that they earned without complaints or demands. And often, after their initial success in the 1920s, the course of the black blues singers' lives took

springboard for another kind of career. In 1928, Hunter won the role of Queenie opposite Paul Robeson in the London production of *Show Boat*. Nightly, her rendition of "Can't Help Lovin' Dat Man" brought the house down. Afterward she toured Europe, and took over Chez Florence in Paris. She hobnobbed with everyone from the Prince of Wales to Cole Porter to Noël Coward, who wrote "I Travel Alone" for her. As special as Hunter was, she later left singing to become a nurse, assuming no one would ever think twice about her. For a long time, she was right. Then, she surfaced in the late 1970s, popularizing the blues all over again. For the most part the early blues singers, for all their uniqueness, often retired or disappeared or struggled on at tiny clubs and cafés, slowly fading into oblivion, never seeing their work fully appreciated. That almost happened to the woman considered to be the greatest blues singer of them all, Bessie Smith.

Bessie Smith:
the Empress
Comes to Town

In the 1920s, Bessie Smith was *the* blues singer. Her title, *The Empress,* was rightly hers and hers alone. Not only was hers the big, powerful voice of the era, but her very style was also the distillation of those other blues singers struggling to make themselves heard in a man's world. In many respects, it was also a dazzling tribute to the woman who influenced Bessie most: Ma Rainey. With Bessie Smith's arrival too, there came the idea of a black woman's life as a drama, a lopsided morality play with the mythic cycle of birth, life, death, rebirth. Through her records, her road tours, her inimitable high-diva stage style, and her hotly discussed lifestyle, Bessie Smith possibly became the most famous black woman of her age, marking the end of one tradition— the diva enclosed solely in the Black Community—and the beginning of another: the diva coming aboveground, openly affecting the dominant culture. Bessie Smith was a distinctive 1920s–diva persona so powerful that later she was transformed into social symbol, legend, myth.

Born dirt poor in Chattanooga, Tennessee, around 1894 (she was never eager to give out her birth date!), the second of seven children of a part-time Baptist minister, Bessie was nine when her parents died. She took to singing on the streets to earn pennies. By 1912, she had left Tennessee and was performing in a troupe with Pa and Ma Rainey. A year later, she was singing at the 81 Theatre in Atlanta. She married a young man named Earl Love, who died not long after the union.

Through the teens of the 20th century, Bessie spent long, lean, tough years performing on the black vaudeville circuit, the Theatre Owners' Booking Association. She worked anywhere: in tents, carnivals, honky-tonks, performing in her street clothes, often dancing as much as she sang. By the early twenties, when she settled in Philadelphia and married a former policeman named Jack Gee, her reputation was established. But her great fame came with her recordings.

Incredibly enough, three different record companies rejected her. They thought that she sounded too raw, too loud, too unso-phisticated, no doubt downright too *cullid* too. In 1923, Frank Walker of Columbia signed her. Within a year, her first recordings had sold one million copies, surpassing the sales of all the other female blues singers. Records broadened her audience. She continued to tour, eventually starred in her own show and played in some of the larger cities such as Nashville, Memphis, Detroit, Chicago, Philadelphia, New York, Cleveland, Atlanta, Birmingham, Cincinnati, and Indianapolis. Soon her reputation preceded her, and for many in the tiny rural towns or the big cities, seeing Bessie Smith was a once-in-a-lifetime experience.

Bessie's stage persona in the 1920s was similar to that of Ma Rainey's: the emotionally well-traveled woman, returning to relate her troubles and triumphs. Nothing was ordinary about Bessie, not even the way she looked. For she was a large woman, big-boned, massively built, and very dark. She stormed stages, circling and courting her audience, dressed in outrageous getups: short horsehair wigs, sequined gowns, ostrich plumes, furs and jewels, and outlandish hats. Her style was in keeping with the uninhibited, far-out air of the era, making her the personification of the big-hearted, good-time gal out for lots of fun. Her emblem was her huge, joyous smile, which, as a great artist, she knew when to turn on and off. In no time the sensual, hepped-up, partying sister could give way to the reflective, pragmatic, soulful woman recording the woes of the world.

Bessie's material was varied. She sang of love and heartache, coming on as a woman who understood men, their good points and their bad. Characters in her songs needed men to complete the story of their lives. Yet, in Bessie's hands, often having a man seemed her divine right. Bessie sang of men in general, using them as a backdrop (on occasion as an explanation) for a story of weariness and pain.

At the same time, her attitudes toward men were similar to those that men expressed toward women. In "Do Your Duty," she sang that if she called her man three times a day to come and drive her blues away, then he should naturally be prepared

In her music, she never feared the thing that women were always cautioned against: self-assertiveness. Her nontraditional role drew female followers to her.

to play, to do his duty. Bessie demanded from the man all the service he could supply. And in an era when the conventional flapper sought independence, Bessie already had hers.

In her music, she never feared the thing that women were always cautioned never to be: self-assertive. It was precisely her self-assertion and her nontraditional role as a woman that drew female followers to her. In the song "Put It Right Her (or Keep It out There)," she emphatically laid down the law to a man who had been playing around while living on her money. And in her bawdy songs, "Need a Little Sugar in My Bowl" (she sang that she was tired of being lonely and blue, and needed not only a little sugar in her bowl but also a little hot-dog in her roll), "I'm Wild about That Thing," and "You Gotta Give Me Some," Bessie represented the sensual woman stepping forward, expressing her needs, appetites, and fantasies.

Other Bessie Smith songs struck different moods. In "'Taint Nobody's Business If I Do," a song that was a favorite for other divas as well, she announced that if she had the notion to jump in the ocean, then it wasn't nobody's business if she did, adding that if her friend didn't have any money and that if she should say take all hers, honey, then again it wasn't nobody's business if she did. Bessie approached this song as if it were an anthem proclaiming a woman's independence, her right to her own follies and idiosyncrasies. "Nobody Knows You When You're Down and Out" tells the story of a woman who once lived high and has now fallen low without money or a friend to

help, and sounds as if it came straight from the hard-luck 1930s. "Gimme a Pigfoot and a Bottle of Beer" remains one of her best pieces, capturing the energy of Harlem rent parties, speakeasies, and bootleg gin.

Offstage, Bessie was a fascinating figure as well. In this period when the black press was still evolving, black newspapers such as the *Philadelphia Tribune* and the *Chicago Defender* (as well as the powerful black grapevine) had a field day with Bessie's offstage antics. Bessie's biographer Chris Albertson points out that in the 1920s black audiences came to theaters anticipating the legend as much as the entertainer. Everyone had some Bessie story to tell. According to Albertson, there were tales of her flights of fancy when she might desert her traveling troupe and rush off to another town for some fun and loving. There were stories about her spending sprees. In one summer alone, she and husband Jack Gee were said to have spent $16,000 (a tremendous sum at the time), and she was known to have paid cash for cars. Her drinking binges were famous. She would enter a local tavern, tell the bartender to lock the door, not to let anyone out or in, and then lay a hundred dollars on the counter, after which there were unlimited drinks for everyone as they all partied, sometimes for days. Her temper was legendary, too. She hit anybody who annoyed or messed with her, man or woman. When she thought her husband was fooling around with some other woman, she would haul off and slap him. On one occasion, she even chased him down a railroad track while firing a pis-

A reflective Bessie at the end of a long and flamboyant career.

tol at him. Her lovers, male and female, were talked about. At one time, when a young woman buckled and withdrew after being publicly kissed by Bessie, the girl was given such a dressing down by Bessie that thereafter she was kissed where and when the Empress wanted—without a word of complaint! She was extravagant. She traveled with her own entourage and in her private railroad car, which would be detached at the local depot, after which Bessie's workers would set up tents, then roam the streets, passing out fliers that said the Empress was here in town for a performance.

Bessie was a woman no one tangled with. She was tough on any entertainer whom she thought might be a possible threat. During Ethel Waters's early days as a struggling young performer, she appeared on the same bill with Bessie in Atlanta. The Empress laid down the law that Waters, whom she called "long goody," could not sing any blues. When the audience cried out for Waters to sing some blues songs, she broke Bessie's rule. Backstage, a loud Bessie let it be known what she thought of those "northern bitches." And later, Waters quoted Bessie as saying: "You ain't so bad. It's only that I never dreamed that anyone would be able to do this to me in my own territory and with my own people. And you damn well know you can't sing worth a shit."

Throughout the 1920s, Bessie's records and personal appearances were tremendously successful. On rare occasions she performed before white audiences. She also did radio shows and starred in the 1928 film *St. Louis Blues*. By the 1930s, some white college students started to collect her records. Even Mae West may have picked up her hands-on-hips pose from Bessie.

The high period of Bessie Smith's career came to an end by the late 1920s. Blues fell out of favor. New stars, with a different kind of refined flash, came into vogue. Bessie's engagements became few. Her money was running out. She was drinking steadily. Eventually even her husband, Gee, took off with another entertainer, Gertrude Saunders. Then, the Great Depression nearly wiped her out. Record producer John Hammond ran across her working as a hostess in a North Philadelphia dive, singing pornographic songs for tips. In 1933, she made her last recordings for Hammond on the Columbia label. (Three days later, a youngster named Billie Holiday made her first records for the same company.)

Bessie fought to regain her stardom and went so far as to modify her flamboyant style. She wore simple, elegant gowns, without the wigs or the wild hats; her hair brushed back, revealing a striking middle-aged woman. Although she never made a big comeback, Bessie never stopped working in the 1930s. In 1937, she set off on a tour through the South with a new man by her side, Richard Morgan, Lionel Hampton's uncle. During the tour, Bessie's car, driven by Morgan, crashed into a truck. Her right arm was nearly severed and she lay bleeding for hours on a lonely country road. Bessie Smith died at a hospital in Clarksdale, Mississippi.

A massive crowd turned out for her funeral. Far from diminishing her legend, her years of decline simply intensified it. After her death, the story spread that she had bled to death when she was refused admittance at a nearby white hospital. Although the story has been discounted by Bessie's biographer Chris Albertson *and* by the physician who attended her at the roadside where the accident occurred, it remains a potent part of her legend; the story that her fans and followers preferred to believe. In 1961, Edward Albee used this story of her death as the basis for his play *The Death of Bessie Smith*, which was a denunciation of bigotry in America.

Bessie Smith was the last of a specific type: the dark diva firmly entrenched in the Black Community. The black beauties who followed, from Baker to Waters to Holiday, started in the African American community

The young Bessie.

but eventually met with great success in the white world, too. And perhaps what disoriented some of the later figures was that, unlike Bessie, they were torn from their roots and found that they could never really go home again. Although Bessie took the diva into the mainstream culture, she was never part of it.

Chorus Girls:
Café-au-Lait Cuties

Two promising young dramatic actresses of the 1920s: Edna Thomas (left) and Fredi Washington.

During this era of accelerated fun and frivolity, Bessie and the blues singers were not the only type of popular entertainment around. There were also the serious stage actresses and the show girls. In the twenties, black theater (or black-oriented theater—plays with black characters or themes) really seemed to be taking off with new opportunities for everyone. Eugene O'Neill's *All God's Chillun Got Wings*, focusing on an interracial romance, appeared in 1924, followed by Garland Anderson's *Appearances*, then *Black Boy* with Paul Robeson, and David Belasco's spectacular *Lulu Belle*, which boasted a cast of sixty or more, three-quarters of whom were "colored." It told the shocking story of the rise (from Harlem to Paris) of a beautiful, wanton girl!

In the new black theater, new dramatic African American actresses appeared: Inez Clough (in *Earth* and *Harlem*), Abbie Mitchell, Edna Thomas, Evelyn Ellis, Georgette Harvey, Fredi Washington, and the magnetic Rose McClendon. Throughout the 1920s, McClendon was no doubt the most talked-about black actress around. She starred opposite Charles Gilpin (and later Paul Robeson) in the 1924 production *Roseanne*, played the mother in Paul Green's Pulitzer Prize–winning play *In Abraham's Bosom*, and appeared in the original 1927 production of *Porgy*. Her 1926 performance in *Deep River* was critically acclaimed by New York theatergoers. Even the feisty critic of the *New York World*, Alexander Woollcott, reported that when Ethel Barrymore had slipped in to see the play, she had been told by her friend Arthur Hopkins to be sure to stay until the last act just to watch McClendon descend a flight of stairs. He told her, "She can teach some of our most hoity-toity actresses distinction." Wrote Woollcott: "It was Miss Barrymore who hunted *him* after the performance to say, 'She can teach them *all* distinction.'" McClendon was a tall, slender

Guitar-strumming Adelaide Hall, the star of *Blackbirds of 1928*.

brown beauty with a regal bearing and a high sense of the dramatic. In the thirties, producer John Houseman launched elaborate plans to star McClendon as the dark queen, Medea. With a white actor playing Jason, there were to be mulatto children and a stunning chorus of black women. The rest of the cast would be white. This would have been a daring piece of theater, but McClendon fell ill, and the project was shelved. For a short time in the 1930s, she

and Houseman headed the Works Progress Administration's Negro Theatre Project. After a long and painful illness, McClendon died just before the project took off. For years afterward, Rose McClendon remained one of those unsung heroines whose fundamental success had proved there could be a place for black women in the legitimate theater.

Of all the new black theater projects, none, however, could hope to compete with the new style of black musicals. *Shuffle Along* set the tone and pace for such shows. Created by black composers Noble Sissle and Eubie Blake, and the black comedy-writing team of Flournoy Miller and Aubrey Lyles, *Shuffle Along* opened on Broadway in 1921, immediately winning raves from critics and public alike. During this era of the Harlem Renaissance, when black writers Langston Hughes, Claude McKay, Zora Neale Hurston, Alain Locke, Nella Larson, and Jean Toomer injected some black culture into the history of American arts and letters, the success of *Shuffle Along* indicated that there was also a place for African Americans in popular, commercial theater. It ushered into vogue the whole notion of the all-black Broadway show that could please whites as well as blacks, and inspired an array of other black musicals: *Runnin' Wild;* Miller and Lyles's *Rang Tang*, and *Keep Shufflin';* Lew Leslie's various editions of *Blackbirds* and *Hot Chocolates*. Emerging from these musicals were show girls Lottie Gee, the haughty Gertrude Saunders, Valaida Snow, Elida Webb, Adelaide Hall (who, for a spell, was almost as great a European sensation as Josephine Baker), Minto Cato, Ada Ward, Marion Gant Tyler (who married Eubie Blake), Baby Cox, Florence Mills, Fredi Washington, Ethel Waters, and Baker. Even the great Paul Robeson got a break in the musicals when he replaced one of the Four Harmony Kings in a road-show version of *Shuffle Along.*

No other figure was as firmly grounded in the animated flip spirit of the flapper or Jazz Age as the show girl. Sharp and sassy, slick and slender, the chorus and show girls all seemed to be making a frantic bid for attention: Junior League divas struggling for self-definition (or self-escape) through movement, song, and a display of energy. In the new musicals, the chorus girls set the pace and tone, often operating much like a chorus in an ancient Greek play: standing as one character, commenting through music, dance, and jokes on the action.

When they weren't working in legitimate theaters, the chorus girls found other work in the sporty new black night spots then coming into vogue—the Cotton Club, Connie's Inn, the Plantation Club, the Shuffle Club, the Savoy, and later, Small's Paradise. It was during the 1920s that whites first started wandering uptown to Harlem for a good time, much of which was provided by the girls performing nightly in the clubs. Some of the so-called black clubs actually were no such thing. They might have had only black entertainers, but the establishments were owned by whites and often had only white customers. A few *sepia joints* were even located downtown. Regardless, the colored chorines were seen. Producers Florenz Ziegfeld and George White were even said to have hired black chorus girls to teach the downtown white chorus lines the new jazz dancing.

What distinguished the black chorus line was its rhythmic, exhilarating energy level. Having grown up exposed to such popular dance forms as the cakewalk, buck dancing, and ballin' the jack, the dancers were well prepared for the fast turns, high jumps, and kicks demanded by their black choreographers. The dance numbers themselves were a clever fusion of the styles of the minstrel shows and burlesque, all in all creating a large-scale carnival of activity. The high point was the sweeping, dramatic, sometimes comic strut.

The black chorus line was also distinguished by the fact that its members were almost always café-au-lait cuties: light-skinned black women with straight hair and keen features. In photographs of the old chorus lines, occasionally a brown face appears, but there is never a dark one. In the 1890s, black revues such as *The Creole Show* and *Octoroon* had glorified the Afro-American Girl, who actually was the light-bright-damn-near-white kind of black beauty. Such shows simply intensified a color-caste system that had long existed in the Black Community. The same was true of the 1920s black night spots, particularly a place like the Cotton Club, which catered exclusively to whites and had to have light-skinned women. The great irony is that the few women who rose from the black shows to become stars were brown beauties such as Baker, Mills, and Waters.

Florence Mills: Make Way for Little Twinks

Florence Mills was one of the lucky ladies from the black shows to emerge as a bona fide star. Born in Washington, D.C., Mills had been in show business all her life. As a child, she was known as Baby Florence when she performed in the drawing rooms of various Washington diplomats. Later she and her sisters, Olivia and Maude, performed as the Mills Sisters. By the 1920s, Florence was working with her dancer-husband, U. S. (Slow Kid) Thompson, on the Keith Circuit in an act called The Tennessee Ten. The big break came when *Shuffle Along* lost its ingenue, Gertrude Saunders. Somewhat uneasily, the producers brought Mills in as a replacement. And then, with the kind of a-star-is-born magic the theater and theatergoers thrive on, her rendition of the hit song "I'm Craving for that Kind of Love" made the replacement an even greater sensation than the original star. Later, Mills successfully appeared at the Plantation Club, then traveled to London and Paris, and other European capitals where she became a tremendously popular international star in *From Dover to Dixie*.

Onstage, Florence Mills introduced the adorably innocent little black girl with a playful wild streak. She would don a sky-high blond Afro wig and throw herself into an exuberant Charleston. Or she dressed up innocently as a hitchhiker off on the road to find love. "I'm a Little Blackbird Looking for a Bluebird," she sang, and the audience took her to its heart. She was a small woman as "delicate as Dresden china," the perfect gamin lost and alone in a cruel world. She had great spunk and vigor, and was one of the few important black female stars who succeeded with the little-girl bit, the kind of woman for whom all the big guys on the block felt they had to look out. Firsthand accounts of her skill have always been flowing. Black critic James Weldon Johnson wrote:

She was indefinable. One might best string out a list of words such as: pixy, elf, radiant,

exotic, Peter Pan, wood-nymph, wistful, piquant, magnetism, witchery, madness, flame; and then despairingly exclaim: "Oh, you know what I mean." She could be whimsical, she could be almost grotesque; but she had the good taste that never allowed her to be coarse. She could be risqué, she could be seductive; but it was impossible for her to be vulgar, for she possessed a naiveté that was alchemic. As a pantomimist and a singing and dancing comedienne she had no superior in any place or race.*

Florence Mills's career did not last long. By the latter years of the decade, the star, sometimes affectionately known as Little Twinks, looked edgy and tense, moody and overworked. In 1927, Florence Mills died after an appendectomy. According to columnist Whitney Bolton of the *New York Morning Telegraph*, over 150,000 people lined the streets of Harlem for her funeral.

A Mills legend developed soon after her death, that of the tragic artist struck down much too early. Later generations would remain intrigued but baffled since she left behind no recordings. (Strangely enough, her life was so rushed that she simply never got around to making records.) The other important divas acquired staying power because long after their heydays had come to an abrupt end or long after their reputations had been tarnished, there were either records or films to reveal the way that they had once dazzled. Bessie Smith and Ma Rainey were brought back into the cultural mainstream by the re-release of their records. Also important to a diva's longevity have been tales about the turbulence and disarray of her life, all of which could be incorporated into her myth. No such dramatic stories about Mills survive. Today, all that remains are a handful of striking photographs that capture her playfulness and at times her endearing vulnerability. But perhaps another reason that Mills is not well remembered now is because of Josephine Baker.

Josephine Baker: the Woman Who Got Away

Josephine Baker obliterated the reputation of just about every other show girl in sight. Her legend took hold in the twenties with a firm, tenacious grip. With various clever modifications, it held on and endured for some six decades. Ultimately, Josephine Baker stood as the personification of the rip-roaring 1920s as well as the archetypal symbol of the black flapper and International Exotique. She perhaps understood her legend—her image, her career, her audiences—better than any other diva. She was a showbiz personality to her bones. And with insight and skill, she fused her public and private personalities in such a way that she witnessed the ultimate fantasy come true: the transformation of the world into her private stage.

Even before she hit the stage, Josephine Baker had steered past a hazardous course. Like Bessie Smith and the other divas of the period, Baker was born into poverty—in 1906 in the heart of the ghetto of St. Louis. Her birth name: Freda J. McDonald. Her mother was a washer woman named Carrie McDonald. For years, there would be much discussion about the identity of her father. Some believed it was musician Eddie Carson. Baker herself—forever romantic—said her father was a Spaniard who did not want to marry the colored girl he had impregnated. Her mother also gave birth to three other children and married a man named Arthur Martin, who hauled gravel for his livelihood. As a lanky, skinny child who stole to eat or who cleaned for whites to earn a few pennies for her family, Baker exhibited the grit and ambition that would eventually bring her the fame that she so desperately craved. Everything about Baker suggested a woman who had to get out, to break loose, to find herself and her own notion of freedom. At thirteen, she married an older man, Willie Wells, but left him, not realizing that because she had been a minor, the marriage had never been legal.

Still a teenager, she ran away from home to join a traveling road show. She also had a second, short-lived marriage to Willie Baker, whose surname she would keep for the rest of her life. By the early 1920s, she found herself in Philadelphia. It

was there that she decided to audition for *Shuffle Along*.

At first, so she later said, she was turned down because she was too young, too thin, too dark. The next time around, she auditioned wearing the lightest face powder that she could find, and was hired as a dresser for one of the show's various road productions. Baker was clever enough to prepare herself for the inevitable. She immediately learned all the songs and dances of the show since she knew at some point some chorus girl had to miss a performance. When a dancer dropped out because of a pregnancy, Baker persuaded the stage manager to let her go on.

That night lingered on in the memories of many. This unknown, skinny, young girl strutted onto the stage, crossed her eyes, made faces like crazy, and shook, shimmied, and wiggled her backside. Taking an ordinary dance slot, she transformed it into a high-falutin', ferociously energetic theatrical event. She brought the house down and word-of-mouth spread quickly. Audiences came to the theater hoping to see the "little cross-eyed, out-of-step girl" at the end of the chorus line. Eventually, Baker became the highest-paid girl in the chorus, the most acclaimed, and, among her fellow chorines, possibly the least liked.

Fredi Washington, another black beauty who worked with Baker in *Shuffle Along* and who became a friend, has recalled the theatrical pettiness that Josephine was the victim of. She was referred to as The Monkey by the other girls, who never forgave her for stealing the show right from under their noses. They never hesitated to let her know what they thought. One evening, when Washington entered the dressing room, she saw that all of Josephine's makeup had been lifted from the dressing table and dumped into the hallway. Washington found the culprits and demanded that they put everything back in place before Josephine arrived at the theater.

Baker has also been remembered as an ambitious, tense young woman, perhaps uneasy and insecure since she was the brownest girl in the chorus line. During the early part of her career, the idea was that, as

During her Folies Bergère period, La Baker went topless long before it was fashionable. She also became the darling of Parisian society.

a brown woman, she could never get attention on her looks alone, the way the high-yellar chorus girls did. At this time, she was hardly the white or black ideal of beauty or appeal. Baker was acutely aware, however, that the one thing that could save her was her own incomparable effervescence. So she used it to provide comic relief every night at the theater. She became known primarily as a high-steppin' clown, something of a ribald joke. But the clowning, coupled with her fierce drive and energy (and her formidable talent), enabled her to steal scenes from everyone in sight.

Josephine Baker used *Shuffle Along* to break through and establish herself—but as an important chorus girl. She was not yet a star. That was true even in 1924, when Sissle and Blake wrote special material for her in their new all-black Broadway show *Chocolate Dandies*. Baker entered wearing a clinging-silk dress with a sexy slit up the side. But for the most part, she still crossed her eyes and grinned widely as she climbed about the stage in outsized shoes and a sash with a huge bow. She was still the cutup. Some of the photographs of Baker during this period are shocking because the woman who most now think of as the symbol of European chic played a pickaninny figure. And the flagrant, hot sexuality that was later to drive audiences wild was then sometimes buried under layers of grotesque makeup and unbecoming costumes.

After *Chocolate Dandies* closed, Baker appeared in the chorus of the Plantation Club, the downtown Broadway night spot that had launched Florence Mills and was then starring Ethel Waters. Baker was now developing an offstage style that made her a noticeable Harlem figure. Her bobbed hair and the insolent spit curls on her forehead gleamed. One day, she walked the streets decked out in an outfit that could

Baker with the man who believed he was her Svengali, Pepito Abatino.

She dazzled European audiences with her version of the Charleston. Baker leaped onto the Paris stage wearing nothing but a festoon of bananas and a smile.

not help but draw attention: a blazing orange jacket, bright-green shoes, a jaunty silver-lamé hat cocked to the side, pearl gray golf pants that clung to her firm buttocks and flared down to her ankles.

Hungry for success at the Plantation Club, she learned without any hesitation all of Ethel Waters's material, in hopes of replacing the star should she ever miss a show. When Waters took ill one night, Baker went on, winning audience approval as she sang Waters's hits. Afterward, Baker was ready to move in with her own act at the club. What she had not taken into consideration was Ethel Waters herself. Throughout her career, Ethel Waters was a difficult and demanding woman, a figure suspicious of almost everyone and an extraordinary talent whom no other entertainer dared mess with. (Waters could be as tough as Bessie—and as evil, too.) When she learned of the Baker triumph, Ethel laid down the law to the club managers—and Josephine. Baker tangled with Ethel only once and never had a second chance. Ironically, her biggest break—the chance to go to Europe with an all-black revue—came about when Waters, the producers' first choice, was unavailable. In later years, this was probably a subject neither woman was eager to discuss. Waters's attitude was always that Baker had done all right abroad—with *her* stuff.

The show was *La Revue Nègre,* which startled postwar Europeans in 1925. The company consisted of twenty-five black dancers, singers, and musicians. The rest of the cast faded into the woodwork when Baker made her sizzling appearance, con-

sidered one of the most sensational of the first half of the century. Nearly fifty years after the event, Janet Flanner, who wrote about Paris for *The New Yorker,* still had vivid memories of Baker's extraordinary presence:

> *She made her entry entirely nude except for a pink flamingo feather between her limbs; she was being carried upside down and doing the split on the shoulder of a black giant. Midstage he paused, and with his long fingers holding her basketwise around the waist, swung her in a slow cartwheel to the stage floor, where she stood, like his magnificent discarded burden, in an instant of*

A casual Baker in a relaxed mood.

Making it to the movies: Baker in the French film *Princess Tam Tam*.

complete silence. A scream of salutation spread through the theatre.

Flanner said that within a half-hour after the curtain had fallen, news of Baker's stunning appearance made its way through the cafés and haunts on the Champs-Elysées. Those who had seen the show retold its wonders time and again, never tiring of the tale, hoping through talk to recapture the spectacular moments. In no time, the nineteen-year-old runaway from St. Louis found herself the most acclaimed and sought-after woman in Paris.

A year later, Baker starred in the Folies Bergère in a show that took months to rehearse, had 500 cast-and-crew members, and 1,200 costumes. She dazzled European audiences with her version of the Charleston. Baker leaped onto the Paris stage, crossed her eyes, swung her hips, and wore nothing but a festoon of bananas and a smile.

Josephine Baker was now an international celebrity. She floated through French theatrical, literary, and intellectual circles with the greatest of ease. She met many of the most prominent European personalities of her age: Max Reinhardt, Colette, Jean Cocteau, Le Corbusier, Marcel Pagnol, Luigi Pirandello, Albert Einstein, and Erich Maria Remarque, who said that she brought "a whiff of jungle air and an elemental strength and beauty to the tired showplace of Western civilization." Those captivated by her onstage exoticism were eager to see if the woman away from the footlights was just as exciting.

Wisely, Baker understood the connection between her public and private personalities. And she promoted the stories that circulated about her extravagance, her hauteur, her unconventionality. One night, she might roam the dance floors with a snake wrapped around her long neck. The next

WINTER GARDEN

1634-1646 BROADWAY REALTY CO., INC.

THE · PLAYBILL · PUBLISHED · BY · THE · NEW · YORK · THEATRE · PROGRAM · CORPORATION

BEGINNING
THURSDAY EVENING,
JANUARY 30, 1936

MATINEES
THURSDAY AND
SATURDAY

1936 EDITION OF THE

ZIEGFELD FOLLIES

A National Institution, Glorifying the American Girl

with

FANNIE BRICE

BOB HOPE	GERTRUDE NIESEN	HUGH O'CONNELL	HARRIET HOCTOR
EVE ARDEN	JUDY CANOVA	CHERRY & JUNE PREISSER	JOHN HOYSRADT

NICHOLAS BROTHERS	DUKE McHALE	RODNEY McLENNAN
STAN KAVANAGH	BEN YOST'S VARSITY EIGHT	GEORGE CHURCH

and

JOSEPHINE BAKER

ENTIRE PRODUCTION STAGED BY
JOHN MURRAY ANDERSON

Famous for her exotic menagerie, Baker cuddles up to her pet, Chiquita.

day, she might be spotted on the Champs-Elysées with a leopard on a leash. Fashion editor Diana Vreeland recalled sitting in a Parisian movie house with Baker *and* Baker's pet cheetah. (Vreeland also said that, along with Isadora Duncan and Consuelo Vanderbilt, Baker was one of America's few authentic women of style.) When the French press learned that she had a Louis XVI bedroom, they thereafter insisted that she slept in Marie Antoinette's bed. She was said to have received 46,000 fan letters within two years. There were 2,000 marriage proposals and scores of suitors, one madman who pursued her through Europe, another young man who, enamored of her, shot himself, then fell at her feet. In France, Baker also later starred in such movies as *Zou Zou* and *Princess Tam Tam.* Siclian Count Giuseppe "Pepito" Abatino became her jealous lover—manager. Maybe he was a count. Most likely, not. She liked to think of him as her

husband. Maybe they married. Most likely, they did not. Baker and dashing man-about-town Jean Lion actually did marry, but the union ended in divorce. Later, she would wed bandleader Jo Bouillon, who would let his own career fade as he became her consort, her housekeeper, her babysitter. Incredible as some of the Baker stories sound, most are true or at least have a truth at their base. Were all the stories simply fabrications of a shrewd press agent, Baker might have been a more relaxed figure. Instead, even at this early stage, while still in her twenties, Josephine Baker seemed hell-bent on constructing an elaborate mythology that would cast her as the most glamorous and exciting woman of her time. Few people ever really knew the woman behind the extroverted personality, the figure who made the legend, and crystallized the style. "Why spoil the illusion?"' she asked (in the 1970s) an eager-beaver New

York City reporter whom she felt was trying to get too close.

Yet, despite whatever confusions even Baker may have had concerning her personal identity, she was just what post–World War I Europeans were in desperate need of. For a generation that had been denied much and had been forced to take everything seriously in order to survive, here stood *"La Ba-Kair"* (later she would be simply "Josephine"), a towering ebony Venus, to teach everybody how to relax and live again. In this period, Baker's particular style and attitude—an outrageous delight in her own prettiness (something that she discovered late), a delight that even then often slipped over into exhilarating self-parody—startled and invigorated audiences. Baker—with her daring (she was going topless long before it was fashionable), her imagination, her outlandish costumes, her gorgeous chocolate shoulders—was a one-woman extravaganza, the most shamelessly assertive form of self-pride any audience, black or white, had ever seen. Throughout the 1920s, she toured the great European capitals—Berlin, Budapest, Amsterdam, London, Madrid—and epitomized the new freedom

Early Baker: a grinning, cross-eyed pickaninny figure in *Chocolate Dandies.*

and festivity with a hint of decadence always just beneath the surface. And so before anyone knew it, she had taken America's flapper spirit to new heights and in an unexpected direction. When people were just beginning to collect *art nègre* and the world was discovering *le jazz hot*, Josephine Baker represented the new black talent and the new black music about to sweep through Europe. She cleared the path for scores of jazz musicians and black beauties such as Adelaide Hall, Elisabeth Welch, the Peters Sisters, and Florence Mills, all of whom would find European audiences much more receptive to their talents than the folks back home.

In the long run, hers was probably the 1920s' most compelling diva personality—and maybe its most disturbing.

For it has to be admitted that Baker succeeded with European audiences in part because she played on their view of the black woman as something of a super-sexy noble savage. Those Europeans with disdain for aggressive, coarse Americans could contentedly pride themselves on being superior to a culturally deprived nation that had, after all, completely overlooked this Eighth Wonder of the World. She seemed the perfect object, a glittering artifact that could never fail to please. At the same time, White America never seemed at ease with this woman who would eventually speak openly about its racism and bigotry, who would often also speak with dramatic romanticism of having had to flee the home of the brave in order to find her freedom. On those occasions when she returned to the States for appearances, even critics seemed skeptical, to put it mildly, not wanting to acknowledge her talent or appeal. When she opened on Broadway in *The Ziegfeld Follies of 1935*, with such stars as Fanny Brice, the reviews were devastating. "After her cyclonic career abroad, Josephine Baker has become a celebrity who offers her presence instead of talent," wrote critic Brooks Atkinson in *The New York Times*. "Her singing voice is only a squeak in the dark and her dancing is only the pain of an artist. Miss Baker has refined her art until there is nothing left of it." Worst was the review in *Time:* "In sex appeal to jaded Europeans of the jazz-loving type, a Negro wench always has a head start, but to Manhattan theatergoers last week she was just a slightly bucktoothed young Negro woman whose figure might be matched in any nightclub show, whose dancing and singing could be topped practically anywhere outside France." American culture has rarely taken to its expatriates, particularly those who fail "to repent" and come back home for good.

But that hardly bothered black women in America who read of Josephine Baker's triumphs with great curiosity and pleasure. In the Black Community there had long been a fantasy of another world, another place and time, where the black woman would be seen for her unique brown beauty. In essence and act, Josephine Baker had escaped and lived out the fantasy for women back home. Black women reveled in her success, identified with her, and had the utmost respect. Blacks loved hearing the stories of the way that Baker, when around whites, flaunted in their faces her chocolate color; her height; her big, beautiful hips. "What a wonderful revenge for an ugly duckling," she said of her fame. The statement reveals that Baker never forgot her early torments or her roots. Ironically, Baker's great theme song would be "J'ai Deux Amours"—*I have two loves, my country and Paris*. In the twenties, she put Harlem on the map of the world.

Ethel Waters:
Sweet Mama
Shakes Her Thing

Just at the time that Josephine Baker was hypnotizing Europe, Ethel Waters's career took its first mighty upward swing in the United States. Waters injected the giddy flapper spirit with a new kind of social realism, introducing the ghettoized flapper, a *hincty* (difficult, arrogant), raunchy girl determined to make good. Hers was also the pure city girl, no longer just singing the blues but exposed to pop music. Ethel Waters fully understood her girl-from-the-school-of-hard-knocks persona because it was so close to herself.

Waters's early life had been a harrowing experience, full of city terrors. Born out of wedlock in Chester, Pennsylvania, in 1896, she had moved, as a child, from one tenement to another, quickly picking up the ways of the street. She ran errands for whores, was a lookout for pimps, and early acquired a reputation as a tough, foul-mouthed girl. At thirteen she married. Two years later, the marriage was over. Afterward, she took a job as a chambermaid and laundress at a Philadelphia hotel. Always a large girl, big-boned and awkward, she felt forever the outsider. The one person she stood in awe of, the one figure who showered Waters with much-needed attention, was her grandmother, Sally Anderson, who died when Waters was still young. Later, her great dramatic characters of stage and film were to be modeled on this strong, tragic figure.

When young, Ethel Waters often stood in front of mirrors, bowing to imaginary crowds applauding her. But she never gave serious thought to a professional career until she performed informally one Halloween night at a Philadelphia club. The audience enthusiasm propelled her. Soon, she was traveling on the road with the Hill Sisters as part of their singing act. Later, she learned that she was being cheated out of money, an experience that she never forgot. Finally, she took off on her own, hitting one tiny town after another, building a large following. Before long, this lanky girl with sweet curves all over the place was packin' 'em in at Edmund's Cellar in New York City where, by then, she was billed as Sweet Mama Stringbean. Although never a pure blues singer, she became the first woman to perform W. C. Handy's "St. Louis Blues."

The Waters of this period was a startling far cry from the strong-as-a-rock maternal figure she would later popularize. In the twenties, she was a good-natured girl with a chip on her shoulders. She was rough and knew how to handle men, too. Often, she talked during her numbers—about and to men, ever ready to shake them up some. Songs such as "Shim Me Sha Wabble" and "I Want to Be Somebody's Baby Doll so I Can Get My Lovin' All the Time" were playful crowd favorites. But with "Brother You've Got Me Wrong" and "Go Back Where You Stayed Last Night," she set the male population straight. In the latter, she commanded that the dude take it where he had had it the night before and to move away from her door, or she would call the law. Somehow, she miraculously made the words *door* and *law* rhyme. But all of this kind of thing could change when she did bumps and grinds to an insolently sexy number like "Shake that Thing," in which she knowingly gave males a heady come-on although she was sure to pull back at the crucial moment. Her attitude seemed to be: You can look, baby, but you damn well better not touch! Black men went wild over her; the greater the challenge, the better the woman.

Gradually, during this time, Waters's work took on a new sophistication, and her stage presence cooled down some to the point where this mix of ghetto raunch and rowdiness, this *exotique*, had become, in the words of Alberta Hunter, "a very refined performer." Her big 1920s hits "Dinah" and "Sweet Georgia Brown" were smooth, easygoing pop tunes. More than any other star of the period, she legitimized the Harlem clubs. Whites were going uptown to see this woman who could sing songs by important white composers in a new *cullid* way.

In 1927, her first Broadway appearance in the short-lived, all-black revue *Africana* marked her emergence out of the clubs and onto the legitimate stage. By the end of the 1920s, Sweet Mama Stringbean was about to undergo some dramatic changes and eventually would become the first dark diva to make Broadway her domain.

Nina Mae McKinney:
Country Girl Gone
City Gone Hollywood

The twenties came to a fitting close with the appearance of Nina Mae McKinney, a South Carolina–born teenager lifted from the chorus line of Lew Leslie's *Blackbirds of 1928* and transported west, where she opened the door that most African American women thought would be permanently closed: Hollywood. With the arrival of the Al Jolson movie *The Jazz Singer* in 1927, American motion pictures learned to talk. Afterward in 1929, the film industry released two all-talking, all-singing, all-dancing, all-colored musicals: *Hearts in Dixie* and *Hallelujah*. Of the pair, King Vidor's *Hallelujah*, despite its stereotypes, has remained impressive, not only because of the skill and sensitivity of his direction, but in large part because of its star—McKinney, a footloose, fancy-free Kewpie doll of an actress, one of the few authentic film delights of this period of transition. In *Hallelujah*, she was cast as Chick, a high-strung, high-yellar strumpet who lures a good, clean-cut colored boy (played by Daniel Haynes) away from his family and the church. Her rival is a homely, dark-skinned girl (played by blues singer Victoria Spivey), who is content to spend her days picking cotton. Spivey's sincere and sensitive good girl was no match for Nina Mae's tantalizing tart.

Tremendous break that *Hallelujah* was, McKinney soon found herself up against a wall: Hollywood's rigid color fixation. Originally, Vidor had wanted Ethel Waters as the star of his film. Had Waters, a brown woman, played the leading role in this picture, the history of black women in American movies might have taken a different course. What happened in films, however, was that black women were divided into color categories. Browner or darker African American women would be cast as dowdy, frumpy, overweight mammy figures. Those black women given a chance at leading parts and glamorous stardom would have to be close to the white ideal: straight hair, keen features, lighter skin. These women would become Hollywood's treasured mulattoes, women appearing (sometimes as a subtext) to be doomed in their films seemingly because their blood was mixed. This tradition started with

McKinney and continued with Fredi Washington, Lena Horne, Dorothy Dandridge, and later Halle Berry. Never would a black movie actress have a chance at fully developing her own persona as had Bessie Smith and Josephine Baker. It is interesting to compare the work that some divas did onstage, when they were in control, and onscreen, when instead of playing characters, they played against them. In the case of Dorothy Dandridge, the tension—and basic dissatisfaction with some of her film roles, especially in *Porgy and Bess* and *Malaga*—brought out a jittery vulnerability that makes her always a fascinating film presence.

Onscreen, McKinney was the consummate tease. For a brief spell, it looked as if she would be the one sepia female star in Hollywood's lily white heaven. Everyone from director Vidor to producer Irving Thalberg predicted a glorious future for her. But McKinney learned what other African American love goddesses of the screen were to discover: after one great triumph, there were no significant follow-up roles. In such later films as *Safe In Hell*, *Sanders of the River*, and *Dark Waters*, she was generally misused, although she was always splendidly appealing.

For the most part, the later years of her career were not happy ones. At one point, McKinney appeared abroad in cellars and cafés, elaborately dressed and coiffed, and billed as the *Black Garbo*. Then, she returned to the States to do her black-vamp bit in all-black shows, clubs, theaters, and independently produced black movies. In the late 1940s she popped up, looking older, heavier, and far less energetic in a supporting role in *Pinky*. But unable to duplicate the success of *Hallelujah*, she seemed forever haunted by it. Nor did she have a stable private life. For a time, she was married to Jimmy Monroe, who also was once the husband of Billie Holiday. McKinney's last years were spent in New York City, and she died in 1967.

At the close of the 1920s, America's dark divas remained confident and optimistic about their respective futures. And they took pride in their accomplishments. Few dealt explicitly with racial issues. Baker, the

It Blasts the Lid off Harlem Rackets!

GUN MOLL

WITH

NINA MAY McKINNEY

GANG SMASHERS

ALL COLORED CAST
LAWRENCE CRINER · MONTE HAWLEY
REGINALD FENDERSON · MANTAN MORELAND

A TODDY PICTURE

McKinney remained a star on the race-movie circuit. Note the spelling of her name on this film poster.

defiant expatriate, was quick to comment openly on racism in America. Often enough, however, the blues singers, with their tales of two-timin' men who had cheated or mistreated them, obviously indicated that they lived within the walls of an oppressive system. Men, in general, represented the constraints and controls of society itself.

Most significantly, throughout this period, the divas lived in a world of new opportunities, and perhaps because they still performed mostly for their own communities, they were indeed "freer" than they would be at any other time. They had been able to set their own stage, to call the shots, to decide what clothes to wear and what material to perform, and finally to create whatever stage personalities that they themselves desired. Of course, the situation would soon change as the diva fully entered the mainstream culture.

In the trumped-up heat of the twenties and in the guise of the carefree flapper, the basic outline of high diva style, her way of dealing with the world and in looking at it, had taken its foremost evolutionary shape.

Pop Myths
The 1930s

S uddenly the stock market crashed, and the diva found herself smack in the middle of the Great Depression itself. Although analysts and government officials spoke of the "great slump," or "temporary setback," the diva beauty knew only two things for sure: first, it was tough to find work, and second, many of the tricks of the trade—the flashy, flamboyant, overblown 1920s style—would no longer do.

In the thirties, American audiences determinedly searched their popular culture to find workable myths. The old-style twenties vamp or flapper was replaced by the working-girl heroine, smart brassy women such as Jean Harlow and Jean Arthur. Actresses Sylvia Sidney, Loretta Young, Bette Davis, Claudette Colbert, and on occasion even Marlene Dietrich and Katharine Hepburn personified the woman up against hard times. The divas also toned down their styles. They were aware of the demands of White and Black America.

By 1930, there were over eleven million blacks in the United States. And every day, in one form of another, this ten percent of the nation's population was becoming increasingly more mainstream—and more politically outspoken, too. In 1930, the all-black show *Green Pastures* was Broadway's hottest ticket. In 1931, the first of the Scottsboro trials (nine African American youths accused of raping two white women) made headlines across the country, becoming a major cause célèbre. That same year, the NAACP launched a full-scale attack against segregation and discrimination in North Carolina. As the era moved on, Mary McLeod Bethune came to national attention when named president of the newly formed National Council of Negro Women. And Olympic runner Jesse Owens and heavyweight champ Joe Louis emerged as black folk heroes.

What with Black America's social changes and the nation's economic upheaval, the divas intuitively understood that the new kind of personality Depression—era audiences craved was one whose personal control might be taken as a comment on a larger theme: the restoration of order and balance to the social system itself. New stars such as Billie Holiday and Ivie Anderson offered a soulful mellowness that Depression audiences found reassuring. An actress like Fredi Washington in *Imitation of Life* raised questions about the nation's ongoing racial inequities. Sometimes, the new stars had a wacky joyousness that provided comic relief. For the most part, since the black beauties kept their collective cool equilibrium intact, they seemed to tell Depression audiences that nobody could keep a good woman down.

Isabel Washington, the thirties diva: mellow, controlled, self-assured.

Page 58: Ethel Waters.

Ella Fitzgerald, with Babe Wallace (right), leads the band.

The Girl-Singers

Ella Fitzgerald got her big break at the Apollo's amateur night contest.

The first of the 1930s new-style divas was a collective one, the *girl-singers*. During this era of Swing and the big bands, almost every orchestra, be it Duke Ellington's, Count Basie's, or Artie Shaw's, had a female vocalist. Swing was really a man's thing. The guys played the instruments, worked out the arrangements, held the baton, and bought most of the records. Usually, the last thing traveling musicians wanted was a woman in the troupe, who they believed could hardly cope with their rough-and-ready lifestyle. (They had short memories. For Ma, Bessie, and all those twenties blues sisters had helped make the road par-for-the-course for all musical entertainers.) But the big-band managers, aware that audiences latched onto female vocalists in a way that they never connected to males, came up with the idea that it never hurt to have a woman by their side. For a spell, Billie Holiday traveled with Basie. From 1938 to 1942, Helen Humes worked with the Count. She also recorded with Harry James in 1938.

Valaida Snow appeared with Earl Hines. Not only did she sing, but she also played the trumpet. Noble Sissle's orchestra employed Lena Horne, the new girl beauty of the era. Chick Webb took a chance on a plump teenager from Newport News, Virginia, who seemed timid but mighty eager to please, the young Ella Fitzgerald. And Pennsylvania–born Maxine Sullivan appeared with bandleader John Kirby, whom she later married. Sometimes, the girl-singer sang the hit that overshadowed the band. Sullivan not only had the popular swing version of the Scottish folk tune "Loch Lomond," but she appeared in the 1939 movies *St. Louis Blues* and *Going Places* and also worked onstage opposite Louis Armstrong in the 1939 pop version of *A Midsummer Night's Dream* called *Swingin' the Dream*. And Fitzgerald had jukeboxes jumping to the beat of "A-Tisket a-Tasket." Once she hooked up with Webb, the two of them reigned as the King and Queen of Harlem's Savoy Ballroom. When Webb died in 1939, Fitzgerald took over management of the band and kept it going for three years. Countless other women such as June Richmond, Velma Middleton, and May Alix performed with various groups.

Closely aligned to the girl-singers were the other women on the sidelines of the big bands, pianists Lil Hardin Armstrong (Louis's first wife and an important jazz artist in her own right), Vivian Smith, Irene Wilson (at one time the wife of orchestra leader Teddy Wilson and also the composer of three of

Billie Holiday's favorite songs: "I'm Pulling Through," "Ghost of Yesterday," and "Some Other Spring"), and Mary Lou Williams. In Kansas City, Mary Lou Williams joined Andy Kirk's Clouds of Joy, arranging, composing, and performing as pianist from 1931 to 1942. Eventually, Williams came east where her radio performances won her a national following. She also wrote for Benny Goodman.

Almost automatically, the girl-singers stood as symbols of resourceful, knowing women on the move, hip and clever enough to travel on the band's bus with the boys, to play cards with them (and win), and to swap stories.

But at night when the house lights went down, the girl-singers stood under the spotlight and took on another dimension. As they sang of loneliness or despair, of hard times or low ones, they represented woman alone, coming to grips with feelings in a way no male singer would have dared. Finally, what distinguished them was that, unlike the raucous Bessie out to shake society up, these women, even when singing of hot, wild times, had a quiet, restrained, comforting approach.

June Richmond was a vocalist with Jimmy Dorsey's band.

Ivie Anderson: the Duke's Lonely Co-ed

For many, the quintessential-1930s big band girl-singer was the sleek, sometimes chummy, sometimes aloof Ivie Anderson. For audiences, black and white, she represented a wholly new statement in black womanhood, her look and manner entirely different and distinct. Neither a hefty mama like Bessie nor an exuberantly high-spirited gal like McKinney, Ivie Anderson was slender, with a rich brown coloring, expressive eyes, and a long, sensual face that could convey a variety of moods. She slipped onto stage often wearing white gowns that were long, silky, slinky, elegant, and very, very sexy. Often, entertainers had been given to overstatement or to showy expressions of their affluence. Ivie Anderson ushered in the look and demeanor of the classy colored girl—the kind of figure that she seemed to be singing about in her big hit "A Lonely Co-ed"—from a good black girls' school like Bennett or Spelman (known as the black Vassar and Radcliffe of the South).

Surely, what contributed to Ivie's well-mannered style was her early training. Born in Gilroy, California, in 1904, she had been reared in a convent until her early teens. Throughout the 1920s, this ladylike young singer worked the West and East Coasts, appearing with such bands as Curtis Mosby's, Paul Howard's, Sonny Clay's, even for a brief spell with the white band of Anson Weeks. By the 1930s, she had joined Earl Hines at the Grand Terrace in Chicago. Here, her career took a dramatic turn when Duke Ellington, eager for a girl-singer to spice up his debut at the Oriental Theatre, hired Ivie (then spelled *Ivy*). Originally, he had wanted May Alix, but some thought she was so light-skinned that she might be mistaken for white and that there might be problems. Finally, the Duke settled on hiring the browner Ivie but he never had any regrets because Anderson was an extraordinary presence and a singer of great skill.

During the twelve years that Anderson toured throughout the States and Europe with Ellington's orchestra, she was often considered the group's high point. If anything, she may have blended in too well with the Ellington sound for she never became a major solo artist.

Onstage, she was perceptive enough, like the Duke, to instantly gauge an audience's mood. Blessed with a comic flair and an impeccable sense of showmanship, she worked up an act with drummer Sonny Greer in which they exchanged playful banter that had sexual innuendoes flying all over the place. Anderson always kept the upper hand because she was too cool ever to be done in by a souped-up cat. With a nonchalant shrug or a toss of a head, Ivie Anderson was above everything, operating in her own magical kingdom where maintaining your cool meant more than anything, except music.

As a singer, she was versatile too. Such songs as "When My Sugar Walks down the Street," "Truckin'," and "All God's Chillun got Rhythm" were delivered with enthusiasm and a wonderful sense of fun. She performed the last in the Marx Brothers movie *A Day at the Races*, announcing to Depression moviegoers that troubles didn't mean a thing and that it was time to turn those frowns upside down. She also calmly mastered the song considered the battle hymn of the period, Ellington's "It Don't Mean a Thing (If It Ain't Got that Swing)." Here, she captured the era's sentimental longing for a return to happy days. As Ivie sang it, the idea was: let's have a great time together—even now in the worst of times!

Generally, she favored the sentimental compositions. In her hands "If You Were in My Place," "There's a Lull in My Life," "Isn't Love the Strangest Thing," and "A Lonely Co-ed" became memorable, haunting ballads, brimming over with loneliness and melancholia as well as with technical virtuosity. Her renditions of Ellington's "Mood Indigo" and "Solitude" remain definitive. When she is inevitably compared to Billie Holiday, about all that can be said is that she never gave in totally to emotion as Lady Day did. (Nobody else did either.) Ivie Anderson had an objective correlative in her work. She gave Depression audiences the emotional content, yet always held herself and the listener at a distance, so that they might not only hear but understand, too.

Years later, when commenting on the Ellington Orchestra in the 1960s, music critic Ralph Gleason wrote: "In only one respect has this band lost with the years. There never was, nor will there ever be again, a vocalist of the caliber of Ivie Anderson. She was unique and irreplaceable. There have been other good singers with the band, but only Ivie sounded as if she were born to sing to this music."

And in the autobiography *Black and White Baby*, entertainer Bobby Short said:

Like Gertrude Lawrence, she could sing the worst songs in the grandest way. And she had a rare gift. She was a popular singer who listened to the lyrics and stayed within the character of the song. She was into the words and music at a time when most girl singers flounced out and warbled lyrics about heartbreak and despair with bright smiles on their faces.

He added that she was his favorite singer "for all time."

In 1941, Anderson was one of the stars, along with Herb Jeffries and Dorothy Dandridge, of Ellington's groundbreaking musical *Jump for Joy*. But later, Ivie Anderson left Ellington's orchestra, much to his great regret and hers. It is doubtful if there was ever another girl-singer he liked as much. But for most of her life, the young woman who was reared in a convent had suffered terrifying attacks of asthma. In time, the wear of the road, the tension of the performances, the anxieties, left their mark. Advised by her physician to give up traveling, she returned to California, performed for a spell as a solo attraction, and later opened her Chicken Shack restaurant, a favorite watering hole for musicians in the west. Ivie Anderson died in 1949.

Anderson with master arranger/composer/vocal coach Phil Moore.

Billie Holiday: the Essence of Cool

Of all the era's girl-singers, Billie Holiday became the most famous. Even in the early days of her career, everyone knew something about her past. She was born Eleanora Fagan in 1915, the out-of-wedlock child of a domestic, Sadie Fagan, and a musician, Clarence Holiday, who abandoned mother and child to resume his career on the road. His attitude about the daughter who would worship him for years was that she was simply an accident, "something I stole when I was fifteen."

While her mother worked in New York City, young Eleanora lived with relatives in Baltimore. Sensitive, unhappy, and mistreated, she often hung out at the local

Billie's childhood fantasies come true—furs, jewels, and an escape from poverty.

brothel since that was the only place in the neighborhood with a Victrola (decades before there were CD players). There, she would sit for hours and listen to her idols, Louis Armstrong and Bessie Smith. Little Eleanora had quite a childhood. She ran errands for prostitutes, was sexually attacked at the age of ten, and was then sent to a

Catholic institution because it was assumed that she had "enticed" the man. She sat silent when her grandmother died with her arms wrapped around her. By thirteen, she quit school, having gone only to the fifth grade, and by fifteen she was working as a maid in New York with her mother. For a short time, she worked as a prostitute and was thrown into jail when she shunned the attentions of a Harlem man, who had connections all over town.

Billie Holiday's early experiences and humiliations were so terrifying that they stuck with her for the rest of her life, spilling over into her personal relationships and often making her suspicious of everyone. The experiences obviously had a bearing on Billie, the artist, for in her music she was determined to explore the emotional territory of a woman smothered by feeling, who had to sing the things that she could not say.

Holiday began to sing in tiny Harlem clubs, where she acquired a reputation among musicians as a remarkable jazz vocalist who used her voice the way Louis Armstrong played his horn. In 1933 at age eighteen, she made her first recordings for Columbia. Producer John Hammond, who signed her up, said that "she sang popular songs in a manner that made them completely her own....She was absolutely beautiful, with a look and bearing that were, indeed, ladylike, and never deserted her, even in the degraded final years....She was the best jazz singer I had ever heard." Her first recordings (with Benny Goodman), "Riffin' the Scotch" and "Your Mother's Son-in-Law," were fast-moving, lively numbers, a far cry from the sometimes sentimental romantic ballads or the torch songs that she later became famous for. Her high spirits gave no indication of the somber, relentless brooding quality that would permeate her late work.

In 1935, she was booked at the Apollo, then the most talked-about showplace in the world for black entertainers. Throughout the 1930s, Ivie Anderson and the Duke performed there as did the up-and-coming Moms Mabley. And in time the Apollo's famous amateur nights would see the lies of Sarah Vaughan, Billy Eckstine, LaVern

Baker, and the Isley Brothers. Even Ella Fitzgerald had her big break there. With Holiday, everyone seemed caught up in the excitement of seeing a major talent coming into her own. According to Holiday biographer John Chilton, Apollo emcee Ralph Cooper saw that she was so nervous that he went out and bought her clothes for the appearance and even rehearsed her numbers for the band. The night she opened, comedian Pigmeat Markham had to push her onto the stage.

Her initial shyness and vulnerability, not at all lost on the audience, simply added to the intensity of her performance. There she stood, an awkward, good-natured country girl, weighing almost two hundred pounds, scared out of her wits. She was neatly dressed and nicely coifed. All she had to do was smile—and she was perfect. But when she sang—"Them There Eyes" and "If the Moon Turns Green"—the enthusiastic black audience screamed for an encore that brought the house down. She sang "The Man I Love." Billie Holiday was booked for a return engagement and was now on her way.

Throughout the thirties, Holiday hopped from one club to another, worked with the prominent musicians of her day (Teddy Wilson, Fletcher Henderson, Count Basie), reached a far wider audience than her predecessors, received good press, and, upon agreeing to appear with Artie Shaw's band, became one of the first black women to travel through the South with a white group.

She was a remarkable performer, able to turn the trite lyrics of pop tunes inside out, coming up with individualized phrasings/interpretations that made an audience think twice about a number it might have heard for years. Then, too, there was the unexpected emotional depth. The direction of her career (and lifestyle) was unheard of for a black entertainer. For Holiday eventually integrated the chic, glittering supper clubs, paving the way for women such as Lena Horne, Carmen McRae, Sarah Vaughan, and Ella Fitzgerald. The darling of sophisticated café society of the late thirties and forties, she represented for Black America the modern, sometimes feisty, and foul-mouthed black woman who had made

it into the system without losing her roots. Even as she went from job to job, band to band, she was part of a progressive dream.

In terms of the professional African American woman's image, she introduced a new kind of glamour. She was hardly your run-of-the-mill girl-singer. Already she was known as *Lady*. (In time, her good buddy Lester Young would tag her *Lady Day*.) And while still young, she had the look of a well-decked matron with expensive, full-skirted, low-cut dresses, plenty of jewelry, and lots of makeup. Later, she luxuriated in furs. And, of course, there was her trademark, the gardenia pinned to her hair. Although viewed as a working girl, Billie Holiday would never have thought of doing the stricken-Depression-child bit. Throughout her career, like all the other great divas, she refused to look tacky, poor, or ordinary. Clothes always had a significance for women like Holiday, assuring them that their childhood fantasies of escape had indeed come true.

But what with all her success, something else was happening to Billie Holiday in the 1930s. The personal myth was emerging from behind troubled shadows, gradually pushing aside the professional image with which her public was so taken. Her lucky breaks had made it look as if the American system was holding up. But Holiday lived the problems her mainstream public didn't care to see. No other diva was ever as disoriented by success. And for no other did personal and professional deterioration set in as quickly.

Of course, often enough she created problems for herself. When appearing at a Philadelphia theater, she was informed by the theater owner's wife that the song she planned to sing ("Underneath the Harlem Moon") was the same one headliner Ethel Waters had intended to perform. By all rights, Holiday should have deferred to the older, established star, but she wouldn't budge! A terrible row followed, in which Billie spared not a word, letting the theater owner's wife know exactly how she felt. (Nobody knows what she said to Ethel or what Ethel said to her. Later, Waters did comment on Billie's style: "She sounds like

But when she sang—"Them There Eyes" and "If the Moon Turns Green"—the enthusiastic black audience screamed for an encore that brought the house down.

her feet hurt.") Holiday was shown the door. She should have learned but she didn't. Later, when successfully traveling with Count Basie's band, she was asked to change some of her material, to sing more blues rather than pop tunes. She flatly refused, and soon she and the Count parted ways.

Other times, Holiday was hassled by club bookers insensitive to her originality. According to Holiday biographer Chilton, at Chicago's Grand Terrace, owner Ed Fox, infuriated by a performance he thought too slow and too somber, yelled at her, "Why the fuck should I pay you $250 [actually, it was $75] a week to stink my goddamn show up. Get out!" She left, but not before speaking her mind and throwing furniture at him.

On other occasions, Billie Holiday fell victim to the blatant racism of her period. In 1935, when she appeared at the Famous Door in New York City, she was told not to mingle with the patrons, not to sit at a table or the bar. Before going on, she waited upstairs outside the toilets. The atmosphere was so tense that it affected her performance. Finally, she was let go from the club. Afterward, when traveling with Basie, she was repeatedly turned away from hotels and restaurants. Her worst experiences were with Shaw, who was considered "daring" for hiring a Negro girl-singer. But in time, this extraordinary career boost proved an emotionally debilitating experience, with the familiar problems simply intensified. It was still a hassle finding a place to sleep or eat. In Boston, there were complaints about her style. The bookers wanted her to speed things up. In St. Louis, a pro-

moter insisted that she be replaced with a white singer. Helen Forrest was brought in. By far, the most depressing business was that of the radio broadcasts, which became fewer and fewer since music publishers griped that she did not stick closely enough to the written melody and lyrics. When she appeared with Shaw at New York's Lincoln Hotel, she was not permitted to visit the bar or the dining room and was told always to use the kitchen entrance. It was getting to the regal Lady Day and the tension showed.

Black America watched the drama of Billie Holiday, connecting to this troubled, restless young woman as it did with no other diva. For whatever problems she had in such "high" places were no different from their own.

By 1938, Billie Holiday had left Shaw. She had left Basie. She had left Teddy Wilson. She had left innumerable clubs. She probably had been fired more frequently than any other major star of the time. And she was rapidly becoming even more of an introspective, withdrawn, difficult woman. Her love affairs weren't going right. Her eating habits were erratic. Her reputation as a hell-raiser and carouser had grown. She was always being hassled by men. And she was drinking. Clearly, she was headed for a tragic decline that she seemed to invite. In conversation, she started painting herself as the victim: of a terrible childhood, of men, of callous club managers, of racism, of you-name-it. She loved to dramatize her woes and tribulations. In the beginning, all her talk may have been nothing more than a public pose with which she

Holiday with her childhood idol Louis Armstrong in the film *New Orleans*.

felt more comfortable. One of Holiday's most tender songs, "God Bless the Child," became her anthem, touching on her feelings of isolation and alienation. Unfortunately, Holiday later became trapped in the persona she had at first played with. What eventually took over was the other Billie, the drug-ridden, magnetic star who, frankly, could be unbearably temperamental and impossible to deal with.

The 1930s may have been Billie Holiday's musical high-water mark, the period of intense creativity, when her voice was clearest, strongest, and most vibrant. Her most stabilizing experience was at Café Society, one of the first New York–white nightspots to integrate not only its perform-

ers but its audiences, too. There, in 1939, she introduced "Strange Fruit," the moody dirge about a Southern lynching. Her rendition of the song drew the intellectuals to her: now, popular music had a social–political consciousness. For years, it played on jukeboxes throughout the United States, particularly in tiny, hidden black bars and restaurants. And so, paradoxical as it may seem now, in the days of the Great Depression, audiences saw in Billie Holiday a hopeful sign for the future, a representative of the basically decent young African American woman who, having survived the toughest of times, was bound to get through anything else without any pain. As Duke Ellington said, she was the essence of cool.

Clockwise from upper left: Hattie McDaniel with Ben Carter; McDaniel with her assistant; Louise Beavers (seated on the right), always in a stoic role; and Beavers with Fredi Washington in *Imitation of Life*.

Louise Beavers and Hattie McDaniel: the Diva Goes West

Nowhere in American popular culture of the thirties was the black-woman-as-pop-myth more prominently displayed than in Hollywood. During the Depression era, more African American women worked in important American movies than ever before. The hitch was that the place the film industry found for the black actress was in the kitchen or pantry or servants' quarters. The divas of the stages and clubs, girl-singers and actresses, may not have had control over the way the public chose to view them. But at least many had shaped their own personas and exerted some control over their material.

The Hollywood diva, however, was dressed by the studio in gingham and rags and made to speak a *dem-and-dose* dialect. Audiences saw black movie heroines playing servants—and rigidly stereotyped ones at that. Yet, the history of American cinema has always been known for its contradictions, unexpected complexities, and oddball triumphs. And demeaning as Hollywood's casting system was, some remarkable African American women were able to inject vigor and some pizzazz into their cheap, trashy roles. Interestingly enough, the black woman of the 1930s films came—on her own terms—to represent beneath the stereotype the idea of energy, drive, spunk, and that good-old American virtue of self-reliance and self-sufficiency, too: the ability to get through, no matter what. Throughout the thirties and into the forties, certain women presented distinct personas, giving in the long run intensely interesting, idiosyncratic performances. In *Flying Down To Rio* and *Gold Diggers of 1933*, Etta Moten held onto her grand-dame hauteur. Theresa Harris emerged as the intelligent, pretty (without having to be a "mulatto type") brown black girl, and was able to land unusual roles with Barbara Stanwyck in *Baby Face* and Jean Harlow in *Hold Your Man*, in which she was more of a hip sidekick than a ditzy maid. She did, however, have her share of dim-maid roles as in *The Toy Wife*. Gertrude Howard, Libby Taylor, Marietta Canty, Lillian Yarbo, and Ruby Dandridge (the mother of Dorothy) were the giddy, happy-go-lucky numbers. The Randolph sisters, Lillian and Amanda, had careers that stretched into later de-

cades. Both would work in the 1950s television series *Amos 'n' Andy*. On that show, Amanda could so easily push people around that no one would have wanted to tangle with her. And there was the cold-eyed, mean-looking Madame Sul-Te-Wan, one of Hollywood's strangest characters, whose friendship with D. W. Griffith was known throughout the film industry. The high-pitched, diminutive Butterfly McQueen always had the gift of operating in a world entirely her own, set apart from the culture of the film. In the Black Community, no one ever disliked these women themselves. What was despised was their movies' gross distortions.

Out of this stereotype system, there appeared two powerful forces, Louise Beavers and Hattie McDaniel, who managed to come up with workable pop myths that reached huge audiences. Sometimes, the myths were so entangled with the stereotypes and misconceptions of the scripts that the actresses had trouble making personal statements through their characters. Much of the conventional way in which America in the 1930s was to view the black woman grew out of these women's performances.

Cincinnati–born Louise Beavers came to prominence portraying overweight mammy figures ready to take on the troubles of the world. Beavers was a big-boned woman, dark, full-faced, wide-hipped. She perfected the optimistic, sentimental black woman whose sweet, sunny disposition and kindheartedness often saved the day. In such features as *Rainbow on the River, She Done Him Wrong, Bombshell, Big Street, Bullets or Ballots,* and the classic tearjerker of 1934, *Imitation of Life*, she emerged as the Depression era's embodiment of Christian stoicism and goodness, lending a friendly ear and hand to down-on-their-luck heroines, who knew that when the rest of the world failed them, Louise would always be there. In *Made for Each Other*, when Carole Lombard and James Stewart are down to their last penny, who shows up with food for the hungry but their former servant Louise! In *Big Street*, when Lucille Ball lies ill and lonely in the hospital, who suggests to Henry Fonda that by pawning Ball's jewelry there will be money for medical expenses?

Why, good old Louise. And in *Bombshell*, when platinum-blond Jean Harlow, as a movie star surrounded by sycophants, finally has had it, who is the one person she screams has ever really done anything for her? None other than her friendly maid Loretta, played by Beavers. Her roles, of course, were absurdities, white myths about black lives. But Beavers approached them with the seriousness and integrity of a true trouper. She also appeared in independently produced black movies made outside the studio system—such as *Reform School* and *Life Goes On*. Because of her skill as well as her own awareness of what the scripts neglected to say about her characters, she herself said much, with a look or a gesture.

In *Imitation of Life*, Beavers played her most famous character, Aunt Delilah, a domestic who, because of hard times, shares a house with a white woman who becomes a friend. The makers of the movie undoubtedly prided themselves on its theme of racial harmony. White and black could unite and make a go of things during these hard times. But no one who has seen the film could fail to be haunted by the image of the tender, sensitive Beavers, still living with the white woman once they have both struck it rich, descending the stairs late at night to return to her quarters in the basement. And in another scene, when Beavers's heart is breaking because her only daughter has decided to pass for white, American movie audiences, for a few minutes, were no longer in a Hollywood-fantasy world, but were confronted by a complex social situation that is disturbingly real.

Although Beavers was relaxed and easygoing, Hattie McDaniel was anything but. Also a large, dark, African American woman typed as the mammy, McDaniel was as well one of the most charismatic performers, black or white, to work in American motion pictures. In scores of movies, McDaniel kept her own with some of the most famous stars of the decade: Gable, Hepburn, Harlow, Vivien Leigh, Shirley Temple, Olivia de Havilland, Henry Fonda, and Barbara Stanwyck. Boldly, she looked her white costars directly in the eye,

never backing off from anyone. Her extraordinary sonic boom of a voice delivered perfectly timed one-line zingers with the greatest of ease. Sometimes, McDaniel seemed angry. Although the filmmakers through their movies never explained it, her undercover hostility, even when coated with humor, was never lost on the audience. She set her own standards and sailed through many films with an astonishing sense of self and personal dignity. For her work as the cantankerous character Mammy in *Gone with the Wind*, Hattie McDaniel became the first African American performer to win an Academy Award for Best Supporting Actress of 1939.

The characters that Beavers and McDaniel created were given more complex, treatment by Ethel Waters in the late 1940s and 1950s. And in the late fifties, Lorraine Hansberry created a character, the mother Lena, in *A Raisin in the Sun*, who finally had a chance onstage and in film to say all the things about a black matriarch that Beavers and McDaniel had fought to bring to the forefront of their shallow films.

With these actresses, though, audiences saw the appeal of the black-matriarchal myth in American pop culture. The myth turns her sexless, has her more caught up in someone else's life than her own, makes her entirely faultless, the essence of Christian goodness, and teaches that she is noble for adjusting to a trying situation without complaining. Looking at the life of Hattie McDaniel, one can see what nonsense the popular myth was. Hattie had four husbands, lived in a plush home in Los Angeles, loved entertaining, and, if pushed, she pushed back. But the matriarch has become one of the staples of the culture: the dark-skinned, all-knowing, all-seeing, all-understanding spiritual force that we can go to when all else fails. In later decades, such gifted actresses as Olivia Cole and Whoopi Goldberg sometimes would get caught up in just such an obsessive conception, one part true, one part national wish-fulfillment. Brilliant as these actresses' characterizations were, here again were acceptable matriarchs out to heal and soothe everybody's wounds.

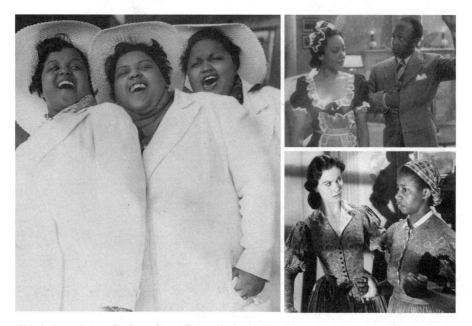

We're in the movies now: The Peters Sisters; Theresa Harris with Eddie "Rochester" Anderson; Butterfly McQueen with Vivien Leigh in *Gone with the Wind.*

Louise Beavers and Hattie McDaniel had careers that spanned some four decades. At the time of her death in 1952, McDaniel was starring on radio and television in the series *Beulah.* Ethel Waters and Louse Beavers also played the lead role in the television series. Beavers's last movie performance was in *The Facts of Life* in 1961.

Other performers, like the Peters Sisters, did a few films, then left Hollywood. Butterfly McQueen might have had an ongoing movie career playing helpless, hysterical maids. But even by the early 1950s, when she joined the cast of television's *Beulah* to play the daffy neighbor Oriole, she was ready to give up on the movies since the industry had failed to give her a chance to grow as an artist. In 1929, Ethel Waters sang "Am I Blue?" and "Birmingham Bertha" in *On with the Show,* then did not appear in a major movie for almost ten years. The delightful Edna Mae Harris appeared in *The Green Pastures* and *Bullets or Ballots,* then soon left Hollywood. But she continued working in independently produced all-black movies. Bee Freeman and Ethel Moses also worked in race movies filmed in the East. The very

young Dandridge sisters—Dorothy, Vivian, and their friend Etta Jones—appeared (sometimes briefly) in musical sequences of such films as *The Big Broadcast of 1936, A Day at the Races,* and *Irene.* Ivie Anderson also played in *A Day at the Races* and with Duke in *The Hit Parade.* Billie Holiday performed in the musical short "Symphony in Black," and later worked with Louis Armstrong in *New Orleans.* (The shocker of this last film was seeing Holiday playing a maid.) Eventually, Lena Horne, Hazel Scott, and Katherine Dunham had a chance to carry their stage personas intact to films. Scott and Dunham did not stay long in Hollywood. But they all realized that exposure in movies added to their glamorous auras: nightclub customers were eager to see the movie star in person.

All the divas, though, had a passionate hope that the movies would eventually find a place for a sensitive, serious black woman. That place was a long time in coming. But on no other thirties figure did the dream seem to have so great a chance of being fulfilled as with Fredi Washington, who emerged as one of Black America's most compelling, electrically charged pop myths of the era.

Bill Robinson, Fredi Washington, Adam Clayton Powell Jr., Isabel Washington, and Fannie Robinson.

The Washington Sisters: Orphans of the Storm

You would never know she was Negro or considered herself such to look at her. She can "pass" whenever it is necessary or convenient, but she makes no attempt to pass: in fact, she feels herself to be entirely identified with the Negro group. Yet Fredi, in a white environment, would be considered white.

Earl Conrad, The Chicago Defender

Fredi Washington, well known on New York stages…[is] not seen on them so frequently as she would be if skin color were not of such surpassing importance…. Fredi is one of those people who find color a special problem in this country for the odd reason that she has little of it. You could describe her in two ways. She is a white girl who could pass as a Negro girl or a Negro girl who could pass as white. Elsewhere there might be no question of being either, but here in this democracy Americans are supposed to be one or another and they have to make a choice. Fredi Washington made it when she was a kid.

Arthur Pollock, The Daily Compass

Today, the words of these newspaper columnists aptly touch on some of the peculiar racial dynamics of American life during the 1920s and Depression, and World War II years. What happens to the black woman who does not look black? What kind of career can she have if she refuses to pass? How is she viewed by her society? These were questions that confronted the legendary Washington sisters, Fredi and Isabel. In theater and social circles, the two were among the most talked-about African American beauties of their age. And whenever their names came up, so too did their color.

They were light-skinned with straight hair and Caucasian features. Slender and green-eyed, Fredi (her full name was Fredricka) looked like a fiercely intellectual career girl on the move. She was something of a mystery, a lovely, quiet woman seemingly given to melancholy. Isabel was less intense: an extroverted, happy-go-lucky young woman ready for a good time. For a number of very prominent people, perhaps most particularly white men, they represented the ultimate taboo: *miscegenated*

beauties cursed by that drop of "negra" blood, which somehow, so the myth said, made them more exciting and passionate than your ordinary white lady. No doubt, in the popular imagination they were viewed as objects that should not freely mingle in society. Instead, they had to be kept locked away, pampered, and glorified. The sisters never saw themselves in this way. If they had, they would have been able to clean up, to run New York City dry. (Years later Eartha Kitt, aware that whites saw her as a classy *exotique*, would play up the exoticism bit to the hilt.)

For the Black Community the two sisters, who spoke without dialects, who understood the social codes and manners of both cultures, and who gave no indication whatsoever of having come from a harsh urban-ghetto experience, were considered highborn, upper-class beauties, representatives perhaps of the old Southern Negro aristocracy. This was what the women were assumed to be. Actually, their background was not so much privileged, or moneyed, as simply different.

Born in Savannah, Georgia (there were nine children in the family), the two sisters—after the death of their mother—had been sent to a convent in Philadelphia for orphaned black and Indian children. Once teenagers, they left. Isabel returned South, married at sixteen, and had a son. Fredi journeyed to New York City to live with her grandmother and to finish school. At sixteen, she dropped out and worked in a dress-company stockroom, making seventeen dollars a week. Later as a bookkeeper at the Black Swan Record Company, she heard of auditions for *Shuffle Along*. Never having danced professionally, she decided to take a chance anyway. After all, the pay was thirty-five dollars a week. When she told her grandmother of her plans, the older woman simply looked at her and said, "If you do it, make something of it." Fredi replied, "Don't worry." With the help of black choreographer Elida Webb, Washington landed a spot in the chorus.

So began a career that had many high points, many disappointments, and that was often enough governed by the response

Sophisticated, sensitive, and political, Fredi Washington was known in New York theater circles as the black girl who looked white.

of theatergoers to Fredi Washington's looks. After *Shuffle Along*, she appeared as a dancer at New York's Club Alabam', and was spotted by Lee Shubert. Obviously dazzled, he suggested that she audition for a new play, *Black Boy*, starring Paul Robeson as a prizefighter. Opening in the play on Broadway, Washington had what remains for her an archetypal role: a fair-skinned black beauty who decides to pass for white. With good notices, she was soon one of the most talked-about ingenues on Broadway. Inside the theaters, some came simply to see if the girl that they had heard of looked that white. Outside theaters, stage-door Johnnies, black and white, pursued, chased, and harassed Fredi Washington like mad.

Millionaire Otto Kahn, who told her she looked French and could easily be French, was so persuaded of her potential to become a star, if freed from "the burden of her race," that, according to printed theater gossip of the day, he even offered to pay for her dramatic education if she changed her name to a French one. "But I want to be what I am," Washington told him, "nothing else."

During the 1920s, Washington toured the smart night spots of Paris, London, Berlin, and Monte Carlo with Al Moore, billed as the dancers Moiret and Fredi. Mingling with European royalty, she even taught the black bottom to the Prince of Wales. The late 1920s found her back in the States in *Hot Chocolates*. Later, she appeared in such plays as *Sweet Chariot* and *Run, Little Chillun,* and in short musical films with Cab Calloway and in *Black and Tan* with Duke Ellington, who was Washngton's great love. For a time, they had a discreet but passionate love affair. Later, she married Lawrence Brown, trombonist with the Duke's orchestra.

During the 1930s, she emerged as one of Black America's most talked-about dramatic actresses. There had not been many. Rose McClendon's dramatic career had been cut short by her premature death. Edna Thomas was a spectacular Depression–age Lady Macbeth in the Orson Welles–John Houseman WPA Federal

watchable. The film tells the story of two women, one white (Claudette Colbert), one black (Louise Beavers), each a widow with a young daughter to rear, who meet and decide to live together. The white woman goes out to work every day. The black woman takes care of the house. One morning, the black woman is fixing breakfast for the white woman, who is so impressed with her friend's pancakes that she wants to know the recipe. It is a family secret, the black woman explains, passed down from generation to generation. Eventually, the white woman strikes it rich with the black woman's pancake mix and has everything money can buy—furs, jewels, beaux.

The tragic side to Washington's dilemma was that she never had the opportunities for strong new roles that might have wiped away the Peola myth.

Theater all-black production of *Macbeth,* which was set in the court of the 19th-century Haitian leader Henri Christophe and was often referred to as Welles's *Voodoo Macbeth.* But Thomas had few opportunities to sustain her dramatic career. Years later, Thomas appeared in the small but showy role of the Mexican woman in the Broadway and movie versions of *A Streetcar Named Desire.* Washington, however, had strong roles in such movies as *The Emperor Jones, Imitation of Life, One Mile from Heaven,* and the play *Mamba's Daughters.* For a spell, it looked as if Hollywood had a serious young black actress it would have to reckon with. But, ironically, Fredi's greatest success almost did her in.

Her big triumph was as Peola, the light-skinned young black woman who passes for white in the original 1934 version of *Imitation of Life.* Seen today, the movie is a classic weepy. But it is also compelling and

Everything is going so well that she offers her black friend a twenty-percent interest in the company. The black woman, submissive and kind, refuses.

Heartache follows when the black woman's light-skinned daughter, Peola, having grown up in a household with whites no lighter than herself, but for whom there is now a world of opportunities, rejects her mother's submissiveness and crosses the color line, going so far as to tell her that if they should ever meet by chance they must act as if they are strangers. The movie ends with Peola returning home for the funeral of her mother, who has died of a broken heart, falling onto the casket, crying, "I killed my mother." There was not a dry eye in the movie house.

A runaway box-office success, *Imitation of Life,* no matter how corny its story might seem today, had an uncanny impact on both Black and White America in 1934, for it was one of the few films even remotely to suggest that there was such a thing as a race problem. In the Black Community, a nerve had been hit, and emotions and sentiments flew high. Ministers preached sermons about it. Intellectuals wrote articles about it. Everyone seemed caught up in its fever, the focal point of which was daughter Peola. On one occasion, as Fredi Washington sat in a beauty parlor, she overheard another woman telling a beautician that she knew Fredi Washington and that that high-yellar so-and-so was, in real life, just the way she had been onscreen. Of course, the woman did not know Washington at all, and when Fredi introduced herself, the lady promptly shut up. On another occasion, as Washington was leaving a Chicago theater that had shown the picture, she was grateful not to be recognized since all the conversation centered on the ingrate daughter. "I bet that Fredi Washington is just like that, too," was a comment the actress heard too often.

The feelings about Washington were ambivalent. In one sense, she was a classy woman audiences loved to hate, the kind of villain contemporary soap-opera viewers endlessly criticize, but whose every move they are sure to watch. Peola's dilemma, whether to pass or not, in essence whether to submit or rebel, was a far more serious issue than the moviemakers had realized. Black audiences could understand how a woman felt when denied such a fundamental right as personal freedom. Aware of the girl's frustration, many responded to her determination to break the rules of a trumped-up, exploitative, decadent, capitalistic society with a *why not?* Then, too, Fredi Washington, because of what the Black Community thought it knew about her personal lifestyle of privilege, sometimes was viewed as a princess entitled to all that she could get.

There were other reactions. The movie had been so manipulative that no one could forgive the woman's treatment of her mother. Here, another issue arose: that of identification and loyalty to one's racial heritage. Peola seemed to have broken not only the white world's rules, but those of the Black Community, too.

Of course, much of the ambivalence was due to the slipshod way the character had been written. *Imitation of Life* had failed

Much ado about a much-talked-about wedding: Adam Clayton Powell Jr. and Isabel Washington, surrounded by Mrs. Powell, Adam Clayton Powell Sr. (second from right), and New York's mayor Fiorello La Guardia.

Fredi Washington (third from left) is joined by actor Canada Lee (left), classical music star Dorothy Maynor, and actor Fredric March at a New York radio broadcast.

to deal squarely, so Fredi Washington herself believed, with a woman who does not want to be white for the sake of *whiteness* but rather wants *white opportunities*. But to the film and the print media that had established a Washington persona, Fredi and Peola were one and the same. As such, Washington emerged a gorgeous oddity, no longer an actress, but one of the most dazzling myths of the period. The popular imagination always simplifies complex experiences. And for Depression audiences, white as well as black, eager to point the finger at someone or something responsible for the loss of order, she would remain an ideal target: the guilt-ridden, troubled mulatto in whom were embodied the best and worst of the races.

The tragic side to Washington's dilemma was that she never had the opportunities for strong new roles that might have wiped away the Peola myth. In 1939, she made a triumphant Broadway appearance as Ethel Waters's lovely daughter Lissa in

Mamba's Daughters. Fresh, alive, energetic, her character was a symbol of a new day, the well-brought-up child who would have all the advantages denied her mother. This role, however, was an exception, and impressive as Washington's Lissa was, the type did not take hold. Fredi Washington once said that had she remained in Hollywood, she would have had to play the standard black-maid bit that Beavers and McDaniel perfected. But even the coarsest movie moguls were not that nearsighted. Far too sleek and sophisticated in even their eyes ever to be cast as a "realistic" black woman—in essence, a domestic—she was a scary problem that they chose to do without. (Even earlier in her career, during the shooting of *The Emperor Jones* opposite Robeson, Fredi learned one afternoon that all their intimate scenes had to be re-shot. It was thought that she looked too white and that there might be an uproar throughout the country if movie audiences believed Robeson was holding a white woman in his arms. So, Fredi was darkened for new sequences.) Unfortunately, neither the movie moguls nor audiences nor even sophisticated theater producers had enough imagination to see Washington as an actress able to do any part. White actresses had played black women in plays and films. In fact, even when *Imitation of Life* was remade in 1959, the role of the mulatto was not played by a black actress. Instead, Susan Kohmer was cast in the part originated by Washington. But no African American actress was given this kind of freedom.

Washington in her dressing room during the production of *Mamba's Daughters*.

Around this time, Washington's professional frustrations may have started getting to her. She threw herself into politically oriented activities. She was a founding member and Executive Secretary of the Negro Actors Guild, which aided the black performer in fighting discrimination in show business. Later, her articles and reviews ap-

peared in *The People's Voice*, published by her onetime brother-in-law, Adam Clayton Powell Jr.

As the years moved on, she appeared in such plays as *A Long Way from Home* and the all-black version of *Lysistrata*. In the fifties, she was the casting consultant for the film *Cry, the Beloved Country*, starring Canada Lee and the young Sidney Poitier. During that era, she also married a Connecticut dentist and retired from show business.

Shortly after Fredi's unexpected success in *Shuffle Along*, her sister Isabel (spelled *Isabell* for a time), captivated by the costumes, the bright lights, the glamorous atmosphere of Harlem night life, hit New York, determined to have a crack at showbiz herself. She debuted in *Runnin' Wild*, later danced at Connie's Inn and the Cotton Club, and appeared in the stage shows *Bamboola*, the extraordinary *Harlem*, and *Singin' the Blues*. In the latter, she worked with Fredi, a fact on which the press was quick to pick up. When the *New York Herald Tribune*'s critic reviewed it, he seemed more caught up in the sisters' celebrity (and in getting off some swipes at one of their admirers, Walter Winchell) than in the play. He wrote:

> It was interesting last night to learn from the all-knowing Mr. Winchell that the two most startling Negroid players in the play (the Misses Washington, Fredi and Isabell) are sisters, that they live in exclusive hotels, that they take themselves and their art with a smiling and a cunning semi-seriousness. Miss Fredi Washington acted the evil intrigant with all the poise of a déclassé, pale patrician; and Miss Isabell equipped the heroine with many of the noble qualities known to weak though sacrificial, womanhood, blonde or brunet.

Like other reviewers, this one may not have done much for the play, but he certainly helped in further establishing the celebrity personas of the sisters. As for Walter Winchell, then America's most influential columnist, he remained an ardent fan, almost fawning over Isabel when he wrote of her as an "irresistible siren," as pretty a "high-yellar as they come"! *Singin' the Blues* also gave Isabel her typical kind of role, that of the good-natured, sweet, soft ingenue, falling victim to a trying situation. In time, this was a role her public believed she played in her private life, too.

Like Fredi, Isabel also had her share of admirers, and her marriage ended during this New York period. At the Cotton Club, she was almost run ragged by the attentions of a well-to-do white clothing manufacturer who sat ringside, staring her down, three nights a week. Today, the fact that Isabel and Fredi were pursued by white men may not mean much. But in the twenties and thirties, this was a startling social phenomenon that had never before been engaged in openly.

Isabel, however, spurned the attentions of the clothing manufacturer and an array of others, waiting no doubt for Mr. Right to come along. He did too, during the run of her play, *Harlem,* in 1929. A student on spring break from Colgate College, he was more than just Mr. Right. He was the Black Community's darling crown prince, Adam Clayton Powell Jr. In no time, he was courting her. Once Isabel had fallen, then the hassles began.

As the minister of one of Black America's most prominent religious institutions, the Abyssinian Baptist Church in Harlem, Adam Clayton Powell Sr. assumed, as did the church deacons, that his son would one day take over the ministry. Now with talk of his son's romance with a previously married entertainer six years his senior, Harlem's social world was thrown into a tizzy. Isabel was viewed as the typical woman of the theater—wild, frivolous, and callous. But young Powell, never a man to back down from anything he really wanted, had a confrontation with the church deacons in 1933. He announced that he was determined to have Isabel. Finally, the two married.

Florenz Ziegfeld was said to have wanted her to play the mulatto in the road-show company of *Show Boat.* But Isabel gave up her career, immersing herself in church affairs, working with youth clubs, including the Abyssinian's Tiny Tots Choir. (One little girl in the choir who everyone predicted would go far was Diahann Carroll.) For elev-

en years, Isabel Washington Powell remained in the news and limelight as the gracious, attractive young wife of a very assured, aggressive young man, and won the respect of Adam's family, the churchgoers, and the Black Community. Then Powell's political hungers grew more intense. Isabel once said she had no idea just how ambitious he was. After Powell's election to Congress, she was prepared for a new life until Powell informed her one evening that she would not be going to Washington with him. The marriage was over. Shortly afterward, in 1945, he married another diva, Hazel Scott.

For Isabel Washington, the breakup and divorce were the toughest experiences of her life. The man for whom she had reshaped most of her life had walked away. She admitted later that she fell into shock and lost fourteen pounds in two weeks. Her anxieties and sorrow were not helped by her status as a celebrity. The black press seemed to know as much about her private life as she did. The story had the makings of a wonderful romantic melodrama. Attractive people. Money. Power. Position. Another woman. The wife who never knew. Earlier, Fredi Washington had starred in a glorious, gaudy Hollywood soap opera. Now Isabel was the star of a real-life one. Publicly humiliated, Isabel found her greatest friend was sister Fredi, who helped her put the pieces of her life back together. Entertainer Bobby Short recalled seeing the sisters at Grand Central Station as Isabel was on her way to Reno to divorce Powell. He always remembered their glamour. "Here were the two beauties being escorted to a flower-banked drawing room on *The 20th Century.* The sisters were in their finest spring finery—Fredi in black and a silver fox jacket, her black-felt beanie with a red rose tilted to just the right angle." He asked Isabel where the two would be staying "out there in Nevada, in racist country. 'There was a Negro woman who took in lodgers,' Fredi assured me." Afterward, Isabel considered a return to show business, but finally decided that she wanted no more of the footlights. She remained in Harlem, continued sponsoring youth groups, and for a spell, contentedly worked as a barber.

Ethel Waters:
Sweet Mama Goes Legit

The diva who brought the thirties to a much-needed, roaring crescendo, who remains one of the quintessential creations of the Depression era, was Ethel Waters. During her sixty-year career, Waters underwent a series of startling image changes, greater than that of any other star, black or white. In the 1930s, audiences saw Sweet Mama Stringbean undergo a distinct transformation right before their very eyes: from the high-kicking figure given to flash who popped up at the start of the decade, to the been-through-hell-but-still-holding-on matriarchal figure at the end of the era. Both were types Waters, the woman, was more than familiar with.

By the thirties, Ethel Waters had had even a stormier personal life than the young Billie Holiday. She had survived a terrifying childhood and the exhausting, backbreaking, and backbiting road tours. She had been cheated out of money and kicked around by a steady stream of men. In the autobiography, she related a nightmarish experience that took place on an early road tour. Outside Birmingham, she had been seriously injured in a car crash, which had left her lying on the road, pinned under a car for hours. Shattered glass from the window shield had cut her badly. Boiling water from the damaged radiator scalded her breasts and stomach. A tendon had snapped. And her left leg was ripped open from the knee to the hip. Whites passing by at first had refused to help. Only after her desperate pleas was Waters taken to a hospital where, as leg wounds were being dressed, she had screamed out in agony, only to be told by the attending white physician, "You needn't holler, gal. This is what all you niggers should get when you wreck...cars." Afterward, she was promptly deposited in the "nigger" quarters, there left unwashed, uncared for, unattended by a doctor.

Later, out of the hospital, recuperating at the home of friends, Ethel Waters learned that hundreds of blacks in the Birmingham area, upon hearing of her accident, had contributed pennies, nickels, dimes, to help pay her medical bills. The soft, sentimental side of Waters never forgot the kindness of the poor "little" people who had helped a stranger.

But the other side of Waters never forgot the cruelty. To her, this all seemed but one more in a long line of experiences of deprivation, humiliation, and terror that had hounded her for years. Later, she would be remembered as one of America's warmest dramatic actresses. But most who worked with her have agreed that, like the charming Bill "Bojangles" Robinson, this model of sobriety onstage was a raging, holy terror off.

During the thirties, her paranoia grew as she became increasingly more restless and difficult. Few got close to her. Whenever there was a dispute, she saw only one side of an issue—hers. Often, she was dead right about the wrongs done to her. But often, too, her fierce suspicions caused her unneeded problems. Her repeated bickering with club managers, her associates, producers, and fellow entertainers not only rattled them but drained her, too.

Despite the problems, Ethel Waters was able to reach full artistic maturity in the 1930s, although at the start of the era, growth hardly looked promising. She had hoped to become a Broadway star. But when her shows *Blackbirds of 1930* and *Rhapsody in Black* had failed to become bona fide hits on the Great White Way, she just gave up and returned to singing in clubs.

Ethel Waters singing "Heat Wave" in *As Thousands Cheer.*

Ethel Waters's rendition of "Stormy Weather" marked a turning point in her career.

As a singer, many had thought she had already peaked. Waters herself, however, felt that she had not yet fulfilled herself artistically as a singer. When she performed, everything was refined and distilled. But unlike the singers whom she admired (Ma and Bessie), who went all the way with a gut response to their material, Waters seemed to hold her feelings in. All her life, she had had few emotional supports. Ma had a husband to protect her. Bessie had an unreal toughness and the love of the battle itself. But all Waters had was her sense of self, and that was pretty shaky. In song, it seemed as if she were afraid to pull out all the stops for fear that if she went too far emotionally she would end up right back in hell with too many bad memories. Ethel Waters was always in need of controls and structures to keep herself together. In time, she would find the one lasting thing that could sustain her—religion, her private sense of God. During the Depression era, Waters got a new taste of emotional freedom. And her first liberator was the Harold Arlen song "Stormy Weather."

Today, the legend persists of her splendid live rendition of the song. Standing on the floor of the Cotton Club in 1933—a big-boned woman who looked like a black Madonna—she transformed a tale of love gone sour into one of a life gone wrong. Waters admitted that she had introduced the song at a time in her life when she was feeling particularly low, and had used it as self-therapy to sum up "the things I couldn't frame in words." It marked a turning point in her life. "I was singing the story of my misery and confusion," she said, "of misunderstandings in my life I couldn't straighten out, the story of the wrongs and outrages done to me by people I had loved and trusted."

Irving Berlin heard her perform the song at the Cotton Club and soon afterward offered her a part in his Broadway–bound show *As Thousands Cheer*, a revue written by Moss Hart and Sam Harris, and starring Clifton Webb, Marilyn Miller, and Helen

As Thousands Cheer firmly established Ether Waters in the legitimate theater and marked the beginning of her peak years when she became the highest-paid woman on Broadway.

Broderick. Waters leaped at the chance, although she had her doubts. After all, she would only be "local color material" in an essentially white-oriented show. She would not have top billing, and she had only four numbers to perform. But she took the dare, opening in the show on Broadway in 1933.

For her sexy number, "Heat Wave," she strutted onstage dressed in colorful rags with an elaborate headdress of bananas and apples, and other fruit. The audience went wild. In the song "Harlem on My Mind," she cast herself as a would-be sophisticate who missed the folks back home. Here, she openly parodied Josephine Baker, the rival who had taken her chance and gone off to Europe. Then, she delivered "Supper Time," a mournful song about a black woman preparing her family's dinner, aware that her husband will not be returning home since he has been lynched. Waters had not known how a white-theater crowd coming to see a lighthearted revue would respond to this number. (At one time, the producers had thought of dropping it altogether because it might be too much of a downer.) But as she performed it, she kept in mind that this song touched on "the whole tragic history of a race." "In singing it," she later said in the autobiography *His Eye Is on the Sparrow*, "I was telling my comfortable, well-fed, well-dressed listener about my people." "Supper Time" moved Broadway audiences in a way never before experienced. And here, Waters emerged as

the first diva to deal with racial matters in a very popular song. (Holiday's more explicit "Strange Fruit" came a few years later.)

As Thousands Cheer firmly established Ethel Waters in the legitimate theater and marked the beginning of her peak years when she became the highest-paid woman on Broadway. Later elevated to star billing, she toured with the show, becoming the first African American personality to costar with white performers below the Mason–Dixon line. While on Broadway, she doubled at a nearby nightclub, earning $2,500 a week. And her radio broadcasts with the Jack Denny Orchestra on Sunday nights were considered major breakthroughs for a black entertainer. During this time, she also lived in style, ensconced in a ten-room apartment (with one room given over entirely to religious artifacts and objects). When asked abut her luxurious lifestyle—fur coats, jewelry, big cars—she explained: "The main reason I have for buying such extravagant objects is because a Broadway star cannot dress like a waif or ride the subway. People will talk and you can say, 'The hell with them!' but they are my customers and I gotta live and appear in public as they expect me to."

In 1935 she was back on Broadway in *At Home Abroad*, and finally, by the end of the era, Waters had what she longed for most, the dramatic starring role in Broadway's *Mamba's Daughters*. This new melodrama by DuBose and Dorothy Heyward,

Waters with Herb Williams, Eleanor Powell, and Beatrice Lillie in Broadway's *At Home Abroad.*

so excited, so moved, so carried away by "make-believe." The fact is the audience and the critics were enjoying what is known as "great" acting, a phenomenon so rare that any generation is permitted only a few examples of it, a phenomenon almost unheard of on our contemporary stage. A great actress should not be confused with a celebrated actress....In the final scene Miss Waters, so far as the effect she makes is concerned, might be playing the Love–Death of Isolde, or Juliet in the potion scene....I have only admiration for the rest of the cast....The fact remains that in the presence of a star of such magnitude as Ethel Waters these matters sink into secondary importance.

What is to become of Ethel Waters in the theatre? Few roles immediately suggest themselves as appropriate. Perhaps some playwright...will be inspired by her genius to create a new part worthy of her...but I cannot help feeling confident that in a Greek play, particularly in "Medea," Ethel Waters would more securely establish herself as the world actress of the first rank she indubitably is.

the husband-and-wife team who had written the book for *Porgy,* told the story of three generations of black women, focusing mainly on the character of Hagar, a large, half-crazed mother with a singular passion: seeing that her beautiful child, Lissa, has all the things in life that the mother missed out on. During the emotionally charged climax of *Mamba's Daughters,* Hagar, in a fit of uncontrollable rage, strangles a "sporting man," who has raped her child.

Originally, the backers had doubts about a musical-comedy star carrying a heavy dramatic play. But in January 1939, with a case that included Georgette Harvey, Canada Lee, Jose Ferrer, Alberta Hunter, and Fredi Washington (as Lissa), Waters's performance in *Mamba's Daughters* won her seventeen curtain calls, made her the most talked-about dramatic actress on Broadway, and garnered the following praise from Carl Van Vechten:

Whatever may be said for or against the play, the performance of Ethel Waters in the role of Hagar calls only for superlatives and has received them from all the critics. Rarely have I encountered such unanimity of opinion, such consistent enthusiasm. Seldom have I seen a first night audience

Somewhat inflated as some might now find Van Vechten's praise, it captures the extraordinary impact that Waters had on the theatrical community of the day. When Brooks Atkinson of *The New York Times* wrote an unenthusiastic review of her work in *Mamba's Daughters,* an advertisement was taken out in the following Sunday *Times* by a group of theater people (including Tallulah Bankhead, Norman Bel Geddes, Dorothy Gish, Aline MacMahon, and Burgess Meredith), who, in essence, announced that the very influential *Times* critic was wrong, that Waters's performance was indeed an altogether remarkable one. Atkinson went back to see the play, re-reviewed it, and admitted he had made a mistake. *Vogue* did a photo layout on Waters and *Life* ran a splashy spread on the play. Even Eleanor Roosevelt mentioned the production in her "My Day" newspaper column, saying: "Ethel Waters really achieved a remarkable dramatic success in the character of Hagar. For me, it was an unforgettable evening, so real that I could hardly believe that I was not actually on the plantation.... It is to me an extraordinary success." And, indeed, it was of significance since Waters had shattered the long-standing myth that black women could perform only as singers, dancers, or comediennes. Here, she brought to fruition what actresses Rose McClendon and Edna Thomas had worked so hard for: the establishment of an African American woman as a major American dramatic actress. Waters never had the chance for a classic role. But she did give other fine dramatic performances.

Her future dramatic roles sometimes seemed an elaboration on the character of Hagar, in time taking on a solitary-mythic structure so etched in the public consciousness that she would be thought of only as that pop myth come true: the ever-endurable black woman, a figure capable of rage and anger, ready to fight if wronged, yet a woman of towering heroic compassion. Finally, Waters had been able to do in theater what her idols Bessie and Ma had done in song: to go all the way emotionally with a work of art.

For years after *Mamba's Daughters*, Ethel Waters, the woman, remained something of a mythic heroine and she may have felt trapped. Part of the price she paid was relinquishing her sexuality, becoming matronly, far too early in her career. Rival Baker never gave hers up. She also seemed so superhumanly strong that it was thought by her public that she could handle anything. Later, too, the religious fervor and conviction that had inspired one era would become a bore for another. And the Ethel Waters myth would be considered obsolete by a public in search of new entertainers to distract and delight them. Yet for a long time, there was no black star like Ethel Waters, held in affectionate high regard by white and black audiences.

By 1939, the divas and their careers were well established. Waters was on Broadway as was Fredi Washington. Ivie Anderson was still touring with the Duke. Holiday was at Cafe Society. And the young Lena Horne was debuting on Broadway in *Blackbirds of 1939*.

All in all, the divas had made remarkable inroads in the mainstream of American cultural life. Broadway, the clubs, radio, and movies had been integrated. There was even an optimistic sign in the world of serious music when a round-faced, wide-eyed baby doll of a woman named Dorothy Maynor had suddenly shown up at the end of the era, glowing with a gold mine of publicity. For years, the friends of this Virginia–born soprano had tried arranging an audition for her with the conductor of the Boston Symphony Orchestra, Serge Koussevitzky. Once the maestro had finally heard her, he exclaimed, "Marvelous. Marvelous. The whole world must hear her." The next day, at Koussevitzky's request, she sang German *Lieder* and spirituals at an informal picnic outside Boston. *New York Times* music critic, Noel Strauss, happened to be present and the following day startled the music world with a full column devoted to this new discovery. The story was picked up by the Associated Press and ran throughout the country. Three months later, Dorothy Maynor had a sold-out debut at Town Hall. Olin Downes wrote in *The New York Times* that she had a "voice of a golden quality," adding that she was "one of the most remarkable soprano voices of the rising generation." Maynor's success made it look as if a dark diva would soon crack the world of grand opera. It did not happen until 1955, but for late–Depression audiences, Maynor embodied the dreamy notion that now progress might be in store for everybody. There was also Marian Anderson, whose legendary People's Concert in 1939 was another symbol of progress. Curiously though, Anderson herself would remain a thorny problem for many Americans until the 1940s.

Throughout the great slump, the various personas and moods of the divas—be it the mellowness of Ivie and Billie or the humor and energy of Hollywood actresses Louise Beavers and Hattie McDaniel—as well as the popular myths some had embodied, all had had a part in making the era endurable, perhaps even a bit more comprehensible.

Social Symbols
The 1940s

The forties opened with a roar. But not from the divas. Instead, it came from Europe.

From the moment the Japanese bombed Pearl Harbor in 1941, American society underwent another series of dramatic changes. In the early 1940s, a call rang out for patriotism and national unity. By the second half of the decade, a triumphant America-as-Giant-World-Power basked in its new national prosperity and the international prestige that the war had brought.

During this period the divas, like everyone else, also witnessed a great awakening within the African American community, which was becoming increasingly more vocal. Black America was invigorated by protests, demonstrations, arguments, many directed by black leaders toward the gut of wartime America, the military, still segregated and blatantly racist. Race riots shot up in the early 1940s in Detroit, Harlem, Atlanta, Philadelphia, and parts of Tennessee and Texas. And before the forties ended, Black America had an array of new-style political heroes—A. Philip Randolph, Walter White, Ralph Bunche, Adam Clayton Powell Jr., Paul Robeson, and those sports figures Jackie Robinson and Joe Louis. At the same time, as the NAACP rose to the height of its power, the idea of full racial integration was slowly taking root in the mainstream of American political and social thought.

What with Black America's determination to make it into the system, and what with the determination of part of White America to show that the system could work for everybody, the forties gave way to a figure both White and Black America saw as positive: the bourgeois diva as social symbol. Such forties women as Lena Horne, Hazel Scott, Katherine Dunham, and Marian Anderson emerged not only as performers of skill, but symbols of the new black who could easily fit into the dominant culture. The idea was that the ordinary hardworking black youth could grow up to be like these heroines who, as seemingly educated, articulate, poised citizens, had seized the golden opportunities that the nation offered.

As a figure everyone felt comfortable with, the bourgeois-black-beauty-as-social-symbol soon fully crossed over, finally "making it" into mainstream American culture. As she did so, often performing for white audiences more than black ones, her "rough" ethnic edges were almost completely wiped away. Forties audiences accepted those black beauties whose color could, when so desired, be overlooked. White audiences could watch a Horne or a Scott without feeling "uncomfortable," without being reminded of ghettoes or poverty or social ills and inequities. Gradually, audiences became more and more fixated on color, or again the absence of it. Now, the most successful black beauties would be those with "mulatto looks" (best exemplified by Horne) or high-mulatto style of dress or manner (like Eartha Kitt and Diana Ross later). Now for some years to come, Ethel Waters would remain the last of the big-time brown ethnic stars.

And this was also the period when the diva's interracial romances became of national interest.

But most importantly, in the 1940s America's black beauties realized that they could talk—in print. Newspaper accounts—interviews, reviews, news stories, feature stories—all trace the diva's metamorphosis. Comments flew all over the place. Sometimes, the comments were on America's racial situation. For a spell, the divas got by with their talk. Only after the war may they have wondered if they had said the wrong thing at the wrong time.

But in the beginning, none of this mattered. All anyone knew or cared about was that the black beauties who came to prominence during the war years were the right dreams at the right time. And none was dreamier or more right than Lena Horne.

Page 90: Lena Horne.

Lena Horne: the Girl
Beauty Comes of Age

Lena Horne and Hazel Scott (at the piano) sing a duet in *I Dood It*. In movies, they performed their songs, then usually disappeared.

For many, the young Lena Horne represented bourgeois haughtiness. She was the pampered black girl-woman never required to do anything. Who cared what she said or thought when it was more than enough just to stare at her? In the history of American popular entertainment, no woman had ever looked like Lena Horne. Nor had any other black woman had looks considered as "safe" and non-threatening. Past mulatto types such as Fredi Washington and Nina Mae McKinney had been so close to the white ideal that troubling questions had arisen. What, indeed, were notions of white superiority based on? Skin color? Features? Hair texture? What kind of insane system was it that denied opportunities to these women who met the culture's beauty standards far more closely than even Joan Crawford and Bette Davis? Lena's looks, however, were less disturbing and more acceptable. Most importantly, she had color, a rich, glowing coppertone. She wasn't too dark or too light. Her hair was straight. Her

features were keen. For a spell, she was labeled the café-au-lait Hedy Lamarr, and when she first started to perform, she was even urged to change her name and pass as a Latin. But looking back on the period now, it is obvious that nobody would ever have wanted Lena to be anything but Lena.

At the same time, the Horne demeanor—distant and aloof—suggested that she was a woman off somewhere in a world of her own. Of course, it was unheard of to find a black woman who became a star without doing anything (Where was the fierce aggression that all the fabled past divas had?), who appeared as if all her life she had been placed on a pedestal and everything had come easily to her. That was the way she appeared to be. The reality was another matter.

She was born Lena Calhoun Horne into a respectable middle-class Brooklyn family in 1917. Her grandfather liked Verdi and fine cigars. Her grandmother, a suffragette and an early member of the NAACP, was an ardent fighter for equality on all fronts.

Singing of love and loneliness . . . .

Three's not a crowd: Horne with Bill Robinson (left) and Cab Calloway in the movie *Stormy Weather.*

Shortly after her birth, Lena Horne's parents separated. For years, as her mother, Edna, struggled to become an actress, the young Lena—separated from the father she adored—was shifted and shuttled throughout the South, staying in one home or another of friends and relatives. She never forgot the loneliness of those early years.

Her career took off in 1933, when sixteen-year-old Lena appeared in the chorus line at the Cotton Cub. Later, she was the girl-singer with Noble Sissle's Orchestra, and then appeared on Broadway in the short-lived *Blackbirds of 1939.* A year later, she performed with Charlie Barnet's Orchestra, then went on to exciting performances at Barney Josephson's Café Society Downtown, which put her on the showbiz map. (For a while, she was known as *Helena Horne.)* In between all these activities, she married Louis Jones, the son of a middle-class black family in Pittsburgh, had two children, also appeared in the race movie *The Duke Is Tops,* and eventually divorced Jones. In the early 1940s, she went to Los Angeles for a nightclub engagement and quickly became the West Coast's latest "in" sensation.

MGM spotted her, signed her up, and afterward Lena Horne, no longer simply a cabaret singer, was transformed almost overnight into a national social symbol. Civil rights groups took a keen interest in her budding movie career. NAACP Executive Secretary Walter White felt that as the first African American woman with a long-term contract at a major Hollywood studio, she could do much to alter the image of the Negro women in American motion pictures. Everyone was determined not to let the movie capital turn her into the conventional clownish black maid.

Well, Hollywood didn't turn her into a housekeeper, but it didn't turn her into another Harlow, either. At heart, Lena Horne knew that she was a celebrated token who could be picked up and dropped or used however MGM saw fit. And with the exceptions of *Cabin in the Sky* and *Stormy Weather,* her eleven movies of the 1940s represented case studies in Hollywood duplicity. Usually, she did not play characters. She just came on as herself (her glamorous-nightclub persona intact), looking terrific, singing her number, then disappearing from the picture. Since she seldom appeared with white stars of the features, such as Mickey Rooney or Judy Garland, in sequences integral to the movies' plots, her scenes—should they ever "offend" Southern audiences—could easily be scissored out. Still, her movies took her fully into the mainstream of American popular culture. Featured in the pages of such mainstream publications as *Life, The New Yorker,* and on the cover of the movie magazine *Motion Picture,* she became one of the most famous African American personalities in the country.

Whether in movies or back in nightclubs, Lena Horne's style and presence remained fresh and exciting. For a black star, her material was different, never the blues, spirituals, or jazz. Instead, she performed the kind of sophisticated Cole Porter or Gershwin ballads her audiences in the classy supper clubs favored. The voice was smooth and vibrant and, as the years moved on, it seemed filled with edgy tensions. But what distinguished her was her intelligence and sophistication. She had a total understanding of a lyric situation. Then, there was her inimitable style. The diction was impeccable. She almost spat out each word. The eyes were eager and afire. The teeth gleamed. And the mouth was magnificent.

There was also the Horne aloofness, which never went unnoticed, that became the hallmark of her style. Sometimes as she sang, her face went vacant. But always, she held something back. In the middle of her career, *The New Yorker* commented on her unusual detachment: "Curiously, as her style has developed, she seems to have withdrawn further and further from her audience and into herself. She never addresses her listeners directly, and her eyes are closed or nearly closed, a good part of the time. In acknowledging applause, she tilts her head, eyes cast down, and bends and turns with...self-effacement."

But no one was more aware of the withdrawal than Lena Horne herself, who no doubt used it for therapeutic reasons. More than any other diva before her, Lena Horne had grown up in front of white audiences, repeatedly encountering the same slights and indignities every other African American female star knew. "Even as a performer I sensed that white people in the audience saw nothing but my flesh and its color onstage. I was not ready for this," she once said. "I didn't know anything about white people."

She also experienced an extraordinary loneliness onstage, feeling that she was being fully exposed. "I don't know how to say it," she explained. "It's so physical, it's all body. There's whiskey, there's sex, there's something that is experienced when people are drinking in a nightclub and having a good time. There are so many ways they look at you, their emotions aren't disciplined.... It's you and you are at the mercy of their thoughts." It was a rough experience

Horne's marriage to MGM arranger–composer Lennie Hayton was the first of the big postwar interracial unions.

that got to her as much as it did to Holiday. Horne was every bit as unsettled by her white audiences. In time, she remembered Noble Sissle's advice: "Remember, you are a lady, and you are not a whore—don't let them treat you like one." So she learned always to pull back from her white audiences, developing a guile and toughness, using her remoteness, her high-flung inaccessibility as an aggressive-protective shield. She developed also a hostility and an edge that often she felt her audiences overlooked since,

> they were too busy seeing their own preconceived image of a Negro woman. The image that I chose to give them was of a woman whom they could not reach. I think this is why I rarely speak to an audience. I am too proud to let them think they can have any personal contact with me. They get the singer, but they are not going to get the woman. I think many Negro performers feel much the same way, and they find their own methods of letting people know it. In other words, we all find our own means of rebellion.

Lena Horne summed up the feeling most divas had when appearing in clubs. Different ones used different techniques, and the techniques had different effects. In Lena's case, she was telling her audiences that she was a black woman who could not be had. The irony is that during the war years, her withdrawal, which alternately puzzled or put audiences off, was accepted nonetheless, perhaps as a byproduct of the war itself. She became a symbol of the melancholy girl back home, ill at ease because her man was off somewhere in combat.

For black GIs who viewed *Stormy Weather* and *Cabin in the Sky* on Army bases around the world, she was, as Rita Hayworth and Betty Grable were for whites, a luscious pinup, a dream girl for those long nights away from home.

Even the military brass was not blind to Lena's special appeal. Like other glamour girls pitching in to help at USO shows and the Hollywood Canteen, she was asked to entertain at Army camps. She was shocked to find segregated audiences. Often, she did not see the black soldiers until the next day after her big appearance. When at a performance for the troops, she spotted German prisoners of war sitting in the best seats in the front of the house, she stepped from the stage, whisked past them, then sang to the black soldiers in the back.

By the late 1940s, Lena had career problems. MGM, having sunk money into the all-black Broadway show *St. Louis Woman*, in which the studio hoped to star her, was hardly pleased when she turned the lead role down. Matters were not helped either when, in 1947, she married Lennie Hayton, a white composer-arranger at MGM, in Paris. This was the first big interracial romance of the postwar era. The marriage was kept secret for three years. But when revealed, it did not sit too well with anyone. In 1951, when MGM remade *Show Boat*, it cast Ava Gardner in a role Horne had her heart set on, that of the mulatto Julie. Finally, there was the business of the Horne politics. By the end of the period, the Communist hunts had started, leading to numerous investigations, subpoenas, and hearings. Once newspapers attacked Café Society Downtown as a "red hangout," many of the artists who had worked there could not find work anywhere else. Lena Horne had also remained friendly with Paul Robeson, even when he was so hotly denounced. Eventually listed in Red Channels, a compilation (put out by the rightist group Counter Attack) of entertainers said to be either Communists or Communist sympathizers, she was blacklisted from television work. But in the late fifties, Horne made a triumphant appearance on Broadway in *Jamaica*. She also became involved in the civil-rights movement. During the sixties, when so many old-time black stars were viewed by the new generation as being "politically obsolete," Lena still held on, her style becoming both looser and more gutsy. In the long run, she was not only the war years' most glorious siren, but also its most durable.

Katherine Dunham: Undercover Sex Goddess

Dancer–choreographer Katherine Dunham was another major 1940s black social symbol. Dunham was known in and out of dance circles as a brainy, scholarly young woman with degrees in anthropology and ethnology. But sex appeal may have had as much to do with her uncanny success as the books or her great artistry.

Dunham grew up in Joliet, Illinois, where her father ran a dry-cleaning business. Her mother, who was French–Canadian, died when Dunham was very young. Enrolling at the University of Chicago, where she studied anthropology, Dunham was also a student of ballet with the Russian master dancer Mme. Ludmilla Speranza. At twenty-one, Dunham founded her first company, Ballet Nègre, and performed in Chicago. From the start, she sought to bring ethnicity to modern dance. One evening during a public performance she gave in an abandoned Chicago loft, she was spotted by the daughters of philanthropist Julius Rosenwald, who promptly suggested that she apply for a Rosenwald Foundation grant. For almost two years, she used her fellowship to travel, study, and take notes on "primitive dance and customs" of various island peoples. In Jamaica, she lived with the Maroon peoples of the high country, who taught her the Koromantee dances remembered from Africa. In Martinque, she saw for the first time the wrestling dance *L'Ag'ya*, from which she later drew inspiration for a number of her famous *Bal Nègre* revue. In Haiti, she studied voodoo. Returning to the States, she was armed with enough material for a master's thesis—later a doctorate—as well as for a full-length book on the Maroons. Her account of her experiences, *Journey to Accompong*, published in 1946, reveals a perceptive young woman with a lush, romantic sensibility.

In the States, Dunham also put her field studies to work. She moved to New York City, and by the forties she had formed a new dance company. In a short time, the city was awash with stories of this innovative and highly dramatic dancer–choreographer, whose series of ballet recitals entitled *Tropics and Le Jazz Hot* introduced audiences to "Primitive Rhythms," "Rumbas" (Cuban and Mexican), "Island Songs,"

"Plantation and Minstrel Dances" (including "The Ballet Bre'r Rabbit"), and "Le Jazz Hot" (with everything from boogie-woogie to honky-tonk numbers). Later, she opened a school to teach Dunham technique. Among those who studied there were Butterfly McQueen, James Dean, and heiress Doris Duke. Charles Mingus and Marlon Brando sometimes stopped by the school. Brando would end up playing on the bongos. Eartha Kitt also became a member of Dunham's company. Almost single-handedly, Katherine Dunham saw to it that Negro dance was taken seriously. Critic John Martin wrote in *The New York Times*:

> With the arrival of Katherine Dunham on the scene, the prospects for the development of a substantial Negro dance art begin to look decidedly bright. Her performance with her group . . . may very well become a historic occasion, for certainly never before in all the efforts of recent years to establish the Negro dance as a serious medium has there been so convincing and authoritative an approach.
>
> Miss Dunham has apparently based her theory on the obvious fact so often overlooked that if the Negro is to develop an art of his own he can begin only with the seeds of that art that lie within him. These seeds are abundant and unique. Indeed, it would be difficult to think of any people with a richer heritage of dance begging to be made use of. Yet in the past . . . there have been those who have started out by denying this heritage and smoothing it over with the gloss of another alien racial culture that deceives no one. The potential greatness of the Negro dance lies in its discovery of its own roots and the crucial nursing of them into growth and flower.
>
> . . . It is because she has showed herself to have both the objective quality of the student and the natural instinct of the artist that she has done such a truly important job.

In 1940, she appeared on Broadway in *Cabin in the Sky*, the all-black musical extravaganza starring Ethel Waters and Dooley Wilson, directed and choreographed by George Balanchine. *Times* dance critic John

"Friends, this is the last time I shall play Louisville because the management refuses to let people like us sit by people like you," announced Katherine Dunham.

Martin had his say again, summing up the attitudes many theatergoers would have about Dunham for the duration of the decade:

> Throughout the evening it is Miss Dunham's chief business to sizzle, and that is one of the things that will seem most extraordinary to those who have followed her work in its previous phases. In her personal programs she has frequently represented women of distinctly torrid temperament, but never before has there been one at all like Georgia….In her own creations she is never without comment, presenting the character and telling a wealth of secrets about it at the same time; as Georgia, however, she has no chance for comment, no chance for the very quality that gave her art its charm and its validity. She is a hundred percent seductress.

Following *Cabin in the Sky*, Dunham and her company were able to reach a far wider audience with *Tropical Revue, Carib Song,* and *Bal Nègre*. Yet, serious artist that Dunham was, some audiences seemed to focus on her as the kind of sultry, sexy vixen she had played in *Cabin in the Sky*. In time, Katherine Dunham, the dancer, was an ideal undercover sepia sex symbol. American audiences of the period still were not ready to officially parade or accept an African American woman as any kind of feminine ideal, not even a sexual one. But there were always covert ways in which a woman was discovered nonetheless. So while audiences congratulated themselves on appreciat-

ing Dunham's skillful renderings of island ritual dances, what many also responded to most was the healthy sexual ambiance that Dunham and her troupe exuded. Excerpts from reviews of the company's performances simply spotlight the general fascination with Dunham's sexuality. Of *Tropical Revue*, the critic of the *New York Mirror* wrote: "A tropical revue that is likely to send thermometers soaring to the bursting point…. Tempestuous and torrid, raffish and revealing." The *New York Sun* said: "Shoulders, midsections and posteriors went round and round. Particularly when the cynosure was Miss Dunham, the vista was full of pulchritude." The *Daily News* commented "The program notes read: 'The fertility ritual here associated with marriage or mating.' Amen, brother!" *The New York Times* added: "Sex in the Caribbean is doing all right."

None of this sexuality business was lost on Hollywood, which, seldom known for spotlighting a serious dance company, let alone an African American one, soon imported Dunham's troupe West for appearances in *Star-Spangled Rhythm, Stormy Weather,* and *Casbah*. Dunham also choreographed *Pardon My Sarong*. Mainstream movie audiences no doubt viewed Dunham and her company as colorful, exotic black entertainers with plenty of rhythm and pizzazz. Interestingly, when MGM filmed *Cabin in the Sky*, it chose the mild-mannered, less exotically sexy Lena to play Georgia. For a movie industry that both enjoyed and feared the idea of black sexuality, Katherine Dunham may well have been considered *too* sensual to be cast in a proper role in a film that cut her off from the cultural veneer that generally made her sex acceptable.

During a 120-city tour of her *Tropical Revue* in 1944, Dunham made newspaper headlines following an incident at a Cincinnati hotel. Arriving at the hotel with reservations made for her by her white secretary, only to be told by the management that there was no room and that she would have to leave, Dunham flatly refused to budge, informing the hotel, "You'll have to carry me out!" Later she sued. Then in Louisville, when she discovered that, except for six African Americans on the lower floor, the rest of the black audience at her performance in the Municipal Auditorium was made to sit in "a special section" in the balcony, she interrupted the applause at the conclusion of her show to make an announcement. "Friends," she was quoted as saying, "we are glad we have made you happy. We hope you have enjoyed us. This is the last time I shall play Louisville because the management refused to let people like us sit by people like you. Maybe after the war we shall have democracy and I can return. Until then," and at this point it was said in newspapers that she shook her finger at the audience, "God bless you, for you will need it!" Needless to say, the white audience was in an uproar. But afterward, the management did announce that there would be no more segregated audiences if Miss Dunham chose to play the house again. Of course, the management neglected to say whether or not there would be segregated audiences for other Negro performers. Nonetheless, Dunham had made her point.

Later, when she played the Army camps, she again took a strong stand against the segregated policies of the military.

No one can say for sure what effect Dunham's outspokenness had on her career. But it is now obvious that the forties were her peak years. She kept the company alive for three decades although there were always financial difficulties. In the 1950s, she was back in the movies for the Italian production *Mambo* and segments of *Green Mansions* in Hollywood, which she choreographed. In 1962, she launched a spectacular theatrical production, *Bamboche*.

By the end of the forties, Dunham's use as a symbol had had its day. For White America, she had been at first an agreeable social symbol, a sign of the Negro making progress in a free society. But once she took that symbol business seriously and spoke out, she was no longer needed. Then, too, who is to say what effect her marriage to white costume designer John Platt had? In the fifties, Dunham, no doubt feeling the stings of bias against her company, publicly asked why the State Department had not backed a group that had already performed in over thirty-eight countries. The familiar fighting spirit was still there. But by the mid-1950s, the serious black-beauty social symbols were anachronisms. And at the same time, when sepia sirens Eartha Kitt and Dorothy Dandridge emerged as open, aboveground sex symbols and were publicized as such, Dunham's reign as underground sex goddess came to an end. Katherine Dunham's career—her position in popular American culture—was never a relaxed affair. In 1963, Dunham became the first African American to choreograph an opera—*Aida*—at the Metropolitan Opera House. Later, Dunham accepted a position at Southern Illinois University and moved to East St. Louis, where she created a community-based arts-education program.

Like Lena Horne, Dunham in the forties introduced the idea that the black entertainer indeed did have a specific responsibility to her or his community. And, perhaps most importantly as an artist, her striking dance innovations were to remain a source of inspiration for generations of black dancers and choreographers to follow. Dunham died at age ninety-six in 2006.

Hazel Scott at her marriage to Adam Clayton Powell Jr. in 1945.

Hazel Scott:
Swinging the Classics

Scott, the child prodigy.

Jazz pianist Hazel Scott was another diva whose career indicated a shift in political consciousness. She, too, was something of a covert-sex symbol. During the forward-looking forties, most chose to view her as an example of a Black American woman who had made it into the system.

Scott was born in Trinidad in 1920, the only child of R. Thomas Scott, a black scholar, and Alma Long Worrell, a ranking debutante in local black society as well as a talented music student. When her parents migrated to the United States in 1924, little Hazel was the family's pride and joy and, in every conceivable sense, a remarkable child. She read at three, was discovered to have perfect pitch at three-and-a-half, played the piano at four, and was improvising at the piano at five. A Juilliard professor who heard her play, proclaimed her a "genius," then began teaching her privately since she was too young to study at the school. Having mastered the classics by age thirteen—Bach, Chopin, Rachmaninoff—Scott was also growing impatient with them and soon jazzing up the classics with a contemporary beat. Then a year later when her father suddenly died, Hazel and her mother were left on their own. Mrs. Scott joined Lil Hardin Armstrong's all-girl

band, then organized her own women's orchestra, the American Creolians, with Hazel playing the piano and doubling on bass. In 1938, Hazel appeared on Broadway—at eighteen—in *Sing out the News*, stopping the show cold with her number "Franklin D. Roosevelt Jones."

Two years later, when she opened at Café Society Downtown, Hazel Scott took New York by storm—and in an unprecedented way. She played the classics. Had anyone before ever come to a New York nightclub to hear a pianist perform Chopin or Lizst? Scott, however, had so perfected her unique way of transforming the classics into swing ballads that audiences could not resist her. She began her classical numbers in a conventional way, then gradually changed the rhythm, letting boogie-woogie notes creep in until, finally, Hazel Scott just gave in to the sounds within her and pounded the keyboard as if any minute might be her last. And the entire nightclub swayed and jumped to her original sounds. Initially brought into Café Society as a three-week replacement for ailing blues singer Ida Cox, Hazel was such a knockout success that the club became her home. When Café Society Downtown moved uptown to Fifty-eighth Street, Hazel Scott went with it.

Her album *Swinging the Classics* nearly broke sales records. Her non-classical discs "Mighty Like Blues," "Calling All Bars," and "Boogie Woogie" sold well, too, and remain definitive period pieces. Throughout the era, she had class bookings: the swanky Rtiz Carlton Hotel in Boston; the huge Paramount and Roxy theaters in New York; and the prestigious Carnegie Hall, where in 1940 she played Liszt's Second Hungarian Rhapsody to rave reviews. Of the latter performance, a critic wrote: "It was the most impudent musical criticism since Bernard Shaw stopped writing on the subject. It was silly, daring, modern but never irreverent. I think Liszt would have been delighted." And the stories run on her in the leading mass publications of the day verified her complete crossover into the cultural mainstream.

Not long afterward, Hazel Scott found herself in the movies: *Something to Shout About, I Dood It* (with Horne), *The Heat's On, Broadway Rhythm*, and most memorably in

Sophisticated Lady: Hazel Scott, who became a nightclub star at age twenty by giving the classics a boogie-woogie sound.

Rhapsody in Blue. In this last film, in a brief interlude where she was seen playing Gershwin's "The Man I Love" in a Paris nightclub, Scott was about as elegant and sophisticated as they come, a blazing symbol of the contemporary black woman completely at home in the most continental of settings. Striking as Scott's movie appearances were, her scenes were sometimes cut when the films were shown in the South. Still, she reached a large audience, appearing always as herself, beautifully dressed and coifed.

As a social symbol, her classical bent placed Scott in a rarefied atmosphere. Yet eager to promote and publicize herself, she was aware that although white patrons came to hear new renditions of classics, it never hurt to give them something to look at at the same time. On occasion, she was criticized for exploiting her sexuality. Usually, she wore low-cut dresses that exposed her sensuous round shoulders and gave a fair amount of attention to her breasts. Her eyes were flirtatious. And sometimes, she had an insolent smile that was a bit suggestive: part come-on and part pull-back so that she still remained a lady. When she went into her swing music, her sexy body movements snapped the audience to attention.

She was also the most outspoken of all the forties divas. Like Horne, she refused to appear before segregated audiences. When a restaurant in Pasco, Washington, refused to serve her, she not only raised a stink but sued for $50,000. In 1945, political momentum was added to Scott's public image when she married Adam Clayton Powell Jr. amid much to-do from the press. But Scott, whose Trinidadian background may explain her haughty demeanor, seemed oblivious to criticism as she went from one dazzling concert performance to another, never giving up her career, and for years remaining more famous than her husband. The two had a son and were seen as the then modern Negro couple: educated, well-traveled, attractive go-getters and doers.

Following the war years, Hazel Scott's career was not as glowing. In this era of blacklisting, when Paul Robeson and Canada Lee could not find work, Hazel Scott was listed in Red Channels and her engagements fell off, too. Her open criticism of America's racial problems may have been looked upon as anti–American comments; so, too, was the fact that in 1943 she had performed at a rally for Benjamin Davis, an avowed Communist running for the New York City Council, which, of course, in the minds of some meant that she had to be a Communist, too. No one seemed interested that Scott might have gone to the rally since Davis was the only black running for the council.

Hazel Scott spoke up, going before the House Un–American Activities Committee in 1950. In an impressive fourteen-page statement, she denounced Red Channels as "guilt by listing," "a lie," and "a vile and un–American act." Going a step further, she later proposed that, in the future, musicians' and artists' unions should boycott those very radio networks and sponsors that had suspended entertainers listed in the book without proof of disloyalty. She was one of the few performers, black or white, determined to fight it out.

Following these troubles, her career was never the same. In 1950, despite good ratings, her television show was not renewed. That same year she was back in the newspapers when she refused to perform before a segregated audience at the University of North Carolina. Although she was respected as a fine pianist in serious music circles, the new mass audience came to think of her musical innovations as relics from the past. Even Scott may have felt that she rode to fame on a classy gimmick since later she stopped jazzing up the classics. In the late 1950s, she left the States. After her divorce from Powell in 1961, she had a short-lived marriage to a European, Anzio Bedin. That same year, she appeared in the film *Night Affair.* And she was back in the papers once more when Powell was accused of having falsified her 1951 income-tax returns. During Powell's tragic decline in the 1960s, Hazel Scott took on yet another new admirable dimension when she refused to criticize him publicly. In the 1970s, after a long absence, Scott successfully returned to the world of New York nightclubs. Scott died in 1981.

Marian Anderson:
the People's Woman

New York mayor Fiorello La Guardia and Marian Anderson.

Of all the forties social symbols, the greatest surely was Marian Anderson. Even as a child, growing up in Philadelphia, Anderson was something of a legend. Her father, who had sold ice and coal, died in 1914 when she was twelve. Her widowed mother, formerly a Virginia schoolteacher, reared Marian and her other two daughters amid great hardships. There was always something both extraordinary and sad about the young Anderson. She was large and awkward for her age. For as long as anyone could remember, the girl had sung in the Union Baptist Church choir, demonstrating her vocal skills early by singing soprano, alto, tenor, and bass. *"Come and Hear the Baby Contralto, Ten Years Old,"* an early church handbill read.

During these early years, Philadelphia's Black Community, keenly interested in her future and determined that her voice be heard, took up a special fund at church so she could have money for singing lessons.

Even then, Marian Anderson must have realized the special responsibility with which she was saddled. No success (or failure) that she ever had would be simply hers alone. Already she was becoming a social symbol for a community that felt its destiny was tied to hers. Soon, Negro America pinned its hopes on Marian Anderson, believing that she would crack the walls of prejudice and become the first major Negro concert hall performer in American history to appear in the grand showplaces of the world.

In 1921, at age nineteen, Anderson studied with Giuseppe Boghetti. He groomed her for an important musical competition, which came in 1926 at Lewisohn Stadium, on the campus of The City College of New York. Anderson won first prize over three-hundred other singers. Afterward, she had a short engagement with the Philadelphia Orchestra, performed at Carnegie Hall, and won a Julius Rosenwald scholarship. She continued studying intensely, vigorously, with astounding reserves of discipline and stamina.

Throughout the 1930s she toured Europe, singing German *Lieder* and spirituals. The reactions to this contralto were overwhelming. The roof of his house was too low for her, composer Sibelius told her. In Salzburg, Arturo Toscanini made the pronouncement that has never died: *A voice like yours is heard only once in a hundred years.* None understood her triumph abroad better than La Baker, who, upon meeting Anderson, bowed and curtsied: one diva homage to another.

Finally, impresario Sol Hurok brought Anderson to New York's Town Hall in 1935. The next year, her Carnegie Hall appearance was packed. Then, she returned to Europe. Then back to the States, where in 1938 alone she performed seventy recitals, hitting cities all over the country, including the South, giving the longest, most intense tours in concert history. In time, Anderson probably also made more celebrated international tours than any other performer, traveling throughout Scandinavia, performing in all the great European capitals, as well as in Japan,

Throughout the long, exhausting European tours of her early years, Marian Anderson may have struck many as a woman on the run, without a home. For the truth of the matter was that Marian Anderson, the greatest contralto of the 20th century, was neither fully recognized nor wanted in her own country.

The great hurricane blew in at the tail end of the 1930s, Anderson was scheduled to appear at Constitution Hall, which was owned by the Daughters of the American Revolution. Playing on a hunch, a shrewd newspaper woman named Mary Johnson called the DAR's president, and asked what was the position of the organization on the matter. The position was clear: neither Marian Anderson nor any other Negro was going to appear in Constitution Hall.

Suddenly, through no design of her own, Marian Anderson was in newspaper headlines, as the star of the biggest racial flap of the decade. Across the nation, blacks and liberal whites were enraged by the inci-

dent. Walter White, Executive Secretary of the NAACP, stepped in to suggest a way to best focus on the racism of the DAR: by staging a large outdoor free concert in the nation's capital. Anderson agreed to the concert, although at the time of the incident she was so busy touring that the full impact of the situation had not hit her.

A surge of publicity arose as Eleanor Roosevelt and Secretary of the Interior Harold Ickes agreed to sponsor the concert. Mrs. Roosevelt even resigned from the DAR in protest. Supreme Court justices, senators, congressmen, Cabinet members, and other distinguished men and women announced their support of the event, too. On Easter Sunday, 1939, the concert was held at the Lincoln Memorial. Seventy-five thousand people attended. Marian Anderson opened with "America" and closed with "Nobody Knows the Trouble I've Seen." Afterward, the enthusiastic crowd went wild, trying its best to get to the singer. For a

Two of America's icons: Anderson and baseball star Jackie Robinson.

few scary moments, it threatened to be a stampede. In the end, though, the event signaled a new era in the history of the fight for civil rights in America. And Marian Anderson became one of the most famous women in the world.

Throughout the event and afterward, she remained a gracious, quietly commanding but shadowy figure. No one can ever say exactly how she felt about any of the

commotion. Even years later, when she did write of the concert in the autobiography *My Lord What a Morning,* her account was moving, but her gut feelings seemed politely veiled. "What were my own feelings?" she wrote of her response to the news of her rejection by the DAR:

> I was saddened and ashamed. I was sorry for the people who had precipitated the affair. I felt the behavior stemmed from lack of understanding. They were not persecuting me personally or as a representative of my people so much as they were doing something that was neither sensible nor good. Could I have erased the bitterness, I would have done so gladly. I do not mean that I would have been prepared to say that I was not entitled to appear in Constitution Hall as might any other performer. But the unpleasantness disturbed me, and if it had been up to me alone I would have sought a way to wipe it out....I have been in this world long enough to know that there are all kinds of people, all suited by their own natures for different tasks. It would be fooling myself to think that I was meant to be a fearless fighter.

Of the plans for the outdoor concert, she said: "In principle the idea was sound, but it could not be comfortable to me as an individual. As I thought further, I could see that my significance as an individual was small in the affair. I had become, whether I liked it or not, a symbol, representing my people. I had to appear." The night before the concert, Marian Anderson knew that no hotel in Washington would accept her. She styaed with friends. Yet, throughout the entire affair and for the duration of her career, she functioned by somehow miraculously detaching herself, stoically accepting a symbolic role thrust on her because of her formidable talent and her color.

During the Roosevelt–Truman years, Anderson continued her record-breaking tours. She also became one of the most decorated women in the world, winning countless awards and citations from groups black and white. In 1946, she appeared on the cover of *Time.* Finally, even Constitution Hall was opened to her. But even with the new honors, her position as a black artist in America had not been greatly altered. Doors were still closed to her because of her color. It would be almost a decade before she would finally sing at the Metropolitan Opera House.

When she commented on the racial attitudes of her own country (or her own situation), Anderson was often gentler than the other divas and never defiantly critical. One wonders now what her place in history, as well as her significance as a social symbol, might have been had she ever lashed out at American society. Surely, she would have been the most threatening lady around. Often, much of White America seemed to value this sensitive, private woman because of her restraint and her reticence.

By the end of the 1940s, as well as throughout the 1950s and 1960s, Anderson became a textbook commodity, written up as a model Negro for elementary and high-school students who often found the simplified version of her that was presented (like the lives and triumphs of George Washington Carver and Joe Louis) a bit remote, even tiresome. The world had heard Marian Anderson sing. Young Black America longed to hear Marian Anderson talk. And so for years among younger blacks, there was a terrible ambivalence toward her. In the late 1960s, her name was seldom mentioned. Only in the 1970s did some idea of the complexities enveloping her once again come to light.

If there was a tragic aspect to Marian Anderson's career, it was simply that later generations, black and white, would view her as something of a past social symbol, rather than as the greatest contralto of the 20th century. Her position, with its layers of meaning and the relentless flow of myth, legend, symbol, image, and dream that swirled about it, was a complicated one. Yet, Marian Anderson handled her situation with unending reserves of intelligence and poise. She died at ninety-six in 1993.

Sister Rosetta Tharpe.

Postwar Optimism

For the most part, the postwar audience seemed eager for new faces and dreams or modified old ones. When it was revealed that Josephine Baker had worked during the war with the French Resistance, she again was a news item. As photographs of Baker entertaining the troops circled the globe, mainstream Americans accepted her no doubt as a local gal who had gone off and made good after all.

Other familiar faces prospered. Never a great social symbol, Ella Fitzgerald, the perennial girl-singer in search of her place in the scheme of things, continued to work in clubs, becoming so popular a singer's singer that for a spell she gave even Holiday a scare. Shy pianist Mary Lou Williams, as private a person as Ella, remained a musician's musician, too. She had her own band for a short time. (Her second husband, Shorty Baker, played trumpet with the group.) Her arrangement, *The Zodiac Suite*, which she introduced in 1945 at Town Hall, was played by the New York Philharmonic in 1946. Singer Ada Brown remained popular. So did newcomer trumpet player Clora Bryant. Dorothy Maynor, yet in the shadow of Marian Anderson after some ten years, was still an active concert-hall favorite and still a viable social symbol. And Anne Brown, the dazzling singer who originated the character Bess in *Porgy and Bess*, also gave impressive concert performances.

New faces popped up: actress Hilda Simms, a dramatic knockout in the black version of the play *Anna Lucasta;* Ruby Dee, who was also making a name for herself in the touring version of *Anna Lucasta;* pianist Dorothy Donegan, who shook and grimaced while jazzing up the classics as Scott had done; former child prodigy and accomplished teenage pianist sensation Philippa Schuyler; singers Joya Sherrill, Betty Carter, Sarah Vaughan, and Dinah Washington; comedienne Pearl Bailey; dancers–choreographers Pearl Primus and Marie Bryant; and the ravishing Dorothy Dandridge, who in the 1930s and early 1940s was still teamed with sister Vivian and singer Etta Jones as the Dandridge Sisters in films

and, for a time, with the Jimmie Lunceford Orchestra. But eventually she went on her own, appearing as the young lead in Duke Ellington's West Coast musical *Jump for Joy* and in such films as *Hit Parade of 1943* with Count Basie and in *Atlantic City* with Louis Armstrong.

There was also the rambunctious gospel singer Sister Rosetta Tharpe, who strutted with a guitar as she performed. In 1938, Tharpe had come to prominence when she appeared in revues with Cab Calloway at the Cotton Club. By 1940, she took her gospel music around the country and also recorded for Decca, sometimes teaming with Marie Knight. In 1949, the rousing Sister Rosetta also recorded a duet with her mother, Katie Bell Nubin.

Now that the war was finally over, Americans were eager for the good times to begin. And all in all, these new stars were seemingly less troublesome figures than some of their predecessors.

Still going strong: Ella Fitzgerald.

Ethel Waters in her Oscar-nominated role in the film *Pinky,* with Jeanne Crain.

Postwar Mania

As the 1940s swept to a close, however, the most talked-about divas, Ethel Waters and Billie Holiday, were hardly malleable types. One shakily symbolized endurance. The other presented a woman-on-the-edge. But both were somewhat out of whack with the rhythm and pace of the era. Each, too, was the star of her own disturbingly significant soap opera, which Americans viewed with open fascination.

At the start of the era, Billie Holiday, the artist, was maturing beautifully, more poised and assured than ever, with no excess gestures or emotions. But Billie Holiday, the woman, was still headed for trouble. In 1941, she married Jimmy Monroe (the one-time husband of Nina Mae McKinney). For years she had smoked marijuana, and she had been able to drink even hard-nosed musicians under the table. But now, she started using heroin. She left Monroe and took up with musician Joe Guy, whom no one seemed to think was good for her. She formed her own band and it failed. When her mother died in 1945, it was a great loss from which she never fully recovered. There were incidents at the clubs, too. On evening, when a rowdy naval officer caller her a *nigger*, she just about turned the place inside out, smashing a beer bottle on a table, then heading for the man. She was held back, but that was one of the few times.

For now, Billie Holiday went public with her manic madness. She was uncomfortable, restless, angry, and she didn't care if the whole goddamn world knew it. In fact, she seemed to relish her growing notoriety as the beautiful, talented woman verging on a breakdown.

Word also spread that dope was getting the best of her. Living with it was hell enough, she once said; working with it, worse. Sometimes, she clutched the mike with both hands to prop herself up. Sometimes, she fell behind on the beat, was inaudible, forgot lyrics, or seemed completely withdrawn. On other occasions, she miraculously caught hold of herself in the middle of a disastrous performance and came back strong. Nightly, there was a disturbing figure hanging around the clubs; her pusher, silently waiting to be summoned. In time, the whiskey, the reefer, the heroin, took their toll. Yet the supreme testament to her artistry is that when the voice started to go, there was a new emotional intensity and depth, so perfectly controlled that today there is no such thing as a bad Billie Holiday recording. All her work still holds up.

In 1946, Holiday gave her first major solo performance at Town Hall. The next year, she wisely took time off for a "cure" treatment, managed to kick the habit, then rose like a phoenix ready for action all over again, only to discover that while no one had bothered her when she had been on the stuff, they were eager to catch up with her now that she was off.

In 1947, Billie Holiday became a tabloid queen, the star of a drug-ridden nightmarish saga as far as members of the press were concerned. Her Philadelphia hotel room was raided by drug agents. She fled the scene, later turned herself in, and was sentenced to a prison term in a Virginia institution. Newspapers informed their readers that the very talented, innovative colored singing star was a dope fiend. Released from prison in 1948, she gave a triumphant comeback concert at Carnegie Hall. But her career was in a shambles. Since New York clubs could not issue a cabaret card to any performer convicted of a felony, she could get no work. She did perform illegally, however, at some small clubs and also was able to work in the big theaters where the law did not apply. All this simply intensified the interest of a public eager to see the legend in the flesh. New incidents and arrests fed the legend: a brawl in a Hollywood hotel in 1948; another drug incident a month later in San Francisco. The press ran countless stories on her goings and comings, her fights, her arrests, her hassles, her never-ending round of difficulties.

Billie Holiday learned the power of the image. "They come to see me get all fouled up," she once said of her performances. "They want to see me fall flat on my can." Now so caught up was the public in her self-destructive *mythos* that it soon lost sight of Billie, the very creative artist.

Ethel Waters was also having problems, but in a far different and less public way. In

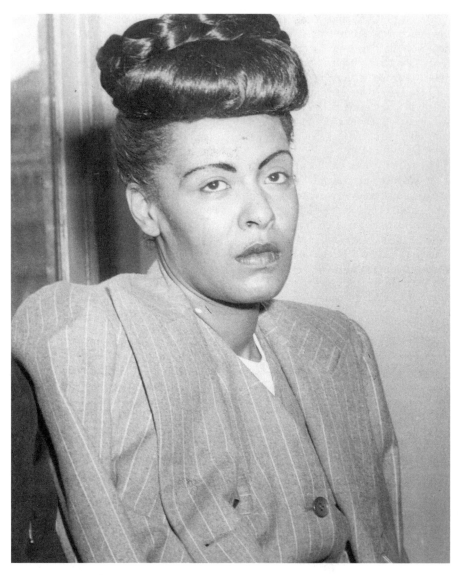

Troubled times for Lady Day.

the early forties, she had great success in the stage and film versions of *Cabin in the Sky* as well as such movies as *Cairo* and *Tales of Manhattan*. For wartime audiences, she remained a glowing symbol, the noble, big-hearted Christian woman who kept the home fires burning in times of trouble. But offstage and screen, Waters was as difficult as ever. Throughout the filming of MGM's

Cabin in the Sky, she fussed and fumed and just about drove everybody batty, particularly the young Lena Horne, whom Waters feared was getting better treatment from the studio. One day, there was a terrible blowup when Waters was to parody a song performed by Horne. How, she wanted to know, did they expect her to imitate a style that was an imitation of a style that she had

One evening, when a rowdy naval officer called her a *nigger*, Holiday just about turned the place inside out, smashing a beer bottle on a table, then heading for the man.

originated years before? (One of her best moments in the picture occurred when, after having looked over rival Horne, Waters put her hands on her full hips and announced that she had everything Lena had—only a whole lot more of it!) Waters won all her battles with MGM. But as she later said: "Like many other performers, I was to discover that winning arguments in Hollywood is costly. Six years were to pass before I could get another job."

During those six years, much else went wrong in her life. The Internal Revenue Service closed in for payment of back taxes from 1938 to 1939. In Hollywood, a young man she had befriended robbed her of over $10,000 in cash and $35,000 worth of jewelry (both large sums at the time), and the newspapers picked up on the story. To some, it looked as if Ethel Waters were a lonely star fallen prey to a young gigolo. Her bookings dwindled. She blamed bad agents for her decline, but her fiery temperament contributed, too. Her money was running out. She had an ulcer and was on a half-cream, half-milk diet. She could not sleep and was on pills. She moved to the homes of various friends in Harlem and sat daily with time on her hands while word spread throughout the community that one of America's greatest Negro stars was down to her last penny. Ethel Waters did not see or talk to anyone. To be down and out was one thing. To have everyone know it was more than she cared to bear.

Somehow, Ethel Waters held on. In early 1949, she was asked to test for a new film (an unusual request for a star of her magnitude), in which she would play the grandmother of a light-skinned young black woman who passes for white. Waters made the test and ended up giving one of her finest performances in *Pinky*. She won an Academy Award nomination for Best Supporting Actress. Ether Waters's career was back on solid ground. But emotionally, she was hardly at ease. Like Holiday, she remained restless and edgy.

Despite the personal problems of Waters and Holiday, and the professional troubles of Lena Horne and Hazel Scott, the forties still closed on an optimistic note. Nothing could have daunted the professional hopes of the new black goddesses coming on the scene at the tail end of the period. Such upcoming stars as Pearl Bailey and Dorothy Dandridge knew, after all, that a war had been won, that the nation was more prosperous than ever before, and that black women had played a significant part in the cultural history of the past era. Then, too, the ambitious new beauties, eyeing the success of Horne and Scott, hoped that there was a place in movies now for glamorous, dignified African American women. And so, with her optimism intact, the emerging goddess of the postwar years rightly anticipated that there would be even more recognition and fanfare for the black beauty in the next era.

Sex Symbols
The 1950s

The fifties in America is now rightly remembered as a period of national conformity and apathy. What with the cold war and Senator Joseph McCarthy's Communist "witch hunts," when dissent of any kind was discouraged, America had turned quiet and sullen. America was soon bored with itself, too. And throughout the era, there were subtle signs everywhere of that boredom as well as of a brewing unrest. If anything, the various fads of the period and its trends simply revealed a great, secret national desire to break through all the lethargy. The new movie heroes—Marlon Brando, James Dean, Montgomery Clift—were all rebels who tapped the undercover dissent and dissatisfaction of America's Lonely Crowd.

The new heroines also had rebellious streaks. Marilyn Monroe shocked Americans when her nude photo ran in *Playboy.* Elizabeth Taylor's marriages kept her in the news. Often, Americans thought that they preferred the wholesome stars—Doris Day, Debbie Reynolds, and Grace Kelly. But Monroe and Taylor, the Light and the Dark of the era, were the 1950s' most famous females, touching on the avid interest in sexy rebelliousness. With Taylor, too, we see the first dark white goddess to become a major American star. Before her, such women as Gene Tierney, Hedy Lamarr, and Dolores Del Rio were successful but none was mythic like Greta Garbo. Taylor became a legendary heroine, although Americans often viewed her as the Scarlet Woman, the Other Side of Womanhood to be feared, even rejected.

Sex opened new doors for the fifties' black beauties. New stars—Eartha Kitt, Joyce Bryant, and Dorothy Dandridge—often played with or dramatized sex to mock or defy traditional middle-class values, taboos, and hang-ups. Neither Bryant nor Dandridge, however, felt comfortable with her sexy image.

Aside from sex, the fifties diva also found this bland new age surprisingly receptive to the cult of personality. Kitt and Pearl Bailey had huge egos and striking public personalities, far more idiosyncratic (and at times more neurotic) than Lena Horne and Hazel Scott.

Dorothy Dandridge: always glamorous.

Page 118: Dorothy Dandridge.

Dorothy Dandridge with Ed Sullivan.

Pearl Bailey: the Sexy Girl Next Door

In this new gamy atmosphere of sex and personality, Pearl Bailey, the first black beauty to make waves, was hardly anyone's idea of a woman who might use sex to track a man down or to lash out at society. Instead, Pearlie Mae personified the lively, down-home diva: the ordinary, chatty, wise-cracking, neighborly lady who was telling a generation scared of its own shadow just to cool it, honey, sit back, relax, and have some fun. She became a star by often laughing at and joking about the birds and the bees, romance and men.

Pearl Bailey had been around since the 1940s, stumbling here and there, trying to find her niche. Born in 1918 in Newport News, Virginia, one of four children and the daughter of a minister, she had gone to live with her mother in Washington, D.C., following the divorce of her parents. After her mother remarried, the family moved to Philadelphia. Her career began at amateur-night shows in Philadelphia and Washington. At first, she was known as the kid sister of dancer Bill Bailey, who was then a far bigger star.

In the forties, Bailey performed at New York clubs, did USO tours, had a hit record called "Tired" (a woman's lament about the way that life and her man have been treating her), and dazzled Broadway audiences in 1946 in *St. Louis Woman.* In a cast that included the Nicholas Brothers, Ruby Hill, June Hawkins, Rex Ingram, and Juanita Hall, Pearlie Mae, with only two numbers, almost stole the show. "Pearl Bailey was a special favorite on opening night," wrote *New York Morning Telegraph* critic George Freedley, "and . . . stopped the show twice which is as unusual as anything I can think of now . . . . Pearl Bailey positively triumphed." Later, Freedley saw the show again and was as enthusiastic as ever, writing:

The highlight is still the wonderfully comic Pearl Bailey who can take any number and make it sound better than it is . . . . Her handling of the highly moral "Legalize My Name" is a joy to behold . . . . The audience was eating out of her hand before she finished. When she saunters into "A Woman's Prerogative" in the last act, the spectators began to laugh before the first lyric was out of her mouth. That is how great comedi-

ennes are born and Pearl Bailey certainly has what it takes to achieve high rank among the comic singers of our stage.

For her performance, Pearl Bailey walked off with the theater world's Donaldson Award.

Bailey was aware of her limitations as well as her assets. Because she was not much of a singer, she shrewdly learned to talk as she sang (or to sing a bit as she talked), providing lively, seemingly spontaneous banter in which she pushed the song aside. What really counted were the direct, personal comments. So, when performing "Toot Toot Tootsie, Good-bye," Bailey would interrupt herself, look at the audience, throw her hands forward, and say, "Good Riddance!" to indicate that she was glad the darn rascal was out of her life. While she performed "Ma, He's Making Eyes at Me," audiences saw a whirling delight. Pearl might be twisting and turning, fidgeting nervously but happily, her eyes widening, her face hot with romantic anticipation, 'cause she was tickled pink that the guy was giving her the once-over. Her hit song, "Takes Two to Tango," was filled with sexual innuendoes. No matter what the song, Pearl Bailey's impromptu conversations presented a portrait of a daffy romantic trapped by her own sense of realism.

Another comic selling point was her fatigue. "Why should I stand? Everybody else is sittin'," she would tell her audience, then take a seat onstage, immediately setting up a free-and-easy rapport with the crowd. Sometimes Bailey's act was criticized as a throwback to prewar stereotypes. Actually, the humor was both old and new. She was influenced by the chitlin-circuit stars such as Moms Mabley and Redd Foxx. Like them, she set herself up as a deliriously engaging community leader of sorts. "Now, looka here, Honey," she might begin a routine. Bailey had also learned from Hattie McDaniel, who could be funny, charming, and downright hostile or rebellious all at the same time. Yet, influenced as she was by the old-timers, Pearl never pushed her humor to the point that it might disturb an audience. Sometimes Moms or Redd, and later Richard Pryor as well as others after him, seemed bent on driving audiences up a wall with their incisive barbs. Bailey, however, was always a soothing figure. She used humor to communicate her view of the world as a joyous, harmonious place that had no great problems or tensions. (This point of view, so much admired in the 1950s, often distressed younger black audiences of the following decade.)

In the late forties and early fifties, Bailey, determined to make the big time, was an ambitious, competitive performer who seemed to be running in circles. She popped up on Broadway, in such disappointing shows as *Arms and the Girl*, *House of Flowers*, and *Bless You All*. In Hollywood, she appeared in such films as *Variety Girl* (in which she sang "Tired"), *Isn't It Romantic?*, *Carmen Jones*, *That Certain Feeling*, *All the Fine Young Cannibals*, and *Porgy and Bess*. But neither Broadway nor Hollywood seemed to know what to do with this magnetic personality, whose timing and delivery were always letter perfect.

During the fifties, Bailey finally became a national celebrity due to her nightclub appearances where, in the middle of her act, she would talk to and tease her patrons, and most importantly, due to her highly successful appearances on a new phenomenon called *television*. Appearing on everything from the Ed Sullivan to the Perry Como shows, she became one of America's first black television stars. She was lucky that

Controversy: Bailey's marriage to musician Louis Bellson.

she showed up when there was a place for her high-flung, far-out broadness. Seeing television for the communal vehicle it was, Bailey was clearly at home, exchanging quips and chitchat with Ed or Perry in her casual style. She knew just how far to go, too. She played more with the idea of romance than sex, and stayed clear of racial material that was then taboo. Moreover, although good looking, she played down her looks. Nothing was going to set her apart from the other gals. Television divested Pearl Bailey of some of her sexuality and some of her originality, too. But her appearances helped middle-class, conformist American viewers to slowly grow accustomed to seeing a black face in their homes. Even at that, she did not star in her own series until the early 1970s.

For the most part, Pearl Bailey was an ethnic diva who knew exactly how far to go with the whole ethnic business. She was an immensely likable woman who, as far as fifties audiences were concerned, made but one mistake. Bailey had an early marriage (which few knew anything about) to the chitlin-circuit comic Slappy White. But the nation came to know much about her 1952 marriage to white drummer Louis Bellson in London, amid a storm of controversy. His father's objection to the interracial match was picked up by the wire services, and the two were besieged by the press, making front-page headlines throughout the country. Later, Bailey was back in the papers after an incident at a New Jersey nightclub where she had been beaten and kicked by a group of unidentified white men.

But the good-natured Pearlie Mae stayed on the scene. A great professional triumph came in 1967 when she starred on Broadway in the all-black version of *Hello, Dolly!* One of the Great White Way's legendary events, her performance won her a special Tony Award. During this later phase of her career, she seemed to enjoy her fame, posing for photographs with one American president after another. During a performance of *Hello, Dolly!* in Washington,

D.C., which was attended by President Lyndon Johnson, Bailey spotted him from the stage and told the audience, "I didn't know this child was going to show up." She brought Johnson onstage to sing the title song of the show with the chorus. "It was probably the first time," commented *The New York Times*, "that a President of the United States served as a chorus boy." But a younger generation—vehemently opposed to the war in Vietnam—did not see Bailey as

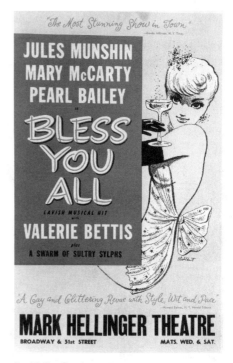

Pearl Bailey, Broadway star.

one of its heroines, especially when she later appeared to be chummy with President Richard M. Nixon. In those later eras, Bailey's humor was less saucy and ribald, more sugary and more openly calculated to disarm. Among entertainers Bailey also had a reputation—for years—for being difficult and flat-out mean-spirited. Some considered her next-to-impossible to work with. Yet, that side of Pearlie Mae was never seen by the public.

Eartha Kitt:
the Cat Woman

The era's next important black beauty was Eartha Kitt, an energetic tiny terror of a performer. A sex symbol who was part alluring, part campy, part pleasingly absurd, she purred, snarled, scratched, and acted up like crazy. Performing at the smartest supper clubs in America, she strutted out in Balmain gowns. Before she even opened her mouth, patrons sat in eager anticipation, aware of the stories circulating abut her temperament, her lifestyle. Men were said to have lavished gifts on her—yachts, cars, furs, diamonds. No one may have believed such stories, but it was fun to hear about them. Her songs, "Monotonous" and "C'est Si Bon," touched on a life of sheer, unadulterated pleasure and self-indulgence. Onstage, sex and money were what she treasured most. She was the ultimate temptress, who sometimes used her audiences, sometimes made fun of them. Her hypnotic coldness, the eyes that stared and blazed, the petulant pouty mouth, the simmering air of arrogance and indolence, the metallic quality of the voice itself, were all knowingly used to entrance her audience. She was the fifties high priestess of the cult of personality. With her, audiences witnessed briefly a blatant triumph of will, a poor backwoods colored girl who provided the silent generation with a far-flung fairy tale, a Cinderella story turned sepia.

Eartha Kitt with Nat "King" Cole (left) in *St. Louis Blues*.

As befitting a fairy tale, the Kitt beginnings were humble. She had been born the daughter of a sharecropper (so it was publicized early in her career) who named her Eartha in homage to the goodness of the earth. When Eartha and her sister were still youngsters, the father deserted their mother. In later years, Kitt appeared to rewrite her life story, saying that her mother was black, her father white, and that she never learned his identity. Again, her followers may have wondered if the story was based on fact. But, again, it made good copy. Still young, Kitt was sent to live in New York where she was a country girl dumbfounded by such big-city mysteries as indoor plumbing, electricity, and the radio. In 1943, she left high school to work as a seamstress in a Brooklyn factory. One day when a girl asked for directions to the Katherine Dunham dance studio, Eartha tagged along, later auditioned for Dunham, and by age twenty was a featured dancer, traveling with the troupe through Europe and Mexico. By 1950 she had left Dunham, embarking on a career as a nightclub chanteuse that carried her to Paris, London, and Turkey. A transfixed Orson Welles—who met her in Paris in 1951—dubbed her *the most exciting woman in the world* and audaciously cast her in his European production of *Faust*. She played Helen of Troy, "the face that launched a thousand ships."

During her early period abroad, Kitt, by some accounts, was a tough, ambitious, driven young woman who refused to slow down since she felt that time might be running out. In each country, during off hours from work, she had studied the people, soaking up the sights, the cultures, the customs, and the languages. For a girl who had grown up with nothing, she seemed desperate to discover herself by means of another cultural experience, one free of American prejudices and pruderies. Early in her career, Eartha Kitt seemed to hold America in disdain, never forgiving this land of opportunity for her early sufferings. Her entire professional stance—everything from her particular kind of elegance and arrogance to the way she spoke with a strange accent—always suggested exotic Eurasian chic. Consequently, although

it took Americans time to discover and appreciate her, in Europe she immediately got attention.

In America, Kitt's career did not take off until her Broadway appearance in *New Faces of 1952*, in which she cleverly mixed sex with humor. And she was rewarded by becoming an instant celebrity, hotly coveted, courted, and promoted by the press. She played the posh clubs, made movies *(Mark of the Hawk, Anna Lucasta)*, was a guest performer at the 1957 Newport Jazz Festival, appeared on television shows (everything from *Voice of Firestone* to *Toast of the Town* to the title role in Oscar Wilde's *Salome)*, bounced back to Broadway for lead roles *(Mrs. Patterson, Shinbone Alley, Jolly's Progress)*, and had one hit record after another with songs that bristled with sex and decadence ("C'est Si Bon," "I Want to Be Evil," and "Santa Baby"). Her first album, *RCA Victor Presents Eartha Kitt*, sold over two million copies in little more than sixteen months, followed by another hit album called *The Bad Eartha*.

Records, shows, movies, and television spots kept her in the public eye. Her life was described as an endless round of benefits, parties, dinners, luncheons, trips to photographers, the hairdresser, a whirl of railroad stations, international airports, studios, dressing rooms, rehearsal halls, press conferences. Well publicized as a sex kitten, she was linked by the press to such celebrities as Orson Welles, playboy Porfiro Rubirosa, and millionaire Arthur Loew Jr. She interviewed Albert Einstein, had tea with Winston Churchill, and dinner with Prime Minister Nehru. In 1954, the undergraduates at Yale voted her the girl that they would most like to take to the Senior Prom.

The press was infatuated not only with her grand style but her fiery temperament, too. When she performed for visiting monarchs King Paul and Queen Fredericka in Los Angeles, the mayor, Norris Poulson, was offended by her selection of suggestive songs. In 1955, when an illness cut short the national tour of the play *Mrs. Patterson*, rumors flew that it wasn't Eartha's kidneys that had acted up: it was her temper. That same year, newspapers reported

The movie version of the Broadway hit that made Kitt famous.

that she had been named defendant in a $200,000 damage suit by a nightclub that charged that a rude Eartha had dumped champagne onto patrons. Despite all the ballyhoo, it is safe to say that she was never as great a public heroine as Baker, Horne, or Waters. Her attitude eventually antagonized not only some of the press, but some of her fans as well. As early as 1954, a columnist for the *New York Morning Telegraph* wrote:

You idly wonder why a girl who has reached such fame and position from such a humble start allows herself to behave as rudely as she does . . . . You remember what another actress told you about how Miss Kitt acted at the party given for her . . . . A noted man of theatre came up and said: "Miss Kitt, you were quite wonderful," and Kitt languidly replied: "Of course." . . . Is this an egotist doing her best to alienate people, or a frightened girl who covers her panic with rudeness?*

Then you remember what Jimmy Kirkwood told you of how charming and simple she was in her early success at the Churchill Club in London and what a change he found a year later when she was in "New Faces." . . . "She was a simple kid working hard for success in London," he said: "Backstage at 'New Faces' I found a bored, languid girl in leopard skin slacks, black satin waist, foot-long cigarette holder and an affected, 'Oh, hello,' said with a vague 'Now I wonder who you are' manner. People haven't got time for that kind of nonsense." . . . Which is something Miss Kitt should learn: people haven't got time for that kind of non-

sense . . . . There were great performers before her and there will be great ones after she has been forgotten.

One could dismiss these comments as those of a white columnist put off or threatened by Kitt's unbridled confidence. Why should her humble beginnings stop her from behaving as rudely as she pleased? But even the black press commented on Kitt's rudeness. *Ebony,* that bastion for the values and sentiments of America's black bourgeoisie and a publication that seldom ran critical articles on African American celebrities, nonetheless carried a 1954 cover story with the banner: *"Why Negroes Do Not Like Eartha Kitt."* The piece was hard-hitting:

> *Eartha Kitt . . . was approached one Sunday afternoon by a. . .Negro who had. . .watch[ed] her play a ball game of "catch" with a little white girl . . . . He interrupted to hand Miss Kitt a note. She took it, frowned slightly as she read it. "Why don't you come out...and visit some Negro places and be with other Negroes?" the note read.*
> *Miss Kitt . . . said she was sorry but she would have to decline . . . . In much less polite language she told him what he could do with his "Negro places." . . .*
> *What he apparently did not know was that . . . many Negroes find Eartha Kitt cold and a little hard to take. Up to now, it has seldom been mentioned that this rejection of her by other Negroes has become almost contagious and that her aloofness has become a subject of much talk.*

Later questioned about her reaction to the piece, Kitt was quoted as saying: "I don't have to defend anything. I do not carry my race around on my shoulders. My work is not racial and neither am I a racial personality."

There is no reason to believe that Eartha Kitt ever regretted this statement nor any other that she might have made. Had she, there might have been more sympathy for her when her career decline set in. It is hard to say exactly what went wrong. But perhaps the haughtiness, which had long been an integral part of the black beauty's style,

now seemed out of control with Kitt. Her dilemma may point up the fundamental uneasiness the black sex symbol felt with her new role. Kitt pushed to extremes the idea that she could not be taken for granted, that her public had to show her respect. Every black goddess would cherish the fact that she was a sexy lady, but every black goddess also felt compelled to let everyone know that she was more than simply *that.*

Finally though, Kitt's problem may well have been that she was too much a personalized fairy-tale heroine ever to be a woman of myth. Eartha had lived out her dream of herself as the poor backwoods girl alone in the world who triumphs over hostile or seemingly insurmountable forces to become a star. Her success gratified her personal wishes. But unlike every other diva on record, she did not seem to share her triumphs with the community. In the end, Kitt may have surely alienated her power base, the African American community.

By the time that the Eisenhower era ended, so too had much of her blazing appeal. (Her marriage in the 1960s to white businessman William McDonald did not help matters.) In the 1960s, she toured the country in a production of *The Owl and the Pussycat* and turned up as Cat Woman on the TV series *Batman.* Then in 1968, she was back on the front pages when at a luncheon with Lady Bird Johnson, then the First Lady, Kitt denounced the Johnson administration's involvement in Vietnam. Kitt later announced that an angered President Lyndon Johnson did all that he could to wreck her career, instructing the FBI to gather a dossier on her. Club and café owners were pressured into canceling engagements. Could it be that Kitt's career would never again have its earlier provocative luster? But almost a decade later, she returned to the spotlight with the Broadway production of *Timbuktu!,* in which upon entering the stage, Kitt stared directly into the audience, announcing haughtily, "I am here!" It was one of her great moments. At the end of the 1970s, the slinky, sexy Cat Woman of the 1950s was once again a star.

Joyce Bryant: the Bronze Blond Bombshell

In the early and mid-fifties, one of Eartha's only real rivals was Joyce Bryant. She was known as the *Black Marilyn Monroe*, the *belter*, and the *voice you'll always remember*. But, sadly, through her own design, she had a surprisingly short reign.

Bryant was the daughter of a San Franciscan who worked as a chef for the Southern Pacific Railroad. Her father was a carouser. Her mother was a devout Seventh-Day Adventist. Young Joyce, the oldest of eight children reared in a suffocating atmosphere of religious dos and don'ts, was a quiet, lonely child. As a teenager on a visit to a cousin in Los Angeles, Bryant joined a

But she generated most of her heat during live performances. She was known for her backless, fishtail, skintight dresses. *Life* reported that the costumes were so tight that often she could barely walk in them and had to be carried to the stage. The dresses revealed enough cleavage to make even Marilyn do a double take. Onstage, she burned up so much energy—twisting, turning, gyrating, shaking—that newspapers reported that she lost as much as four pounds at each performance.

In due time, though, Joyce Bryant's great trademark was (like Marilyn again) her blond hair. She had been born a bru-

Like her contemporary, Monroe, Bryant exuded sex. So provocative were "Love for Sale" and "Drunk with Love" that both were sometimes banned from radio play.

sing-along with other patrons at a local club. No sooner had she opened her mouth than everyone else became silent, impressed by her four-octave miracle of a voice. She was immediately offered a job as a professional singer. She went from club to club, slowly acquiring a reputation and a following.

By the middle of the decade, Joyce Bryant was a star not only because of her voice, but also because of her image as a kooky, dreamy woman. Like her contemporary, Monroe, Bryant exuded sex. Sometimes when she sang, she was cool and relaxed about sexual matters. Her tones were mellow. But other times, as she belted the tunes out, she became a steamy performer. So provocative were her big sexy hits "Love for Sale" and "Drunk with Love" that both were sometimes banned from radio play.

nette. But the hair color change came about one evening when she found herself appearing on the same bill with Josephine Baker. Terrified of competing with a legend, she finally hit on a surefire gimmick. That night, she arrived onstage in a tight silver dress, with silver nails, silver floor-length mink, and silver hair. She had grabbed a bottle of silver-radiator paint and painted the stuff all over her head. As she herself said, when she appeared, "I stopped everything!" (Bryant recalled that even Baker gave a nod when the two passed each other in a hallway, as if to say *"Touchez!"*)In no time, the bronze blond bombshell was plastered all over newspapers and magazines, and even started a fad among some more adventurous African American women. Eventually, the silver hair became her trademark, turning her into a glorified national oddity.

With the gimmick and voice intact, Bryant picked up as much as $2,500 to $3,500 a performance, earning as much as $150,000 a year. She was called one of the most beautiful black women in the world. And now, for the first time, a dark African American woman had become a certified national sex symbol. A 1953 *Life* magazine layout ran steamy photographs of her, the kind that readers seldom saw of white love goddesses. In one shot she was bent over, her backside in full view. In another, she lay on her dressing-room floor with feet propped up, her midriff showing, her open blouse barely managing to cup her breasts.

Eventually, the image unnerved even Bryant. Just when she had hit the real big time—when Earl Wilson or Walter Winchell was eager for an interview or a quote, when the Copacabana, the Fontainebleau, and Miami's Algiers Hotel signed her for appearances, when no less than the queen of Hollywood social arbiters, Louella Parsons, was happy to be photographed by her side—Joyce Bryant's fairy tale was already about to come to a bad end. The silver radiator paint made her hair fall out, and everything else seemed to fall to pieces, too. Because of her early religious indoctrination, she was never at ease with the sexy image. She fretted about working on the Sabbath and rebelled inwardly against "acting like a sexpot." She hated the atmosphere of the nightclubs and the men who eyed her or gave her a hard time.

"I never enjoyed my career," she later told *Essence*. "I was a pound of flesh and an object of lust in my last years, and I've no one but myself to blame."

Her private tensions became so great that before an appearance, she would cry that she could not perform. But she discovered that there was no such thing as "couldn't perform." Soon the managers, agents, promoters moved in, ready to take control. On those hard nights, when her nerves, rattled and frayed, drove her up a wall, pills and drugs were often available to calm her down or pep her up. "I had no peace," she said. "Pills brought sleep or pills brought energy, but never peace. I felt so alone. There was no one to talk to. I was such a big star, but I was such a little girl." And then, suddenly, she decided to leave show business. In November 1955, the headline over Earl Wilson's column read: *Joyce Bryant Ends Show Career for Church.* Later, a United Press article carried another headline: "*Torch Singer Joyce Bryant Starting on Evangelical Tour.*" *Ebony* ran a lengthy feature under the banner: "*The New World of Joyce Bryant: Former Café Singer Gives up $200,000-a-year Career to Learn to Serve God.*"

Joyce Bryant enrolled in Oakwood College, a Seventh-Day Adventist institution in Alabama. Here, she followed a strict regimen. No smoking. No drinking. No profanity. No dancing. No theater. No sex either. While a student, she did evangelical singing tours. And for a spell, she popped back up in the papers. As the bad-woman-trying-to-go-straight, she held a new fascination for readers caught up in the idea of repentance.

Once the blond hair was back to its natural black, she looked far less exotic; also heavier, strained, and lost. No doubt, she struck readers as a woman who had suffered. Oddly enough, once Bryant's conversion was accepted as the real thing and not some publicity stunt, she was virtually forgotten by the public.

As Bryant later revealed, the years away from show business were almost as bleak and hellish as those in. Disillusioned, she left her religious studies to return to performing in the sixties. She appeared with the Washington Symphony and later toured with the Italian, French, and Vienna Opera companies. But work was hard to find, and at one point she found herself demonstrating beauty products at the department store Lord & Taylor. Only in the late seventies, after further disappointments and more personal nightmarish experiences, did she return to the New York club scene, no longer a gimmicky blond bombshell but a magnificent dark-haired earthy woman.

Dorothy Dandridge:
Tragic Venus

Having come of professional age at the same time as Kitt, Bailey, and Bryant, Dorothy Dandridge rose higher and emerged as America's first bona fide black movie star. In time, she had her share of problems, ending up, like Holiday, a tragic heroine. But while Dandridge rode the crest of success, there was, quite simply, no one like her.

She was a child of Hollywood, growing up with her older sister Vivian in a heady showbiz atmosphere. Born in Cleveland in 1922, she was the daughter of Cyril Dandridge, a draftsman, and his wife Ruby Butler Dandridge, an aspiring comedienne. Shortly before Dorothy was born, Ruby walked out on Cyril, taking Vivian with her. Under the tutelage of Ruby and her live-in female friend Geneva Williams (called Auntie Ma-Ma by the children and who was actually Ruby's lesbian lover), the sisters, who grew up without knowing their father, were trained to perform—singing, dancing, doing acrobatics. Billed as the Wonder Children, they appeared at churches and schools, first in Cleveland, then in parts of the South. In the midst of the Great Depression, Ruby and Williams settled in sunny Los Angeles with dreams of finding movie work for the girls. Ruby herself appeared in such films as *Tish* and *Cabin in the Sky,* and was a regular on such radio programs as *The Judy Canova Show* and *Beulah.* Ruby also teamed Dorothy and Vivian, as noted earlier, with another little girl, Etta Jones. Now known as the Dandridge Sisters, the trio appeared in such movies as *A Day at the Races* and *Going Places,* as well as at theaters and then, as teenagers, at New York's Cotton Club on the same bill with popular dance stars, the Nicholas Brothers, Harold and Fayard.

Vivian Dandridge was always known as the more aggressive, more outgoing of the two sisters. But by the early 1940s, Dorothy had ventured out on her own, playing roles in such movies as *Bahama Passage, Lady from Louisiana,* and *Sundown,* and performing the classic "Chattanooga Choo Choo" number with the Nicholas Brothers in *Sun Valley Serenade.* By then, she and Harold Nicholas had fallen in love and soon married. The union, however, was fraught with problems. Nicholas admitted years later that he

had been a womanizer and that he had been too young to marry. But the greatest heartache for Dandridge came after the birth of the couple's only child, a daughter named Harolyn, who had been born brain damaged. "She always blamed herself for the child's condition," Vivian Dandridge said. "She never got over it," said Dorothy's closest friend Geri Branton, who had married Fayard Nicholas. Later, Dorothy and Harold divorced. During this period of great personal depression, Dandridge, feeling she had failed as a wife, as a mother, as a lover, was finally determined to prove that she could do something right.

The idea that an African American woman could become a dramatic film actress was still unthinkable. Dandridge was also introverted and an extremely private young woman. But an extraordinary drive took over in the late 1940s, and she pushed herself beyond even her limits, channeling all her energies and frustrations into her career. She enrolled in the prestigious Actors Lab in Los Angeles, where her classmates included Marilyn Monroe and Sydney Chaplin. She worked hard on her voice, knowing that if she perfected her style and became a success in nightclubs, she would have a foot in the showbiz door. Whatever money that she made from early singing engagements was poured into costumes. When she was not in a rehearsal hall, she was studying—acting, singing, dancing. Or she was meeting people, off to a benefit, party, interview, or audition. "My sister worked twenty-four hours a day at being a star," Vivian once said.

And it paid off, especially when Dandridge worked with Phil Moore, one of the first African American arrangers–composers at MGM and the Svengali who had been the singing coach for Lena Horne, and who later worked with Diahann Carroll and Julie Wilson. Moore played an important part in shaping their styles. He also coached such stars as Marilyn Monroe and Ava Gardner. Horne and Dandridge (also Carroll) had striking similarities in looks, in dress, in hairstyles, in delivery. Phil Moore knew exactly what type of material they should use in order to appeal to a broader audience. Not one of them sang rhythm-and-blues. They stuck to the acceptable sounds of Gershwin and Rodgers and Hart.

In 1951, Dandridge's breakthrough performance occurred at the Club Gala in Los Angeles, a chic hangout for hip showbiz folk, intellectuals, and transplanted sophisticated Easterners working on the West Coast. Dandridge started off disastrously, so nervous according to her manager Earl Mills, that she could not stand and had to be seated onstage while she feebly performed. But Phil Moore, by then head-over-heels in love with her, joked and talked with her onstage. He loosened her up and coaxed her out of her shell, touching on the fiery personality for which she became famous. She won rave reviews from the critics. Afterward, entertainer Bobby Short recalled, there were long lines waiting to get into the club to see her. Her act at the Club Gala was so talked about that Dandridge was booked into the Mocambo, the most glamorous nightclub on the Sunset Strip, where stars such as Gable and Dietrich as well as movie wheeler-dealers came for a night of festivity. Dandridge broke all existing attendance records.

The press promptly latched onto her, as it did with no other black beauty. When she reopened at the Mocambo, *Life* ran a splashy picture layout, touting her as "the most beautiful Negro singer since Lena Horne." Two years later, *Life* ran another Dandridge photo layout. And the following year, she became one of the first black women to ever grace a *Life* cover. She also appeared on the cover of *Ebony*.

Soon, Dandridge made major appearances at important clubs around the country. When she performed at La Vie en Rose in New York City, then a popular nightclub in the midst of serious financial problems, her two-week engagement was such a sellout that she stayed on for some fourteen weeks, and single-handedly saved the club from bankruptcy. Later becoming the first African American performer to appear at the Waldorf Astoria's deluxe Empire Room, she also became a headliner in Las Vegas, that desert city which was a playground for the stars in the 1950s.

As Dandridge was ushered in, it looked as if Lena was being eased out. No doubt,

Black America's most cherished star of the 1950s: Dorothy Dandridge, who once said that she had everything—and nothing.

the name of Dorothy Dandridge was thrown in Lena's face numerous times. What she thought of her fifties rival is anyone's guess. But surely there had to be occasions when, eyeing Dorothy's triumphs, Lena felt that her own heyday had come and gone, particularly when Dandridge won movie roles in *Tarzan's Peril*, *The Harlem Globetrotters*, and the lead in MGM's *Bright Road*.

Then in the mid-1950s, Dandridge finally got the big prize, the black woman's movie role of the decade, the lead in Otto Preminger's all-black musical *Carmen Jones*. Initially, Preminger rejected her because she looked too sophisticated to play a *cullid* temptress. When she met with him in his office, he explained that when he saw her, he thought of Saks Fifth Avenue, not the earthy Carmen he sought. He thought she was better suited to play the good girl in the film, Cindy Lou. Arriving on her second interview with him, Dandridge had completely changed her style. She sexily sauntered into the office darkly made up and dressed in a tight skirt and low-cut blouse. Preminger took one look and proclaimed, "It's Carmen!" He immediately set up a screen test. Afterward, the role was hers.

In this lavish, Technicolor, CinemaScope modernization of Bizet's opera *Carmen*, Dandridge played a sexy young black woman working in a parachute factory, who lures a good, clean-cut colored boy (played by Harry Belafonte) away from the Army and his sweet innocent girlfriend (played sweetly by Olga James). Later, she dumps him for another man, only to be strangled by the hero at the climax of the film. No one thought an all-black movie would do well at the box office, but what with Dandridge's rousing performance, it was the surprise hit of 1954.

Life celebrated Dandridge as something of a grand natural wonder when the magazine wrote: "Of all the divas of grand opera—from Emma Calvé of the 1900s to Risë Stevens—who have decorated the title role of Carmen and have in turn been made famous by it, none was ever so decorative or will reach nationwide fame so quickly as the sultry young lady...on *Life*'s cover this week." After a nationwide poll of film critics, *Film Daily* selected her as one of the top five performers of the year. In 1954, she became the first African American woman to win an Academy Award nomination as Best Actress.

Afterward, everywhere she went, everything she said or did, was of public interest. A host of publications publicized and fawned over her in a constant whirl of attention and adulation. Newspapers ran photographs of her arriving at airports or strolling along Fifth Avenue. Formally invited by the French government to the Cannes Film Festival, where *Carmen Jones* had a special screening, she arrived with Preminger, triumphantly aglow amid a horde of international photographers and reporters. The following year, she was invited to England for a celebration at Oxford. In an elaborate ceremony that lasted until dawn, thousands of students crowned her the Queen of May.

For Black America, then about to launch its massive civil rights offensive, Dorothy Dandridge was part of the new day. Athletes Jackie Robinson and Roy Campanella had integrated major league baseball. Now, a dramatic black actress integrated American motion pictures in a distinctly new way.

But sadly, her decline came soon after her triumph. Dandridge realized that she was but a token figure within the movie colony, her position not much different from Lena Horne's in the forties. There were no great follow-up roles to sustain her fame. Three years passed before she appeared in another film, *Island in the Sun*, in which she costarred with Harry Belafonte, James Mason, and Joan Collins. In this drama about politics and miscegenation in the tropics, she was cast as a lovely island girl in love with a white Briton. In *Tamango*, *The Decks Run Red*, and *Malaga*, she was cast opposite white actors—Curt Jurgens, Edmund Purdom, Trevor Howard, James Mason, and Stuart Whitman. But the films, provocative for the time, always pulled back at the crucial moment. Dandridge's manager, Earl Mills, has said that the creators of *Malaga* (filmed abroad) could never decide what nationality her character should be. In that film as well as *Island in the Sun*, there were no dramatic love scenes in which Dandridge and her leading men passionately kissed. Filmed abroad, *Tamango*, which dealt with interracial love, was released in two versions: a more explicit one for European audiences; a sanitized version for American moviegoers. Even so, the film was poorly distributed in the States. It was a frustrating, debilitating experience that broke her. By 1959, five years after *Carmen Jones*, when she appeared in Otto Preminger's all-star *Porgy and Bess* (with Sidney Poitier, Sammy Davis Jr., and Pearl Bailey) she knew that even if it were a hit, she might have to wait five more years for another decent role.

She returned to nightclub work but hated it. The clubs made her feel like a failure, a dramatic actress unable to get dramatic parts.

Dandridge's offscreen life was in shambles, too. Ugly stories circulated that she was no longer attracted to black men and now, suffering from what blacks call *white fever*, she could only find fulfillment with white men. She was romantically linked with Preminger, Peter Lawford, Michael Rennie, and Curt Jurgens. No doubt, this kind of talk was the cruelest blow of all. Dorothy Dandridge's involvement with white men grew in large part out of her pe-

The many faces of Dorothy Dandridge, clockwise from top left: major nightclub star; with her abusive second husband, Jack Denison; with *Island in the Sun* co-stars Stephen Boyd and Joan Collins; with her sister Vivian (right) and friend Etta Jones in the singing trio The Dandridge Sisters; with co-star Stuart Whitman in *The Decks Ran Red;* showing the team how to hold the bat.

culiar position as a love goddess in a system that black men never got anywhere near. Her sister, Vivian, once said that Dorothy would have gladly married someone like a Harry Belafonte (with whom she was said to be romantically involved). But the few important black male stars of her day were already married. At the same time, the African American female star, like any other kind of star, black or white, male or female, often needs someone willing to take a back seat, permitting the star to glow in the light of fame. The mate often simply has to be there when the star has no one else, and, on occasion, to be dumped on by the star. Those black males Dandridge did encounter seldom understood the world in which she op-

money into Denison's new restaurant. "They had met in Las Vegas, where he had been a *maitre d'hôtel*," Preminger later said of Dandridge and Denison. "'Did you invest money in this restaurant?' I asked. She laughed. 'You know me. You know I wouldn't put money into anything.' She married that man and they spent all *her* money. She had to sell her house and everything of value she owned. Then he left her."

The rest of her life was a sad, tragic affair. After three years of marriage, she divorced Denison in 1962. Once her creditors closed in, Dandridge was forced to file for bankruptcy. According to her manager Earl Mills, she was never again the same person. Dandridge drank heavily during this

She made a trip to Mexico, worked out at a health farm, and optimistically signed a new movie contract. But a few days after her return to Hollywood, she was found dead in her apartment.

erated. A female star has enough problems finding someone within the business who can cope with stardom. (A relationship with someone outside the business, unless perhaps he himself is another kind of star—as was the case with Adam Clayton Powell during his marriage to Hazel Scott—could be disastrous.)

Isolated, desperate, older, still haunted by her daughter's condition, and aware that if the career did not go right at least her private life should, Dandridge made a terrible mistake. She married white restaurateur Jack Denison. For years she had been thrifty, terrified of poverty, carefully saving every penny. But once her mania had taken over, once the equilibrium had been thrown off, talk spread that she was pouring her

time and her health was also poor. Mills has said that a new physician had given her drug prescriptions to cover a multitude of ills. There were pills for energy, for dehydration, for relaxation, for sleep. Yet, she attempted to resurrect her career. With Mills, she made a trip to Mexico, worked out at a health farm, and optimistically signed a new movie contract. But a few days after her return to Hollywood, she was found dead in her apartment. She was forty-two. Later, an autopsy attributed Dorothy Dandridge's death to an overdose of an antidepressant, prescribed by her doctor. For later generations of African American actresses, she would be a haunting symbol: the one truly tragic black film goddess of the 20th century.

Gospel star Clara Ward and her singers.

Other Faces, Other Voices

Other sepia ladies appeared in the fifties. Some became prominent partly because there was a black audience so eager for a magnetic African American female star it could glorify or identify with that, on occasion, it would take almost anyone it could get—or anyone that offered some kind of promise. The fifties love goddess was also fortunate because of a new black press on the rise. Now, such national African American publications as *Ebony, Jet, Hue*, and later *Sepia*, as well as revitalized black newspapers in major cities, all helped feed Black America's appetite for new faces.

In 1952, *Jet* ran a cover story on talented actress Mildred Smith (who appeared opposite newcomer Sidney Poitier in *No Way Out)*, satisfied that it was able to come up with at least one other black film actress besides Dandridge. Had it not been for a tragic automobile accident that left her partially paralyzed, Smith might have developed into an important dramatic actress. Later in the decade, actress Juanita Moore came to national attention after she appeared in the 1959 remake of *Imitation of Life* and won an Oscar nomination as Best Supporting Actress.

Hilda Simms, who now seems to belong almost exclusively to the postwar Truman years, was often reported on by the African American press, particularly after her performance in the low-budget film *The Joe Louis Story*. But few actresses could match the gifts of Ruby Dee, who appeared in such films as *Tall Target* and *Edge of the City*.

Also drawing a fair amount of attention were newcomer Diahann Carroll and pianists Natalie Hinderas, Dorothy Donegan, and Philippa Schuyler. On the Broadway stage, spunky Juanita Hall turned up regularly. Having played non-black roles in *South Pacific* (as Bloody Mary) and *The Flower Drum Song*, she also appear ed in *House of Flowers*. Opera singers Leontyne Price, Mattiwilda Dobbs, and Camilla Williams emerged on the scene, each waiting for the big break, the chance to appear at the Met. (Price got it in the next decade.) Making it to the Metropolitan Opera House—as its first African American prima ballerina in 1951— was Janet Collins, who had earlier performed with the Lester Horton dance com-

pany in Los Angeles. Collins's cousin, dancer Carmen de Lavallade, performed in such films as *Lydia Bailey, Carmen Jones*, and as a lovely young handmaiden to Susan Hayward in *Demetrius and the Gladiators*. Then she left her home in Los Angeles, having also appeared with the Horton company, to perform in New York where eventually she followed in Collins's footsteps and also became a prima ballerina at the Met. Waiting for a big break of another sort—a serious dramatic stage role—was Jane White (the daughter of NAACP executive secretary Walter

Lady Day later in her career.

White), who appeared on Broadway in *Strange Fruit*. Pint-sized newcomer Leslie Uggams played the little girl next door on television's *Beulah*. As a teenager, she appeared on television on Mitch Miller's *Sing Along With Mitch*. Later she had her own network television series, and eventually won solid dramatic roles in such television productions of the 1970s as *Roots* and *Backstairs at the White House*.

There were the glamour-girl singers: Savannah Churchill, Damita Jo (appearing with or without the Red Caps), and the engaging Ruth Brown. In a career that saw many ups and downs, Brown sang the big-selling pop singles "Teardrops in My Eyes" and "Mama, He Treats Your Daughter Mean," later dropping out of show business, then resurfacing to play Motormouth Maybelle in John Waters's cult film *Hairspray*, and triumphing in a Tony Award–winning performance in Broadway's *Black and Blue*.

Performers Sarah Vaughan, Ella Fitzgerald, Carmen McRae, Della Reese, Dakota Staton, Big Maybelle, Big Mama Willie Mae Thornton, Gloria Lynn, LaVern Baker, and Dinah Washington all had faithful, adoring followers. Had these women been more flamboyant or, in keeping with the demands of the age, sexier, they might have well developed into legendary public heroines. But for the most part, whatever personal dramas, pains, or joys these women experienced, they kept under wraps. Many of Fitzgerald's fans did not even know whether she was married or not. The same was true of Vaughan. Her nickname, Sassy, however, often did lead audiences to speculate about exactly what went on after a performance.

A knockout creation like Dinah Washington, known for being hellishly difficult and demanding, did shake fifties audiences up. During her career, Washington insisted on being called the Queen; she once dyed her hair as blond as Bryant's and dared anybody to make a crack. By one account, this talented jazz–blues singer had at least eight husbands. They included her first, a seventeen-year-old fellow student of hers in Chicago; four others, all musicians; a cab driver; a youthful Dominican actor; and the last, football hero Dick (Night Train) Lane. Throughout the fifties, she made scandalous newspaper headlines: *"Blues Singer Escapes Death by Gift of Glass Candy"* (a box of chocolates that had arrived in the mail for her, presumably from a fan, contained quarter-inch slivers of glass); *"Dinah Washington Will Be Tried in Third-degree Assault"*; *"Dismiss Rap in Baltimore vs Dinah Washington;"* *"Charge*

Dinah Washington, "the Queen"; LaVern Baker; and Lena Horne—voices of the 1950s.

Sarah Vaughan: jazz singer extaordinaire, sometimes known as Sassy, sometimes as the Divine Sarah.

Dinah Washington Walks Out on Concert in Winston Salem Area." Washington made for juicy reading. But once onstage, she never let anything interfere with her performance.

To the surprise of many, gospel music was finally carried into the cultural mainstream by two charismatic gospel queens: Clara Ward and Mahalia Jackson. Few could yell, cry, or talk to the Lord like these women.

Based in Philadelphia in the 1950s, the Clara Ward Singers had been founded years before by Clara's mother, Gertrude, who was known to her fans as Mother Ward. Originally, she performed at churches, carrying her two daughters, Clara and Willa, with her. In time, Clara led the group with other women, eventually taking them in the late 1950s into the gut of American popular culture. They played Las Vegas, Disneyland, night spots like the Blue Angel in New York, and turned up at jazz festivals everywhere from New York to Paris. By the 1960s, the group was appearing on *The Tonight Show* and *The Jack Benny Program*. "Make a joyful noise unto the Lord" was what the Bible had said, and that seemed to be the Ward Singers's attitude as they performed with hands and arms flailing, feet stomping, hips bumping and thumping, hand clapping and shoulders shaking, all part of an elaborate extroverted showbiz theatricality that made gospel even more direct than before, its ties to rock 'n' roll never more apparent. Clara Ward herself was a tiny dynamo who promptly posed for photographs with any celebrity who turned up at a performance. And there were plenty: Judy Garland, Peter Lawford, Dinah Shore, Jack Benny, Liberace. She had a magnificent gold tooth right in the front of her mouth, rode in a special custom-built, eight-door limousine, and surely led the way for a later gospel titan like Shirley Caesar.

Mahalia Jackson, while not as energetic, was no less theatrical. A small, heavyset woman, who had been born in New Orleans and had worked as a domestic, Jackson belted out tune after tune. Her big hit was "He's Got the Whole World in His Hands." So popular was she that in the late fifties she took her gospels and spirituals to Hollywood where she sang in *St. Louis Blues* and most

movingly during the funeral sequence of the 1959 version of *Imitation of Life*. Even before the guilt-ridden black girl who has passed for white returns to her mother's funeral, Mahalia's hard-driving, deeply felt performance kept the audience in tears.

A new kind of black beauty appeared during the end of the Eisenhower era: the African American fashion model. At the time, executives at black publications, particularly *Ebony*, realized that the best way for major advertisers to reach the black buyer was by using black models in ads. Although most advertisers still dismissed the idea, a few took a chance, and a black model named Helen Williams appeared in ads. She was a striking woman, tall and slender, with a radiant smile and dark, penetrating eyes — she never graced the pages of *Vogue* or *Harper's Bazaar*, but certainly she led the way for such models who later did as Donyale Luna, Naomi Sims, Norma Jean Darden, Pat Cleveland, Beverly Johnson, Alva Chinn, Iman, and Gail O'Neill.

Finally, the late fifties marked the formal comeback of Lena Horne, who triumphantly returned to Broadway in *Jamaica*. Old-timer Adelaide Hall also appeared in the production. And in 1959, a newcomer named Cicely Tyson made her stage debut in the Harlem production of *The Dark of the Moon*.

But the fifties would have hardly been complete without some word from the classic old-time divas. Josephine Baker, now a feisty veteran, remained as outspoken as ever. In 1951, she was asked to appear at the plush Miami nightclub Copa City. This was a historic engagement because Baker signed her contract only after it had been agreed that African Americans would be admitted to the club to see her. Like most southern cities, Miami was still openly segregated. When Baker arrived in the city, many white citizens were astonished to see a black woman driven in a car down the streets of Miami by a white chauffeur! The engagement was hugely successful.

Shortly afterward, Baker went to New York for an appearance at the Roxy. One evening, at the invitation of a white friend, opera singer Roger Rico, she went to dinner with him and two others at Manhattan's

Carmen McRae began her career as Carmen Clarke, an intermissions singer and part-time typist.

Singer Josephine Baker has snubbed a State Department representative seeking to ask her about her anti–U.S. statements in Argentina, Harlem's Rep. A. Clayton Powell revealed in a blast at the entertainer for her "deliberate distortion and misrepresentation." Assailing the St. Louis–born performer who later became a French citizen, Powell said that the State Department inquiry was made at his request. An official tried three times to see Miss Baker in Buenos Aires but was refused. Powell assailed Miss Baker for "wild imaginings," in which she stated she had seen "daily lynchings" and concurred in a State Department report to him which said the singer had "become the tool of foreign interests notoriously unfriendly to the U.S." Powell noted that he and his wife, pianist Hazel Scott, had been friends of Miss Baker for a long time and "we cannot allow this gross misrepresentation to go unchallenged." He then noted: "She has seen no lynchings and has been present at no electrocutions. Miss Baker seems to be a manufactured Joan of Arc."

chic Stork Club. The theatrically regal Baker entered with all eyes glued to her. After various delays, however, it was apparent to Baker that the restaurant did not want to serve her. But refusing to quietly leave, Baker demanded service. When she was finally served "a pathetic little steak," she was infuriated. She immediately called the NAACP's Executive Secretary Walter White, asking him to send over an officer to certify that the Stork Club had refused to serve her. The incident made news around the world. The NAACP and other liberal groups attacked the Stork Club. Baker's flap incurred the wrath of powerful columnist Walter Winchell, who set out "to get her" in his columns. Winchell had been sitting in the restaurant the night of the incident.

Throughout the fifties, Baker spoke her mind, sometimes upsetting even prominent Black Americans by her behavior. In 1952, one of Baker's staunchest supporters, *Jet*, carried the following news item titled *"Jo Baker Snubs State Dept. Official"*:

Of course, Powell had his point. Yet, the article also reveals that America remained uneasy with Baker, particularly during a period when "reds" and "pinkos" were still being hunted.

In the 1950s and 1960s, Baker was very much a part of America's civil rights movement. Because she often lived on instinct and intuition, some might have thought a serious decline had set in, that emotionally she might be headed for trouble. But Baker proved all her critics wrong. In the 1970s, she came back strong.

Throughout the era, Marian Anderson remained regal and aloof. In 1953, news accounts reported that the Lyric Opera House for Theatre in Baltimore had refused to book an Anderson concert. The theater refused to discuss its standard segregation policy. True to form, no one knew how Anderson felt about this most recent insult. But in 1955, she nervously glowed when she had one of her great triumphs as the first African American performer to sing a major role, Ulrica in Verdi's *Un ballo in maschera,* at the Metropolitan Opera House. She later said her nervousness almost overcame her. But when the curtain rose, the mere sight of Anderson onstage was enough to send the entire audience into thunderous applause. Once again when Black America needed a symbol, the glorious Anderson stepped forward.

Billie Holiday and Ethel Waters remained as wildly unpredictable as before. Holiday's 1957 autobiography *Lady Sings the Blues* was a bestseller, indicating that Americans were as taken as ever with her image. For the most part these were troubled times, when she would forget lyrics onstage or miss a performance. An appearance at a festival in Monterey had gone so badly that afterward the musicians had refused to speak to her.

Holiday also had cirrhosis of the liver and was still drinking too much. She was separated from her husband Louis McKay. In 1959, Holiday died in a New York hospital. The *New York Post* reported that she had $750 strapped to her leg and seventy cents in her bank account. Newspaper serials told the story of her life. Record sales went up again. In time, the dead Billie was to be even a greater legend than the living one.

Ethel Waters, hopped up after her great performance in the highly acclaimed stage and film productions of Carson McCullers's *The Member of the Wedding* and the huge success of the best-selling autobiography *His Eye Is on the Sparrow,* seemed off on a brilliant revitalization of her career until the IRS closed in again. The indomitable, debt-ridden Waters soon found herself appearing before the nation on the television-quiz show *Break the $250,000 Bank,* trying to win enough money to pay off her debts. In 1959, she appeared in her last film, *The Sound and the Fury,* as Dilsey. But the movie was disappointing and did nothing for her career. As quickly as she had re-risen, she fell. Now, alone in a career that had always encompassed an array of ups and downs, the white-haired Ethel Waters slowly drifted in and out of show business. She later did guest appearances on several TV shows. But her heart did not seem to be in her work. She looked old and disheartened.

The divas had made great professional achievements in the fifties. Not only had they continued crossing over into the mainstream culture, but they had received a new kind of official recognition. The magazine covers and the big nightclub engagements were testaments to the divas' ongoing mainstream success. What with the coming of television, they found more work and greater opportunities. This was the era when American popular culture was almost completely integrated. Sometimes it may have been token integration, but most saw it as positive integration nonetheless. And any

Americans watched teenager Leslie Uggams grow up on television.

casual observer would have optimistically looked forward to the future—to the gains and rewards to be had in the next era. Yet despite the accomplishments, the fifties, in retrospect, had been a difficult period for the black beauty. As successful as were such new stars as Dorothy Dandridge, Joyce Bryant, and even Eartha Kitt, they had not been at ease with that success. The optimism and innocence that had propelled the careers of divas in the past were slowly vanishing. The troubled diva life of the fifties simply brought into focus once again America's traditional racial attitudes. The big stars had run fast and hard to make it into the system. But it was precisely the system itself that was about to be questioned.

Political Symbols
The 1960s

The sixties opened with a dazzling display of optimism. John F. Kennedy stormed into the presidency with talk of his New Frontier and his lofty dreams for a modern Camelot. Martin Luther King Jr. led a triumphant March On Washington. Over two-hundred thousand Black Americans, and many whites, descended peacefully on the capital to demand civil rights.

Most Americans looked on calmly, confident that the troubles—be they civil rights, poverty, or a war abroad—could be resolved. But in time it was apparent that the old remedies, as well as the old confidence, would no longer work. The familiar problems had escalated and become far more complex. Suddenly, Americans witnessed incredible horrors that they had thought would never happen in their country. The nation was stunned by the assassinations of John and Robert Kennedy, Medgar Evers, Malcolm X, and of the one figure most Americans, black and white, felt might be a conciliatory force: Martin Luther King Jr. Ghettoes throughout the country—in Harlem, Watts, Detroit—shot up in flames as the disaffiliated and deprived of America finally announced their anger and their rage. Soon, there was a rise of the black power move-

ment, the Black Nationalists, and the Black Panthers. New black political leaders such as Stokely Carmichael, Fannie Lou Hammer, Eldridge Cleaver, H. Rap Brown, and Huey Newton came into national prominence. From Vietnam there also came word of new corruption and atrocities, of the Tet Offensive and the My Lai Massacre. What with the riots, and the new demands for basic human rights as well as the war protests and demonstrations, American society was undergoing some of the most dramatic changes of the 20th century.

During this time, the old-style diva was a dying breed, so much so that by the end of the era she would be supplanted by a new-style figure. For the duration of the sixties there was a restless, determined search for new images and symbols, for a fresh set of fantasies and dreams that would touch on Black America's evolving militancy. Just as in the thirties, when the harsh nature of the times demanded that Waters, Fredi Washington, Ivie Anderson, and Holiday be glamorous but still close to the experiences of everyday life in the United States, so too, in the sixties, there was a call for social realism in all the arts. And that call obviously again touched the divas. Slowly, political heroines came into vogue.

Roberta Flack, who came to prominence with her mellow sound.

Page 146: The Supremes.

Nina Simone, transcendent artist and symbol of black pride.

Diahann Carroll:
the Right Beauty
at the Wrong Time

Guess who this cute teenager named Carol Diann Johnson grew up to be?

Few black beauties could have been more affected by the changing attitudes of the period than Diahann Carroll. At the start of the era, it was confidently assumed that she would inherit Dandridge's crown as deluxe international siren. But gradually, as a need developed for stars of grit and grime, the mass audience may well have found it hard to identify with so slick and polished a performer as Diahann Carroll.

Prior to the sixties, however, Diahann Carroll had done all the right things. She was born Carol Diann Johnson in the Bronx, the daughter of a transit-company worker father and a homemaker mother. In school, she worked hard for scholarships and embarked on a modeling career by the time that she was a teenager. In the beginning, her roots were tightly tied to the Black Community. Years later, old-timers at *Ebony* loved reminiscing about the young Carroll showing up at the New York office, portfolio in hand, hoping to be used in *Ebony* ads.

In these early days, as this slim, frail girl made a steady round of auditions, she had ferocious drive and energy. She sang and acted as much as she modeled. By her late teens she had made it to Hollywood, playing a supporting role in *Carmen Jones*. Afterward, she appeared on Broadway as the ingenue in *House of Flowers* and later in another Otto Preminger film, *Porgy and Bess*. At this time, she was neither glamorous nor strikingly beautiful. In fact, in her early films she looked like a good-natured homebody. But she had her professional admirers nonetheless. Richard Rodgers was so taken with her talents that he wanted her to star in his Broadway musical comedy *Flower Drum Song*. Had she played the leading role, that of a Far Eastern ingenue, she might have dramatically altered the history of American musical theater. It would have been the first time an African American woman starred on Broadway in a non-black role, proving to audiences that a talented black performer should be free to tackle any kind of part. (Already, that pint-sized powerhouse Juanita Hall had brilliantly portrayed non-black heroines on Broadway. But Hall had played supporting characters and surprisingly, many people outside theater circles were not even aware that she was black.) But the audacious plans to star Carroll in the show fell through.

In the 1960s Diahann Carroll's career really picked up momentum, and her professional image was greatly changed. She emerged as a sleek sophisticate with never a hair out of place nor a false eyelash badly applied. Her makeup was perfect, shrewdly used to play up her lush coloring, her high, refined forehead, her spectacular high cheekbones, her sensual mouth, and her sensational sweeping chin. She had magnificent shoulders and the lines of her body were perfect. Yet with all this, there was something not quite natural about her. She wasn't loose, didn't flow. She seemed to stand still like a mannequin unable to breathe or feel.

But the new look was on splendid display when Carroll returned to Broadway in 1962 as the star of Richard Rodgers's *No Strings*. Although *No Strings* was hardly a great show, it was still a golden opportunity. Rodgers had created the musical with Diahann Carroll in mind. She had a chance to sing a beautiful song, "The Sweetest Sounds." And in theater circles, because she had been cast "daringly" opposite white actor Richard Kiley and because of the in-

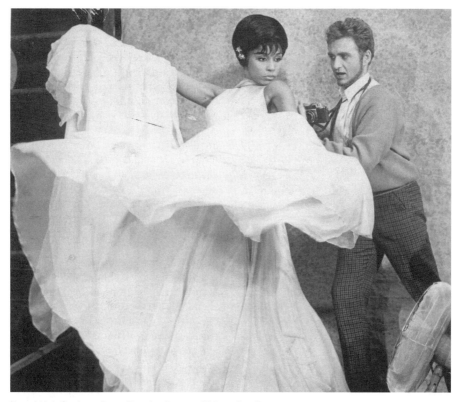

Presto! Little Carol transformed into the glamorous Diahann Carroll.

terracial theme of the play (a black fashion model involved with a white writer in Paris), the show had an impact. In Black America, however, *No Strings* may have communicated good intentions; but it had come too late in the day. In this era of sit-ins, protests, and of an evolving black nationalism, the idea that a black woman might have an affair with a white man was viewed by the younger generation as almost being politically treasonous. *No Strings* functioned as a pacifier for White America, a way for it to pat itself on the back for being above the old prejudices.

Diahann Carroll, however, emerged from *No Strings* as a star. She won a Tony for her performance. Afterward she appeared on television shows, had successful nightclub engagements, and played important roles in the films *Paris Blues* and *Hurry Sundown.* Her great professional coup came in 1968, when she landed the title role as a widowed nurse on the television series *Julia.* This marked the first time since the

sitcom *Beulah* with Ethel Waters that an African American woman was the star of her own weekly network series. Carroll played an educated, middle-class woman, seemingly unfamiliar with ghetto life, something of a cloistered Goody Two Shoes Sister living off in some Neverland (despite the fact that the series was set in Los Angeles) to which many younger Black Americans could not connect. Initially however, *Julia* was a hit. Yet often, Carroll was hampered by scripts with patently false situations and little feel for African American life or culture. Sometimes, she had a pleasant rapport with Diana Sands, who played her cousin on various episodes and also with football-star-turned-actor Fred Williamson, who sometimes appeared as her boyfriend. *Julia* ran for three seasons. Carroll, however, said she did not want to continue the series, which was taken off the air. Afterward, Carroll may have been a bit frazzled because now she had to take a long, serious look at her career.

Carroll, star of the TV series *Julia*.

And the cold, hard fact was that despite the big breaks—the Broadway starring role, the big-budget films, the *Look* and *Ebony* magazine covers—she seemed a woman out of tune with her era. At a time when Black America was adopting the political philosophy of cultural separatism, and when the Black Community looked for entertainers who were openly political (or openly against the established order), Diahann Carroll stood as a figure from the past: a proper bourgeois lady able and willing to integrate into White America. She herself said that she had become a star because she had a look and style acceptable to whites. For some, she represented a well-behaved, well-mannered beauty who, during a period of great racial turmoil, was not going to rock the boat. Carroll seemed to be a woman without ethnic flavor. In the past, the great gift of divas Baker and Waters had been that, while operating as stars in the white world, they had still known when and how to give all audiences a tantalizing glimpse of their "other" black world. Through dress, speech, behavior, and attitude, they informed everyone that they had not forgotten their roots. In fact, one of their great selling points had been the ethnic flair and flavor that always crept through. Finally,

black audiences may have been turned off by Carroll's private life. She was seen dating white males, and her romance with British talk-show host David Frost was well publicized.

Ironically enough, in another age Diahann Carroll's particular bourgeois image might have been tolerated or even valued as being as socially significant as Lena Horne's image had been in the 1940s. But now the times had changed. The old values and ideals were being hotly questioned and denounced. Also, the typical crossover mulatto-style diva was just about dead and done during this period. Of course, all of this would change in subsequent decades.

Also affected by the changes in the social atmosphere was Barbara McNair, who assumed the lead role in *No Strings* after Carroll left the cast. McNair was a ladylike, demure young woman with magnetic dark eyes and a warm, lush smile. She performed in clubs and films *(If He Hollers, Let Him Go* and later *They Call Me MISTER Tibbs!)* and on television, eventually hosting her own syndicated-variety series. As the *Jet* and *Ebony* articles of the period prove, she had a certain rapport with the Black Community and never offended it. But the era of the sixties, while seeming at first to offer her promise, never fulfilled it. In the seventies, her career and image took an unexpected turn when newspaper headlines exploded with stories of McNair's arrest for the alleged possession of heroin. Rumors of her connections with the mob flew all over the place. It was said that she would never be cleared of the charges, that her career was over anyway. In the midst of all the newspaper flap, McNair, rather courageously, appeared on Dick Cavett's talk show. She seemed in control, yet obviously troubled. The charges were later dropped. But McNair was back in the papers later in the seventies when her husband was found shot to death in their Las Vegas home. McNair, so often tense and vulnerable in her public appearances of the seventies, continued on with her career, but later faded from public view.

Diana Sands.

The New Serious Dramatic Actresses

Other women appeared, introducing audiences to totally new concepts on what being a black woman was all about. Black acting companies such as the New Lafayette Theatre, the Negro Ensemble Company, and the Free Southern Theater, as well as a host of others, provided a chance for artistic growth and exposure to a number of new actresses: Clarice Taylor, Esther Rolle, Barbara Ann Teer, Denise Nicholas, and Rosalind Cash. Onstage and screen, other serious dramatic actresses—Claudia McNeil, Abbey Lincoln (in the films *Nothing but a Man* and *For Love of Ivy*), and the incomparable Beah Richards—gave impressive, invigorating performances. Of the group of new actresses reaching maturity in this period, four stood out: Ruby Dee, Diana Sands, Gloria Foster, and Cicely Tyson. Playing anguished heroines, these women seemed as if they had touched base with life's harsher experiences and were scarred or bruised by their pasts.

Ruby Dee came to prominence first. This Cleveland–born actress grew up in New York and graduated from Hunter College. In the late 1940s, she studied and worked at the American Negro Theater in Harlem. Her classmates included other newcomers—Sidney Poitier, Harry Belafonte, Lloyd Richards (who later directed her on Broadway in Lorraine Hansberry's *A Raisin in the Sun*), and Ossie Davis, whom she later married. They became one of Black America's great couples of the theater. In the 1950s and 1960s, Dee appeared in a lineup of films: *No Way Out*, *The Jackie Robinson Story*, *The Balcony*, *The Incident*, and *A Raisin in the Sun*. She also costarred with husband Davis in *Gone Are the Days* (the film version of his play *Purlie Victorious*).

In the sixties this performer, who often seemed vulnerable and introverted, emerged as a master of the tiny telling detail. Her emotions were perfectly pared down until the moment when her characters' hearts simply broke—or exploded. Often she seemed to wander about quietly, unobtrusively, almost as if she were terrified of someone looking twice at her. But at her crucial moment, she was able to grab the audience by the throat and not let go. Most significantly, this small woman, almost birdlike, sensitive,

and unassuming, managed (particularly with her bravura performance in *A Raisin in the Sun*) to go against the stereotyped conception of the emotionally strong black woman as one who is also physically large or loud. Ruby Dee helped usher in a portrait of the contemporary troubled black woman. Dee kept working in subsequent decades. In the 1970s, she gave strong portrayals in the film *Buck and the Preacher* as well as such stage plays as *A Wedding Band*, by black playwright Alice Childress, and *Boesman and Lena*. Later, she won an Emmy for her performance in *Decoration Day*.

At the same time, Diana Sands represented for many the modern, bright, educated African American woman aware and proud of her roots, and confident and independent enough to speak out on any issue. In theater, Sands seemed to want to do everything to herald the new black woman's arrival. On Broadway, she starred opposite Alan Alda in *The Owl and the Pussycat*, playing a high-strung hooker who falls for a testy intellectual. Because it was the first Broadway production in which white and black costars had been cast romantically without any mention of race or color, the play drew much attention. In James Baldwin's *Blues for Mr. Charlie*, Sands played an aggressive civil rights fighter. Of her long, chilling monologue at the climax, critic Walter Kerr wrote: "Miss Sands [performs]...with a pulsing hysteria that is still just within control. I know of no other single sequence as powerful in New York today." Later, Kerr said that Sands "is one of the most exciting of young American actresses." Diana Sands also took on classical roles in theater productions of *Caesar and Cleopatra*, *Antony and Cleopatra*, *Saint Joan*, and Robert Lowell's *Phaedre*. In films, she repeated her stage role as the restless kid sister Beneatha in *A Raisin in the Sun*, and later gave effective performances in *Georgia, Georgia*; *Willie Dynamite*; and *Doctors' Wives*. Her most successful movie performance was in *The Landlord*. Also appearing on such television dramas as *East Side, West Side*; *The Nurses*; *Dr. Kildare*; and *I Spy*, Sands played a variety of challenging, complex characters until her early death — at thirty-nine — in 1973.

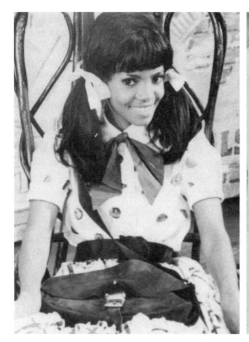 

A big voice for a little girl: former schoolteacher Melba Moore went from *Hair* to a Tony Award–winning role as Lutiebelle in *Purlie*.

Claudia McNeil and Ruby Dee in *Raisin in the Sun*.

Another actress—one of great interior power—was Gloria Foster. Foster grew up in the small farming town of South Beloit, Illinois, studied at Illinois State University, and taught school for two years. But she grew restless and soon enrolled in Chicago's Goodman School of Drama. In 1963, she opened in the New York production of *In White America*. It was a stunning debut. "Most moving of all," wrote Howard Taubman in *The New York Times*, "is Gloria Foster, a young actress with talent and intensity to burn. Three of her [vignettes]...are in themselves justification for a visit to *In White America*." Foster won the Obie and Drama Desk–Vernon Rice Awards for best actress of the year in an off–Broadway production. Afterward in the stage productions of *Yerma* and *Medea*, she gave searing, defiant performances, perfectly scaled to the demands of the big stage. Foster also gave impressive performances in the films *The Cool World*, *Nothing but a Man*, and *The Comedians*. She seemed born for films since, unlike most theater people, she did not need dialogue. She did everything with her eyes.

And of all the new-style dramatic actresses, her presence was the most troubling. She was always ill at ease, brooding, and burning over some private hurt.

By the end of the 1960s, Foster's promising career had a setback when, with her husband Clarence Williams III, who was then starring in the television series *Mod Squad*, she moved to Los Angeles. She appeared on several television programs, and Bill Cosby, quite impressed with her talents, had influence enough in the industry to have her signed up as his costar in some promising projects. The most satisfying was the likable, disjointed film *Man and Boy*. Foster and Cosby always played well together despite the fact that they often seemed mismatched. Whereas Cosby was skillful at articulating the basic, everyday dilemmas that perplex or trouble any ordinary man, there stood Foster, looking as if she were Medea trapped in a world that could not comprehend big emotions. Wonderful as Foster could be, television wasted her. She was one of the few actresses who should have been back on the stage, taking on one heavyweight role after another. When she finally returned to New York in the mid-1970s, Walter Kerr wrote of her performance in *Black Visions:* "Gloria Foster's work in the opening monologue is as breathtaking as anything the American theater can come up with just now." Foster also appeared in *The Cherry Orchard, Agamemnon,* and *Coriolanus* at the Public Theater. But she remained one of those great actresses about whom the mass audience never seemed to know enough.

During the sixties, Cicely Tyson also came to prominence. She energetically went from one television appearance to another, whether it be a guest role on *The FBI* or a continuing part on the series *East Side, West Side,* or from one supporting movie role to another, in *A Man Called Adam, The Comedians, The Heart Is a Lonely Hunter.* Like Foster, she had an edge and great power. Yet, her career seemed to go nowhere.

Often, many of the new serious dramatic actresses found themselves in conflict with audience anticipation. On the one hand, the audience had to have typical women who, operating in the black world, were not out to integrate into the larger white culture. On the other hand, the audience yearned for some breathtaking, larger-than-life (somewhat romanticized) heroine who not only touched on the real, but soared above it, too. In the game of symbol and image, these actresses did not yet have the mythic thrust and power of Waters. For the most part, they emerged as art-house or theatergoer favorites. Of the group, only Tyson became a real diva, and that was not until the next decade.

Finally, closely aligned to these actresses were the poets of the late sixties—Nikki Giovanni and Sonia Sanchez. They became popular on college campuses. In time, they also heralded the coming of the deeply committed-fiery-black-woman-as-political-symbol.

Ruby Dee with the hero himself in *The Jackie Robinson Story.*

Leontyne Price:
Making It to the Met

In the world of classical music, operatic divas Grace Bumbry, Martina Arroyo, Reri Grist, Shirley Verrett, and Leontyne Price (and later Jessye Norman and Kathleen Battle) found that doors, even those of the hallowed Metropolitan Opera House, were finally opening for African American women. True to a tradition long an integral part of the opera world, these women, before, during, and after the opening of those doors behaved like classic, temperamental stars. Indeed, if haughtiness were the only requirement for *divadom,* these women would have been at the top of the list. Of the group, however, Leontyne Price was the only operatic diva to become a national heroine.

Price was a fascinating woman to watch. She had a special, unconventional kind of beauty: golden brown skin, high cheekbones, compelling eyes. And she carried herself as regally as Marian Anderson. Yet with Price, there was a striking mixture of high and low. One minute, she was all mink and ermine; the next, she was a downhome, unpretentious girl from Mississippi. She also had a biting sense of humor. Once, upon hearing a well-known tenor remark that his "lovely, pure, full, and beautiful" voice moved her to tears, Price interrupted to say, "I hate to bring this up, but it is *my* voice so warm, full, and beautiful that moves me to tears." On another occasion, when she heard that a well-known soprano was about to marry and retire, she haughtily asked, "Retire from what?" And during a Christmas spent in Mississippi (where she returned as often as possible), she helped out serving at her family's dinner table, remarking, "I'm keeping my hand in. The first flat C and I'll be back here."

Price had grown up in the tiny town of Laurel, Mississippi. Her father was a carpenter. Her mother worked occasionally as a nurse and midwife. After graduating from Central State College (a black school in Ohio), Leontyne (originally spelled *Leontine)* was set to become a schoolteacher. But when a white neighbor, who had heard the young Leontyne sing (and for whom Price's aunt had worked as a maid), offered to help finance her studies at Juilliard, Price jumped at her chance.

At the music school, her voice and superb musicianship won her a circle of influential followers: Florence Page Kimball, the opera star who became her teacher; composer and critic Virgil Thomson; composer Samuel Barber. In 1952, Thomson selected her to perform on Broadway in *Four Saints in Three Acts.* Later that same year, she played Bess in the stunning revival of *Porgy and Bess.* She married the Porgy of the production, baritone William Warfield. In 1955, in what was considered a landmark production, this young black woman appeared on American television in the title role of *Tosca.* She sang *Aida* at the San Francisco Opera, at Covent Garden, at the Vienna State Opera, and finally, at La Scala. Like Anderson, she toured extensively, traveling wherever there was a chance to perform a great role. She may well have wondered if she would ever win great recognition in her own country. Stories still circulate of the young Leontyne's romantic melancholia. At a party on New York's Riverside Drive, a dancing, barefoot, dramatic Leontyne decided that she had had it with life and announced that she was running out to throw herself into the Hudson River. Fortunately, a friend calmed her down.

In 1961, Leontyne Price finally—triumphantly—debuted at the Metropolitan Opera as Leonora in *Il Trovatore.* Her debut, however, was not without its political overtones. The Civil Rights Movement was spreading throughout America. At the Met, Rudolph Bing and his staff surely must have realized that some gesture again had to be made to prove the cultured world of grand opera was without biases. By this time, Price had become too great an international name and talent to be ignored. Afterward she briefly became something of a media sensation, appearing on the cover of *Time* and in the pages of *Look.* Later, she was selected to launch the Met's next season in *The Girl from the Golden West.* And in 1966, a great honor (and tribute to her box-office clout) was bestowed on her when she opened the new Met at Lincoln Center in *Antony and Cleopatra.* Her role was especially tailored for her by composer Samuel Barber.

Leontyne Price struck many Americans as being a warm, intensely likable opera star. But perhaps the tensions and pressures of her fame weighed on her because after all the fanfare, she soon withdrew from the public eye. As her appearances at the Met became fewer (from 1961 to early 1969, there had been 118 performances; from late 1969 to 1973, there were but 6), she was the only great opera singer who never seemed to work.

Occasionally, she spoke up about some of her tensions. "That 1966 opening was the most grueling experience of my life. It really left me almost traumatized for two-and-a-half years," she once said. "So much was hanging on it. A new house, a premiere of a new work. I felt that if I caught a cold and couldn't perform, it would be worldwide news. So much to do, so much to think about, so much to cope with in so short a time. It got to the point where it wasn't a matter of how well one performed, but just being able to perform. Maybe that was a kind of turning point. For the next season or so I kept on doing opera and other things, and sometimes it seemed I just didn't know where I was. Pressures all the time."

For the most part, though, Price remained silent about the professional or private difficulties plaguing her. And perhaps it was precisely the insistence on privacy that prevented her from becoming a legendary figure along the lines of a Maria Callas. Nor did Price become a Marian Anderson: a stoic, majestically heroic figure accepting the weight of being an international social symbol.

In a way, she was also affected by the times. For great as her triumph had been, many of young Black America now viewed the world of opera as "irrelevant," "politically obsolete," a "decadent art form" about which American blacks had no business being bothered. An evolving black aesthetic then demanded that all art forms of Western culture be seriously examined: it insisted, too, that black artists return to their roots, that their art connect directly to the political goals and aspirations of the Black Community. Such attitudes would change in subsequent eras. But as was true of many other black artists in every period, Price was in a complex situation. The white world demanded one thing of her. The Black Community expected something entirely different. And her particular art itself had its peculiar demands.

In an interview in the September 9, 1972, issue of *Saturday Review*, Leontyne Price once touched on her dilemma, saying (without self-pity):

> Some people criticize me for not being "militant" or not being "involved" or whatever. Being black and accomplished, as I am proud to say I am, gets you invited to be with a lot of people who wouldn't pay you any attention otherwise. I don't go to cocktail parties or social meetings, where you "get the word" and are supposed to take it back to the "lowly ones" who look up to you. What I do for my own people, to whom I might be a token black, I do in my own way, on my own level....I've been that [a token figure] for years, and I accept it as a responsibility in my own way.

By the era's end, Leontyne Price was aware that she would always be some kind of symbol for Black and White America. But she was determined never to let the symbol business overpower her.

Jackie "Moms" Mabley: the Funniest Woman in the World

With the rise of black cultural nationalism, the old standards and the old values—the do's and don'ts preached to Black America by White America for centuries—were quickly eroding. Black Americans turned away from those artists who had made it within the system, who were part of something now dubbed *the establishment*, and sought out those personalities who somehow had maintained a gritty ethnic quality. And it was primarily for this reason that finally there came aboveground a woman who seemed to have been around since the year one, an old-time hipster who called herself *Moms* and who in the 1960s discovered herself appearing on national television. In the past, some might have thought of Jackie "Moms" Mabley as a stereotyped figure. But oddly enough, she became a cultural heroine of sorts for a new audience that saw her as feisty, resilient, and enduringly tough. Never had she expressed any desire to make it in the white world. In fact more often than not, she was a knowing satirist of the ways of white folks.

Certainly, no one could have been more surprised at the sudden sixties popularity of Jackie "Moms" Mabley than Moms herself. She was doing what she had been doing for years, ever since that day in 1913 when, at age sixteen, she had run away from her home in Brevard, North Carolina, to pursue a career as an entertainer. She soon changed her name from Loretta Mary Aiken to Jackie Mabley. It had been the name of a boyfriend. Somehow, the *Moms* title was picked up along the way. One story has it that she was so sympathetic to the problems of her fellow performers in black vaudeville, mothering them when they were down and out, that they dubbed her *Moms*.

For fifty years she toured the country, hitting the legendary black theaters such as the Regal and Monogram in Chicago and the Apollo in New York City, where she was the undisputed queen. Her fans called her the funniest woman in the world. During these early years, she was aware of her place as a woman operating in a world dominated by men. In vaudeville, female stars were often a part of a team or used as a foil for the man's jokes. For a time, Mabley herself

teamed up with other legendary chitlin circuit performers—Dusty "Open the Door, Richard" Fletcher, Tim Moore (who became Kingfish on the *Amos 'n' Andy* television series), and the great "Spider Bruce," John Mason. As the years passed, she influenced newcomers Redd Foxx and Slappy White, whom audiences often referred to as the sons of Moms. (There were even rumors that both men actually were her children.) But Mabley turned the male-oriented comic world of vaudeville into her own arena, emerging as the first distinctive black female comic star able to run an act on her own, using men as her foils, developing such a strong shtick that no one was ever able to take the spotlight from her.

Mabley's early monologues were written by herself and comic Bonnie Drew Bell. Moms would amble onto the stage, wearing tattered Raggedy Ann dresses with plaids, polka dots, and checks mixed every which way. She sported outsized shoes, large drooping argyle socks, and an old floppy hat, and she would give a broad smile to show she didn't have a tooth in her head. Her audience was wild with laughter even before she opened her mouth. When that happened, she would stand silent, giving everybody the once-over or the evil eye, 'cause she was here to deliver the *word*, the gospel according to Moms. "Now lissen here, chil-run," she would announce, and the audience was prepared for a monologue that touched on current events and that always bristled with sly folk wisdom and keen insights.

She was the mistress of spicy, raucous, blue humor. Unlike a white comic like Martha Raye, Moms knew sex was something on the mind of any audience. She played the part of the little old lady in search of a handsome young man. The last thing she ever wanted was a man her own age. "No," her classic line informed the audience, "there ain't nothing an old man can do for me except bring me a message from a young one." Another of her better-known lines was that "a woman is a woman until the day she dies, but a man's a man only as long as he can!" In comic terms, she handled men as roughly as Bessie Smith sometimes did in song.

In the fifties and sixties, Moms Mabley began her slow ascent into the mainstream of American popular culture with her successful record albums *Moms Mabley—The Funniest Woman in the World*, *Moms Mabley at the UN*, *Moms Mabley at the Geneva Conference*, and *Now Hear This*. She boasted of talking to presidents and prime ministers who called for advice on the world situation. "Now what you want, boy?" was the

Negro humor *A Time for Laughter*. In one skit, she played the maid of an uppity black bourgeois couple (Godfrey Cambridge and Diana Sands) trying to be white, living in hoity-toity Westchester County (which, ironically enough, was precisely where Moms Mabley was living). Whenever Cambridge and Sands put on airs, there was down-to-earth Moms giving them a look, a grunt, or a groan to remind them of their roots. (Years

Moms knew sex was something on the mind of any audience. She played the part of the little old lady in search of a handsome young man.

way she always addressed them. She also said that she and Eleanor Roosevelt were good friends who liked to get together and talk about young men.

In the 1970s she poked fun at political figures, saying of Richard Nixon after the Watergate scandal: "Even old Moms couldn't do nothin' for that man, 'cept give him a few licks upside the head, that is...he was just too far gone. Only thing I got to say about him is, your sins will find you out. Like old Joe Louis says, you can run but you can't hide." Of President Gerald Ford, she added: "I hear, now mind me, I hear he's a godly man, but Moms is keeping her eye on him."

In 1967 Moms made it to network television, appearing in the all-black tribute to

later, Marla Gibbs would play the maid, Florence, much in the same way on the television series *The Jeffersons.*) Moms also appeared on *The Smothers Brothers Show*, *The Mike Douglas Show*, *The Merv Griffin Show*, and *The Flip Wilson Show*.

Moms Mabley's popularity continued into the next decade. She starred in the movie *Amazing Grace* as Grace, a spry old lady who decides that she has had enough and is going to rid Baltimore of all the corrupt politicians exploiting the common little man. In one sequence, Moms goes to the all-black campus of Morgan State College where she addresses the students. Moms at the podium was no different from Moms on the stage of the Apollo.

The Marvelettes, Motown's first big girl group.

New Sounds:
Pint-sized Sirens

THE SHIRELLES

Clockwise from upper left: the enduring Gladys Knight; the Shirelles, who sang of love that any teenager would understand; Mary Wells, who would never have been caught dead without her wigs; and the sensitive, socially conscious Odetta.

Almost at the very start of the decade, the emerging new generation was humming and hopping to the tune of pop, rock, and soul: innovative musical styles growing out of the heat of the ghetto and the Black American experience.

In the recent past, older Americans had been able to sit back and relax to the soft and slow ballads of Nat King Cole and Billy Eckstine. These men had invigorated standards (as well as standard approaches to music) with their own sense of style and phrasing. But their most popular material was seldom jolting. Now, in the sixties, no longer was popular music those familiar soothing chords delivered in the acceptable idiom and beat of the mainstream, dominant culture. The new music, influenced by gospel sounds and such black rock 'n' roll–rhythm-and-blues stars as Chuck Berry, Hank Ballard, Little Richard, and Fats Domino, used language and beat in a startling fashion. The idiom was distinctly black since the new artists were performing—at least in the beginning—for an all-black record market. In time, the new sixties music acquired a fresh sound and tone all its own, sometimes fevered and anxious.

The attitude about the music was different, too. In the past, Black America's popular music had never been sanctioned by the dominant culture. Now, however, young Black Americans could not have cared less what the official white culture thought of its sounds. There was a new confidence and pride in the worth of the music. Eventually, the white kids in the affluent suburbs would not care what their elders thought of the music either. For they knew, too, that the music was simply good. In time, all of young America turned to black music not only as a source of pleasure, but of protest too. "Way Over There," as Smokey Robinson's song had announced, were innovative artists with totally different material and points of view, with songs calling for new rights and dreams. And leading the way were groups of pint-sized, wide-eyed sirens, the pubescent, Junior League teeny-bopper divas who had no idea at first what *image* or *persona* meant. All they knew was that they wanted to perform. And perform they did.

Not since the blues singers of the twenties had so many talented black women had a chance to sing their songs.

In the beginning, the new groups were certainly influenced by LaVern Baker who, during the 1950s, had been a full-fledged rock 'n' roll, rhythm-and-blues diva. At that time, the popular soul group the Platters had a female harmonizing with them. But Chicago–born Baker was a star attraction on her own, a knockout entertainer with a truly large, confident voice. Performing her big hits "Jim Dandy," "See See Ryder" (a song Ma Rainey had recorded), and "Tweedle Dee," Baker wore skintight dresses and developed the persona of the familiar bronze mama who, like Bessie her idol, was in control of any situation. In the fifties, Baker worked the black theaters and movie houses. In the sixties, she was determined to take her rock 'n' roll persona into the important clubs. In 1961, she successfully appeared with Louis Armstrong at Basin Street East. But although her hefty personality was intact, she left behind her music, choosing to sing such conventional ballads as "After You're Gone" and "Yes, Sir, that's My Baby." Baker soon lost her audience because she was going establishment almost at the very point when the mass audience was ready to accept rhythm and blues. Still, LaVern Baker's gutsy rock 'n' roll renditions helped pave the way for others. The same was true of Ruth Brown.

During the fifties period of Baker's initial rise, black girl groups had also come into their own. The Chantels tapped a nerve with their tune "Maybe," a pulsating, dazzling wail of a woman wanting a second chance with the man she had lost. Then there was the great group of the late fifties and early sixties, the Shirelles, who had a string of hits—"Everybody Loves a Lover," "Soldier Boy," "Tonight's the Night," and "Will You Still Love Me Tomorrow?" They also sang the tune that became a national anthem for love-struck high-school girls everywhere, "Dedicated to the One I Love." Here they sang: "Each night before you go to bed, my baby / Say a little prayer for me, my baby / And tell all the stars above, / 'This is dedicated to the one I love.'" During a

Dancing in the streets—girl-groups, sporting wigs and fancy dresses, sang love songs that told American teenagers the facts of life: Martha and the Vandellas.

time when sex was not something that kids were supposed to know anything about, the Shirelles's music served as an outlet for pent-up tensions and romantic confusions. Almost all their numbers were love statements or love warnings, all delivered with a teen intensity that today still taps the tender aches and subconscious fears of adolescents caught in the grip of first love. The Shirelles set the style for the groups, dressing alike in sexy, tight dresses. They were about the same age as their fans, which helped the young to identify with them.

Once the Shirelles's records started selling, the market opened up to another group—Patti LaBelle and the Bluebells ("I Sold My Heart to the Junkman," "Down the Aisle") and the Crystals ("Da Doo Ron Ron"). And Ruby and the Romantics (one young woman backed up by three young men) came up with a well-styled piece called "Our Day Will Come."

Black music was in vogue for the young. Etta James, Carla "The Queen of Memphis" Thomas, Dee Dee Sharpe, Little Eva, Barbara Lewis, the feverish Tina Turner, and sweet-tempered Baby Washington were getting their records played on radio and going on tour. All these young women had an individual style and presence. Yet, few had long careers. Some lacked drive. Others became disillusioned after having been exploited by record companies and shifty promoters. Unfortunately, most were not encouraged to think of a future in the music business. One day a record was a hit. Next day, it was dead. There still was no center for the young black woman; no one to groom or promote her; no one to help her branch out. So many with talent faded into oblivion. But their sweet, pop-soul tunes have lingered.

The situation changed when founders and executives of Motown, a new record company out of the Motor City, Detroit, realized the commercial potential of black music and urban-soul artists. Through costuming, choreography, and specific tunes for specific artists, Motown's chief Berry Gordy Jr. came to grips with the creation of rock-pop-soul personas to which the American young, male and female, black, then white, could firmly connect. In the sixties, no other single record company touched on the needs and desires of a whole nation of teenagers as effectively as Motown.

The first important female headliner for Motown was Mary Wells. For a time, she was the biggest star in the stable, coming out with hit after hit. Her songs "You Lost the Sweetest Boy" and "Bye Bye Baby" were almost uncontrollably energetic. The latter, which she wrote, was about a girl who was jilted. But she was not feeling blue: hell, no. He had taken her love, thrown it away, but he was gonna want her love back someday, so, bye-bye baby, she wailed. She added a warning, too: that he better not come back running, knock, knock, knocking on her front door! Here Mary Wells broke loose, screaming, acting like a churchgoing sister who decided that she was tired of the preacher's sermon—and was determined to deliver her own. The gospel beat and drive let the listener know that this song was about personal salvation. Other times, with such songs as "What's Easy For Two" and "Two Lovers," she was sweet, simple, and enduringly melodic. Her biggest hit, "My Guy," became a standard for young girls in love. With lyrics by Smokey Robinson, Wells delivered a hymn of praise to the guy of her dreams.

Mary Wells was a rambunctious bundle of energy and glee. In personal appearances, she often came across as a petulant, bratty kid, the kind audiences loved to hate. She looked small, had an insolent pout, big baby eyes, and a collection of wigs without which she would never have been caught dead. One day, she might sport a short, blond hairdo. Next day, Mary would be wailing with a blond ponytail flying all over the place. Sometimes, her super-confidence about her appeal could be amusing. Why should she care a hoot whether people called her tasteless or gauche or a mess? In the long run she introduced the hip, swinging, modern girl from the other side of town that loved the brash music that only she could sing. In the late fifties and early sixties, she was a teen fantasy come true, for she represented the spunky kid who got to play with sex and romance, the lucky runaway no longer having to put up with parents or tenements. She was living a glamorous life on the road.

Shortly after Mary Wells's success, two hot Motown female groups came on the scene. From 1961 to 1967, the Marvelettes were a big attraction. They won a gold record for "Please, Mr. Postman," the wild wail of four girls waiting, hoping, then just pleading with the mailman to look and see if there was a letter—from the boy of their dreams. Later, with their moving ballad "Don't Mess with Bill," they assumed the pose of tough little mamas, announcing that nobody was to trifle with their guy, Bill. And with "Forever," a slow grind about enduring love, the quartet reached its artistic peak.

Martha and the Vandellas was the second big female group for Motown Records. With them, the company attained a new artistic maturity. The writing team of Holland, Dozier, and Holland hit its stride, became confident of its talent, and acquired an understanding of the basic pop rhythms and formulas that would sell.

Led by Martha Reeves, the group never lost its ethnic beat and pulse. More often than not, their feverish hits ("Come and Get These Memories," "Heat Wave," and "Quick Sand") touched on a new restlessness among the young. The lyrics explained that love was the reason for all the fuss and bother. But these ghetto girls had something else on their minds. It was precisely such rebellious undertones that made their song "Dancing in the Streets" so controversial. Here, they announced that summer had come. They wanted to know if folks were ready for a brand-new beat. This was an invitation, they sang, for people throughout the nation to meet. So come on, they said, because it was time for dancing in the streets. On the surface, the song simply called for some communion everywhere through dance. But during the period of city-ghetto riots, some radio stations, fearing the record was a call for some kind of street action, an announcement meant to incite Black America, banned it from airplay.

The original Supremes with Sammy Davis Jr.

The Supremes:
Ghetto Goddesses

But the greatest of the Motown female groups was the dazzling Supremes. With the Supremes, audiences saw everything that Motown had been experimenting with—in terms of group image, style, dynamics—fully worked out. Also important was the fact that the Supremes, in the early part of their careers, were models for every black ghetto kid in America who dreamed of getting out.

Theirs was a sixties-style-rags-to-riches saga for an audience that had the harsh urban experience very much on its mind. The three members of the group had grown up dirt poor in the Brewster Projects of Detroit. There had been twelve children in Florence Ballard's family; three in Mary Wilson's; and six in Diana Ross's. (Ross's first name was actually Diane.) As adolescents, the three girls—and another teenager, Betty McGlown, later replaced by Barbara Martin— had met and decided to form a group. When they went to Motown chief Berry Gordy, he turned them away, telling the girls to finish school before embarking on a career. They returned to the classroom, but spent most of their time performing at churches, hops, dances, block-and-basement parties, wherever and whenever possible. Then with their high-school education completed, they went back to Motown, were signed as the Primettes (the female counterparts of a male group, the Primes, who later became the Temptations), and used as backup vocalists for Marvin Gaye and Mary Wells. Once Barbara Martin left the group, the Supremes became a trio. They recorded nine singles of their own that went nowhere but finally hit the jackpot with "Where Did Our Love Go?" Their entire world changed. "That's when," Diana Ross said later, "we started doing the hard work—meeting disc jockeys, interviews, charm school, being nice to build ourselves up." Motown, the fairy godmother in the tale, groomed the girls to be the stars.

The Supremes's ascent began in Detroit in the early 1960s. By the time it ended, they had twelve number-one singles, sold over fifty million records, and were more famous than any other black performing group in American history. They played Vegas, the big supper clubs (formerly closed to rhythm-and-blues and rock 'n' roll stars), national television (*The Ed Sullivan Show, Hullabaloo, Shindig, The Mike Douglas Show)*, college campuses, and royal command performances.

Their early big singles, "Where Did Our Love Go?," "Come See About Me," "Baby Love," and "Stop! In the Name of Love" were familiar themes on love, but presented with a new musical sophistication. The Supremes were still not adults, but they were not pubescent bubble-gum kiddies, either. No longer was it simply whine and pine, ache, throb and sob. Instead, here stood young women who understood something of the teen experience.

They were also a perfect ensemble group, precisely in touch with their material, their collective and individual personas, and one another. Like so many other Motown groups, this trio genuinely seemed to enjoy entertaining, exuding self-confidence, and inviting everyone to join in. They had a controlled, dramatic intensity as well.

Whenever they came onstage, the three were dressed alike and to the nth degree—clothes that were expensive and swanky. Their lacquered wigs and sequined gowns sparkled whenever they moved. Together, the three Supremes represented one ideal girl. Mary was the sweet, sexy one; Florence, the high-hat, no-nonsense one; Diana, the lively, skinny one. Onstage, between numbers, they kidded one another as only girlfriends could. After Diana had made all the introductions, she would laugh about her skinniness, saying, "But you know what they say. Thin is in." "Yeah," Florence would interject, putting her hands on her full hips, "thin may be in. But fat's where it's at." Their banter kept them in touch with their audiences, and they were seen as positive figures by young black kids and their parents: for these were ghetto girls making good.

Finally, of course, the Supremes, as crossover figures, represented for young white audiences (and some older ones, too) new-style black girls whose ethnicity had been made more acceptable. The Supremes set out to charm, to offer escape. Energetic

After Cindy Birdsong (left) replaced Florence Ballard, the group became Diana Ross and The Supremes, and the fairy tale turned sour. Ballard tried to make it as a solo performer but died penniless at the age of thirty-two.

Earlier times when there were four Supremes: Diana Ross (top) with (left to right) Barbara Diane Martin, Mary Wilson, and Florence Ballard.

as their music was, it was pure soul–pop without the tension of Bessie's disturbing, disorderly blues, without the haunt and taunt of Billie's moody style. And as their interviews in *Time* and *Look* stressed, they were supposedly not really any different from any other American girl who wanted marriage, a home, and kids, and who hoped to do something to help her family.

But everything was not perfect with the group. There were problems: they were often overworked, underpaid, and extremely tense. In 1967, the group became Diana Ross & The Supremes. Stories circulated of Diana's temperament, her flaming egotism, of Florence's outrage and bitterness because Motown reaped most of the profits from their work, and Diana always reaped most of the attention. In time, the fairy tale turned sour. Florence Ballard left the group in 1967, tried to make it as a solo performer, but ended up back in Detroit, broke, and living on welfare. She died at the age of thirty-two in 1976. Cindy Birdsong, who had previously worked with Patti LaBelle and The Bluebells, replaced Ballard.

But soon, the social temper of the period changed. Black audiences now demanded undiluted soul as well as music that touched on social issues, politics, *the system* (which the Supremes were now so much a part of). Motown altered the music some. "Love Child" and " Living in Shame" were specific ghetto-oriented songs about ills and problems of inner-city black victims. But these tunes were temporary postponements in the group's demise. Finally, it was announced that Diana Ross would become a solo act, with Jean Terrell replacing her as the Supremes's lead singer. Shrewdly, Motown, even at the end, kept the Supremes's legend machines working: the last single with Diana as lead was a sentimental tune entitled "Someday We'll Be Together."

The celebrated history of the group may have been tainted by its closing chapter, but the early legend still glows. It would be the inspiration for the movie *Sparkle* and the Broadway show *Dreamgirls*. And their early music, no matter how pop or commercial, still captures much of the mid-1960s idealism and energy.

Singers Nancy Wilson, Della Reese, Roberta Flack, Nina Simone, and folk singers Odetta and Miriam Makeba also acquired followings. For Black Americans with an emerging awareness of their roots in Africa, Miriam Makeba was a triumphant symbol, bringing her African folk tunes to college campuses and theaters around the country. Her marriage to Stokely Carmichael, the hero of the Black Power movement, was seen as a revolutionary fairy tale, the union of a strong black warrior and his beautiful black woman. But Carmichael's politics alienated theater managers and booking agencies, many of whom closed their doors to Makeba.

Throughout most of the 1960s, it looked as if Dionne Warwick (spelled *Warwicke* for a while) would also become a major diva. With her hit renditions of Burt Bacharach's songs "Don't Make Me Over" and "Walk On By," she represented the reflective young African American woman caught in the heat of a trying emotional situation. As she struggled to get the song out, there was always a plea in Dionne's voice and a moment of desperation. She was also one of the few song stylists with the range to sing Bacharach's intricate melodies. Warwick had hugely successful concerts and won gold records, too.

Performer Nina Simone was surely a political diva if ever there were one. With her songs "Four Women" and "Mississippi Goddamn," she spoke directly—and bitterly—about America's racial situation. Simone also had a haughty, testy, hot-tempered personality. Audiences never knew what to expect during one of her concerts. Sometimes, they were not even sure that she would show up. Sometimes, they feared that she might begin a performance by telling everybody off. In retrospect, it might be safe to say that because of her irascible attitude and, surprisingly—and, sadly—because of her looks (the dark color), the mass audience may never have been fully at ease with her. But musically, no one could touch her.

Winning an international following, The Supremes — Cindy, Diana, and Mary — with Paul McCartney.

Aretha Franklin:
Lady Soul Brings
It All Home

Finally, the sixties closed with the full discovery and appreciation of the greatest ethnic down-home diva of the era, Lady Soul Herself, Aretha Franklin. No matter what her private feelings or sentiments, she was the perfect heroine for an age now caught up in political fervor. When she sang, Aretha was described as the brilliant distillation of several streams of Black American music. She was considered part spiritual, part gospel (like Mahalia Jackson and Clara Ward), part raunchy blues (like Bessie Smith), part moody, mellow blues (like Billie Holiday and Dinah Washington), part rhythm-and-blues (like Ruth Brown and Ray Charles), part field holler (like Ma Rainey), part work song, part jazz, part holiness shout. Aretha brought everything home, down front in the open for White and Black America to see and hear. For a new movement of black political separatists, activists, and cultural nationalists and for an age caught up in Black Pride, she emerged as a splendid symbol, a woman whose *soulfulness* flowed out of her effortlessly and whose music at every turn was a comment on the Black American experience, a summation of its pain, joy, trials, and triumphs. David Llorens of *Ebony* proclaimed the late 1960s as the period of "Retha, Rap, and Revolt." (The rap in this case refers to political hero H. Rap Brown.) She was one of the few cultural heroines to bridge all gaps, appealing to rural African Americans as much as to inner-city folks, her records also being played in college dorms as well as in *nighttime-is-the-righttime* big-city bars. In time, every imaginable cliché, every late-sixties trend, almost every important black political ideology of the time was, in some way of another, laid on Lady Soul. And like Marian Anderson, Aretha endured the weight of the symbol business, since at heart none of it seemed to matter as much as her music and her art.

Like the other important divas, Franklin's personal life was an important part of the legend that enveloped her. She had had a lonely, chilly childhood. She never had the harsh ghetto experience of a Holiday (or even a Diana Ross), but nothing had been rosy, either. Born in 1942 in Memphis, she and her four brothers and sisters were reared in Detroit, where her father, C. L. Franklin, was pastor of the New Bethal Baptist Church. When Aretha was six, her mother left the family and then died four years later. And Aretha's father, a popular,

Aretha (left) with Clara Ward (next to her) and Della Reese (third from right). Even though she was one of the world's biggest stars, she seldom looked happy. "Somebody else is making her sing the blues," Mahalia Jackson once said.

dynamic evangelist, was on the road barn-storming at churches and gatherings throughout the country.

As a shy child whose only refuge was music, Aretha saw many of the greats of black music visiting her father at their home: such legendary figures as Mahalia Jackson (who eventually wanted the world to know Aretha was her prized protégée), Clara Ward, James Cleveland, Arthur Prysock, B. B. King, Dorothy Donegan, Lou Rawls, Sam Cook, and even the queen herself, Dinah Washington. Aretha watched and

Aretha, during the early period of stardom.

studied them all, taken by their talent, their passion for their art, and their sense of the dramatic. At the funeral of one of Aretha's aunts, Mahalia Jackson sang the gospel tune "Peace in the Valley." In her fervor, Mahalia tore off her hat and flung it to the ground. "This," Aretha said later, "was when I wanted to become a singer."

As a child, she crisscrossed the country on gospel tours. In the tiny towns and hamlets, she was often turned away from res-taurants and hotels. The town streets themselves were closed to African Americans after certain hours. By the age of fourteen, she cut her first gospel single for Chess Records. Then in 1960, she went to New York City, taking dance-and-vocal lessons, and signing with Columbia Records in 1961. Here, in the legend that shaped her career, she emerged as the sensitive, bruised, brooding young artist being told what to do and be by a culture that had no idea what she or her art were all about. Columbia had her singing standards. Tense and withdrawn, she cut nine albums for Columbia (one of which was *Unforgettable*, a tribute to Dinah Washington). The sales were lackluster. She refused to renew her Columbia contract, choosing instead to sign in 1966 with Atlantic Records, the company that had handled rhythm-and-blues artists Ruth Brown, Ray Charles, and Wilson Pickett. Aretha could select her material and block out her arrangements. She worked with legendary producer Tom Dowd. And here, the artist finally flowered.

Her first Atlantic single, in 1967, "I Never Loved a Man," sold over a million copies, followed by two other hits, "Respect" and "Baby, I Love You." The sales soared on her albums *I Never Loved a Man* and *Aretha Arrives*. In 1967, she also made her first European tour and appeared at New York's Philharmonic Hall, accompanied by her back-up group the Sweet Inspirations (led by her sister Carolyn). By this time, Aretha was the biggest name in the world of popular music.

With her success came stories of her unhappy private life. She had married Ted White. In its cover story on Aretha, *Time* described White as "a former dabbler in Detroit real estate and a street-corner wheeler-dealer." Soon, he was managing her career. The couple had three children, but it was hardly an ideal marriage. In the popular imagination, White was a man who was manipulating Aretha's career for his own ends. (Before White, many people thought Aretha's father had exploited her, too.) Word spread of an incident at the Regency Hyatt House Hotel in Atlanta, where White had reportedly roughed up Aretha. Even Mahalia Jackson commented, "I don't think she's happy. Somebody else is making her sing the blues." *Time*, too, described Aretha as a young woman "cloaked in a brooding sadness, all the more achingly impenetrable because she rarely talks about it." The magazine added that she often retreated into her huge Detroit home to wrestle "with her private demons. She sleeps till afternoon, then mopes in front of the TV set, chain-smoking Kools and snacking compulsively." But whereas *Time* and other publications said this or that about her, Aretha herself remained silent.

The troubled Aretha image was, of course, readily accepted since, in the eyes of her fans, Aretha like Bessie, sang what she lived. Aretha's songs sometimes focused on pained women pushed and pulled here and there by love, by gut emotion.

What also added to her particular troubled image was the way Aretha looked, She was big-boned and heavy. And at times, she seemed awkward, nervous, guilty, embarrassed about the weight, about the fact that she was not a glamour girl. At one point, she wore wigs and billowing dresses that camouflaged her figure. Later Aretha went natural, sporting an Afro. In the 1970s, she lost weight and appeared in soft, sexy, diaphanous gowns. Her vulnerability—the pain in her face and eyes—coupled with her fierce, gritty determination to get through a song in spite of its emotional demands, drew audiences to her. But even as her fans saw all of Aretha's raging power and glory, it seemed to pass Aretha by. In a rare television interview she was fine when at the piano, but when asked to speak she seemed lost, her eyes liquid and looking frightened.

In the mass imagination, Aretha took her place in a line of dedicated, tortured artists such as Holiday, Charlie Parker, and Lester Young. Sometimes, an Aretha Franklin concert was a stirring ritual for a mass audience. When Aretha suffered onstage, so

Aretha and Bill Curtis at a radio station.

did her audience. She was the perfect cathartic performer, though, because Aretha took her audience down *with her* to the level of *their* despair. But she always brought them back up. Afterward, many may have forgotten that the great pleasure and satisfaction of an Aretha Franklin concert was that they had left with an uncanny high.

Aretha Franklin had brought soul to America. Like Ethel Waters in the late 1940s and 1950s, Aretha was a glowing, full-bodied, rock-of-ages matriarch (a twenty-six-year-old girl going on a hundred) who symbolized endurance. And her tribal chant helped bring the restless, culturally split sixties to its dramatic conclusion. The idea was that things could and would change in America. Although the next decade would not need her as a symbol as the sixties had, Aretha would be there nonetheless, with not a drop of magnetism or power diminished.

Survivors
The 1970s

In the seventies, the political fervor and turmoil of the previous decade slowly faded. And the diva discovered a nation eager once again for pure rituals and diversions. In a short period of time, the seventies shaped up as a sometimes wickedly slick, trendy, fiercely contradictory era with a multitude of incongruities. The decade opened with Cambodia and Kent State, the Soledad Brothers and Angela Davis, the Pentagon Papers and Attica, Muhammad Ali and Joe Frazier, Vietnam and Watergate. Before its end, it would boast of or be haunted by other images, as well as new fads or trends, all testaments to its eerie unpredictability.

The mood that came to dominate the era seemed to be a longing for escape and adventure, which may have simply revealed America's basic uncertainty about itself and its overriding sense of alienation. Losing oneself somewhere outside the present, blotting out the harsh realities the sixties had been so determined to confront (the war abroad; the problems of an industrial culture polluting itself to death), seemed the one great mad hope of the slick seventies; an era aptly dubbed the Me Decade by

Chaka Khan.

Page 176: Donna Summer.

writer Tom Wolfe. Perhaps, better than anything else, that explains the rise of the discos, where everyone could dance his or her problems away.

And, of course, the era's desire for escape affected the styles and images of the divas. Often, the important black goddesses were women seemingly operating in deluxe fantasy lands that audiences also eagerly sought. What audiences cherished most about the new black heroine was that by way of the American success ethic, by way of the treasured American status of star, she had escaped and survived the kind of humdrum existence with which audiences felt that they themselves were saddled. Of course, stars had functioned in this way in the past. But now, the audience need for escape was intensified. And soon, a new generation seemed off on a giddy star trip unlike any that anyone had experienced before. In a gossipy, celebrity-oriented period, the American black beauty found herself fully emerging (for the first time) as a true superstar celebrity, as famous and adored as any white goddess, sometimes even more. No matter how talented an African American goddess might be, it never mattered so much what she did (politically, socially, artistically) as long as she could sustain the illusion of stardom, or that of the survivor who could not be kept down. Curiously, too, the era's star fixation (and the superficial star trappings: the clothes, the money, the look, the media attention) as well as the interest in the-woman-who-had-held-on now helped bring about the formal apotheosis of the classic dark diva spirit.

Oddly enough, the first important seventies divas still had some political fall-out power from the sixties. In the early seventies, audiences still searched their popular entertainment for comments on America's political system. Consequently, the two divas who launched the era were women who, while definite stars, also were political heroines. And in them, Diana Ross and Cicely Tyson, the great dichotomy of the early seventies was best summed up. One was pure political heroine with touches of glitter in her personal style. The other was glitter goddess bathed in the waters of politics.

Diana Ross: the Superstar Ascends

By the early seventies, Diana Ross was already internationally famous and fully on her own. Having left the Supremes, she could boast of hit records—"Ain't No Mountain High Enough" and "Reach out and Touch." She also played the big engagements. But something still was not right. There was already a national nostalgia surrounding the Supremes. If the public fully accepted Ross on her own, it meant that something else had to be accepted, namely that the original Supremes, a great sixties vision touching on the idealism and dreams of the era, were now dead and gone, and could never return. A kind of national innocence had died. Ross herself was often thought of as the selfish, superficial, overly ambitious sister who had stepped on everyone else. Motown and Ross's Svengali, Berry Gordy Jr., aware of the sentiments, knew that something had to be done to change the image as well as broaden her stardom.

Diana Ross soon underwent a metamorphosis. During this early part of a period that still saw Aretha Franklin as the undisputed queen, Ross in all likelihood knew intuitively that she would not be accepted as a goddess until she symbolically had gone back to the holy waters, been re-baptized, and born again. What brought about her metamorphosis was a diva from the past, Billie Holiday.

In the early seventies, Billie Holiday was treasured all the more by young Black America since mass White Americans still had not hooked onto her legend. All that sixties' worship of Holiday as a tragic victim was still around. Black America identified with all of Billie Holiday's sufferings. The bigoted system that had helped destroy her was the very same system that had denied dignity and full freedom to millions of other African Americans throughout the nation. In essence, Billie Holiday's troubled story was Black America's story too. And now there was a demand that the story be told. Interestingly, had Holiday's life been dramatized in the late sixties, Diana Ross would have been totally unacceptable. That heated period would never have settled for the 1972 movie version of Holiday's autobiography, *Lady Sings the Blues*, which would have been dismissed as but one more symbol of the exploitation of a black artist by a decadent capitalistic culture. But in the 1970s, the more relaxed social and political attitudes as well as Motown's clout permitted Ross to take the role.

When word first spread that Motown planned to bring Holiday's story to the screen and that Ross would play Holiday, there was open astonishment. She seemed the least qualified of actresses for the part. Her voice did not have the shading or depth of Lady Day's. She was skinny and small-boned; Holiday had been large and full. And the personality contrasts were astounding. Holiday had been still, remote, moody, withdrawn, intense, the essence of quiet fire. Diana was all razzle-dazzle, all get-up-and-move-extroversion, all show and flash and dash. In the minds of many, Motown chieftain Gordy had gone cuckoo over his protégée. But Diana Ross proved everyone wrong.

Lady Sings the Blues was a lush, romantic melodrama dressed up with some political rhetoric and social trappings to alleviate any guilt feelings audiences might have about enjoying old-fashioned soap opera. Holiday's life was transformed into a standard rags-to-riches saga with the trying, unnerving experiences (the early jail experience, the tension in her Baltimore household, her sense of isolation as well as the tensions she herself laid out on others) all either neatly reduced to mild comic fare or ignored altogether. Nor did the film focus on her loves. Had *Lady Sings the Blues* dealt explicitly with Holiday's love life, the movie might have been too disturbing. At this point in history, audiences were desperate for "positive black images." Already in such films as *Shaft* and *Superfly*, too many black women had been seen too readily dispensing with their sexual favors. So, for the mass audience there had to be a mass-acceptable Billie, one who was a bourgeois lady. Billie Holiday herself no doubt would have loved some of the phony business of the film, but she would have seen it for what it was too: a motion picture that could be appreciated and enjoyed as an elaborate escapist romantic fantasy, but a film, in the final analysis, which simplified a very complex life.

What gave *Lady Sings the Blues* its driving force and charge, as well as its particular

Billie Holiday, whose legend became more powerful than ever before. Black Americans identified with her and longed for her story to be told.

Diana Ross as Billie in *Lady Sings the Blues:* a shrewd piece of image-merchandising. Although the film was pure escapist fantasy, it reaffirmed Ross's star power, winning her an Oscar nomination.

poignancy and pull, were the performances of Billy Dee Williams, Richard Pryor, and mainly Diana Ross. Richard Shickel of *Life* wrote that whereas the film did an injustice to Holiday's life by trying to "shoehorn one of the legendary tragedies of popular music into one of the most trivial and convention-alized of screen forms, the showbiz biogra-phy," it still had the Ross performance to recommend it. "Singing," he wrote, "she does a fair imitation of the Holiday style. Acting, she does even more. Billie Holiday personified the vulnerability, terror, and confusion of the performer who can't hide in a crowd or in a role. Miss Ross, in an unselfconscious, bravura performance makes us feel all of that." In *The New Yorker,* Pauline Kael wrote: "Diana Ross, a tall skinny goblin of a girl, in-tensely likeable, always in motion...[is] like a beautiful bonfire: there's nothing to ques-tion—you just react with everything you've got...because she has given herself to the role with an all-out physicality, not holding anything back."

And William Wolf of *Cue* added: "If there's any justice, Diana Ross should be the biggest movie superstar to come along since Barbra Streisand, and she possesses deeper acting ability." In the end, Ross walked off with a Golden Globe for her work in the film as well as the highly prestigious Academy Award nomination as Best Actress of 1972.

But with all this aside, the ritual inherent in *Lady Sings the Blues* is obvious: Diana, the princess of ghetto chic, a girl–woman known as *plastic,* goes through Billie's horrors and humiliations. By doing so, she acquires a certain depth and relevance. Thus, the queen of pop (who is loved precisely because she is that, although no one is quite ready to ad-mit it yet) is transformed into an acceptable commodity for an age that thinks of itself as still being politically motivated. Shrewdly, the movie ends on a high note, not with Lady Day alone and lonely in her Manhattan apartment, but with an image of Diana standing tall and proud and triumphant at Carnegie Hall (superimposed newspaper clips tell of Holiday's death), an appropriate way, of course, to announce the death–rebirth of a major star myth for the new era. Diana Ross and *Lady Sings the Blues* ushered black pop into the seventies with great pizzazz.

When word first spread that Motown planned to bring Holiday's story to the screen and that Ross would play Holiday, there was open astonishment.

Afterward, Ross never looked better—her skinny body perfectly decked out in glittery but "tasteful" gowns. Eventually, the wigs would go, the hair pulled severely from the forehead and tied in the back. She was becoming, a bit prematurely, an exuberant grande dame, living in the Hollywood Hills, granting interviews selectively, making rare personal appearances, always traveling in style in limos, in furs and diamonds. And she was accorded status symbols reserved only for the real big-time goddesses: a cover portrait on *Life* just before its demise at the time; sensational covers throughout the era on *Ebony, People, Jet, Rolling Stone, Cue,* and countless others; a prestigious *Blackgama* mink advertisement with simply a photograph of Diana wrapped in mink and the words *"What Becomes a Legend Most;"* and the big-star status symbol of that age, an interview by Barbara Walters. And with all the attention and the hugely successful concert performances, it was apparent the 1970s mass audience had caught up with her. But it did not end there. In time, Ross would lead her audiences into the land of ritual glamour and glitter, where it did not matter what she said or sang. She merely had to be.

Seldom was her star power more apparent than with the arrival of her second movie *Mahogany.* Directed by Berry Gordy Jr., this disjointed and disorienting tale of a black fashion model was met with terrible reviews. Yet, the picture was a smash and Diana succeeded in taking her fans on a star trip. Cast as an upwardly mobile woman determined to be a success, she delighted in wearing fine, flamboyant, sometimes over-the-top clothes, while not caring what the world had to say about sometimes histrionic, melodramatic scenes. Rarely had her glamorous narcissism been on such an enjoyably splashy display.

The same was true in the mid- and late-seventies, when Diana Ross went on to play huge houses—the Palace in New York and Radio City—where her ritual, usually carefully prepared dramatic entrances and exits, and carefully programmed romps through the audience while being protected by guards, gave the impression that the queen was humble enough to mingle with the hoi polloi. During these performances, too, she was more confident than ever, aware of the basis of her appeal and so magnetized by her own celebrity and personal history that her new concerts often openly, with the use of slides and film clips and old Supremes songs, paid homage to her. She presented her fans time and again with her now-legendary life story, which was turned into a sanitized, sentimental journey from Detroit to Hollywood and Vine. Her concerts also paid homage to past divas Baker, Waters, and Bessie, whom she impersonated onstage, and with whom she now knew she was historically linked.

In time, these concerts became part of her new legend. And some of the critics were swept away by her astounding audience rapport. Their reactions touched on the unfathomable power that she had over huge crowds. In the June 15, 1976, edition of the *New York Post,* Jan Hodenfield wrote:

Diana Ross, who opened at the Palace last night for a two-week run, sings as though she's standing on a mountaintop.

Whether or not she's at the height of her career, she is a star of the classic I'm-here-you're-there-and-I'm-always-going-to-be-here school, and she has been provided a superstar act. A lot of glitz.

. . . She is beautiful. She has no cavities. It's all in the hips. And she is up, but carefully so, laid back. From baby panther to

the most teasing of tigers, she always appears almost sure of herself.

... And who else but Diana Ross could sing a children's song in purple, blue and silver sequins and, sitting in a child's chair, actually make it poignant? She may be the only glamorous woman to come out of the 60s.

And of her 1977 Forest Hills engagement. *New York Times* critic Robert Palmer seemed so taken with her he couldn't see straight.

Diana Ross ... has "it." What is "it"? The answer is not simple ... having "it" means having not just sex appeal, but also talent, personality, and the most difficult of all performer qualities to define, charisma. Because Miss Ross has "it," she can get away with the most saccharine sort of monologues. She can talk ingenuously about turning a tennis stadium into a discotheque, sit on the edge of the stage and ask a crowd of thousands to pretend they are sitting in her living room, and finally induce the entire audience to hold hands and sway back and forth in rhythm. It takes plenty of "it" to pull this sort of thing off, and Miss Ross makes it seem easy.

There are perfectly valid musical reasons for Miss Ross's ability to charm an audience. She has been able to move out from her base in her sweet soul sound of early Motown, without sacrificing an iota of the girlish appeal she exuded during those years, into a much broader stylist arena.

There is no truly popular singer in America who can touch her stylistic range or her ability to put across a song's emotional charge without wallowing in either melancholy or bombast. In the light of this talent, even the most contrived stage routines seem to sparkle.

Glowing notices aside, there were moments during her peak years when she showed signs of wear and strain. Her material was not as fresh and imaginative as it had been in the sixties. She could no longer hit the high notes, and she did not move around the stage as she had in the past. It was difficult for her to fake spontaneity, too. Yet, she remained so exuberantly confident of her own powers to entertain and delight that audiences could not take their eyes off her.

Throughout the seventies, Ross appeared to be having great fun. Refusing to

Old-style movie glamour: Diana Ross in *Mahogany.*

hide any aspect of her stardom, she glorified in it all, always making great copy for the celebrity sheets. *People* reported that one evening, upon arriving at Berry Gordy's Detroit mansion for a party in her honor, Ross simply waved to the one hundred guests. Then she calmly shucked her leather boots and dove into the mansion's swimming pool, "swam a length in rust-colored pants and cowled sweater, waved goodnight to the guests, and strutted dripping to bed." Diana Ross was doing much of what Josephine Baker had done in Europe, keeping the troops entertained offstage as well as on, and reveling in all the attention.

Diana Ross also fell victim, however, to a critical backlash. Sometimes, the attacks on her were fierce. Her 1978 film *The Wiz* was met with scathing reviews. This $35

Interestingly, while such critics raged on, the Black Community sat back and watched, its ambivalence about Ross once again on the rise. There had been the business of her marriage to a white music executive, Robert Silberstein, father of her three children, so it was then reported, although there were rumors even than that the father of her oldest daughter was actually Berry Gordy Jr. Indeed, what may have saved Ross here from totally alienating the community were the rumors of her ongoing romantic relationship with Gordy. In the mass imagination, the two belonged together. Yet no matter what the Black Community's feelings, there was never an outright attack on her in the African American press. As with Muhammad Ali, Diana Ross may have unnerved part of White America because there was some-

As with Muhammad Ali, Diana Ross may have unnerved part of White America because there was something unreal about her powers, something almost superhuman about her image and the effect she had on large audiences.

million musical was a flop. But far too often, the responsibility for the failure of the film was attributed to Ross rather than to the sluggish direction of Sidney Lumet. On another occasion, a *Village Voice* article labeled her as "the Last of the Black White Girls." A *Newsweek* article announced that offstage "Diana Ross is not plastic, she's steel," adding that she no longer had "soul." Worse was a *Women's Wear Daily* review, which dismissed her for giving in concert "hack ballad readings and a pimpish charade of egotistical humility better suited to female impersonators. Ross...is merely a grade-B actress fronting a soundtrack of dismal clichés."

thing unreal about her powers, something almost superhuman about her image and the effect she had on large audiences.

For the duration of the seventies, despite friends and foes alike, Diana Ross remained a truly dazzling creation, a woman who, regardless of critics, controversies, and contradictions always survived and never disappointed. She was a hip, giddy gamin of a high priestess who always had the gift of gab and energy, the sense of high-flung fun that the nostalgia-crazed, *discoized* 1970s were eager for. In the long run she, like her audience, may have been a figure of profound isolation and alienation. If so, no one seemed to mind.

Cicely Tyson:
the Incorruptible
Black Artist

The other black goddess rising to super-stardom in the early 1970s was Cicely Tyson, who represented for many the incorruptible black artist. She was something sixties America had been waiting for: a symbol of black consciousness and pride. Hers was an image that worked perfectly as the period opened. Her career also indicated that American audiences still had not completely risen above their familiar color hang-ups and biases.

Cicely Tyson was born in Harlem, the daughter of a West Indian couple who had migrated from the Nevis Islands. Her father was a carpenter; her mother, a domestic worker. At age nine, Tyson was on the streets selling shopping bags. The family was dirt poor but proud, and Tyson's strict and fiercely religious mother sent her three children off to church every chance that she had.

Once out of school, Tyson worked a series of jobs. Her last before the start of her show-business career was as a typist for the Red Cross. One day when she had had it with the grinding routine, she announced for all in the office to hear, "God didn't intend for me to sit at a typewriter all my life." She quit the job, became a model, and soon embarked on an acting career, which did not sit well with her mother at all. But Tyson stuck to her guns, lit up with a gritty determination that showed in her work. Throughout the late 1950s and 1960s, she worked hard, studied tenaciously, slowly learning her craft and year by year winning critical attention in off-Broadway and Broadway productions—*Talents '59; Jolly's Progress* (as an understudy for Eartha Kitt); *Moon on a Rainbow Shawl;* Langston Hughes's *Trumpets of the Lord; Tiger Tiger Burning Bright; A Hand Is on the Gate; The Cool World; Blue Boy in Black; Take Me Back to Morningside Heights;* and *To Be Young, Gifted and Black.* But of all those roles, her most impressive, the part that brought her national attention, was as the prostitute Virtue in the legendary 1961 production of Jean Genet's *The Blacks*, a rousing, revolutionary piece of theater that introduced a startling group of young players: Raymond St. Jacques, Lou Gossett Jr., Godfrey Cambridge, Roscoe Lee Browne,

James Earl Jones, and Maya Angelou. In this cast of heavyweights, Tyson walked off with her first Drama Desk Award as outstanding off-Broadway performer of the year. The next year, she won the same award again for her performance in *Moon on a Rainbow Shawl.*

Tyson soon began working in films and on television, sometimes in bit parts, where if you blinked you missed her; other times in supporting roles, where her striking face and personality were there for all to see.

In appearances on series as diverse as *I Spy*, the under-appreciated *East Side, West Side, The Nurses, The FBI, Medical Center, Gunsmoke*, and the daytime soap opera *The Guiding Light*, what always shone through was her fierce integrity—that sense of her own worth and her rigid refusal to sell herself short. In those days, she did not give out that radiant smile so readily. Often, too, her large luminous eyes seemed to look through, rather than at, her costars. For years, as she struggled with unchallenging television parts, Cicely Tyson, like so many African American beauties before her, was rarely at ease. There was that familiar edge, not too different from Bessie Smith's or Lena Horne's. All that pent-up frustration and disillusionment, about her own career and the fact that as an African American woman it was taking longer to get anywhere, helped make her such a compelling presence. Even then, at the time of the early television spots, the large audience watching her, those millions who did not know her name, but who could not forget the face and the attitude, knew that here was a young woman better and bigger than her parts. Cicely Tyson knew that one of the secrets of great acting is holding something back.

Tyson's main problem may have been that she was too dark. What with her color and her features, and regal way that she carried herself, she did not seem to fit into a Western definition of beauty at all. In a period when the Supremes had donned wigs and glitter makeup, looking from a distance like tiger-limbed mulattoes, Tyson looked African. Even Diana Sands, with her full lips, had the "advantage" of lighter skin to help make her acceptable to mainstream audi-

Tyson, winning critical acclaim and an Oscar nomination for her performance in *Sounder.*

ences. Cicely Tyson would never come anywhere near a mulatto ideal. Ironically, when Tyson did become a star, in spite of national attitudes about her looks and her particular stance, those very things would be most treasured by her devotees. For just at the moment when Tyson appeared before the mass audience in a role just right for her talents, Black America was eager for a dark heroine.

And, of course, stardom finally came with the 1972 release of *Sounder,* the story of a troubled black family living in Louisiana in the 1930s. It focused on several charac-

ters: a father imprisoned after he steals to get food on his family's table; a mother forced to hold the family together during his absence and at the same time to keep her emotions in check; a young son off on the road to maturity. Arriving amid a spate of such black action films as *The Legend of Nigger Charley* and *Shaft, Sounder* looked at first as if it had come at the wrong time. But it became the sleeper hit of the year. The critics had a field day with it, praising Tyson left and right. *Time* announced that "no American actress since Jane Fonda in *Klute*

Tyson in *Sounder:* making audiences rethink their definition of beauty.

has given a film performance of such artfully and varied texture." In *The New Yorker,* Pauline Kael wrote: "Cicely Tyson plays the first great black heroine on the screen. Her Rebecca was worth waiting for. She is visually extraordinary. Her cry as she runs down the road toward her husband is a phenomenon—something even the most fabled actresses might not have dared."

Afterward, Tyson won the National Board of Review's award as Best Actress of the Year and also picked up an Oscar nomination, along with Diana Ross, for Best Actress. For the first time in movie history, two African American women were now vying for Hollywood's most prized possession. Although Liza Minnelli walked off with the Oscar for her performance in *Cabaret,* this remained a thoroughly optimistic experience for black moviegoers who saw this event as a striking new turn for American movies.

But following all the hoopla, even with *Sounder* under her belt, Tyson did not get the big publicity shoves in the national magazines or the plugs in the syndicated columns. The media found Diana Ross infinitely more salable because of her glamorous image. Tyson's success was seen as merited and long overdue, but many also thought it was fluky, a once-in-a-lifetime experience. For a year or so, it almost looked as if the doubters were right. Then Tyson came back strong in another surprise hit, *The Autobiography of Miss Jane Pittman,* a film that was made for television. Based on a novel by African American writer Ernest Gaines, it traced the life of a black woman from the days of slavery to the dawning of the civil rights movement in the late 1950s. Tyson won critical raves for a tour-de-force performance as well as two Emmys: one for Outstanding Actress in a Drama, and another special award as Actress of the Year.

What Tyson had done in this early part of the era was to present ordinary women in a distinctly heroic manner. Her Rebecca and Miss Jane, neither mammies nor mulattoes, stood as symbols. They were low-keyed, sensitive women aware of the bonds of race and gender. They struck audiences as decent but guarded, never fully at ease in the white world since they knew too well its basic hypocrisy and its power to destroy. Yet at the very moment when they must take a stand and grasp full control over their personal destinies, Tyson's women did not hesitate.

After *The Autobiography of Miss Jane Pittman*, Cicely Tyson became something of a national commodity. The wheels of the big-time publicity machines finally turned. Her appearances on the covers of *Ebony, People, Ms.,* and *Jet* confirmed her arrival aboveground. Her persona was now directly in tune with the distinct needs of an age still in transition. There was so much about her now that the public could connect to, offscreen as well as on. Aside from her talent and charm, there was the history of her career that had taken so long to climax. There were also the intelligent comments that she made to the press about the lack of good roles for African American women and of the importance of role models on the screen for black audiences. The statements also endeared her to the politically conscious. There was also a strong identification with her among African American women. And in time, Tyson reached another group too. For during this period, when everyone seemed to be struggling to get back to basics, to abandon psychedelics, to be more in tune with the earth and nature, and away from chemicals, pollutants, and corruptive elements of all kinds, Tyson represented Natural Woman. She was the star who was also the vegetarian, the jogger, the woman who meditated daily, who sewed her own clothes. In a way, her color also made her the familiar dark woman of mystery, closer to the spirit than most mere mortals.

This was the type of publicity a Baker would have howled over. And, of course, it was the flip side of the Ross image. Yet, all these revelations about a new-style, down-to-earth diva had a certain social value at the time. Ironically, there was another side to Tyson: the Tyson who also wore designer duds, who was always impeccably made up and often bejeweled, and who later had a stormy marriage (and divorce) to jazz musician Miles Davis.

Nonetheless, Tyson was eventually affected by changing attitudes. In time, there were artistic disappointments: an all-black stage production of *Desire Under the Elms;* the television films *Just an Old Sweet Song* and *King;* the films *The Blue Bird, The River Niger,* and *A Hero Ain't Nothing but a Sandwich.* Even the critically successful television miniseries *A Woman Called Moses* failed to win a huge audience. Often, Tyson's persona was thrown out of whack by directors who failed to understand that, like Waters, Tyson had to have that big dramatic moment. Worse, a type of backlash sprang up against her. "Why doesn't Cicely Tyson stop playing somebody's grandmother?" seemed to be the attitude in even supposedly enlightened, intellectual circles. What the gripers did not stop to think about was that Tyson herself probably longed for a different kind of role. But had she not played the noble heroic types, all she might have hoped for was a bit as a prostitute. A role that might have been ideal for her was that of the mother in *Claudine.* Here, her dramatic gifts as well as her often-unacknowledged talents for light romantic comedy might have been beautifully showcased. But one wonders if the mass audience would have accepted her in such a role. For the Tyson *dark* look demanded—in the mind of the public—that she play strong black women of spirit but not much flesh.

Throughout the seventies, Tyson refused to budge from her convictions to fit the fashion of the times. Her public personality itself may have become too serious and "political" for an audience insistent on art and entertainment that did not ask questions or present problems. But Tyson did not wilt and die. In the next decade, she appeared in the popular TV movie *The Marva Collins Story,* and also opposite Richard Pryor in the film *Bustin' Loose.* She won another Emmy in the early 1990s for her performance in *Oldest Living Confederate Widow.* And for future generations, her image would blaze on as one of Black and White America's few authentic cultural icons of the 1970s and 1980s.

Vonetta McGee.

Black Ladies of the Silver Screen

Briefly, following the movie success of Tyson and Ross, it looked as if other black goddesses might become stars through film. For the early seventies saw the rise of the new-style black-oriented motion picture that touched on the needs of the African American audience for political heroes. Actresses Vonetta McGee, Sheila Frazier, Brenda Sykes, Marlene Clark, Jeanne Bell, and Paula Kelly suddenly found, even if only briefly, the doors of Hollywood open to them. For the political hero naturally needed a girlfriend. Mostly the actresses appeared in black action dramas, souped-up male fantasies geared to please a large black male audience. In *Shaft, Hit Man, Hammer,* and *Trouble Man* the heroines had little to do, other than to be at the hero's side during times of need. In retrospect, it is apparent that although more African American women had a chance to work, the movies of a male-oriented industry still did not care about telling a black woman's side of the story. Clearly, that was the case with the films of actress Rosalind Cash.

At the beginning of the decade, Cash left the Negro Ensemble Company in New York to go west to costar with Charlton Heston in the highly touted *Omega Man.* At the time, what with Angela Davis still in the headlines, many assumed Cash, with her magnificent puffed-up, larger-than-life Afro and her compelling assertiveness, would be playing a militant, politically committed heroine. There was reason to believe that the studio executives producing *Omega Man* felt the same way, at least when the production was first taking off. Strangely enough, in the first half of the film Cash was glowingly aggressive. She made a dramatic appearance on a motorcycle, rescuing hero Heston, giving him commands to jump on the darn thing if he wants to keep on living. Here she was a glorious symbol, one of those heady dreams of the beautiful black woman who comes out of nowhere and saves man from his own sad plight. Then gradually the Cash character, who looked as if she were about to run away with the picture, was softened by the script and Boris Segal's direction to the point where all her drive and force were watered down

completely. Even at that, Cash's character was never the one-dimensional black superwoman type. For the actress's obvious intelligence and genuine warmth nicely shaded the role.

The same was true of her work in *Melinda,* in which she played a brooding, troubled woman caught up with a man who has become involved with another woman. In one sequence, to aid the hero, she pretended that she was the other woman in order to withdraw some much-need-

Rosalind Cash in *Omega Man.*

ed money from the bank. When the bank executive questions her, Cash launches into a harangue that stands outside the bounds of cheap melodrama: her face tight and constricted, her emotions in a blast of fury and rage, she represented a demanding, unyielding black woman lashing out at a racist culture that repeatedly had told her the trumped-up rules by which she must live.

In the very early years of the decade, Rosalind Cash's work (notably in *Melinda*) had an impact on young black women, who identified with her strongly. Had films such as *Melinda* and *Omega Man* turned out better, had the scripts been ambitious or insightful enough to provide her characters with some kind of dramatic consistency or clarity, Rosalind Cash would have emerged as an important film star and might well have entered the ranks of the great divas. But gradually, the opportunities for exciting, compelling moments onscreen grew slimmer as she drifted from one sweet-tempered role to another in such films as *Uptown Saturday Night, Cornbread, Earl and Me*, and *The New Centurions*. Later, she worked on television.

Seldom in the history of Hollywood was a black woman so repeatedly wasted, so thoroughly trashed by the industry. And the roles this gifted woman found herself playing often revealed the basic contempt in Hollywood for the talented, not-easily typed African American actress. In a way, though, the roles, coupled with Cash's high-strung artistry, created a persona for her. As with Gloria Foster, perceptive audiences sat watching Rosalind Cash, using her as a symbol of their own broken promises and unfulfilled dreams. Something similar would happen with Angela Bassett in the 1990s.

Other gifted actresses seemed to get lost in the shuffle. Lonette McKee gave a blazing performance in *Sparkle*, but was unable to find another film that properly used her talents (though she worked in subse-quent decades in such films as *The Cotton Club, Jungle Fever*, and *Malcolm X*). The same was true of Tracy Reed after her exciting work in *Car Wash*.

The new black television series (such as *Good Times, The Jeffersons, Sanford and Son, What's Happening!*) offered exposure to a number of actresses: Esther Rolle, Isabel Sanford, Teresa Graves, Roxie Roker, Mabel King, Theresa Merritt, and the delightful Marla Gibbs. Unfortunately, some of these talented women found themselves cast as the familiar overweight, mammy figure. Of the TV personalities, surely the most interesting were the women cast in *Roots* and *Roots: The Next Generations:* Madge Sinclair, Olivia Cole, Leslie Uggams, Lynne Moody, Irene Cara, Bever-Leigh Banfield, Beah Richards, and Lee Chamberlain. Cole and Sinclair were two of the best new dramatic actresses around. Sinclair also appeared in the movies *Leadbelly* and *Conrack*. Cole won an Emmy for her work in *Roots* and then went on to give a complex performance in *Backstairs at the White House*. But always, these actresses searched for the big role. The same was true of Ellen Holly, who appeared on the soap opera *One Life to Live*, and Denise Nicholas, who throughout the era gave lively, engaging performances on the tube, as well as Nichelle Nichols of *Star Trek*.

Moms makes it to Hollywood – with Rosalind Cash – in the film *Amazing Grace.*

Pam Grier and
Tamara Dobson:
Macho Matriarchs

In the world of film, the only other names of the period (women who acquired definite followings) were Tamara Dobson and Pam Grier, each of whom was able alternatively to touch on the shifting demands for glitter and guts.

In such films as *Cleopatra Jones, Coffy, Foxy Brown, Sheba Baby,* and *Friday Foster,* Dobson and Grier arrived on the movie scene—and nearly swept it clean. Each a tantalizing male fantasy come true, they personified the tough black mama out to avenge herself and her community on Whitey and his ills. In a way, they were matriarchal figures, beautiful, more-

Grier always came across as a fiercely aggressive, tough, resilient, hot, and surprisingly funny black woman on the move. Her movies themselves were cheap, rowdy comic strips. But she infused them with her energy and had a following, mostly among black makes. The male reactions were purely, openly chauvinistic. Grier herself seemed to play up to the chauvinism: there was nudity when hardly called for. And away from movie theaters, she struck a number of provocative bare poses for the black publication *Players.* She was the woman black college boys drooled over. It may well have

In such films as *Cleopatra Jones, Coffy, Foxy Brown, Sheba Baby,* and *Friday Foster,* Dobson and Grier arrived on the movie scene—and nearly swept it clean.

politicized, self-righteous versions of the Hattie McDaniel no-nonsense mammy. In a way, they were "mulattoes," too: gorgeous, exotic sex objects who were turning the object business inside out. They took men when they wanted. They were always in control of any situation. They had neither a penis nor penis envy. And they fought, shot, bombed, burned, castrated, and caused holy havoc, all in the name of restoring order to the Black Community, of ridding it of the pushers, the pimps, and the exploiters.

Of the two, Dobson was the more sedate. A former high-fashion model, she struck audiences as a classy, inaccessible black woman who stepped high with head held even higher. She was a living wonder to behold, but impossible to possess.

Grier's image was raunchier and livelier. And it lasted longer. The star of low-budget action films, Grier had originally worked her way up from a position as a switchboard operator at American International Pictures to become queen of the lot. Her ambitiousness showed too, because in her films Pam

been the nudity and coarseness of the Grier characters—often objectified by the camera—which alienated her from black women. They could respond to her funky, down-home aggressiveness, and they might have enjoyed the way she spoke her mind to the dimwitted males populating her films. But the movies themselves were travesties, removed from the world and daily problems of most African American women. At the same time, this was a period when black women, openly concerned about their image, were weary of the whole sexy-vulgar-slut image. Interestingly, Grier did have a following among some white women who often saw her as a figure of liberation. She even made the cover of *Ms.*

Both Pam Grier and Tamara Dobson seemed destined to go the route of Maria Montez, emerging as camp delights for audiences eager for old-fashioned kitsch at revival movie theaters. Yet, Grier developed as an actress and kept working in such films as *Fort Apache: The Bronx; Above the Law;* and Quentin Tarantino's *Jackie Brown* as well as on television's *The L Word.* Dobson died in 2006.

Clockwise from top left: Grier battlin' it out with Carl Weathers; Dobson, elegant and sedate; Grier (center) taking aim; Dobson as Cleopatra Jones, kicking up a storm; a raunchy Grier with Robert Doqui in *Coffy*.

Josephine Baker:
Coming Home

And who should appear precisely when needed, but the very woman who, for most, was the personification of old-time classic diva style—none other than La Baker herself, whose seventies return to the States was probably the best indication that audiences were now ready for unadulterated glitter and high style.

In 1973, Josephine Baker returned to the States for an engagement at Carnegie Hall. By this point in her life, Baker was something of a time-worn myth. She had been through much, and she had endured her traumas and terrors publicly, remaining true to the old star tradition of sharing the high and low with adoring fans. For her work during the war years with the French Resistance, she later was awarded the Légion d'Honneur by the French government. After her marriage in the 1940s to bandleader Jo Bouillon, Baker's great dream in the 1950s and 1960s had been to establish a home for her "rainbow tribe," children of every color, creed, and nationality who had been orphaned. Hopped up with what became her mad obsession, Baker adopted a dozen orphans, moving them into Les Milandes, a sprawling three-hundred-acre estate in the Dordogne Valley in southwestern France. Here, she hoped to open a resort with a hotel, restaurant, swimming pool, and theater and golf-and-tennis facilities, all of which would pay the expenses for her family. It was, of course, a lavish, grandiose folly. But she believed that she could pull it off, that in a world in which she, a poor girl from St. Louis, had become an international personality, hobnobbing with some of the most important leaders and artists of the 20th century, anything she chose to do was possible.

But reality came crashing in. The cost of the project, the upkeep of her chateau, and the expenses for supporting her children wiped out Baker's personal fortune, leaving her in debt. Her creditors warned her, then seized her property and belongings, and later sold them at auction in 1969. Until the very end Baker held on, literally fighting off the gendarmes who had to forcibly remove her from her property, carrying her from her chateau out into the rain. The photograph of the evicted Josephine Baker, far from glamorous, bundled in an oversized coat, with her dark glasses hiding the angry, swollen eyes, circled the globe. Here was a remarkable woman who had provided the world with illusion for years and who had as well lived on some illusions herself. In the past, she had been strong enough to make the illusions work for everybody. Even during the difficult war years, one senses that much of what propelled Baker, perhaps even contributed to her great heroism, was her gloriously romanticized view of herself and her uncanny ability always to succeed.

Reaction to the news of her eviction was curiously mixed. Like Ethel Waters during the period of her most intense personal problems, when her public knew as much about her situation as she herself, Josephine Baker had become a legendary heroine seemingly beyond human sympathy. For a brief spell, many followed her "story," content perhaps that she could still entertain them offstage. If she made it through this bad time, that would add another notch to the legend. If she did not, that might give the legend a surprising finishing touch, coloring a triumphant career with pathos and tragedy. Nevertheless, it was Baker's story to work out.

Worse than these reactions to her as a legend were the reactions to her as a performer. For at this point in her history, Baker was seen by many as an over-the-hill legend without much of a career left. In photographs, she looked fat, puffy, a diva who had lost her physical appeal.

But Baker summoned up something within herself. She needed money to keep her rainbow tribe dream alive. She was not about to let go of it. Nor was she about to let go of her world-famous persona. In a way, it was a matter of self-respect. But then, too, all her life she had been an entertainer. Entertaining had kept her alive. She needed that almighty roar of the crowd. From many accounts, she was a driven, restless woman who always had to be on the move, who had to have that mass affection to keep moving and to keep her own view of self from dying. So soon she was dieting, exercising, rehearsing, working on a new act, determined to prove the cynics wrong, determined, too, to live up to the expectations of her fans as an ageless creation who could eternally please.

And all of that brought her to Carnegie Hall in 1973—back to New York City, a place that had never been home, but a place that she was determined to lick this time around. The night she opened, a packed house saw a tiny, red-haired lady walk out onto the stage. Private groans and whispers shot through the audience. Was this small, plainly dressed woman the legend they had heard about for decades? The quiet groans ceased only when the woman was introduced as Bricktop, who years before had left the States and become an internationally famous club doyenne, managing the most chic night spots Europeans had seen. Her Place Pigalle *boite* had been the second home of the so-called Lost Generation of the 1920s and 1930s. In the 1950s and 1960s, her dazzling *nitery* on Rome's Via Veneto had been the place for the Jet Set. She had taught the black bottom to the duke of Windsor, the Charleston to Cole Porter (who wrote "Miss Otis Regrets" for her), and had thrown a rowdy John Steinbeck out of her club. (Later, he had returned apologetically, with a car full of roses for her.) And she had been hostess at her club to Elizabeth Taylor and Richard Burton before their marriage, during the peak of their scandalous love affair while filming *Cleopatra.* Born Ada Beatrice Queen Victoria Louise Virginia Smith DuConge, she had become a celebrity in her own right. And now, she was introducing her friend Josephine Baker to this skeptical audience.

Bricktop's appearance—and the case of mistaken identity—simply set the stage for Baker's spectacular entrance. For suddenly, like a true goddess, she seemed to descend from out of nowhere, magnificently dressed in a skintight body suit with sequins and rhinestones covering the vital areas and a giddy, glittering campy headdress, so towering it looked as if it would kiss the ceiling. Baker let out a hoot of a laugh as her audience gaped, ooooohing and aaaaahing. She knew what they had been thinking and let them know it too, announcing, while clutching her rhinestone-laden microphone, that she was aware of their surprise. Ah, you thought I would be fat, she informed the crowd, adding that no, she did not like fat. She loved thin. And the way she kept thin was by simply not eating. Then, her voice lowering a bit, as she seductively flattered and cajoled her audience as only a great star knows how, she added that she had wanted to be thin tonight for them, and so she had not eaten for days! Cheers, screams, and applause rang throughout the theater. And from then on, the audience was in the palm of her hand. The Baker voice was strong, vibrant, clear. The body was in perfect shape. The old-time chorus-girl strut was as defiantly sensational as ever. And that extraordinary gift—of transporting audiences into another world—was still there, too.

"Forget about Liza. Never mind about Liz," wrote Fern Marja Eckman in the *New York Post.* "Josephine Baker's back in town for 27 hours, lean as a whippet, graceful as a cat ('I'm a black cat with nine lives'), 67 and no trace of bulge or slack, still the mistress of high camp, still the presence that cast a spell over Paris back in the 1920s when she sang and danced and strutted at the Folies Bergère." The years had done nothing to diminish the Baker charisma.

During the New York visit, she appeared before enthusiastic crowds in Harlem, conquering, so *Jet* reported, a whole new generation of blacks. Afterward she flew back to France, then returned to New York for an engagement at the Palace. At the time, there was a musician's strike, and during rehearsals the tension and strain sometimes were telling. Backstage, some of the white stagehands grumbled and complained about their work and *her* demands, unaware of what a legend Baker was. It was a humiliating experience, the same kind of racism that she had fled decades ago. But the indomitable star carried on. Later, back in Europe at a charity benefit given by her friend Princess Grace, Baker stepped in as the last-minute star replacement for the event when Sammy Davis Jr. was unable to appear. Shrewdly, she used this internationally important occasion formally to launch her European comeback. She was a hit all over again. Later, she bought a $100,000 villa on the Riviera for her rainbow tribe. Once again, she was back into the swing of things, living it up in the grand old high style. In 1975, she opened a successful new revue in Paris, celebrating her fifty years in show business. But she had pushed herself too hard. Four days after the opening, Baker suffered a massive stroke and later died—in her sleep—in Paris. Josephine Baker had been blessed. For she was one of the few women, diva or otherwise, who saw almost all her dreams fulfilled.

Josephine Baker's great obsession—her rainbow tribe: she set up a home for war orphans of different races, creeds, and nationalities. The dream led her into debt, but she was determined to see it through.

Helen Humes.

The Old Style Returns

Baker's success lent new air to the entire dark diva phenomenon, endowing it (for those who cared to see) with a kind of political significance. The African American entertainer who had been through it all and was back to deliver the message to a new crowd now arose as a symbol of black endurance and accomplishment. Of course, the divas had always been such symbols. But it took a new generation time to discover that and to appreciate them as survivors. For years, too, black audiences had been aware that great performers such as Dietrich, Hepburn, and Davis had had star careers that spanned decades. Although even these women had sometimes been trashed or ignored by the dominant culture, an honored place was still reserved for them.

With the old black stars, however, there had been no such thing. So many of them, once they had peaked, had been forgotten. Seldom did theater histories even cite their achievements. So it was as if they had never existed. Baker's long career proved that wrong. And her triumphant 1970s return encouraged many to reexamine past popular history.

What also aided in the new discovery of the old-style diva was that as the social atmosphere became increasingly more relaxed, room was being made for a return of the purely pleasurable moment. Not only did discos surge up but the smart supper clubs briefly looked as if they would return. Night life was in vogue once again. In New York, a revamped Cotton Club reopened, amid such fanfare. (This time around, there were no segregated audiences.) And finally women who had been on the scene for years, some working steadily, others not, found themselves called back into public service for appearances at the clubs. The very proper Hazel Scott, the extremely sophisticated Mabel Mercer (a woman who had been a mainstay in New York and European cities for years as well as an idol for an array of performers, from Holiday to Frank Sinatra, all of whom were eager to study her impeccable diction and her sublimely cool delivery), and the grimacing and giddy Dorothy Donegan found work. Joyce Bryant, the ebullient Helen Humes, and the super-tough Maxine Sullivan all were not only working but getting publicity, too.

Someone like Sullivan also appeared in the stage play *My Old Friends*, winning rave notices. Jazz vocalist Betty Carter, who had been around since the 1940s when she had toured with Lionel Hampton, finally received serious critical attention. The music critic of *The New York Times* lauded her as "one of the great improvisatory jazz singers." *Newsweek* reassessed her entire career. At the 1978 Newport Jazz Festival tribute to women in jazz, Carter was honored along with Mary Lou Williams, Hazel Scott, and Maxine Sullivan.

The seventies proved receptive to other old-time divas. Lena Horne, never out of public sight, not only appeared in successful concerts with Tony Bennett, but also turned up as the star of the Los Angeles all-black production of *Pal Joey* with Clifton Davis and Josephine Premice. In 1978, she even returned to films, popping up for a cameo tour-de-force number in *The Wiz*, proving that if no one else knew what to do with this picture, she did.

In the seventies, Pearl Bailey also returned to movies, appearing in *The Landlord* and *Norman...Is That You?* Butterfly McQueen whipped up a nightclub act for New York audiences. By 1978 Eartha Kitt, her purr and scratch intact, returned to Broadway in *Timbuktu!*

Diahann Carroll's turbulent career was also infused with new ironies. Now that the social order was relaxed again, she finally seemed to break through and act up. Her romance with David Frost had ended. Briefly, she married and divorced Las Vegas businessman Freddie Glusman (it lasted four months), then took Robert DeLeon, an African American writer many years younger than she, as her husband. And she did not seem to give a damn what anyone thought of it. In *Jet* she also spoke out, indicating for the first time that she was aware of some of the sentiment against her. She announced that she was black and had always been so. No one was going to dictate her behavior, either. At a time when she could have simply spent her evenings on a disco floor, she took on a feisty fervor. When her husband was killed in a car crash, she briefly emerged as one of those enduring heroines who, having finally found happiness, had it quickly snatched away by the gods. Here, her career and image were touched with that most important of elements for a larger-than-life mythic persona: the element of fate. But refusing to exploit her personal tragedy, she kept a low profile. Most importantly, her singing style became far more dramatic (and she used more pop and soul material). She also gave her most felt film performance, as the title character in *Claudine*, the tale of a Harlem domestic worker living on welfare with six kids and no husband. Even the way that she looked in the film was refreshingly new, her face

Twenties blues star Alberta Hunter came out of retirement to become a nightclub star again.

scrubbed down of the glitter makeup, the brows high and strong, the body occasionally going slack but always sensually alive. Here she stood as a good-looking black woman in her middle years, somehow finding something in the material of *Claudine*—perhaps simply the idea of a black woman off on a quest for personal identity—that she fully connected to. She walked away with an Oscar nomination as Best Actress of 1974. Later, she married (and divorced) Vic Damone.

What with this reappearance of so many familiar faces, none could outclass that of Alberta Hunter, the 1920s blues sister who now returned to knock audiences dead in New York club performances. Hunter became something of a media sen-

sation. Celebrities packed her engagements. *Newsweek*, *The New York Times*, and other publications rushed to do features on her. She also appeared on talk shows, did television commercials, and scored the music for the Robert Altman film *Remember My Name*. Seventies audiences took to her in an unusual way, almost as if by giving this survivor her due, they could make up for oversights of the past.

Diva fever spread, touching even the dead. Billie Holiday, gone almost fifteen years, was now fully apotheosized as an authentic American mythic legend with the release of *Lady Sings the Blues*. Billie-mania led to an awakening of interest in the life and legend of Bessie Smith. In the Broadway show *Me and Bessie*, tribute was paid to the blues singer by the pulsating, lively gospel star Linda Hopkins. Bessie's albums were all reissued and, for a spell, there was talk of a Bessie movie biography to star either Aretha Franklin or Roberta Flack.

Other divas were the subjects of shows and benefits. In the New Federal Theater production of *Mahalia*, Ethel Morrow starred as gospel singer Mahalia Jackson. In 1979, a huge Carnegie Hall benefit was staged to honor Katherine Dunham. Claudia McNeil did a nightclub act centered on the songs of Ethel Waters. And off-Broadway, Charles Fuller's play *Sparrow in Flight*, starring Ethel Ayler, dramatized Waters's stormy life. Sadly, though, during all this revival business, Ethel Waters was a diva who was ignored throughout most of the seventies, seen by a new generation simply as a relic, no more than some tired, old, gray-haired woman who spent her later years singing with evangelist Billy Graham's Crusades tours. There was nothing campy about Waters at this period of her life, so she could not even be embraced for that. Whatever tributes she received came after her death in 1977. Even then, American theater circles still failed to give this extraordinary performer her due.

One of the most exciting events surely had to be the Kennedy Center's tribute to four distinguished American senior citizens: George Balanchine, Arthur Rubinstein, Fred Astaire, and the most queenly of divas, Marian Anderson. At the televised benefit a host of dignitaries and officials sat in attendance, led by President and Mrs. Carter. For the African American Community, the special moments were when a trio of dark divas—Grace Bumbry, Aretha Franklin, and Alberta Hunter—seemed to be performing solely for Anderson. Here the entire business of historical continuity was readily apparent.

And so the old-time diva and that old-time diva style were ushered back into vogue. Baker's influence was felt not only in the supper clubs, but on the stage too, in many of the new all-black Broadway shows—*The Wiz, Eubie, Bubbling Brown Sugar, Raisin, Ain't Misbehavin'*, the black revival of *Guys and Dolls*, perhaps even in Ntozake Shange's choreo-poem *for colored girls who have considered suicide when the rainbow is enuf.* All these shows were imbued with glitter and flash and a great sense of style. Now, as in the past, the African American performers understood that style often had to transcend content, particularly on those occasions when a black entertainer appeared before a white audience. Many of the new Broadway shows may have been accepted by the typical Broadway crowd as nothing more than high-flung entertainments. But for the black groups—coming to Broadway from churches and schools—the shows emerged (like Baker) as emblems of pride, razzmatazz homages to the resiliency and creativity of the African American Community. Onstage a number of exciting female performers were blessed with the old sense of style: Clarice Taylor, Rosetta LeNoire, Ernestine Jackson, Stephanie Mills, Alaina Reed, Josephine Premice, Mary Alice, Laurie Carlos, Mabel King, Clamma Dale, Virginia Capers, Vivian Reed, Nell Carter, Charlaine Woodard, Barbara Montgomery, Trazana Beverley, Debbie Allen, Vinnie Burrows, and the unforgettable Lynnie Godfrey. Behind the scenes, director Vinnette Carroll and composer Micki Grant created the hit musical *Don't Bother Me, I Can't Cope.* Melba Moore used Broadway as a springboard for a career as a pop vocalist. She began her career in Broadway's *Hair*, later won a Tony for her performance in *Purlie*, and returned to Broadway again in *Timbuktu!*

Striking and innovative as so many of these women were, few, however, could establish the kind of mythic identities that brought personal fame and huge followings. Some were on their way. Others would always be members of the show, good, solid, vibrant performers essential to American theater and popular entertainment, and the kind of colorful background material off which the great divas would play. Occasionally, a stunning performer such as Seret Scott, star of the Broadway drama *My Sister, My Sister*, would find herself suddenly cast in the spotlight with critics fawning over her, with the wheels of publicity machines starting to take off. Sometimes too, an extraordinary artist like dancer Judith Jamison could just about turn the world of dance inside out, expressing in dance a dramatically intriguing personality.

Many of the distinctive seventies personalities, the ones who reached and affected large audiences, came, unsurprisingly, from the world of popular music. Here, as in the past, black beauties discovered that, as singing stars, they could create their personas and exert some control over their careers. Once political messages disappeared from pop music early in the decade, such women as Marilyn McCoo and Florence La Rue (of the singing group the Fifth Dimension), Freda Payne, Valerie Simpson, Lola Falana, Natalie Cole, Letta Mbulu, the Pointer Sisters, Chaka Khan, the Staples, Minnie Riperton, Phyllis Hyman (whose suicide later shocked the music world), and Millie Jackson soon reverted to familiar images that exuded swanky glamour.

One of the most enduring was Gladys Knight, who had been performing since childhood and had won, at age seven, a prize on *The Original Amateur Hour.* Later, she joined her brother and cousins to lead the group Gladys Knight and the Pips. At Motown, she had such hits as "Heard It through the Grapevine." But even greater success came in 1973 when she left Motown to perform on the Buddah label. Great hits such as "Midnight Train to Georgia" and "I've Got to Use My Imagination" followed. The fact that here was a women leading the group, never being a part of the background, was not lost on record buyers. On her own, Knight kept performing into the next century.

Labelle: Nona Hendryx, Sarah Dash, and Patti LaBelle.

Tina Turner and Labelle: Funk and Glitter

Of the new stars, Labelle and Tina Turner were the most idiosyncratic performers of the era. Turner was a true star of raunch, as earthy, upfront, and funky as they come. Born Anna Mae Bullock in Brownsville, Tennessee, she and husband Ike Turner had been rhythm-and-blues stars since the 1960s when their record "A Fool in Love" had become a national hit. In the 1970s, Tina led Ike and their back-up group, the Ikettes, to the center of the pop-music scene with new renditions of "River Deep, Mountain High," "Honky Tonk Woman," and "Proud Mary."

Eventually, Tina went out on her own, performing as the Acid Queen in the movie *Tommy,* and appearing on national television. When she first attracted large audiences, disco still had not arrived. But a craving for disco was apparent, and Tina Turner was clearly a predecessor of the disco queens. Her club performances were popular during those anemic mid-to-late 1970s, when audiences were in need of a high priestess to shake them out of their own inertia and lethargy. Tina Turner did all the work for her audiences. Her arms flew and flailed. Her legs bent and split open in a provocative squat. Her head shook up and down, and all over the place, her long, straight-haired wigs defiantly flying up and down with her. Her costumes were brief, with lots of tassels and fringe. She turned and twirled and skittered across the stage like a whirling dervish in search of salvation. During concerts—again, whether with Ike or on her own—she played with her audiences, temporarily slowing the temp, saying softly, "And we're gonna do this easy." Then she would flash a wicked smile and add, "But we don't do nothin' nice and easy. We do things nice and rough." And then she would be off and at it again. Onstage, Turner was pure ritual, one of the great instinctive performers of her age. It never mattered what the words were. It was the sounds, the movements, the crazy world away from this world, a world of incessant delirious action, that Turner offered. Janis

Tina Turner: straight-haired wigs and scanty costumes.

Joplin, who was far more commercial and who often said that she had been influenced by Bessie Smith, actually owed some of her style to Turner.

Other predecessors to the upcoming disco craze were the sirens Labelle, the group known in the sixties as Patti LaBelle and the Bluebells. In the seventies the group—composed of Patti LaBelle, Sarah Dash, and Nona Hendryx—changed its name and revamped its image. The three came on in flamboyantly bizarre space-age outfits. But mostly they performed numbers that touched on the need for sexy, dreamy music that also could offer escape from the social and political passivity of the Nixon and Ford years. The aftermath of Vietnam and the Watergate scandal seemed the last thing Labelle's audiences had on its mind. Instead, this futuristic campy trio offered a world where no one lived by the old values, where almost anything went, where pleasure came easily and perhaps danger, too. Their biggest hit, the spicy and suggestive "Lady Marmalade," asked the question—of a stranger on the street—*Voulez-vous coucher avec moi ce soir?* This was a night, an adventure, which could lead somewhere. The group's mixture of heat, flash, and all-that-trash helped set the stage for the disco divas.

The androgynous Grace Jones: model turned disco star.

Disco Divas

Once the disco scene was established, the high priestess of those head emporiums were almost all black: Gloria Gaynor, Vicki Sue Robinson, Evelyn "Champagne" King, Linda Clifford, Amii Stewart, the singing group Sister Sledge, and the sublimely androgynous Grace Jones. Although the music critics ignored or dismissed disco music as simply a passing fancy, an opiate for the dull-witted, alienated masses, these women led the chants, inviting huge audiences off on a journey. The message of the disco divas was: get away from this troubled world and into another realm, explore the past, and search for the future. Music of-fered perfect escape, particularly electronically frenzied music presented in an atmosphere where everyone could escape together and have a sense of community. The discos also afforded everyone the chance to be special, to take off on a ritualized quest for self-expression. Here was a place where individuality was welcomed, where the more unconventional or freakier, the better. And if, with some luck and imagination, you were flashy enough, you could become, on your own terms, the very thing that the mid- and late-seventies seemed most in awe of: a star. Without restraints in the way you look-ed or behaved, everybody could be a diva.

Donna Summer:
the Queen of Disco

And, of course, from all this, there arose the seventies' final significant pop star, the queen of disco herself, and a bona fide diva for her age, Donna Summer. Almost single-handedly, she not only articulated what was on the minds of the disco crowd, but eventually made disco respectable, legitimized it in serious pop-music circles, and extended its range. In her style and her career were embodied the triumphs and tensions that had been part of past diva history. Like Baker, she was also a great success abroad before she was recognized in her own country.

In 1967, eighteen-year-old LaDonna Gaines left her home in Boston, auditioned for the Munich–based production of *Hair*, and soon appeared in a major role in the play. While in Germany, she briefly married an Austrian actor, Herbert Sommer (later she Anglicized her new last name), had a daughter Mimi, then was cutting records. Two of her singles went gold abroad. Then, she cut "Love To Love You, Baby," a basic rhythm track in which she seemed mostly to moan and groan, caught up in the ecstasy of sexual climax. All in all, *Time* reported, it sounded as if there were twenty-two orgasms on the record. No matter what the actual count, "Love to Love You, Baby," crossed the ocean and became an international hit, propelling Summer to instant fame.

She returned to the States, but no one was ready to take her seriously. For she was a sight to behold. Her puffed-out, blowy hair ballooned to the point of no return. Her eyes were always half-closed. Her legs were hotly exposed. Her mouth was a ripe instrument, opening and closing, the tongue often in motion across the lips. And her hands did overtime with the microphone stand, so much so that *Rolling Stone* wrote that she came "damn close to copulating" with it, "writhing up and down its length with palpable shivers." There was no sex queen like this one. Dubbed the First Lady of Lust, she was part burlesque, part camp, part absurd, but also utterly unique with a blazing talent.

The whole sex business, Summer later said, had been a gimmick, a commercial device to get her over. When some of it backfired, she was openly shaken. Even the reac-

tions of the disco crowd, which idolized her, hurt at times because she was taken too seriously as a sexual myth. She was what she sang, the crowd assumed. Radio stations played her record at midnight, inviting listeners to have "seventeen minutes of love with Donna Summer." Stories circulated that "Love to Love You, Baby," had actually been recorded when her producers slipped into her apartment and simply placed recording devices under her bed while Donna and a partner were in it. There were other rumors. *Ebony* even ran a cover story on Summer with the headline "*Donna Summer Talks about…the Rumor that Hurts Her Deeply*." One story had it that Donna Summer was really a man in drag, a lusty female impersonator. Another said that she was a transsexual.

Worse for Summer was the way some critics repeatedly dismissed her. She fought hard to branch out and develop. When she appeared in the 1978 film *Thank God It's Friday*, *The New York Times* movie critic wrote: "Miss Summer, whose wigs are as elaborate as Diana Ross's, is competition for the superb Miss Ross in no department other than hair." Of course, merely because she was a black singer, Summer had been considered Ross's rival. Actually, the women were different types with different audiences. (Diana Ross eventually sang disco songs, but not out of any great rivalry with Summer; she simply wanted to be in tune with the latest trend in popular music.)

The pressures and tensions took their toll on Summer. The grinding tours and hassles of the music world rattled her nerves. Headaches and insomnia set in. Once, she boarded an airplane gasping for breath and was given oxygen, then carried away. "Sometimes it gets to the point where you've been pushed for so long," she once said, "by those motorous, monstrous forces, this whole production of people and props that you're responsible for, by audiences and everything that trouble you, until you take it upon yourself to be a *machine*. And at some point a machine breaks down. I feel like I want to cry most of the time and just get rid of it, but sometimes I get so pent-up, I can't. And that's when I get afraid."

Donna Summer emerged as a star who extended the range of disco music and forced critics to take it and her seriously.

She survived the tensions, releasing ambitious new albums, notably *Once Upon a Time*, a concept album that transforms the Cinderella story into a tale about an urban girl who does indeed find her dream prince. It marked a new artistic direction for Summer. Gradually, in television appearances, Summer's style was modified. The gowns became longer, sleeker, more sophisticated. The puffy hairdo was modified, too. The moans and groans were toned down. But Summer herself seemed girlish, a bit awkward and wide-eyed, and when she talked, it was not the voice of a siren but that of a vulnerable, slightly uneasy young woman as eager to please as a Marilyn Monroe.

By the end of the 1970s, her albums *Donna Summer Live* and *Bad Girls* shot to the top of the record charts. Even some of the critics did an about-face. In December 1977, John Rockwell wrote in *The New York Times:* "Miss Summer has...built a real career for herself as both a singer and as someone pushing the formal boundaries of disco music even wider."

Almost exactly a year later, in December, 1978, Rockwell wrote of her again:

As a disco singer, however, Miss Summer has a genuine ability to phrase with conviction. The form may seem rudimentary, but there's a gift to projecting personality on top of such a strong, structurally rigid instrumental base, and Miss Summer's success suggests that critics may have been shortsighted or premature to ignore disco as they have done.

Still later, Rockwell said of Summer's "Hot Stuff": "There hasn't been such confident all-stops-out vocalism of this sort since the best days of Aretha Franklin."

And so Donna Summer closed the self-absorbed 1970s, which had shaped up as a period of self-expression rather than a time of communal activism. In some respects, the era set the stage for the next two decades; eras when the celebration of celebrities would grow even more intense, but also when audiences would still salute those divas who proved they could survive through times good and bad.

OLD STYLE
GODDESSES
OF GLITZ,
NEW SCHOOL
INGENUES
The 1980s

Glamorous and gilded, self-indulgent and frivolous: that might best describe the early 1980s. Indeed the first half of the new decade seemed swept up on a wave of optimism, especially in light of the resolution of the international crisis and domestic problems at the close of the previous era. When the United States found itself in the position of having to negotiate for American hostages taken captive in Iran in late 1979, President Jimmy Carter saw his numbers in the polls slide downward. Nor was his popularity helped by the dependence of the United States on foreign oil, which led to huge prices and long lines at the gas pumps. With the 1980 election of Ronald Reagan—and the release of the hostages—most in the nation assumed the bad days were over, and the good times were back in full swing. The press wrote of the return to elegance in the White House.

Within Black America, there were optimistic signs of social/political change. Harold Washington and Wilson Goode became the first elected African American mayors of their respective cities, Chicago and Philadelphia. Colin Powell was named the national security adviser to the president in 1987. Alice Walker and Toni Morrison were awarded Pulitzer Prizes for their respective novels *The Color Purple* and *Beloved*. Socially and professionally, this was also the age of the yuppie (the young urban professional) and then the buppie (the black urban professional), those eager-beaver corporate climbers, ever ready to network and grasp hold of the almighty dollar.

But with these high times, there were the low times too. As investors enjoyed a boom period with record profits, Wall Street was also rocked by scandals. As the wealthy became wealthier, eventually, a disturbing disparity also grew between the rich and the poor in America. In time, the 1980s would be dubbed the Greed Decade; the Reagan Era itself, a daydream decade—as mounting social problems appeared to go unattended and pushed under the carpet. Civil rights groups, which had opposed Reagan's presidency, saw cutbacks and cut-offs in government-funded social programs. Homeless citizens were seen wandering on the streets of America. The unemployment rate for African Americans, who constituted 11.7 percent of the population, was almost 17 percent. Before its end, the 1980s also turned dark and depressing because of a health crisis that had surfaced in the early years but for too long was ignored: the onset of a new illness, Acquired Immune Deficiency Syndrome, known simply as AIDS.

Again the divas stepped forward to touch on or answer the needs of their age. The outright political or socially conscious diva seemed a creature of the past. Curiously, no new-style diva—a woman coming of age within the era itself—appeared during the early years. Instead divas of past eras continued to exert a pull and power over the mass imagination. Could that have been a sign of some covert national insecurity, indicating that audiences (at first) were comfortable only with divas with whom they were already familiar? Some divas of the past were again symbols of survival—and also potent symbols of transformation: women able to reinvent themselves or to adapt to a shift in the national mood. Other divas were very much in tune with the era's fascination with wealth and power. Still others, especially those upcoming divas of a new generation, appeared to be optimistic heroines for this new age: soothing dreamy goddesses of youth and vitality who were hopeful signs that despite darkness and death and societal evasions, life continues on, indeed that progress somehow still can be made.

Regardless, early on no old-style star power proved as resilient and popular as that possessed by a woman who had been on the road and in the public eye since the 1960s. She proved to be the first great diva of the new decade, none other than Tina Turner.

Page 210: Janet Jackson.

Tina Turner:
Life without Ike

Tina Turner's emergence as a pop superstar caught everyone off-guard: the record companies, the fans, the entertainment community itself. Not that this diva was ever completely out of the public's mind. From the 1960s into the 1970s, she had become something of an entertainment fixture as she recorded and played dates around the country with the Ike and Tina Turner Revue. During those years, she was right by husband Ike's side and in the forefront of his whirling, twirling Ikettes. But in the 1980s, her public persona took on new dimensions that eventually made her a far more mainstream diva, the type of star known by people who had never bought one of her records. Her *story*—her life and woes and her determination to survive—also became an important part of her legend, which added a new layer of meaning to many of her songs. Deeply encoded in her life narrative was the theme of female endurance and resilience. Though Tina Turner never called herself a feminist, her story indeed might have been read as a parable for an age now concerned even more with women's rights and self-assertion and the battle against a type of social/marital oppression.

The story went like this. While the one-time farmer's daughter Anna Mae Bullock from Tennessee—born in Brownsville and reared in Nut Bush—had risen to fame as the professional partner of her husband Ike, she also had found herself brutally humiliated by him. Onstage, she was expected to be an energetic crowd-pleaser. Offstage, she was required to be a dutiful wife to Ike and mother to their children. Ike had never been easy to please. Anything could set him off: be it a performance that failed to meet his expectations or a meal not "properly" prepared. Or Ike might just wake up in a foul mood. Often he took it out on Tina. *That* meant physical as well as emotional abuse. Almost every aspect of her life, including her money, was controlled by Ike. It was even Ike who had changed her name. Once she had recorded the 1960 hit "A Fool in Love," Ike—aware that Anna Mae Bullock had become the focal point of his

group and a money-maker—had decided a different name would look better on the marquee. As a kid, he had loved the white jungle queens of the old movie serials. For him, they were wild women. Now he had his own wild Queen of the Jungle. Maybe not Sheena, but his very own *Tina* would work very well.

For sixteen years, Tina had lived by Ike's rules and his moods. But then, as she recalled, came the turning point on the July Fourth weekend of 1976 when the couple arrived in Dallas for a performance at that city's Hilton Hotel. En route from the airport in a limousine, the situation turned ugly when a foul-tempered Ike, who had struck her earlier in the day, struck her again, hard and fast. She fought back but was no match for him. "He kept hitting me, but I didn't cry once. I was cursing him out and I'd keep talking right back to him. He was amazed! He was punching me." She never forgot that the white Yves Saint Laurent suit she wore was soon bloodied. "By the time we got to the Hilton, the left side of my face was swollen out past my ear and blood was everywhere—running out of my mouth," she said.

With some hours to go before show time, Ike fell asleep in their hotel room. Then Turner did something Ike never thought she was capable of—and something she never thought she was capable of either: she walked out on him. All she had was thirty-six cents and a credit card. Making her way out of the hotel, she remembered that she hid in an alley to avoid being seen by his aides, and then walked across a freeway to enter the lobby of a Ramada Inn. There, she asked to see the manager. Explaining who she was and how little money she had, she asked if he could provide her with a room. He complied. She stayed incognito in the hotel. Without Tina by his side, the Ike and Tina Turner Revue tour had to be canceled. Ultimately, she would be held financially accountable for all the missed engagements. For a long period afterward, she struggled to get out of the marriage and then build a solo career for herself. None of this came easy. But her liberation had begun.

Returning to Los Angeles where she had lived with Ike, Turner stayed with various friends. Flat broke, she said the only way she could show her gratitude was by cleaning the homes of those who took her in. "I moved from place to place for two months, working my way at each one," she said. "I know how to clean. I moved junk and stored stuff away and put out the trash and cleaned cupboards and washed dishes and scrubbed stoves—because that was

Fearful of Ike, she carried a .38-caliber gun with her and was once stopped by a policeman in West Hollywood, who spotted it, and then hauled her down to the station.

Once her divorce proceedings began, she found herself in danger of losing everything, including her professional name. Ike Turner told the court that his principle asset was the "good will" of the name "Ike and Tina Turner," which he valued at $750,000. Finally, she settled, forfeiting property the

A young Tina Turner, raisin' Cain with the Ikettes.

the only way I could repay these people. I didn't have any money. I didn't have anything at all. So I paid my rent by cleaning."

Struggling not only to make a living but pay off the debts of those canceled bookings, she also had to provide care for four sons: her own son Craig; her son Ronnie by Turner; and Ike's two sons Michael and Ike Jr., all of whom eventually lived with her.

two had owned and just about everything else, including four cars that Ike kept. She held onto her writers' royalties for songs she had written—*and* her name. The divorce decree was made official on March 29, 1978. That same year she did her first post-Ike album *Rough*. When it bombed, the record company United Artists dropped her. Her debts mounted. The IRS wanted

$100,000 for back taxes plus penalties, which totaled almost $200,000.

For years, she worked long and hard to pay off her debts. In the beginning, she played just about any kind of date: be it a McDonald's sales convention; or the cabaret circuit in Las Vegas and Lake Tahoe, where she performed in glitzy, silver-lamé sequined costumes sensationally designed by Bob Mackie to make her look more like the typical Vegas kind of star. At the Venetian Room of the Fairmont Hotel (a hotel that such stars as Dandridge and Lena Horne had played in the 1950s), she performed songs like "Disco Inferno" for older audiences who were dressed in gowns and tuxedos. She also appeared on television on *Hollywood Squares* and *Donny and Marie*. Tina Turner now looked like a golden-oldies kind of star, good for nostalgia events and for middle-aged patrons trying to relive happy days from their youth. During this time, she found solace in her spiritual conversion to Buddhism.

Though Turner was often ignored by the mainstream media during this period, that was not the case within the African American community. The black publication *Jet* followed and celebrated her. "That's not another underground nuclear test in the Nevada desert rocking the buildings in Las Vegas," *Jet* wrote in its July 28, 1977, issue, "that's just Miss Tina Turner—have mercy—exploding like a bronze bombshell all over the state from Caesars Palace."

In her efforts to land a new recording contract, a turnaround occurred when she acquired a new manager, Australian Roger Davies. To keep her before an audience and to help get her out of debt, he booked a lucrative five-week tour in South Africa. Later she was criticized for appearances in a city where anti-apartheid laws were strictly enforced. Turner, however, admitted that at the time she didn't understand the political situation "beyond the basic fact that it was segregated." Having grown up in the segregated South, she had not thought much about it. Other tours followed in Australia and Southeast Asia. But most important, Davies sat her down and frankly told her that she had to redefine herself if she ever hoped to become a real recording star

again. Not only did Turner need a new back-up group and a different sound, she also had to adapt to changing times and refashion another look for herself. Out went the sparkling Bob Mackie costumes. Gone were the long straight haired wigs, eventually replaced by wigs with a shorter coif. Now she dressed in tight jeans. Or she wore short tight skirts that showed off her legs. When the new Turner toured abroad in London and parts of Poland and what was then Yugoslavia, audiences went wild. But she still was not back in the major leagues. Nor did the record companies believe she could click with a younger generation.

By the summer of 1981, Turner, who had not played New York for ten years, was booked into the city's Ritz, the hippest club in town. Turner recalled that her manager did everything he could to create a buzz about her: a full-page advertisement ran in the *Village Voice*, and arriving at the Ritz to see her was a lineup of celebrities—Andy Warhol, Mick Jagger, Mary Tyler Moore, Robert De Niro, even Diana Ross. The reviews were raves. When she returned to the Ritz a few months later, Rod Stewart showed up at the club, was dazzled by Turner's energy, and asked her to join him for his scheduled TV performance on *Saturday Night Live*. Together they performed a sexy duet of "Hot Legs." Not long afterward, she opened for the Rolling Stones at a New Jersey engagement and also performed a duet with Mick Jagger. Here Turner was reaching a rock-oriented audience that was young and predominantly white.

The record companies paid attention. But still she was a tough sell. Then Capitol Records, the company with the splashy building (shaped like a stack of records) in Los Angeles that it was once said that the music of Nat "King" Cole had built, began negotiations. But not until David Bowie went to see her perform at yet another Ritz engagement—and was accompanied by music executives—did Capitol send over the contract to be signed.

Turner began recording in London. There she could work with new musicians and technicians who used computers and

Ultimately, because of the autobiography and the movie, Tina Turner emerged all the more in the mass imagination as a woman who had overcome much and who indeed deserved her new fame.

synthesizers for orchestration. But after she recorded a new version of Al Green's 1971 hit "Let's Stay Together," Capitol turned it down. The song, however, became a huge hit in Europe, especially Great Britain. Imports made their way to New York where "Let's Stay Together" played in dance clubs. An inexpensive video version—shot with Tina and two backup dancers—ended with the two other women on the floor, each holding onto one of Tina's legs. Some viewers would see a lesbian subtext. But that simply added to its hipness. "Let's Stay Together" became a much-discussed hit. Finally, Capitol executives came to their senses and pushed for Turner to do her album.

On that album, *Private Dancer*, Turner performed the title number as well as a song she had initially balked at recording: "What's Love Got to Do with It." Not realizing that the song had been written expressly for her by Terry Britten, Turner said she "just thought it was some old pop song." As it turned out, "What's Love Got to Do with It" became her first number one hit and launched her amazing comeback.

Private Dancer arrived at a time when the charts were dominated by those androgynous monarchs, Michael Jackson and Prince, as well as hip-hop. Also now proving crucial to the music industry was MTV with its twenty-four-hour rounds of videos. In the youth-oriented business, Turner was a middle-aged woman. That no doubt had been a problem for those music executives who had stalled on recording her. Yet Turner nei-

ther looked nor acted like a middle-aged woman. When she did her Tina Turner strut across stage and in videos with those long legs, short skirts, tousled hair, and her high-voltage energy, she looked contemporary to the young. In many respects, Turner had updated, revamped, and re-popularized her wild woman image from the days with Ike: now she seemed more sophisticated, also more cynical and knowing, even more assured, at times projecting a kind of street-walker-chic image; a woman who knew her way around the block.

Her voice—rough and sandpapery—clearly had the sound of experience. Tough, alienated, and wounded by life, she was still moving on. Past songs like "Proud Mary" and "River Deep, Mountain High" clearly were larger than life; ferociously energetic; and flat out, indisputably brilliant. But now on *Private Dancer*, song after song—"Better Be Good to Me," "Let's Stay Together," "What's Love Got to Do with It," the title number itself—had a storyline and an emotional truth that was not always evident in her earlier music. Sometimes the new songs seemed to spring from chapters in her painful life. Perhaps the message was not that different from Ma Rainey's so many decades earlier: the idea of the experienced African American woman who had been everywhere and done everything and was now emerging as something of a hip Mother Courage ready to tell a new generation the ins and outs of survival.

In a decade that slowly was becoming darker and sadder with the rise of deaths from

AIDS, her rendition of "What's Love Got to Do with It"—on the record, on video, and in concert—had another kind of resonance and meaning; a mournful song for a mournful generation that perhaps saw itself as having been too cynical about love and sex. "What's love but a second hand emotion," she sang. "Who needs a heart when a heart can be broken." Love was something that a generation had believed—and perhaps still believed—couldn't be found. Nor did it need to be found. Was it not best to just live for the day without thoughts of a tomorrow? But indeed a tomorrow had come. Turner seemed very much in touch with the feelings and pulse of this new decade. Yet she still appealed to her old fans. Walking away with a Grammy for Best Female Pop Vocal Performance for "What's Love Got to Do with It" and Best Female Rock Vocal Performance for "Better Be Good to Me," she succeeded in a way that ultimately Diana Ross, though still a major player in the early to mid-1980s, would not be able to do.

What added to Turner's image and appeal—and what made the music all the more a *personal* narrative—was her life drama, which was soon told in the pages of magazines and then with the publication of the autobiography *I, Tina*. After whispers for years about her life with Ike, Turner herself stepped up to the plate and told all. Well, *almost all*. Other divas such as Billie Holiday with *Lady Sings the Blues* and Lena Horne with *Lena* had written about their troubled childhoods and the twists and turns of their careers. And in this decade a diva like Diahann Carroll would chronicle her experiences in the book *Diahann!* Though none would ever write a volume with the force and power of Ethel Waters's *His Eye Is on the Sparrow*, many of the new star memoirs seemed intent in presenting not only the star's story but also the determination to maintain an image. The memoirs of the women did not always separate fact from myth—but now far more of these books appeared.

Though Turner's book did not tell everything, *I, Tina* (co-authored by Kurt Loder) was often candid and surprising. Turner herself appeared on talk shows to promote it. The book made it to the bestseller list. Later a hit movie based on it, entitled *What's Love Got to Do with It* and starring Angela Bassett, made the Turner story even better known.

In the past, such black publications as *Ebony, Jet, Sepia,* and *Our World* had chronicled the ups and downs of black performers, keeping them visible for their African American audiences. That clearly indicated the importance of the black press not only to the Black Community but to the careers of certain black stars. More mainstream coverage of black stars had started in the 1950s with such performers as Dandridge, Nat "King" Cole, and Sammy Davis Jr. But *full* coverage did not come until the late 1970s and then most significantly, the 1980s. Turner benefited from this mainstream exposure as her face popped up on numerous magazine covers: *People, Rolling Stone,* and *Us.*

At the same time, Turner's duets with Rod Stewart and Mick Jagger, especially her performance with Jagger during 1985's *Live Aid* broadcast, seemed to depict her as an age-old white male fantasy: With her punked-out wigs, her bronze coloring, and her strut, here was a woman with a brazen, unabashed sexuality who could tease and taunt, tantalize and torment—and who was capable of providing forbidden pleasures: something of the highly exoticized and highly sexualized black woman that white males imagined they might have a chance of bedding. This same type of fantasy would lie at the root of the character Halle Berry played a later decade in the controversial film *Monster's Ball*. The twist that Turner brought to the eroticized fantasy (which *Monster's Ball* did not) was her own splendid control. Much like Baker, Waters, and other divas of the past, Turner's performances were built on the idea that she could be approached but never *had;* she sent out the message that in such a pas de deux as her duets with Jagger and Stewart, she called her own shots. (The same was true of her movie appearances in *Tommy* and *Mad Max Beyond Thunderdome.*) In some respects, she both embodied and subverted the old fantasy.

With Turner, the dichotomy of her on-stage performances and her offstage reality was surprising and at times amusing. The private Tina remained a devout Buddhist who prayed and chanted daily. The private Tina collected Chinese art. The private Tina also did not speak in the hip, casual manner one might have expected: instead in her television interviews of the 1980s and later, she enunciated every word in a very proper, exacting, almost stilted manner with a strange accent that at times seemed

be known that there was not one sequin dress in her closet. "I'm not that person," she said. "I don't even wear colors. My work is noisy, but my life is quiet."

In other interviews, Turner may also have surprised her fans when she spoke of her identification with the Egyptian Warrior Queen Hatshepsut. But a greater surprise may have been the identity of her ideal contemporary woman. "Above all other women, I have a queen," she once said, "and that is Jackie Kennedy Onassis. I love her and I

The woman—with the streetwaiker-chic image—seemed intent on creating a counter-image offstage, as if she were trying at all costs *not* to be the kind of exotic, earthy woman that audiences might have assumed she was.

forced. Not like Eartha Kitt's strange, vaguely European accent of the past. But rather like a grand lady in the manor on the hill. The woman—with the streetwalker-chic image—seemed intent on creating a counter-image offstage, as if she were trying at all costs *not* to be the kind of exotic, earthy woman that audiences might have assumed she was.

When *Architectural Digest* ran a spread on Turner's villa perched high on a hilltop above the French Riviera, it wrote of her "acquired European politesse." In her master bedroom, there stood an "antique carved armoire, an Empire-style chair and sofa and an Indian-inspired patienated bronze bed." "Decorating is a matter of emotion," Turner said. "I'm drawn to the old much more than the new." Turner let it

always will. I love her for her life, her strength, her education and for herself." Her ideal man: John F. Kennedy. "That's the [kind of] man I want. A perfect mixture of naughty and powerful." She once said her favorite movies were *The Exorcist* and *The Ten Commandments*. Who would have guessed? Away from the spotlight, not much about Turner was predictable.

Turner performed throughout the 1980s. Huge crowds turned out for her concerts. Another album, *Breaking Every Rule*, was released in 1986. Others followed in subsequent decades. When her popularity was no longer at its peak in the States, she remained a huge star in Europe. No matter what, the girl from Nut Bush—once she put her life with Ike behind her—retained her survivor skills and her worldwide icon status.

The one and only Aretha.

Re-inventing Themselves: Divas from the Past

Among the other established stars who held onto their careers and remained in touch with a new generation was Aretha Franklin, who had found herself on a commercial downslide in the late 1970s. Her albums were not brisk sellers. Critics complained that in her concerts she seemed detached from her music. Then after fourteen years, Franklin left Atlantic Records to sign with Arista. There, music czar Clive Davis set out to revitalize her career. In the 1980s, Franklin began working with new musicians. On her first albums under the new label—*Aretha*; *Love All The Hurt Away*; and the Luther Vandross–produced *Jump to It*—the old soulful blast was gone but now a more emotionally involved Aretha came up with a string of hits that were part rhythm and blues, part melodic pop. She transformed the rather plaintive "It's My Turn," previously recorded by Diana Ross, into a brazen triumphant tale of self-assertion. On the single "Jump to It," with backup vocals by Cissy Houston, Darlene Love, and Vandross, fans heard a playful Aretha, yet an Aretha totally in charge of her romantic situation. She also recorded a sexy, mellow version of "It's Your Thing." On the album *Jump to It*, the Queen of Soul also talked to her listeners, letting them know "Miss Re ain't playin' this time."

Working with producer Narada Michael Walden, she later recorded the album *Who's Zoomin' Who?* with a big hit "Freeway of Love," which became her twentieth single to reach number one and won her a Grammy for Best Rhythm and Blues Vocalist of the year. If any one single brought her close to a new generation, it was "Freeway of Love," along with her rousing duet with Annie Lennox on "Sisters Are Doing It for Themselves."

Having long sought a more glamorous image, Franklin also slimmed down, dressed in designer digs, and experimented with different hair colors. At one point, there would be a blond Aretha; at another point, a punked-out Aretha with spiked hair. As the press reported on her weight losses and gains, Aretha seemed unaware that her following could not have cared less about her *look*. What drew so many to her was, of course, still her voice and the ex-

traordinary emotion it conveyed. Many were still moved by the private Aretha who struggled quietly with personal issues and pain. Her greatest heartache grew out of the tragedy that overtook her family. Her father, the Reverend C. L. Franklin, had remained a prominent minister with a 4,500 member congregation at Detroit's New Bethel Baptist Church. Aretha, then living in California, called him three times a day. "She and my dad were very, very, very close," said her sister Erma. "She depended on him and his advice." Then in 1979, he was shot in a burglary at his home and fell into an irreversible coma.

Afterward, Aretha made near weekly trips to Detroit to see him. Said Erma: Aretha "spent over a half million on him, $1,500 a week just for nurses." In 1982, she bought a home in the fashionable Bloomfield Hills on the outskirts of Detroit. After remaining unconsciousness for five years, the Reverend C. L. Franklin died in 1984. A year later, Erma Franklin said that Aretha still couldn't "talk about it, not even with her own family. You can't even say the word 'death' around her. You have to say 'passed away' or find some other expression." A few years later she lost her sister Carolyn (who had written such Aretha hits as "Angel" and "Ain't No Way") and then her brother Cecil, who had managed her career and who Aretha called her greatest friend. For a woman known to let few people get close, these had to have been devastating losses. After six years of marriage, Franklin had also divorced her husband, actor Glynn Turman. During the 1980s, she was plagued by a paralyzing fear of flying that limited her tour schedule and led her to cancel or postpone other appearances. She eventually dropped out of plans to star in a stage biography of one of her childhood idols, Mahalia Jackson, as well as a proposed Broadway musical about Bessie Smith.

Other albums followed in the 1980s. So did concerts at which once again some critics felt the old Aretha had vanished. Reviewing a televised concert at Detroit's Music Hall Center, *New York Times* critic John O'Connor observed that she performed "on minimum voltage" and that she appeared "distracted and even sullen."

Donna Summer, a working woman's heroine with her hit "She Works Hard for the Money."

"Perhaps she just wasn't in a good mood that day," commented O'Connor, who added that very few of her signature songs such as "Chain of Fools and "Respect" worked "up the head of steam for which Miss Franklin is justly celebrated." Other critics had similar complaints. Had live performances lost their charm for her? Perhaps. Only on rare occasions did Aretha seem energized, such as during VH1's 1999 *Divas Live* broadcast, when Aretha, appearing with Mariah Carey, Celine Dion, Shania Twain, and Gloria Estefan, closed the show with a gospel number that brought down the house. Amid the competition, Queen Aretha was letting everyone see who was still the Queen.

Refusing to "sell" her torments to the crowd, Franklin still kept her personal life under wraps. "In an era of talkative tabloid stars and camera-conscious navel queens, Aretha, 43, guards her privacy even more carefully than her five-octave pipes," *People* commented in its October 14, 1985, issue. In its August 26, 1985, issue, *Newsweek* referred to her as "a storied recluse" who "rarely ventures out of her Detroit home."

Though seeming oblivious to what was said or written about her, occasionally she spoke out about the way she or her family was portrayed by the media. In response to an article in *People*'s February 23, 1985, issue, in which she believed her mother had been misrepresented, Franklin wrote that the article "was inaccurate and completely untrue with reference to my mother deserting her family. My mother was a responsible parent who talked to my father on a regular basis regarding our well-being. We spent every summer with her, and she visited with us as well. I appreciate your cooperation in correcting this."

Some years later, an obviously angered Aretha responded to an item by columnist Liz Smith in the April 30, 1993, edition of *New York Newsday*. When Franklin had performed while costumed in a special bustier, Smith commented: "Aretha must know she's really too bosomy to wear such clothing, but she just doesn't *care* what we think. And that attitude is what separates mere stars from true divas!" Taking issue with those comments, Franklin sent a letter that Smith printed: "How dare you be so presumptuous as to presume you could know my attitudes with respect to anything other than music," Franklin wrote. "Obviously I have enough of what it takes to wear a bustier and I haven't had any complaints, I'm sure if you could you would. When you get to be a noted and respected fashion editor please let us all know." Then in a P.S., Aretha added: "You are hardly in any position to determine what separates stars from divas since you are neither one, or an authority on either." The message being sent loud and clear was obviously that Aretha was not to be messed with! Smith's response: "Miss Franklin is correct. I don't know what she thinks. But she does have a lot of divine chutzpah to get herself up the way she often does. Her flamboyant taste in clothes is legend. I am certainly not the first journalist ever to comment on the same. Personally, I *prefer* somebody like Aretha, who says 'Screw you!' to fashion dictates and wears what she likes."

The new generation still had an idea of Aretha's mythic status. But as time moved on, Aretha's "story" would start to fade. Later generations would not readily understand what a great symbol Franklin had been in the 1960s. Yet her greatness remained potent, undiminished, and undeniable.

Patti LaBelle also reached a new generation. Having left the group Labelle in 1977 to perform solo, she had a hit single "New Attitude" on the soundtrack for the film *Beverly Hills Cop*. With her propensity to showboat as strong as ever, LaBelle looked as if she were not about to let anybody walk anywhere near *her* spotlight. She could talk non-stop, and just about everyone no doubt had the desire to tell her, "Enough already!" On the 1985 television special *Motown Returns to the Apollo*, she blasted her way through the evening and just about stole the show from Diana Ross. That was no easy feat. Ross herself may have been surprised by the unrelenting aggressiveness of LaBelle. But then maybe not. With her renewed energy, she told *Newsweek*, "When I saw Tina finally getting what she deserved, it *did* give me more confidence. I did think, maybe I can do that." Her 1986 album *Winner in You*—with her mournful duet with Michael McDonald, "On My Own"—put her back on top. Maybe a career for an old-time rock 'n' roll/rhythm-and-blues diva didn't have to end once she hit thirty. Or forty. Or older.

As Patti LaBelle worked into the next decades, her physical appearance also changed. With her almost over-the-top costumes and her high glam makeup, she sometimes looked like a different person. Maybe it was the spiked hairdo that made her appear *too* punked-out. Maybe later it was the super-straight brownish-red, near-blond hair (or wig). Maybe it was the fact that she looked as if she'd slimmed down or at least toned her voluptuous figure. Maybe it was something else. Rumors ran throughout show business circles. The face was beginning to look sculpted, so much so that she might have been mistaken for a member of the Jackson family. Finally, Patti LaBelle informed the press that she had undergone rhinoplasty: in short, she had a nose job. Recalling her early years when she had been teased by kids about her broad nose, she said, "I realized I wasn't a very good-looking girl." She added, "I didn't like the way that made me feel." Yet she did not want a nose that didn't seem true to the look of an African American woman. A button nose was out of the question. "Nothing drastic, just enough to make me feel and look as good as I could," she said. "If, in a few years, I want to get some more work done on my chin or neck, I will."

Once the new hits stopped coming, LaBelle made image adjustments. In the early 1990s, she played the overly chatty mother of the character Dwayne in various episodes of the sitcom *A Different World*. Later, she spoke openly about her battle with diabetes, became a cookbook author, toned down her personal style, and even curbed some of the notorious onstage showboating. In interviews, she was a rather maternal but still chatty lady eager to tell folks how best to live. In the new millennium, audiences would not forget her appearances on the daytime show *Martha* with domestic goddess Martha Stewart. Patti LaBelle seemed genuinely impressed with Stewart. Stewart was openly impressed with LaBelle, who was perhaps an idol from her youth. Together, the two were a very likable odd couple. LaBelle herself said they were like Lucy and Ethel, which of course was stretching it. But most significant was the remarkable shift in Patti LaBelle's image from the long-gone days of teen divas Patti LaBelle and the Bluebells. The one time girl from Philadelphia now seemed like a well-heeled big-city matron.

For Donna Summer, the 1980s proved to be a mixed bag of hits and misses and ultimately a dramatic change in the direction of her career. As disco's popularity faded, a surprise hit had grown out of Summer's observations at the Beverly Hills restaurant Chasen's. On her way to the ladies' room, she spotted an attendant who had fallen asleep. "I looked at the woman and felt a wave of sympathy. This poor woman had to be cooped up in the bathroom all night long," Summer recalled. "I blurted out, 'She works hard for the money.'" Summer scribbled the words down. "I tried to envision what her day-to-day life was like, how this must be her second job because she was obviously so worn out. In an instant I made up a whole life for her in my head, which became the basis for my song and album." Her single "She Works Hard for the Money" shot to the top of the charts. Did the sexy Bad Girl goddess of the 1970s have a pop social consciousness? Regardless, the song—and the rousing video that ended with Summer leading a street full of hard-working women—made her briefly a champion for working women.

But that was hardly the end of Summer's story in the 1980s. Following a bitter dispute and legal battle with music mogul Neil Bogart over her contract at Casablanca Records, she left the label and signed with David Geffen's record company. Now she no longer recorded with Giorgio Moroder, who had been the mastermind behind the distinctive Summer sound of the 1970s. Instead, Geffen teamed her with Quincy Jones for the album *Donna Summer*. Perhaps the idea was to move her more in the direction of rhythm and blues. But it was reported that Summer, accustomed to more control, clashed with Jones. Upon the release of *Donna Summer*, *People* called Summer "one of the most versatile vocalists in the

pop world." But the album failed to ignite the excitement of Summer's earlier work.

Summer herself appeared to be undergoing personal changes and re-evaluations. Later she revealed a suicide attempt that had occurred at the height of her fame in 1976. Suffering from depression over health problems and the breakup of her marriage to Herbert Sommer and still troubled by her hyper-sexy image, Summer, while staying at New York's Navarro Hotel, had tried to jump from a window but her leg had become caught in a drapery. A maid entered the hotel suite and talked to her. "I didn't know who I was in the business," Summer said. "I lost my freedom and my privacy." Afterward doctors discovered that a chemical imbalance had caused her depression. A few years later, Summer became a born-again Christian. She also married songwriter Bruce Sudano. The couple had two daughters.

As the 1980s moved on, Summer was no longer *the* hot music star. Almost shockingly, a rumor spread that alienated an important part of Summer's core audience, the gay community. Reportedly, Summer had commented that AIDS was "a divine ruling," God's punishment to homosexuals, who were "sinners." "Summer always denied she made the remark," columnist Liz Smith later reported, "but she never sued because the story just floated around—there really wasn't anybody *to* sue." But when *New York* magazine referred to the purported comment in its "Intelligencer" section in its August 5, 1991, issue, Summer did sue. At that time, Summer had a subpoena served on songwriter Paul Jabara, who had written her hits "Last Dance" and "Enough Is Enough," in relation to her lawsuit. Jabara was then dying. Summer's "persistence about prying more information out of Jabara—on his sickbed—stunned those close to him," wrote Smith. "But sentiment apparently meant less to Summer than clearing her name. . . . Jabara's friends say that the singer's 'unending, harassing phone calls and messages. . . were quite the most extraordinary behavior anybody has ever seen.'" Summer appeared desperate to prove the comment attributed to her was untrue. In 1991, she appeared at an

AIDS benefit on Fire Island. But by then, most felt it was too late and that the real decline in her career in the 1980s could be traced partly to the rumor. Of course, musical tastes, as always, had changed. Yet, just when women such as Tina Turner, Patti LaBelle, and Aretha Franklin had reached a new generation of record-buyers, Summer did not regain her position.

In the early 1990s, Summer moved from her home in the Los Angeles area. Spending more time at her 104-acre farm in rural Tennessee and at a home in Nashville, she looked as if she were relieved to be out of the constant hustle and bustle of show business. Still, Summer continued to perform at such unexpected venues as Trump Plaza in Atlantic City and the Concord Resort Hotel in Kiamesha Lake, New York, as well as Radio City Music Hall in 1996. Surprisingly, her 1970s hits became favorites for a new generation in 1990s. She released a live album in 1999, and VH1 aired her first televised concert. Summer also made a triumphant appearance on VH1's *Divas Live* broadcast in 2000. She wrote

the memoir *Ordinary Girl: The Journey* in 2003. Away from the glare of the spotlight, when asked to describe herself, she said: "Donna Summer, empress of herself."

But perhaps the most surprising career/image shift of earlier divas was with Lena Horne, still a gorgeous goddess at the top of her game. Over the years, Horne had developed all the more into being a shrewd song stylist. A hallmark of her style was still her mastery of lyric interpretation in which each word and sound were perfectly measured, calibrated, and thought-out. There was also her icy distance and detachment— with a suggestive underlayer of anger—that audiences found intriguing and appealing. At the same time, she appeared to have won a battle with time: looking magnificent, her glamour was undiminished by shifting trends in popular culture and changing fashions. But always there seemed to be something about Horne that was *unsaid* and left *unexplained*. She *intentionally* was not letting the adoring crowd know who she was, refusing to let the public get close

Still going strong: Lena Horne, star of Broadway's *Lena Horne: The Lady and Her Music*, backstage with Ben Vereen (left), Dionne Warwick, and Sarah Vaughan.

In 1981, Horne made a daring move when she appeared on Broadway in a one-woman show that traced her life and career titled *Lena Horne: The Lady and Her Music*. Because Horne was still known more for her beauty and classy style than anything else, theater-goers and critics alike may have wondered if she could carry a show by herself. Would her voice be powerful enough to keep the Broadway audience in its seats for an entire evening? Would the show tunes and pop standards that she had performed throughout her career still captivate?

All doubts were thrown aside once Horne made her entrance: from the moment the audience saw her, it knew the supremely confident Horne was completely in control of the evening. Horne's sound was grittier now, more seasoned emotionally, as she performed such numbers as "From This Moment On," "Can't Help Loving Dat Man of Mine," and "I Got a Name." Equally compelling were the moments when she spoke of her life, never revealing as much as the audience might have wanted, but revealing enough to make many think twice about who this legend was and what she had endured. Recalling her years at MGM, she explained her disappointment when the studio refused to cast her in the role of the mulatto Julie in the 1951 remake of *Show Boat*. She also commented on her singing style itself and performed two versions of "Stormy Weather": the first was the detached, but nonetheless affecting, way she had sung it in the 1943 movie; the second, a searing, earthy rendition that just about blew off the roof of the theater. *Lena Horne: The Lady and Her Music* was a glorious, soon to be legendary, evening in American musical theater history that was also a bona fide hit. Calling the show a triumph, *New York Times* critic Frank Rich wrote: "Not only have we heard a great singer top what we thought to be her best work, but we've also witnessed an honest-to-God *coup de théâtre*." He added: "For Lena Horne and the audience, the excitement is beginning all over again—right now."

At sixty-three, Horne appeared to be liberated. Newspapers and magazines clamored to interview her. *Vogue* ran a splashy color layout of Horne photographed by Richard Avedon. In some interviews, she talked more candidly about her past. "It's like looking at someone else," Horne said of herself during her MGM period. "She's young and dumb, but working because it's the only place she could work and feed her family. She looked like a little brown copy of the other leading ladies. MGM didn't want any blackness in those days, except in the role of being some native in the jungle or a loving, confidential maid. So, I was made into a kind of neuter. In the old days, I thought, really, that by being a good girl and minding my mother, it would open doors for others, that it would maybe do some good. I used to sing about things like the moon in June and airy-fairy sort of stuff, but I don't do that anymore because life isn't that way. My expectations are less fairy tale-ish now."

Of her husband Lennie Hayton: "He didn't see me as black, and I realized that that was part of my feeling this whole sterility. I suddenly wanted him to see how different I was. I wanted him to *feel* I was black. That he could say to me the day that Malcolm X was killed—'those radicals, they're always killing each other off'—as though I were another white person was like a blow. He didn't see that to me, Malcolm was a kind of hero. I knew it was wrong to feel that anger against him, but I was sick of being taken for granted. I was sick of conforming."

She also commented on that single eighteen-month period that had begun in 1972 when she dealt with the deaths of Hayton as well as her father and her son Teddy. "I let myself feel all that hurt and the hurt seemed to release me," she said. "Maybe it weakened me. It let me feel sorry for a whole lot of people and things I couldn't do anything about. When I finally woke up and realized there was only me and I was still awake morning after morning, I did what I had to do—I went back to work."

Diva stories, of course, are the stuff of legend, myth, fable, and parable from which an audience draws inspiration or a meaning that proves significant to its own lives. Yet Horne, like Aretha, refused to exploit these personal tragedies. Ultimately, her audience would have to draw whatever conclusions it chose from her life narrative. But that didn't matter. She was now a legendary diva in the ranks of a Josephine Baker.

Miss Ross: Über-Diva

Still going strong—early in the decade—was the über-diva herself, Diana Ross. Still a blazing visual creation, Ross became even more diva-like during these years: the hair was longer and fuller (a weave? extensions?); the gowns more elaborate and glamorous, harking back sometimes to the haute couture of the 1950s. Born for music videos, she worked well in the new medium, although for the MTV generation she was never quite its idea of a fresh contemporary star. At times, she was even something of an anachronism: accustomed to the perks of stardom and the adoration of her devotees, she had the air of a grande dame goddess from the 1930s or 1940s, who saw herself as being apart and above the general lineup of divas. That would always be one of the great things about Ross. Who could not respect, even love, her maddening haughtiness? But for a later generation, it would be hard to believe this nonstop glamour girl had come of age in the gritty and politically restless 1960s.

For a time, her career sailed along. Her 1980 Motown album, *diana*, went platinum with dance-crazy singles like "Upside Down" and "I'm Coming Out." Her "Endless Love" duet with Lionel Richie also hit the top of the charts. Her 1981 HBO special, *Standing Room Only: Diana Ross*, drew in cable viewers. But Ross grew restless. For years, she wanted to get out of Motown and from under the control of Motown founder Berry Gordy Jr. For a star like Ross, it must have been grating to constantly hear that Gordy had made her a star. Finally, Ross left the company to sign with RCA in 1981. Now she felt confident at controlling her artistic destiny. There were commercial bright spots. From her first RCA album *Why Do Fools Fall in Love?*, her single of the title song—a cover of the old hit by Frankie Lymon and the Teenagers—went to number one on the charts. Afterward Michael Jackson, who then idolized her, wrote the song "Muscles" for her—a rather campy number about a woman's desire for brawny guys. Most observers felt this hit single propelled her 1982 RCA album, *Silk Electric*, to the top of the charts. Otherwise the album—with mostly uninspired material—was far from being her best. Here were the first signs of cracks in her gilded armor.

During this time, in all likelihood her most memorable and publicized performance occurred on July 21, 1983, when some 400,000 gathered to see Ross perform a free concert in New York City's Central Park. Entering onto a special stage devised by master set designer Tony Walton and dressed in an orange sequined bodysuit with flowing chiffon scarf, Ross's glitzy, goddessy glamour was on brilliant display. But before the concert had progressed very far, the clear sunny skies suddenly turned dark. Ross found herself caught in a torrential downpour with thunder and lightning. Of the fierce wind that enveloped her, she later said, "I felt as if it was a parachute, that it was about to lift me off the ground." Yet true to her training in an old show business tradition that demanded that the show must go on and that if an audience, small or great, awaited you, you indeed performed, Ross remained onstage. "It's taken me a lifetime to get here. I'm not going anywhere," she told the crowd. "Reach out, hold your hands in the air. Are you afraid of the rain? I won't melt. Will you?"

Ross performed as long as she could, but the musicians grew concerned that their equipment would be destroyed. There was also a fear of electrocution. As the severe weather drove the audience out of the park, Ross knew her concert had to end. But she remained onstage, speaking to the crowd, trying to calm the group so there would be an orderly exit. "I was cold, shaken, yet unmoving," she later said. "I knew what I had to do. I took charge. I would be the last to leave after I was certain that everyone else was safe." It turned out to be one of her great public moments. The following day, news programs throughout the country carried footage of her performing in the rain. And photographs of her—drenched in her orange body suit, but triumphant with her arms stretched up to the heavens—ran in newspapers and magazines around the country. Ross returned that next day to give the concert again. It was a triumph. A year later, September 1984, she had a record-breaking engagement at Radio City Music Hall. The good times were still rolling.

But Ross suffered a great personal loss when her mother Ernestine Ross Jordan died of cancer—at age sixty-eight—in suburban Detroit. Its full effect on Ross may never be known, but a former employee would later speak to one of Ross's biographers of the singer's reaction: "That was the only time I had ever seen Miss Ross break down," the one-time employee told writer J. Randy Taraborrelli. "She tried to throw herself into her career, but she would dissolve into tears at any time. There was an older woman working in accounting whom Miss Ross seemed to like and, after Diana's mother died, she hired this woman to be a personal assistant. It was as if she wanted to be around an older woman who reminded her of Ernestine. It was very sad."

Ross stayed in the news. But the public still appeared to have mixed feelings about her. In the past, she had been linked romantically to actor Ryan O'Neal and singer Gene Simmons of Kiss. Some within the African American community read these relationships as a sign of a woman distancing herself from her roots. A comment attributed to O'Neal seemed to confirm such assumptions. When plans fell through for the two to co-star in a film titled *The Bodyguard*, O'Neal reportedly said: "Diana Ross doesn't want to show her body, doesn't want to do sex scenes on the screen, and doesn't want to be black." All of this was fodder for the gossip mill, which obviously could be important or detrimental to a star's image within the entertainment industry itself and certainly with the general public. Later reports surfaced of her infatuation with singer Julio Iglesias with whom she performed the duet "All of You" on her album *Swept Away*.

Then came her big romance of the era—
—and the great publicity that surrounded it. While vacationing with her children in Lyford Cay in the Bahamas in 1985, she met a wealthy Norwegian, Arne Naess, who was also traveling with his children by a previous marriage. Soon, the two were seen together. Eventually, they married *twice:* the first ceremony, a secret affair in October 1985 in New York; the second, a

widely covered public event in February 1986 in Switzerland. Other than her Central Park concert, this latter ceremony proved to be the event that Ross would best be remembered for in this new decade. Here she pulled out all diva stops. The February 17, 1986, *People* ran a cover story on the wedding ceremony that was performed—before 240 friends and relatives—at the 10th-century Swiss Reformed Church in the village of Romainmôtier. It was reported to have cost $1 million. Included in that estimate were a reported $50,000 for a Bob Mackie–designed wedding gown; $12,000 for the wedding veil; $10,000 for a 250-year-old diamond tiara; some $70,000 for security. A $15,000 first class ticket was also provided for a hairdresser, who was flown from Los Angeles to tend to Ross's locks. The cost for the limousines and buses to take the guests to the reception at the five-star Beau-Rivage Palace hotel in Lausanne, along with the cost of the caviar and champagne, totaled another $50,000. Ross herself headed for the reception wearing a satin-lined white mink wrap over her shoulders. Apparently sensitive to stories about her excesses, Ross balked at *People*'s million-dollar estimate. "How could anyone think I could spend a million dollars on a wedding," she reportedly told an associate. "They must think I'm crazy. Actually, it cost me half that much." It was said that her husband, known for being economical, to put it mildly, had refused to pay for the ceremony.

Regardless, Diana Ross had made a point with her extravagance. Here she was once again living out her dream, which she no doubt saw, without any irony, as a typically American one. The ghetto girl from Detroit was still living high, higher perhaps than her idol Josephine Baker, higher than just about any previous pop music diva in American history.

Settling comfortably into some semblance of domestic life, Ross and Naess had two sons. By most accounts, she was a dutiful and devoted mother. Her children also appeared (one could never say for sure) to understand her—and the demands of her career. But as the 1980s moved on, that career seemed to stall. Her later albums—

The diva herself: glamorous, optimistic, and always the center of attention.

Swept Away, *Eaten Alive*, and *Red Hot Rhythm*—proved disappointing and slowly, almost shockingly, her career slipped into a decline. Like many great stars—male as well as female, who are finally on their own—Ross had made questionable choices. She had no one to tell her "no"; no one to advise her, if it meant crossing swords with her, from staying away from lousy material.

Then too the music scene had started to change as it inevitably must. New stars were waiting in the wings. For a pop diva, Ross was now considered "older."

The Ross image was also paradoxically both buffed and battered by a major Broadway musical as well as several tell-all books. Opening on Broadway in 1981 under the direction of Michael Bennett with music by Henry Krieger and book and lyrics by Tom Eyen, the musical *Dreamgirls* was a dark, innovative production that featured a cast of newcomers who made names for themselves in the theater world: Sheryl Lee Ralph, Jennifer Holliday, Loretta Devine, Deborah Burrell, Cleavant Derricks, and Ben Harney. But what openly fascinated theatergoers was that the show's tale of three young singing hopefuls who form a group and are on their way to fame and heartache seemed to spring from the story of the Supremes, more openly than had the 1976 film *Sparkle*. At the center of *Dreamgirls* was its ambitious heroine Deena. In the mind of audiences, Deena naturally was Diana. Like *Sparkle*, *Dreamgirls* indicated how much the story of the Supremes remained a legendary part of the pop landscape—and how powerful an imagination the public still had about Diana Ross.

Then came the publication of the 1986 memoir, *Dreamgirl: My Life as a Supreme*, by former Supremes singer Mary Wilson. Here she detailed life with the Supremes. And while Wilson did not do a hatchet job on Ross, she clearly did not pull any punches either. Ross-with-warts was there on the page: everything from her battles with Florence Ballard, to her strategy for solo stardom, to her conflicts with other stars at Motown, to her relationships with Berry Gordy *and* the then-married Smokey Robinson. From Ross's point of view, this may well have been an act of supreme betrayal. After all, when Mary Wilson had fallen on hard times and was in need of a loan to buy a new home, it was reportedly Ross who wrote out a check in the amount of $30,000. Ross had also been godmother to one of Wilson's children.

There followed J. Randy Taraborrelli's 1989 biography, *Call Her Miss Ross*, which further detailed the Ross romances with the usual suspects—Gordy and Robinson as well as Gene Simmons. Also further revealed were her fierce rivalries with other Motown artists *and* her anger over the publication of Mary Wilson's book. Also explored was Ross's friendship with Michael Jackson, who had once worshiped her (*before* he met Elizabeth Taylor). The title itself came from a comment made by one of Ross's assistants. "Call her Miss Ross," the assistant reportedly informed other employees of the star. "Never, *ever* call her Diana. And never *Ms.* Ross. She hates that." More Ross stories were found in Mary Wilson's *second* book, *Supreme Faith: Someday We'll Be Together*, in 1990.

What emerged in all these books was a portrait of Ross as an ego-mad, fiercely ambitious, self-absorbed, headstrong, and sometimes ruthless woman who could be her own worst enemy. Ironically, Ross also appeared to be as prototypically an American heroine as, oddly enough, Scarlett O'Hara. These were shrewd, calculating women who were determined to live high and well; who had survived deprivation (Ross's being her seemingly impoverished childhood) to become at times heartless, even cruel. The American public found itself admiring of the drive and strength of the women yet ambivalent about, if not appalled by, the tactics the women seemed to employ for their own advancement and survival.

In some respects, the stories did not hurt Ross professionally. After all, this type of story had been whispered about for years. In the mass imagination, Diana Ross wouldn't be Diana Ross if she weren't aggressive and headstrong. So there was nothing new *there—except* that the stories were out in the open and had more credibility because they were in print—and were backed up by some fairly dicey details. Diana Ross was not a star who engendered much sympathy. No doubt with the belief that her side of the story *had* to be told, Ross took to print herself, writing the memoir *Secrets of a Sparrow* that would be published in 1993. Though Ross's book was not quite the self-serving tale that her critics might have expected, it was not an earthshaking revelation either. Instead the book was a tame retelling of her life and career, coming across as a portrait done in gauze, with all the telltale feuds, disputes, and rivalries ignored. After the juicy episodes in the other books, hers held little interest for readers.

By the late 1980s, Ross, though she hit the Top Ten with her single "Missing You," seemed to be struggling to get back on solid ground. For years, she ambitiously sought to play Josephine Baker onscreen. Researching her subject, she was said to have acquired an impressive archive of Baker material. Certainly, it seemed like the right role for her and one fitting her view of herself: here would be another film, like *Lady Sings the Blues* and *Mahogany*, about a poor girl—ambitious but vulnerable with the odds for success stacked against her—who propels herself to the top of her profession. But the proposed movie to star Ross as Baker never came to fruition. And surely, it must have been painful for Ross to see that a younger actress, Lynn Whitfield, later played Baker in an HBO television movie on the entertainer's life—and also walked away with an Emmy for her performance. As new music stars came to prominence and as Tina Turner staged such a highly publicized comeback, Ross—still known for her full body of long hair and her elaborate ballroom-style gowns as well as for albums that no longer sold—looked as if she might be passé.

For many, it was surprising that Ross couldn't manage a real comeback of some sorts. The TV movie *Double Platinum*, in which she played an international singing star who had left her young daughter to pursue her career, left viewers cold. The great fiasco occurred when she attempted a Supremes reunion tour in 2000. There was trouble right away. The *Los Angeles Times* reported that money became an issue. "Wilson and Birdsong balked, saying Ross' deal would have treated them like bit players in the project. Finally, according to Wilson, the two singers agreed to take $3 million each (compared to $20 million for Ross), but then Ross abruptly rescinded the offer." Both women declined to participate. Mary Wilson also let it be known that she had no desire to relive the past with Ross. Ross ended up with two other singers, Lynda Laurence and Scherrie Payne, each of whom had performed with the post-Ross Supremes. Briefly, the tour hobbled along. At Philadelphia's Spectrum arena, seats were noticeably vacant. Ticket prices had been high, with the top seats going for $250 each. Audiences grew disgruntled. Many observers felt that Mary Wilson, the

only other original member of the Supremes, had been treated badly. No one seemed to have much interest now in seeing a Supremes reunion without the real Supremes. It was the first time in decades that Ross actually needed the other two singers, Wilson in particular. The tour was finally canceled.

Despite the career lows, Ross managed to stay in the public eye in the later years. Though there may not have been interest in Ross, the entertainer, there was still an interest in Ross, the woman. Her divorce from Naess received media attention. Later he died in a tragic accident. Cameras recorded Ross's appearances at various events, Always, she seemed to enjoy the attention. She also seemed to thrive on the whole Diva Style. The press also recorded some of the unsavory events in her life. Much attention was focused on an incident at London's Heathrow Airport where a security guard claimed she had been assaulted by Ross. Dressed in "a black leather jacket, tight black leggings, lilac boots" with "purple highlights in her hair," Ross later explained that she had become frightened when the security guard had patted down her breasts "and between my legs" while frisking her. An angered Ross had then apparently decided she had had enough. "How do you like it?" Ross was said to have sniped after reportedly touching the guard's chest. It was then that Ross was taken to a police station and held for five hours of questioning, so reported the September 23, 1999, issue of the *New York Post*.

Around this time, rumors circulated that Ross had a drinking problem. Those rumors seemed to be confirmed in December 2002 when Ross made front-page headlines following an arrest for drunken driving in Arizona. The press reported that Ross had started laughing "as she bungled her field sobriety tests again and again. She couldn't walk a straight line, stand on one foot, tell the time or write the alphabet, which, according to her efforts in police documents, includes two Cs, two Ls, two Ss but no I or N." Most embarrassing was the police video of the arrest. Later Ross was incarcerated at a facility near her home in Greenwich, Connecticut. But the press reported that an

Sheryl Lee Ralph, who played the Ross–inspired character Deena in the Broadway hit *Dreamgirls*.

eyewitness at the facility said it "was one big joke. She had them running around, waiting on her hand and foot. She was ordering take out and had cops running out to pick up her food." The news reports admittedly were fun to read. But underneath it all was a sad drama. At the height of her fame, Ross had appeared perfectly in control of her life and career. Her discipline and focus were among her finest attributes. No one could ever have predicted that a time would come when she would appear to have lost that control.

Yet at other times, Ross seemed poised and mature. Whether this was a performance was hard to say. But when seen in television interviews, especially during one with Barbara Walters on *20/20*, she remained a fascinating and, often enough, charming woman and far more likeable than most were willing to admit. Her children appeared to be a great comfort to her;

the three daughters and two sons. By this time, Ross had also revealed that her first-born child, Rhonda, had not been fathered by Ross's husband (at the time) Robert Silberstein but by Berry Gordy Jr. The only surprising thing about Ross's revelation was the timing. Rhonda was a dead ringer for Gordy, and the stories that he was indeed the child's father had made the rounds for years. Ross did not disappear from public view. Like Michael Jackson, Sammy Davis Jr., and Ethel Waters, she would be remembered as one of the 20th century's greatest entertainers, in concert or on stage. New generations of divas viewed her as a glamour ideal and also as a diva ideal: a woman who was always most alive when performing; a star who would always be larger than life, standing above the adoring crowd that, like it or not, would somehow always look up to her.

Jennifer Beals.

Actresses: Slim Pickings

For African American film actresses, the era was clearly not the best of times. If audiences were looking for a diva film star in the tradition of a Dandridge or a Cicely Tyson or a Diana Ross, they'd be hard pressed to find one. Aside from Tina Turner's performance in *Mad Max Beyond Thunderdome*, there was Grace Jones as a campy villainess in the James Bond film *A View to a Kill*. Cast as willful exotics, neither portrayed the kind of real life women that movie-goers hoped to see. Alfre Woodard won an Oscar nomination for Best Supporting Actress of 1983 for her dated role as the servant to a white Southern woman in *Cross Creek*. Woodard also walked off with Emmys for her contemporary characters on television's *Hill Street Blues* and *L.A. Law.* Proving durable, she earned audience respect into the next decades for her performances in such films as *Down in the Delta* and *Passion Fish* and even played a highly unusual character on the TV smash *Desperate Housewives.*

Newcomer Jennifer Beals looked as if she were headed for stardom when she beat out actress Demi Moore (then unknown) for the plum lead in the 1983 hit *Flashdance.* As a young dancer trying to make her mark while working in Pittsburgh as a *welder* by day (only in Hollywood!), Beals's character—who was befriended by an older white woman (a kind of mother surrogate) and romantically involved with a handsome white man who just happens to be her boss—was without any clearly stated racial identity and lived in a world where race didn't seem to exist, except for some African American break dancers seen in the film. Mainstream moviegoers assumed the light-skinned Beals was a white actress. Yet while the film ignored her racial background, apparently the movie industry didn't. Once her racial background became known—she was the biracial daughter of a white mother and black father—her movie career seemed reminiscent of Fredi

Alfre Woodard in *Cross Creek.*

Washington's: Beals appeared to be too light for black roles; yet not "white" enough for big-time stardom. But there was a crucial difference in her social life: Washington was always identifiably black. Beals, however, was rarely thought of as being part of the African American entertainment community. In some respects in the next decade, the same would be true early in the career of singer Mariah Carey. Through the years, Beals found work in such films as *The Bride* and later *Devil in a Blue Dress*, in which she played a mysterious woman who is passing for white. Oddly, that latter film did little for her career. She had more success when cast in the cable TV series *The L Word.*

Making Whoopi

The most talked-about actresses midway in the decade were those who appeared in one of the most controversial films of the era, the 1985 *The Color Purple*, directed by Steven Spielberg from the best-selling novel by Alice Walker. Criticized for its depiction of African American men as well as its simplification of Walker's story, the film nonetheless was one of the few to focus on the tensions and inner conflicts of black women. In the cast were Akosua Busia and Rae Dawn Chong, along with Margaret Avery, who won an Oscar nomination as Best Supporting Actress of the Year. A newcomer, actually a Chicago talk show hostess turned actress, named Oprah Winfrey also won a Best Supporting Actress nomination. The film's other newcomer, Whoopi Goldberg, won a Best Actress nomination. Three black actresses up for the Oscar in the same year was an historic event. None of these nominees, however, won the award. But Winfrey and Goldberg garnered much attention from the press.

In the case of Goldberg—with the possible exceptions of Jackie "Moms" Mabley and Pearl Bailey—there had not been an African American comedienne who became so well known.

Goldberg's rise to fame had been a long time in coming. Born in 1950, she had grown up in a Manhattan housing project. Her mother was a Head Start teacher. Little was said about her father. Dropping out of high school and living a seemingly aimless life, she joined the fast-moving Village scene of the late 1960s, had a brief marriage, gave birth to a daughter named Alexandrea, then left the East Coast to go to San Diego. There, she lived on welfare for a time and did odd jobs, including a stint as a beautician in a morgue. She also appeared in the San Diego Repertory productions of *Mother Courage* and *A Christmas Carol.* Perhaps because of major shifts in American society and theater, Goldberg, unlike most divas who preceded her, did not begin her career within African American entertainment circles.

In comedy clubs, she performed in improvisational skits with a partner. Her career veered in a wholly different direction one evening when the partner didn't show up for an engagement in San Francisco. Goldberg was forced to perform alone. "The audience went bananas," she later said. "It freaked me out. I had never contemplated being a solo performer." Moving to the Bay Area, she appeared with San Francisco's avant-garde theater group Blake Street Hawkeyes. For a time, she also lived with a playwright-actor. But, mainly, she experimented with character skits that she would ultimately use for her Broadway show: an air-head surfer girl who finds herself pregnant and performs an abortion on herself; a PhD-turned-junkie-turned-burglar; a black girl who longs for blue eyes and blond hair. The moving and sad characters were, in many respects, influenced by Richard Pryor who had mastered the art of giving voice to the rejects of society: the winos, the numbers runners, the junkies. Goldberg's black girl yearning for blue eyes could also be traced to Toni Morrison's novel *The Bluest Eye.*

Goldberg created a one-woman theatrical piece, titled *The Spook Show,* which she somehow took to off-Broadway, no doubt aware that if she ever hoped to have a career that reached a wide audience, she had to win the New York critics. And she did. In the February 3, 1984, edition of *The New York Times,* Mel Gussow called her "a satirist with a cutting edge and an actress with a wry attitude toward life." Director Mike Nichols was so impressed by her performance that nine months later, under his direction, she opened on Broadway in *Whoopi Goldberg.* Working with the same material, Goldberg became a darling of the Great White Way. Yet not all the critics found her gallery of characters well-developed or particularly insightful. Frank Rich, who felt she showed comic promise, wrote nonetheless that

> a still-developing fringe-theater act has been padded and stretched to meet the supposed demands of a Broadway occasion . . . her jokes, however scatological in language, can be mild and overextended, and her moments of pathos are often too mechanically ironic and maudlin to provoke. At least twice, Miss Goldberg announces that she doesn't intend for her putatively threatening outcast characters to make the audience "nervous." How one wishes that such disclaimers were actually necessary.

Movie Comedy Queen: Goldberg with Sam Elliott in *Fatal Beauty*.

Nonetheless, Goldberg made great copy. Clearly, what helped was the seeming irony of her name. While the name Whoopi conjured up the image of a fun-loving, sexy free spirit, no one really expected to see a black comedienne with a "Jewish-sounding" last name. Consequently, when Whoopi Goldberg made her entrance, she had a ready-made laugh, perhaps at her expense. The name worked so well at getting her attention that for a time she kept her real name secret. "The name came out of the blue," she once said. "It was a joke. It's like Rip Torn." Finally, the press learned that she had been born Caryn Johnson.

Wearing what became her signature dreadlocks at a time when dreadlocks did not yet have widespread acceptance, Goldberg had a look that was new to the cultural mainstream. For younger audiences, Goldberg's dreadlocks were a cultural signifier/marker, much like the Afro in the 1960s. The dreads also contributed to the idea that Goldberg was announcing herself as a cultural force in American life: Here she was, by no means considered a conventionally "pretty" woman, who would nonetheless play leading roles and not be consigned to the sidelines; who was coming forward to comment on those, like herself, that mainstream society had ignored or left behind. Yet, ironically, because of her personality and the roles she ultimately played, her dreadlocks may have led to the mainstream perception of her as the oddball Other, ever ready to make people laugh. The political connotations initially associated with Goldberg's dreadlocks by black audiences were also soon neutralized. She never became the type of political icon that the Afroed Cicely Tyson had been in the late 1960s and early 1970s.

Nonetheless, Whoopi Goldberg was now on her way to stardom. But no longer could stars become huge well-known celebrities on Broadway alone. Instead, as everyone knew, Hollywood was the destination point. Yet was there a place in American cinema for the "unusual" looking Goldberg? A call had come in March 1984—around the time of *The Spook Show*—from director Steven Spielberg. "I'd like you to come and perform for me and a couple of friends," he reportedly said. In attendance to see her at Spielberg's private screening room in Los Angeles were such Hollywood heavy-hitters as Michael Jackson and Quincy Jones. Goldberg was a smash. She later said that Spielberg then told her he might be directing *The Color Purple* and that "it's yours if you want it." "My teeth caught cold," Goldberg said, "'cause all I could do was grin."

Telephone, Clara's Heart, Homer and Eddie, Sarafina!, and *Soapdish.* Some films cast her in unlikely roles. In *The Associate*, she appeared in makeup as a middle-aged white man. Surprisingly, she gave an adroit performance. In *The Little Rascals*, she played the mother of Buckwheat. Regardless, no African American woman in Hollywood history had played leading roles in so many features.

But *that* was not all she did. She also appeared on television—on seemingly *everything* from guest spots on such series or specials as *Moonlighting, Saturday Night Live, The Pointer Sisters: Up All Nite, The Arsenio Hall Show, The Tonight Show Starring Johnny*

A serious Goldberg in the film *The Long Walk Home.*

With her Oscar nomination and all the publicity surrounding *The Color Purple*, Goldberg became a nationally famous personality whose face peered out from the covers of such magazines as *Rolling Stone, Ms.,* and *People*, as she leaped from one film to another in the 1980s and the 1990s: *Jumpin' Jack Flash, Burglar, Fatal Beauty, The*

Carson, The American Film Institute Salute to Billy Wilder, The Muppets, The Nanny, and *The Roseanne Show.* She also played the recurring role of Guinan on the series *Star Trek: The Next Generation,* co-starred with Jean Stapleton in the short-lived series *Bagdad Cafe,* and played the lead in the TV movie *Kiss Shot.* Aligning herself with the hip, socially conscious Hollywood, she joined Billy Crystal and Robin Williams as the star of HBO's *Comic Relief* specials, which raised money for the homeless.

Ironically, because Goldberg stayed so busy, perhaps *too* busy, audiences may have grown weary of seeing her. Or they may have taken her for granted. Indeed, Goldberg had overexposed herself. Few things can be worse in Hollywood. Nor had she been be very selective about the films she chose to appear in. Most were dismissed by the critics, sometimes brutally so. In a movie like *Clara's Heart*, which cast her as a Jamaican domestic who nurtures an unhappy white woman and the woman's troubled son, the character sometimes looked like little more than an updated mammy. When *People* magazine selected its "Lows in Acting" for 1988, it listed the Worst Actress as "Whoopi Goldberg in *Clara's Heart*—a deplorable display of Oscar-begging histrionics."

The event that made headlines: Ted Danson, in blackface, with Goldberg at a Friar's Roast.

"Does Hollywood think Whoopi Goldberg recently arrived here from another planet?" critic Roger Ebert asked in his review of *Burglar*. "Sure, she looks a little funny, but why isn't she allowed to have normal relationships in the movies? Why is she always packaged as the weirdo from Planet X?" He added:

Films like Burglar *and* Jumpin' Jack Flash, *her previous film, will continue to be made as long as there are writers with nothing to say, agents with nothing to deal and directors who don't care what their films are about. But let them feed off each other. Don't throw Goldberg to those sharks. . . . Let's face it. Hollywood knows Goldberg is talented, but nobody knows how to handle her in the movies. She is a woman. She is black. She looks goofy. So, they take the path of no resistance. They ignore all of those realities about her. It is one thing to argue that casting directors should be color blind, but another thing altogether to cast Whoopi Goldberg in a role so impersonal that it could be filled by Robert Redford, Seka or Rin Tin Tin—all without a rewrite.*

Within the African American community, the responses to Goldberg were mixed. Many were respectful of Goldberg's talents in *The Color Purple*. But there was resentment of the way she so publicly embraced the film and its director while ignoring the controversy over its depiction of African American men. "To me, it's justifying everything they say about black people and black men in general: that we ain't shit, that we're animals. That's why this film was made," said one of Goldberg's most vocal critics, director Spike Lee. "And Whoopi Goldberg says that Steven Spielberg is the only director in the world who could have directed that film. Does she realize what she is saying? Is she saying that a white person is the only person who can define our existence?" Lee also criticized Goldberg's *acquired* blue eyes. "I hope people realize, that the media realize, that she's not a spokesperson for black people, especially when you're running around with motherfucking blue contact lenses telling everybody that your eyes are blue."

By the time the 1980s drew to a close, Goldberg almost looked like yesterday's sensation—somehow an ever-present has-been who was still working. Yet others hoped she would somehow find a decent movie role in which her talents would be spectacularly showcased. That happened when she appeared in the film *Ghost*, in which she was cast as Oda Mae Brown, a phony medium who enables the spirit of a

Goldberg and Danson, co-stars in the film *Made for Each Other*.

man (killed in a mugging) to reunite with the love of his life. Though Goldberg's character may have looked like another of her updated nurturing, mammy-like characters, she was undeniably *funny*. For her performance, she ended up winning an Oscar as Best Supporting Actress of 1990, becoming the first African American woman to walk off with the award since Hattie McDaniel fifty-one years earlier.

Goldberg was again a presence to be reckoned with. There were those signs of major stardom: a Barbara Walters interview (on Walters's pre-Oscar show on the night Goldberg won) plus something unprecedented—Goldberg was later signed to host the Academy Awards. In 1992, Goldberg also had a new movie hit, *Sister Act*. At the time of agreeing to do the follow-up *Sister Act II*, she was briefly, as she told the television program *Entertainment Tonight* on December 6, 1993, Hollywood's highest paid actress. Though she did not specify

how much she had been paid, she said she had "waited until they had to offer me a lot of money. I wanted them to. I wanted them to have to come to me." When asked why that was so important, Goldberg said, "Because I needed vindication. That point was made. It also made me the highest paid woman in the history of films, which I enjoy also. . . . One thing they will never change. For a little while, I was the Queen Bee." Goldberg may have felt compelled to assert her power and position in the industry at this particular time because only a couple of months earlier, she had found herself in the midst of a national controversy, stemming from an event in her private life.

From the time of her arrival in Hollywood, attention had been focused on her private life. In 1986, Goldberg had a brief second marriage to a Dutch cinematographer named David Claessen who was almost ten years her junior. At a reception for the couple, big name stars turned up: Mel

241

Gibson, Cher, Robin Williams, Carol Burnett, Barry Manilow, Dolly Parton, Penny Marshall, and Kenny Rogers. Not since the days of Sammy Davis Jr. had a black star seemed so eager to meet and mingle with as many big stars as possible, in a very integrated Hollywood in which she appeared to be the only African American in the crowd. Stories circulated about her interracial relationships with such actors as Ted Danson, with whom she co-starred in the film *Made in America*, and later Frank Langella. "Ted & Whoopi in Love" was the title of the June 7, 1993, *People* cover story. Some black moviegoers no doubt felt a certain alienation from this actress who appeared detached from the African American community. But Goldberg seemed oblivious to such feelings.

Then there occurred an incident that many were shocked by. In October 1993, Goldberg was to be roasted by the Friars Club in New York City. Among those on the guest list were: Michael Douglas, Tony Randall, Kirstie Alley, Mr. T, Matthew Broderick, Natalie Cole, Michael J. Fox, Robert De Niro, Farrah Fawcett, Chris Rock, Montel Williams, and Ted Danson. As was to be expected at a Friars roast, the jokes were fast and furious and sometimes off-color. But *not* expected was the appearance of Ted Danson, who showed up on the dais in blackface with exaggerated white lips and a black top hat, looking as if he had stepped out of a 19th-century minstrel show. Many in the audience were stunned by his appearance, not quite sure how to react. Then came his roast, in which he attempted to make jokes about race—and his relationship with Goldberg. "I was very nervous because my parents can be so stuffy and out-of-touch," Danson told the crowd. "But after Whoopi had done the laundry and dusted and finished cleaning up, I could tell my dad had warmed up to her because he offered to drop her off at the bus stop." Danson also reportedly punctuated his routine at various times by using the word *nigger.*

There was laughter. But many were uncomfortable. Others were outraged. African American talk show host Montel Williams stormed out after a few minutes. Arriving after Danson had made his remarks was New York City's mayor, David Dinkins, who was introduced by Danson (still in blackface). Later the mayor was informed of what transpired earlier. The nation was also informed. The *Daily News* and *New York Post* ran front-page stories. Mayor Dinkins issued a public statement: "The jokes today were pretty vulgar and many were way, way over the line. I was embarrassed for Whoopi and the audience and felt a tremendous sense of relief when it was over." Montel Williams sent a telegram stating that he "was confused as to whether or not I was at a Friars event or at a rally for the KKK and Aryan Nation." Goldberg herself was reported to have encouraged Danson to go in blackface and to have even helped him prepare his material.

In the October 12, 1993, edition of *New York Newsday*, syndicated columnist Liz Smith commented: "I am not black, so I can't claim to 'know' how some offended African-Americans feel about Ted Danson's blackface routine, or his repeated use of the word 'nigger.' However, Danson's very good friend Miss Goldberg, who certainly is black, *wasn't* offended. Miss Goldberg pointed out that the Friars roasts are traditionally over-the-top, vulgar, scatological tributes to bad taste and the lowest common denominator of humor. Perhaps Danson's donning blackface took the Friars tradition *too* far. Perhaps common sense on the part of both Ted and Whoopi—they discussed his 'act' beforehand—should have told them this was bad taste on thin ice." On October 13, 1993, *The New York Times* carried an editorial under the headline *"Manhattan Minstrel Show."*

Danson seemed baffled by the reactions. "I don't understand why the Friars are going through this," he was reported (in the October 11, 1993, edition of the *New York Post*) to have asked the dean of the Friars Club. "Did I do anything wrong?" Most assumed Goldberg would apologize for her part in the debacle. But apology was the furthest thing from her mind. When the Friars Club's dean publicly stated that he was "saddened by the racially offensive nature of some of the material," Goldberg criticized the Friars Club. "We were not trying to be politically correct," she told the *New York Post* on October 11, 1993. "We were trying to be funny for ourselves. We knocked Somalia off the cover of the New York newspapers. This is insane to me." In response to Montel Williams's telegram, she said: "Perhaps Montel's show is not doing as well as it could be and this was his way of drawing attention."

"Ted Danson is not a racist," said Goldberg. Black America appeared to collectively shake its head. Was Goldberg that far removed from the realities of racial attitudes in America that she could not understand why many were offended? In the past, when a diva like Eartha Kitt made headlines after she spoke against President Lyndon Johnson's war policies in Vietnam, she was viewed as a woman calling for a change in America. Goldberg, however, appeared to be a woman who was looking backward, not forward. "Ms. Goldberg, who helped craft Mr. Danson's jokes, says she's astonished," read *The New York Times* editorial on October 13, 1993. "But that's naive coming from a black person from New York City, especially a black person who plays with race the way Ms. Goldberg does."

Could Goldberg survive this type of controversy? Actually, she did. Goldberg remained a figure on the national landscape; she participated in major entertainment events, including another year of hosting the Academy Awards. Roles in such films as *Corrina, Corrina; Boys on the Side;* and *Ghosts of Mississippi* followed. So did television appearances. As in the past, the quality of those films and television programs was often negligible. Again she seemed to be accepting just about anything that came her way. Occasionally, she connected rath-er well with black moviegoers, especially when she appeared in a supporting role in the 1998 film *How Stella Got Her Groove Back.* And her comedic skills were on splendid display with her performance as Queen Constantina in the 1997 multicultural television production of *Cinderella.* At times like these, surely audiences were not only entertained but also felt a sense of loss because these vehicles were the exception to the rule of Goldberg's career moves.

Yet Goldberg—a woman of many faces—was not without her complications. Though she seemed naive or misguided on the subject of race, she appeared at other times, certainly for the liberal community, rather politically astute. She aligned herself with women's rights issues. When she returned to television as the star of her own series, *Whoopi,* in 2003, she took new swings at the political right in a rather daring and courageous way. Fans no doubt yearned for the series itself to match Goldberg's wit. Ultimately, the series ran into problems and criticism after Goldberg blasted the administration of President George W. Bush, especially at a fundraiser for then-presidential candidate John Kerry at Radio City Music Hall in 2004. Her TV series lasted only one season. And because of her political outspokenness, Goldberg lost her job as a spokeswoman for a weight-loss product.

Nonetheless, Goldberg remained a talented, intriguing personality, willing to speak her mind and to take a stand, no matter what the risk, refusing to be politically fashionable. Ultimately, there came to be a respect for her durability, that indeed, she held on as a presence from the 1980s into the new millennium, an accomplishment by anyone's estimation.

Talking Her Way
to Fame: Oprah

That other actress in *The Color Purple*, Oprah Winfrey, was certainly the most unexpected new presence on the national scene. No one could have predicted her extraordinary success nor her impact on the nation. Oprah Winfrey was a true cultural phenomenon.

Before *The Color Purple*, Winfrey was a personable young woman known for her work in local television. A graduate of Tennessee State College, she made a name for herself by first winning in pageants: the Miss Fire Prevention title in Nashville in 1971 and, the next year, the Miss Black Tennessee title. She also began working at a local Nashville radio station. Brown-skinned, full-figured, and with lively eyes and an eagerness to please, Winfrey's childhood photographs sometimes suggested a hidden sadness. Yet never was there any indication of the grand vision she had for herself—or the daring drive that led to her fame. By the early 1980s, she was doing the news at a television station in Baltimore and co-hosting a daily program called *People Are Talking*. Baltimoreans took to her almost immediately. The talk show had solid ratings.

Winfrey could have been content with this type of popular local career. But she continually strove to improve herself; indeed to be prepared for bigger things; and perhaps most interestingly, mainly to be as good as possible in Baltimore. Through her perseverance and her ambition she moved to an ABC affiliate in a larger city, Chicago. Again popular with audiences, she might easily have settled for her success here. Why not? She made a good living, was the toast of the town, and though it wasn't New York or Los Angeles, Chicago was not small potatoes. Winfrey even appeared to enjoy the city itself. With all that came her way within the next few years, she kept Chicago as her home base.

In Chicago on business, composer/arranger Quincy Jones happened to see her show. As one of the producers of *The Color Purple*, then in pre-production, Jones called director Steven Spielberg. He had found the actress to play the role of the battered but resilient Sofia. How Jones detected acting talent or even a screen presence from viewing her at this point on the tiny tube is anyone's guess. But obviously he had a sharp eye. Signed to do the film, Oprah, rather than giving up her talk show, simply took time off. Never would she be like all those other black actresses out there on the West Coast who, after one big role, hoped to find another, but mainly sat, waiting for the phone to ring. Not going Hollywood and sticking to what she knew best, the talk show, was the shrewdest move this very shrewd woman made.

Yet with her TV career, Ms. Winfrey played for big stakes. She succeeded in signing a syndication deal that carried her program into homes throughout the country. Her competition at that time was the daytime talk show *Donahue*, hosted by the popular Phil Donahue. She ended up demolishing him in the ratings. For mainstream America, she proved to be a dream come true: a thoughtful and patient woman, willing to listen to anyone's problems and able to dish out some sound common sense advice. In those early days, she seemed eager to comfort, never to be harsh, always ready to hug or embrace. And her appearance proved important too. Had she been a glamorous "lighter" ideal like a Lena Horne or Dorothy Dandridge, that clearly would not have played on daytime TV. The fact that she was heavyset also enabled her television audience better to identify with her. A talk show host perceived as any kind of sexual competition, let alone a threat, for those in her audience, would have found doors slammed in her face. Daytime audiences turned on the soaps for glamorous yet domesticated naughty heroines. But for talk shows, they demanded a certain comfort zone. Of course, true divas had to be larger than life. Winfrey, however, understood a broadcast television star (as opposed to a cable TV star) has to play it small and ordinary to succeed. Viewers don't want to turn on the set each day and be confronted with an explosive personality. They had to feel safe with her.

In time, Winfrey shared *her* problems with the public, whether on air or in interviews. There was the lonely childhood. Born in 1954 in Kosciusko, Mississippi, she once said she was conceived as "a one-day fling under an oak tree." Her father was twenty; her mother, eighteen. As a girl she lived with her grandmother—who "could whip me for days and never get tired"—and then was shuttled from Mississippi to her welfare mother in Milwaukee to her father in Tennessee. "I wanted to be a little white kid because they didn't get whippings," she said. "They got *talked* to." At age nine, she endured a rape by a distant cousin. Others had also sexually abused her. As a teenager, she was "starving to be pretty" and was in and out of trouble: she broke her mother's curfews, stole from her mother's pocketbook, lied, ran away, and once faked a break-in. On her show, she also tearfully confessed that, while in her twenties, she had snorted cocaine. What Oprah did not reveal, others later did. A family member—in a story in 1990 in the *National Enquirer*—informed those enquiring minds that a fourteen-year-old Oprah had given birth to a premature baby who had died. That type of disclosure as well as the others might have damaged another kind of star. But not Oprah. Hers was a tale of overcoming the worst kind of adversities; of not simply self-re-invention, but self-empowerment. In this way, she indeed did strike viewers as being larger than life; so did her extraordinary success ultimately make her seem like a woman blessed by the gods.

Hers was also a tale in which race was obviously a factor. For that reason, African Americans identified with her in a personal way. Yet in the politically conservative Reagan era, the racial components in Oprah's stories seemed to be generic ones of an earlier time. "She identifies herself first as a woman, next as a black woman, not at all as a black spokesperson," *People* magazine wrote in its January 12, 1987, cover story on Winfrey, "although she is in tremendous demand to be one. 'Whenever I hear the words "community organization" or "task force," I know I'm in deep trouble,' she says, adding, 'People feel you have to lead a civil rights movement every day of your life, that you have to be a spokeswoman and represent *the race*. I understand what they're talking about, but you don't have to do it, don't have to do what other people want you to do. Blackness is something I just am. I'm black. I'm a woman.'"

People added that viewers "have found in Winfrey a comfortable and unthreatening bridge between the white and the black culture. She is equally adept at amusing a black audience." That last comment proved significant and telling. To her credit, Oprah Winfrey herself never forgot race. And when it came down to it, she always exhibited racial pride. When she spoke of such African Americans as Maya Angelou (a role model for her) or Sidney Poitier, she beamed, wanting her viewers to understand the contributions of such black trailblazers. An admirer of novelist Toni Morrison, she did much to introduce an even broader audience to the works of Morrison. One of the most famous episodes of her program occurred in 1987 when she traveled to Forsyth, Georgia, where a group of white racists were marching. Still, for that mainstream audience, Oprah mainly seemed representative of someone who had overcome and was now free to live like any other American—a sign that America's race problem was a thing of the past; at the same time, mainstream viewers may have failed to understand the remarkable way in which Oprah was the exception to the rule of black life in White America. Oprah herself seemed rather clear-eyed about her exceptional position in American culture.

In time, her then-current problems were very much the type the general audience could sympathize with. Winfrey openly discussed her weight, openly went on diets, openly regained weight, and then openly lost it again. Her conversations with her best friend, Gayle King, became part of her public record. Her relationship with her beau, Stedman Graham, was also part of her ongoing narrative. Would he ever marry her? In time, even her wealth became part of her appeal. Winfrey understood that the audience members must never see her as being too different from them. So Winfrey, who soon became a millionaire, was depicted simply as a focused hard worker, which in all truth she was. The underlying message was that anyone could succeed if she, or he, too, worked hard and pulled her-

Winfrey's hit miniseries *The Women of Brewster Place* with a lineup of stars (left to right): Cicely Tyson, Robin Givens, Olivia Cole, Lynn Whitfield, Winfrey, Lonette McKee, Paula Kelly, Jackée, and (bottom) Phyllis Yvonne Stickney.

self or himself up by the bootstraps. In this respect, she was similar to those Diva Social Symbols of the 1940s.

Winfrey, the millionaire, also delighted in sharing her wealth, which made her wealth unthreatening. Stories were published of the Christmas gifts she gave her staff. On one occasion, she flew four of her female producers from Chicago to New York. Each was put up in a luxurious hotel. Each was handed $1,500 and given thirty minutes to spend it at the city's plush department store, Bergdorf Goodman's. Another $1,200 was provided for a twenty-minute spree at a leather shop. Time and money were also given for jaunts to a shoe store, then another store. All of this was capped by a ride in Oprah's limo in which each of the women was given champagne—and each was blindfolded. The blindfolds were not removed until the four producers had been led inside a furrier's showroom. Awaiting them was a feast for

the eyes: a dazzling array of fur coats. Each then selected the coat of her choice. Talk about office perks! Those employees loved it. So did Oprah's audience.

At the same time, when she attended ceremonies like the Academy Awards, she gave the public the vicarious thrill of being along for the ride. Dressed to the nines, Oprah always made it look as if she were star-struck and giddy over being lucky enough to attend the big events and yet remain unaffected and as ordinary as her audience. Never did Winfrey put on airs. Never did she appear to be a snob. At big glamorous events, she was, in the minds of her followers, a surrogate for them.

Early on, Winfrey also became so popular and influential that no one was willing to really *mess* with her. A Chicago columnist reported a rumor—first as a blind item—about Oprah and boyfriend Stedman Graham that went like this: Oprah had caught Stedman in bed with her hairdresser. Later the rumor spread—with embellishments, of course—Winfrey was said to have stabbed Graham with a butcher knife after finding him with her *male* hairdresser. Had it been any other star, the story might have appeared without any consequences to the columnist. But a coolly outraged Winfrey let it be known on her television program that the story was a "vicious, malicious lie and no part of it . . . is true. I have chosen to speak up because the rumor has become so widespread and so vulgar that I just wanted to go on the record and let you know it's not true." In the end, the columnist was fired. Though the tabloid press would report on Winfrey's weight gains and losses and various other aspects of her life, it would never really rake her over the coals. Oprah Winfrey in time became a rare thing for an American star: she was fundamentally untouchable.

By the close of the 1980s, Oprah expanded her power base—and her income. Her initial contract with King World—the syndicator of her show—guaranteed her twenty-five percent of the program's total revenues minus production and distribution costs. In 1986, she earned $2 million for the show; the next year, $12 million; the following year, $25 million. Then Oprah announced (or threatened) that she would leave the show when her contract expired in 1991. But before then King World renegotiated with her. Now she acquired ownership of *The Oprah Winfrey Show* plus control of production and a flexible schedule. Forming Harpo Productions (Oprah spelled backward) to produce the show in her deluxe $20 million studios, Winfrey became the third woman in history to own her own studio—Mary Pickford and Lucille Ball had preceded her—and the first African American woman to do so. From the show alone, it was estimated she might earn $45 million in 1989.

Realizing the need for stories about African Americans on the small tube, she also produced and appeared in the hugely successful 1989 all-star mini-series based on Gloria Naylor's novel *The Women of Brewster Place.* Featuring such stars as Cicely Tyson, Paula Kelly, Olivia Cole, Jackée, Lynn Whitfield, Robin Givens, Glenn Plummer, and Lonette McKee, the two-part, four-hour drama told the story of inner city women confronted with problems of race, class, and gender. Afterward, Winfrey produced a short-lived half-hour television series entitled *Brewster Place*, with characters inspired by the Naylor novel.

By 1989, the *Wall Street Journal* named her one of the twenty-eight rising stars in the world of business. Media analysts estimated that Harpo Productions was worth $250 million. In just four years, Oprah had gone from national obscurity to become one of the country's richest and most famous women.

Yet despite the fanfare, this seemingly very open woman who was willing to share so much with her adoring public was something of an enigma. Not like a Garbo or a Dandridge where one felt there was true mystery; where the fans strove to understand the complexities of an unfathomable goddess. Instead the most puzzling aspect, indeed the unspoken mystery, about Winfrey—and surprisingly something usually ignored by the media—was precisely what lay at the heart of her boundless drive and energy. There were no attempts to analyze her, to uncover what made her tick; to understand if there was something "deeper" beneath her public persona, if Winfrey was indeed as she appeared. Eventually, what Oprah saw in herself may have been less interesting than what the public saw in her, what needs she touched on or answered for those hordes of people who sat in the studio audience or watched at home. Nonetheless, Winfrey was only at the beginning of her extraordinary public journey.

Vanessa Williams.

Actresses on the Rise

Though the movies offered few starring roles for black actresses, television proved more fertile ground. In the early years of the decade, Shari Belafonte, also known as Shari Belafonte-Harper, was the television actress that mainstream media briefly seemed most interested in after she was cast in a supporting role on the series *Hotel*. She did not have much to do on the series. But being the sensational-looking daughter of Harry Belafonte didn't hurt. *Vogue* ran her

Nell Carter, star of Broadway's *Ain't Misbehavin'* and TV's *Gimme a Break*.

on its December 1982 cover: concentrating only on that fabulous face. Then *Vanity Fair*, which had resumed publication under the editorship of Tina Brown after having been dormant for several decades, selected her as its cover girl in May 1985. Perhaps had Belafonte been more aggressive or had she sought more challenging roles, she might have moved on to the movies and perhaps become a cinematic glamour girl. But it didn't happen.

Also winning attention was Broadway actress Nell Carter who appeared in a supporting role in the TV series *Lobo*, then starred in her own sitcom, *Gimme a Break*. When her previous Broadway hit *Ain't Misbehavin'* aired on television, Carter won an Emmy in 1982 for Outstanding Individual Achievement. Yet for all her talent, Carter found herself saddled with an updated mammy character in *Gimme a Break*, which in many respects was a remake of the old *Beulah* TV sitcom: the story of yet another hefty maid-housekeeper devoted to her white employers. Appearing with Carter on *Gimme a Break* was actress Telma Hopkins, who later worked on the long-running series *Family Matters*, along with such actresses as Rosetta LeNoire, Kellie Shanygne Williams, and Jo Marie Payton.

Robin Givens first sought to make her mark in the television series *Head of the Class*, playing so slight a supporting role that most were unaware of her existence. Instead Givens became famous because of her private life—as the wife of heavyweight champion Mike Tyson. The press had a field day with the two. Much attention was focused on their very different backgrounds: she was sleek, educated, and seemingly refined, a graduate of Sarah Lawrence, and for a time, so she informed the press, a grad student at Harvard. Tyson was the tough street kid who had fought his way to the top. By the time *Vanity Fair* revealed that Harvard had no record of Givens's ever having been enrolled there, her image had already changed from Ms. Refined to Ms. Golddigger. The media, with the help of Givens herself, then delighted in depicting her as a conniving, manipulative witch of a gal out to take advantage of a plucky but seemingly dimwitted lad. In this bronze tale of the beauty and the beast, Givens was the beast; Mike, if not the beauty, then her hapless victim. Givens's mother, Ruth Roper, was also viewed as a calculating mother-in-law from hell. There was sympathy for Tyson and disdain for Givens. Then, during an appearance by the couple on a Barbara Walters television interview, Givens revealed that Tyson had physically abused her. As she spoke, the champ sat next to her, say-

A rough life with the champ: Robin Givens and Mike Tyson.

ing next to nothing. That interview marked the beginning of the end of their marriage—and a dramatic shift in public perceptions about the pair, although Givens still didn't come across as anybody's dear little push-over. "Why Does Everyone Hate Me?" read the banner on *People*'s December 19, 1988, cover story on Givens. For a time, she shrewdly used all the publicity for her career advancement. Not only did she snare a lead role in the film *A Rage in Harlem*, but also a starring role in a TV vehicle called *Penthouse*.

In the past, those troubled divas that were hotly reported on by the press drew coverage because indeed—beneath the scandal—what had first brought them attention was their talent, be it Billie Holiday or Eartha Kitt. But Givens's fame indicated a new day—and a shift in the attention the mainstream media gave an African American woman. Now a black woman could become nationally known simply because of a scandal. No one really knew anything about Givens before the union with Tyson. Nor later did anyone seem to care much about her. Yet Givens, in a TV movie

like *Beverly Hills Madam* with Faye Dunaway and in the feature film *Boomerang* opposite Eddie Murphy, could be assured and skilled at crafting well-etched portraits of tough-minded, calculating young women very capable of taking care of themselves without being tied to a man. For mainstream audiences, though, her real appeal as an actress may have been that she showed little vulnerability. Underneath the surface hardness there seemed to be only more hardness, solid concrete. In the years to come, Givens's fling with actor Brad Pitt (before his stardom) would be discussed—but primarily within the industry. Otherwise, long after the dissolution of her marriage to Tyson, that marriage would still be what she was best known for.

Another actress embroiled in scandalous headlines was Vanessa Williams. As the nation's first black winner of the Miss America contest in 1983, Williams, then twenty, was as wholesomely American as one could envision. The night she won the crown was historic in another respect: the runner-up, Suzette Charles, was also African

American. Having grown up in Millwood, New York, the daughter of a father who was an arts coordinator for public schools and a mother who was a music teacher, Williams had been a student at Syracuse University. Upon assuming her Miss America crown, the pert and poised, well-mannered and sweet-tempered Williams—with her bright green eyes and beaming girlish smile—was obviously a symbol of changing racial attitudes in the nation. But the ground fell out beneath her when word leaked that Bob Guccione, publisher of the skin magazine *Penthouse*, planned on publishing nude photographs taken of Williams a few years before the contest. The photographs had been sold to the magazine by the photographer who had snapped them. Few wanted to believe the news. Contest officials met with Williams, who was obviously under tremendous duress and embarrassment. One could only wonder (and sympathize) how she informed her parents that indeed such photographs existed. Reluctant at first but with her poise intact, Williams resigned "to avoid potential harm to the pageant and the deep division that a bitter fight may cause." Suzette Charles then assumed the crown. The *Penthouse* issue with the very provocative photographs became the best selling one in the history of the magazine at that time. Talk about profiting off someone else's misery.

Most thought that was the end of the Williams story. "When I was Miss America," Williams said,

> I did an interview with Joan Rivers, and it was like, "Oh-my-God-you're-so-smart-and-you're-so-talented-and-for-once-we've-got-a-Miss-America-who's-got-brains-and-she's-got-no-hips-look-at-her-I-hate-her." You know, just very supportive and holding my hand, and then the pictures came out, and she was like questioning my moral character to get a laugh and that type of thing. I didn't know that as a comedian you

> had to sacrifice your own personal beliefs. Of course, I don't know what her beliefs are. I don't know if she was sincere the first time or the second time.

There were other problems. When Williams attempted to buy a New York apartment, the co-op board turned her down as an "inappropriate person." Director Tommy Tune was impressed by her audition for his revival of George and Ira Gershwin's *My One and Only*, but the widow of Ira Gershwin nixed it. "She said I'd bring the wrong type of audience into the theater," said Williams.

But slowly, she started rebuilding a career for herself, appearing in a small role in the off-Broadway musical *One Man Band* and working whenever she could. Never did she seem embittered, although the psychological toll it took on her will probably never be known. "I knew when everything was going berserk that one day when the dust settled people would see what I could do," she said. She was right. In time, she established a successful singing career, worked in leading roles in such films as *Eraser*, opposite Arnold Schwarzenegger, and *Soul Food*, and stunned New York theatergoers with her performances in the Broadway musicals *Kiss of the Spider Woman* and *Into the Woods*. Marrying her manager Ramon Hervey, who many credited with helping her resurrect her career, she became a proud mother. Later the two divorced, and Williams was married for a time to Los Angeles Lakers basketball star Rick Fox. Preferring a rather low-keyed life, she looked at times as if she wanted to walk away from the spotlight—but not from performing itself. She kept working and succeeded at something Robin Givens did not quite manage in the 1980s: she put the scandal behind her and ironically emerged as a much-admired woman. In the next millennium, she would win raves for her performance on the sitcom *Ugly Betty*.

Phylicia Ayers-Allen Rashad.

Sisters on the Tube

Two Houston–born sisters, Debbie and Phylicia Allen, who had been in show business since the 1970s, saw their careers take off, thanks to television. The daughters of a dentist father and an artist mother (who was a great influence on them), the sisters both graduated from Howard University. The younger of the two, Debbie, a slender, sexy dancer/choreographer, rushed to New York, worked with George Faison's modern dance company, caught the eye of the New York critics in such Broadway productions as *Raisin* and as the Latina charac-

Debbie Allen as Anita in the Broadway revival of *West Side Story*.

ter Anita in the 1980 revival of *West Side Story*. Performing the famous "America," she was a fierce nonstop inferno of pleasure, stomping up a storm, leaving theatergoers with their mouths open. For years, everyone waited to see her arrival at the kind of stardom that had long been predicted for her. Yet her career would stall at various points, then she would jumpstart it, only to have it stall all over again. Roles in Milos Forman's 1984 film *Ragtime* and in Richard Pryor's 1986 feature *Jo Jo Dancer, Your Life Is Calling* took her nowhere in mov-

ies. A part in Alan Parker's hyper *Fame* brought her some attention but mainly just led to a replay of her role in the television series *Fame*. Though she was known in the industry, major stardom eluded her.

Still, Debbie Allen was in better shape than her sister, Phylicia, who for years appeared to be struggling to find her way. An early brief marriage to a dentist in New York ended in divorce. The couple had a son. Afterward, more focused on her career, she appeared in such Broadway productions as *Raisin* and as an understudy for Sheryl Lee Ralph in *Dreamgirls*. But if she was known for anything, it was for being Debbie's older sister and then—with a second marriage— as the wife of Victor Willis, a member of the singing group The Village People. Supporting her career endeavors, Willis said that he spent $100,000 to produce an album she recorded, *Josephine Superstar*, a tribute to Josephine Baker. When the album tanked, plans for a second one were quickly dropped.

By then, no one expected much from Phylicia's career. But she won a role as the publicist Courney Wright on the ABC daytime soap *One Life to Live*. A year later she auditioned for a role as the wife of Bill Cosby in a new sitcom. The odds were against her. The part called for her to be the mother of four (later five) children, the oldest of whom (once the series aired) would be a freshman at Princeton. At age thirty-five, Phylicia not only was too young for the role, she also *looked* too young. But the chemistry between Cosby and Allen was apparent, and she walked off with the coveted part. Afterward, Phylicia Allen's world changed. So did her name. For a time, she was billed as Phylicia Ayers-Allen.

The sitcom, of course, was *The Cosby Show*, the groundbreaking weekly program that followed the experiences of the Huxtable family: father Cliff, a physician, and mother Clair, an attorney, and their children Sondra, Denise, Vanessa, Theo, and Rudy. Forever altering the image of African Americans on television, *The Cosby Show* shot to the top of the ratings and ran for eight seasons. Phylicia Ayers-Allen's Clair was a rarity for television: here was a modern portrait of a professional black woman who was also a wife–mother, who was intelligent, charming, sensible, commanding, and able to match wits with her husband *and* her children. Always maintaining her sexuality and her femininity, she could never be described as "brassy" or "sassy," the terms usually associated with forceful black women in TV series of the past. Here television moved away entirely from that longtime staple of black sitcoms: the mother as hefty, desexed mammy type. Part working woman role model (though she wasn't seen often at the work desk), part domestic goddess (though she didn't seem to do much around the house), her Clair was admittedly something of an idealized dream heroine. Yet Ayers-Allen always played the character realistically with a shrewd confidence.

Though such weekly exposure transformed her into one of the most famous actresses in the country, much about her life was kept private. Living in New York, where the series was taped, she was seldom seen on the red carpet or at the big events. True, that on a national broadcast of a football game between the Detroit Lions and the New York Jets, the former football-player-turned-broadcaster, Ahmad Rashad, asked her to marry him—in front of 40 million people. True, at the time she was hosting Macy's annual Thanksgiving parade in New York City and had to get to a NBC local affiliate where she said "Yes" via satellite. "I wasn't thinking about them," she said of the vast TV audience. "I was being proposed to." True, her name changed again, now to Phylicia Rashad. True, the media made some to-do over the wedding ceremony, which looked like a match made in entertainment heaven—at least *at that time*. Matron of honor was her sister Debbie. The best man: O. J. Simpson. True, magazines ran articles on her. Yet her face did not peer out from a wide array of the big magazine covers, as did those of stars like Goldberg, Winfrey, and Turner. And Phylicia Ayers-Allen Rashad never had a high profile offscreen.

Occasionally, stories surfaced that were at variance with her cool and composed Clair Huxtable image. "She ain't no Goody Two Shoes," her former husband Willis said. "I never watched the [Cosby] show. I have that much bitterness still in me." Reportedly smarting from a half-a-million-dollar divorce settlement with Phylicia Allen, which he said he had no way of paying, Willis informed the press that beneath her almost glacial exterior—"all the manifestations of peace"—there had once beaten "a heart eaten up with jealousy as Willis's singing career and Debbie Allen's acting and dancing career suddenly took off." Rashad's first husband, Dr. Bill Bowles, spoke up for her. So did her sister. Bowles said there was a rivalry but that "it's a healthy one." "Being an old track runner, if somebody shoots past you, you run that much harder to catch them," he said.

Phylicia Rashad rarely defended herself and at every turn appeared to back away from a public discourse about her life, which was admirable. Yet high visibility—and diva struggles or torment—can be important to an actress's shelf life and to diva status.

Once *The Cosby Show* went off the air, Rashad did not disappear, as do some stars of defunct TV series. She returned to what must have been her first love: theater in New York. She even performed in cabaret. When Bill Cosby returned to series television as the star of *Cosby*, he selected anoth-

Keshia Knight Pulliam also starred in successful TV movies.

er actress to play his wife but ultimately replaced her with Rashad, who stepped back into the old rhythm with Cosby as if not a day had passed. But her role didn't seem to give her space enough to breathe; mostly, she appeared confined to the sidelines. Once that series ended, she again did New York theater. As the star of the production *Blue*, she won notice from the critics and then had a rousing critical triumph with her performance as the mother Lena Younger in a revival of *A Raisin in the Sun*. For her wholly new interpretation of the character—still strong but with softer edges and a

Beauf, Tempestt Bledsoe, Keshia Knight Pulliam, and later, Erika Alexander (as Cousin Pam). And it provided new exposure for such theater veterans as Clarice Taylor (who had a recurring role as Cliff Huxtable's mother) and Ethel Ayler (who played an occasional role as Clair's mother). Of the younger actresses, Lisa Bonet proved to be the most visible. As Denise Huxtable—that poetic, dreamy, offbeat daughter—Bonet, thanks to skillful writing, managed to escape the kind of black teenager stereotype that TV was littered with. One wondered what kind of future was in store for her.

Changing the face of the sitcom—*The Cosby Show* with (top row): Sabrina Le Beauf, Tempestt Bledsoe, Malcolm Jamal-Warner, (bottom row) Lisa Bonet, Bill Cosby, Keshia Knight Pulliam, and Phylicia Rashad.

subdued power—she became the first African American actress to win the Tony Award for Best Dramatic Actress. There followed another celebrated role—as a 300-year-old matriarch—in August Wilson's *Gem of the Ocean*.

The Cosby Show also established budding careers for the actresses Sabrina Le

Cosby and the production company, Carsey-Warner, which had produced *The Cosby Show*, created a spin-off, *A Different World*, that starred Bonet in 1987 as a student at Hillman, a fictional Southern black college. During the first season, the quality of the scripts wavered. *A Different World* lacked the strong spine of *The Cosby Show*.

A favorite with younger viewers: *A Different World* with (top row) Charnele Brown, Kadeem Hardison, Mary Alice, Jasmine Guy, (bottom row) Dawnn Lewis and Cree Summer.

Appealing as Bonet was, she apparently grew restless and left the series. When she appeared in a blood-splattered sex scene in the controversial film *Angel Heart*, fans of *The Cosby Show* were shocked. Afterward, a partially clad Bonet turned up on the cover of *Rolling Stone* with a two-page spread inside of Bonet wearing nothing but a bracelet and a nose ring. Could that really be sweet Denise in that tawdry psychological thriller and those provocative magazine photos? In 1989, she returned to *The Cosby Show* as a grown up Denise, who now had the "acceptable" roles of wife to a young Navy lieutenant and stepmother to his daughter, played by Raven-Symone. But Bonet left the series again in 1991. This time around, Cosby appeared angered with

her. Glaringly absent in the final episode of the series, Bonet by then had married future rock star Lenny Kravitz (son of Roxie Roker of *The Jeffersons*) and had a daughter named Zoe. Later, she divorced Kravitz. During the post-*Cosby* years, she gave highly appealing performances in such films as *High Fidelity* and *Enemy of the State*. But this unusual actress never worked as much as she should have.

A Different World also proved important for Debbie Allen. Having found herself in the unexpected position of being overshadowed by her sister after years in the spotlight, Debbie Allen's career veered in a new direction. Aware of the lack of roles for African American actresses, Allen, while appearing in TV's *Fame*, directed eleven episodes of the series. Taking note of her skills, Cosby asked her to direct *A Different World*, knowing that the series needed a strong hand to get it into shape. At first, she turned him down to appear in the Broadway revival of *Sweet Charity*. When the musical failed to click, she accepted Cosby's offer. Under her direction, along with the producing strength of Susan Fales (daughter of actress Josephine Premice), *A Different World*

that she did not seem to want to be at the center of. At times, she could appear *too* extroverted (similar to Patti LaBelle), as if she didn't know when to *turn it off* and just relax. On the other hand, as the reticent Phylicia grew older, there was something of the *grand dame* about her. Could the down-to-earth Clair Huxtable now be taking herself too seriously? One might have thought that the Allen sisters would have been the modern-

A throwback to the days of *I Love Lucy, Amen* starred Anna Maria Horsford with Clifton Davis and Sherman Hemsley.

became a new type of show that thoughtfully dramatized some issues facing the young at that time: be it an episode that focused on AIDS or on the rights of women. Allen and Fales wrote episodes. Later, Allen directed episodes of the series *The Fresh Prince of Bel-Air* and was a producer of the Steven Spielberg feature, *Amistad*. She also choreographed the Academy Awards ceremony for two consecutive years.

The more outgoing of the Allen sisters, Debbie was ever ready to take center stage and never engaged in a public conversation

day equivalent of those beauties from the 1920s and 1930s, the Washington sisters, Fredi and Isabel. But perhaps because of a changing social dynamic and with the presence of so many other African American women on the entertainment scene, the siblings did not have the unique glow of those earlier women. Then too, television was not as receptive to high-flung, drop-dead allure as movies, nightclubs, and the old theater had been. Still, in the 1980s and early 1990s, the Allen sisters were the best-known siblings on the scene.

Following Lisa Bonet's departure, Jasmine Guy became the star of *A Different World*. She too played a wholly new type of character: her Whitley was a black Southern belle; a member of the old-guard black bourgeoisie; sometimes unbearably snobbish and condescending yet confident without any feelings whatsoever of being a second class citizen. Also featured on the series were such actresses as Cree Summer, Dawnn Lewis, Charnele Brown, Loretta Devine, Mary Alice, Karen Malina White, and Jada Pinkett. Always, the women of *A Different World* were far more interesting and developed than the male characters. And the series did not hesitate to make references to such stars as Katherine Dunham, Dorothy Dandridge, and Lena Horne. Its theme song was originally performed by Phoebe Snow and later by Aretha Franklin.

Such series as *227* and *Amen* also featured varied actresses. Created by Marla Gibbs of *The Jeffersons*, *227* focused on women living in an apartment building in a black neighborhood in Washington, D.C. Seasoned performer Helen Martin played the nosy Pearl while Alaina Reed appeared as the building's landlady, Rose. Gibbs herself played Mary, the sensible one in the group with a stable marriage and family. Hal Williams played the husband. Cast as Gibbs's young daughter was actress Regina King, one of the few child stars to have a successful career as an adult. King later appeared in such films as *Poetic Justice, Any Given Sunday, Ray*, and *Miss Congeniality II*. The sitcom *227* proved a breakout for New York actress Jackée Harry, known simply as Jackée. Curvy, busty, perpetually wide-eyed, giggly or pouty, Jackée's character, Sandra, was clearly a gender type: a comic, avaricious, man-hungry gal, constantly clad in tight sweaters, skirts, and dresses *and* constantly on the prowl, with not much else on her mind other than snaring a man, preferably one with big bucks. Black actresses had heretofore not played this type, which seemed to spring from the hip of Marilyn Monroe's ditzy-but-endearing heroines in *Gentlemen Prefer Blondes* and *How to Marry a Millionaire*. In another actress's hands (or hips), the character might have been insipid, embarrassing, and too dull-witted to keep viewers' interest. But Jackée, who infused the character with wit, had a wickedly winning way with a double entendre. The performance was strong enough to win her an Emmy as Outstanding Supporting Actress in a Comedy Series, and also established an offscreen identity for Jackée. Here it was apparent that while television was not the place for larger-than-life goddesses, it was nonetheless territory where stars could be born. Later, Jackée starred in the series *Sister, Sister*, opposite the twin actresses Tia and Tamera Mowry. She also directed episodes.

As the whining, easily rattled, perpetually girlish Thelma in the series *Amen*, Anna Maria Horsford also won a following. Almost as fabulously batty as Lucille Ball, she skillfully stole scenes from her co-star Sherman Hemsley (the one-time George Jefferson of *The Jeffersons*), cast as her lawyer father. That by no means was a small accomplishment. Hemsley was a master of comic timing and the double take, as well as frenetic energy. Also on the series were Barbara Montgomery and Roz Ryan. Watching Montgomery, no one would have imagined that she was an altogether remarkable stage actress with a searing power, born to play a frightening Medea. TV provided her with a steady paycheck—which no one could begrudge her—but never the great roles she was capable of. Horsford also had range, as was evident in her performance in

The Pointer Sisters and Bruce Willis.

the film *Street Smart* (opposite Morgan Freeman). Later, she returned to series TV in such short-lived sitcoms as *Rhythm & Blues, Tall Hopes,* and *The Wayans Bros.*

C.C.H. Pounder also drew well-etched characterizations on TV into the next century. And who could forget Holly Robinson (Peete) at the start of her career as Officer Judy Hoffs on *21 Jump Street?*

But for those aspiring to diva status, television was not of great help. The medium seemed to dwarf its actresses. In the mind of the public, the women of the tube were thought of as being ordinary folks down the street. (Yet it's hard to imagine neighbors like Jackée's Sandra or Horsford's Thelma.) Nor did the private lives of TV stars establish another kind of mythic persona for them. Perhaps the only African American star to keep her high-flung glamour intact

Diahann Carroll with Billy Dee Williams on *Dynasty.*

on the small screen was Diahann Carroll, who returned to series TV as Dominique Deveraux, the biracial sister of Blake Carrington on the hit nighttime soap *Dynasty.* Carroll was then publicized as TV's "first black bitch." She also guest-starred on *A Different World,* appropriately cast as the sophisticated, elegant, sexy mother of Jasmine Guy's Whitley.

As the 1980s moved on, in the absence of a new generation of dark divas, it looked as if white pop star Madonna had appropriated

the diva mantle that black stars of the past had traditionally been able to grasp. Anita Baker and singing groups like the still deliriously enjoyable Pointer Sisters, Sweet Honey in the Rock, and a new-style rap trio like Salt-n-Pepa caught the eye and ear of the new era.

Occasionally, an earthy, raunchy performer like Georgia-native Millie Jackson continued to be a fresh, invigorating presence, who delighted in her delectable trashiness. Mastering bawdy bluesy songs on her 1974 album *Caught,* Jackson sang, talked, and rapped about love and relationships in explicitly sexual terms. On the jacket of her mid-1980s album *Back to the Sh-t,* Millie posed on a toilet seat. Her underwear was around her ankles. Many radio stations would not give her music airplay. A knowledgeable business woman who wrote and co-produced some of her recordings, Jackson, for a time, even managed her career herself. Some might have yearned for an offstage raunchy hellion who carried on the way Dinah Washington had when she suddenly turned up as a platinum blond and ran through a series of husbands. But, oddly enough, the juxtaposition of the verbally flamboyant Jackson onstage with her rather sedate offstage lifestyle made Jackson all the more interesting and likable. In the 1990s, Jackson created a show for herself, *Young Man, Older Woman,* a collection of monologue and comedy bits with some dancing that played almost exclusively to African American audiences. By playing the black venues in an era when crossing over still was important, Jackson may have prefigured what was to come in the late 1990s and the new millennium when chiltin' circuit stage shows like *A Hard Man Is Good to Find* and personalities like playwright Tyler Perry (creator of the Madea shows) would be unknown for years to the mainstream while they amassed huge black followings and fortunes. In the long run, Jackson was not well enough known to the mass audience; her effect on the larger culture had not been significant enough. But if ever there were a root-a-toot-tootin' ethnic, gloriously funny, and funky diva, Millie Jackson was it.

Miss Jackson,
if You're Nasty

But another Jackson, Janet, that is, steadily—and tenaciously—climbed the ranks of mainstream stardom in the mid-to-late 1980s. Though still in her early twenties, she was by then a showbiz veteran. Born in Gary, Indiana, in 1966, Janet Damita Jackson was a full-faced, baby doll of a girl (the youngest in the famous Jackson family) who found herself thrust into a show business career without necessarily seeking it. As the Jackson Five, her brothers—Jackie, Tito, Jermaine, Marlon, and Michael—had become teen idols in the late 1960s and early 1970s, turning out one hit after another for Motown, always under the watchful, demanding eye of their manager father, Joseph Jackson. It looked as if Papa Joe had decided that all his children should be in show business, and in fact, at one time or another, all the Jackson children indeed were performers. The youngest of the brothers, Randy, later performed with his brothers when they were known simply as the Jacksons. After recording a one-time hit, the oldest sister Rebbie shied away from the spotlight. Perhaps aware of the payment that fame demanded, she was not willing to pay the price. Perhaps the most frustrated of all the children was La Toya who, despite her albums and relentless pursuit of stardom, found her career stunted at almost every turn.

In the early years, Janet dreamed of becoming a jockey. But when her father asked her to sing in a Vegas-style review with her brothers, those jockey dreams were about to end. Soon she worked regularly on such television series as *Good Times* and *Diff'rent Strokes*. In those early years, she seemed like a sweet kid, always hoping to please. Yet there was something about her that also seemed vacant, even lost. Some key spark or connection with the characters that she played was missing. She appeared to be following the script (onscreen and off) without much of an emotional investment. That actually worked to her advantage when she portrayed the child abuse victim, Penny, on *Good Times*. Viewers may have felt her Penny had been so damaged by life at such an early age that she could never fully bloom into adulthood, that a part of her

remained hidden or unformed. Still, it looked as if someone had hired her mainly because she was a Jackson with a name recognition that wouldn't hurt a show. On those early shows, though, Janet Jackson was always a professional.

At age sixteen, she started making albums—*Janet Jackson* in 1982, *Dream Street* in 1984—for A&M Records. But whether she had the drive for success was still open to question. The most interesting aspect of this phase of her career was a kind of passive-aggressive rebelliousness that was evident when, at age eighteen, she eloped with the entertainer James DeBarge of the singing group DeBarge. She had known him since she was ten-years-old. How her family responded to the marriage was the subject of countless rumors. DeBarge himself was reported to have referred to the Jackson family home as "The House of Fears." Certainly, the parents must have had their concerns because of her youth and perhaps for Joseph Jackson because the marriage might interfere with the track of her career. From the start, Jackson and DeBarge looked like two kids who had gotten in over their heads, unsure what marriage really meant, unsure of themselves as well. At the time, while she filmed the TV series *Fame*, her young husband was reported to spend his days in her dressing room *sleeping*. At night, he would be in the recording studios, working on material. No one could ever say exactly what had proved to be the breaking point.

Once the marriage ended, a transformation came over Jackson, who now focused intently and exclusively on her career, determined to become a successful recording artist. At A&M Records, the African American executive John McClain suggested she work with the young recording wizards Jimmy Jam and Terry Lewis, who were based in Minneapolis. Janet Jackson reportedly arrived in Minneapolis with a bodyguard and a girlfriend. Before long, the bodyguard was gone, and she was working in the studio tirelessly with Jam and Lewis. Never could it now be said that Jackson lacked discipline or drive. Nor could it be said that she was not willing to

Jackson first caught the attention of audiences when she appeared as Penny – a victim of child abuse – on TV's *Good Times.*

sacrifice whatever it took to become a major entertainer.

The result of their efforts was her 1986 album—appropriately and perfectly entitled—*Control*. Thematically, it held together splendidly. Its message was that Janet Jackson was coming out from under the shadow of her brothers, breaking free from the domination of her father, and now taking full control of her life. The first song of the album, the single "Control," opened with Jackson speaking: "This is a story about control / My control / Control of what I say / Control of what I do." Once she sang, she announced: "When I was 17 / I did what people told me / Did what my father said / And let my mother mold me / But that was long ago. . . / Now I'm all grown up." In the world of popular images, *Control* was the absolute right album for her at the absolute right time. Of *Control*, Jackson said, "There was an added pressure. A lot of people said, 'Ah, she's just running off her brother's success and it's not going to happen again.' That just fueled the fire. It made me try even harder just to prove them wrong." The lines between entertainment and reality had been skillfully blurred.

From *Control*, there were six hit singles, among them "When I Think of You," "What Have You Done for Me Lately," and the playfully insolent "Nasty," in which she informs a guy that her name is *not* Baby; it's Janet, *Miss Jackson*, if you're *nasty*. On this album, which sold some five million copies, she also perfected the kind of dance tunes that would play in clubs around the country and that would also dominate the charts.

In photographs, and soon in videos and concert performances, her appearance changed. The nose was more pointed; the makeup, less girlish and cute, more grown-up (but not too much) and seductive. She had also slimmed down, yet apparently, by her standards, not enough. For some time, she continued to work hard to lose her baby fat and dressed in jackets and dark colors to camouflage suggestions of weight. Now, though, she was all the more able to showcase herself as a breathtakingly stylized dancer, who executed unexpected moves, twists, and turns of the body and dizzyingly rapid twists of her head. Under the guidance of the young Paula Abdul, who choreographed four of Jackson's videos and who would soon have a music career of her own, Jackson looked like a good girl determined to have a good time. The good girl image would plague her in the years to come when she would work hard to discard it for a sexually more mature persona. But that indeed was then the essence of her persona. "Let's Wait Awhile"—a sweet girl telling her fellow to take things slow before "we go too far"—was the most affecting slow tune on the album. Of course, in the past, divas rarely came across as girlish innocents (with the exception of Florence Mills). But Jackson was one of the era's younger goddesses to usher in the image of the diva as ingenue, slowly making her way to womanhood to arrive at a mature sexuality.

A&M Records wanted a follow-up to *Control* in the same personal, quasi-confessional mode. The projected album, to be called *Scandal*, would focus on her family. Now there were murmurs of sibling rivalry between Janet and La Toya who—long thought to be Michael's favorite sister—had appeared in videos with him. Looking almost desperate for stardom and attention, La Toya posed nude for *Playboy* in 1989—and later broke ties with her family, going so far as to publicly criticize the Jackson clan and also to accuse her father of abusing both her and her sister Rebbie. "Lie. Lie. Lie," Rebbie was later reported as saying. "I've never been raped by my dad."

Informing the press that they were perplexed and obviously disturbed by La Toya's statements and behavior, the Jackson family never denounced or rejected her. Instead, the family blamed her comments on the influence of a new man/manager in La Toya's life, Jack Gordon. Despite the ongoing stories then (and in the years to come) that would depict the Jacksons as a dysfunctional family, Janet resisted the plans for the family confessional album. Eventually, such plans were dropped. Janet, however, recorded a single, "You Need Me," about a distant father. But she denied that it referred to Joseph Jackson.

Like Phylicia Rashad, she appeared to retreat from the type of diva stardom in which the public was permitted access to personal dramas. Yet Jackson obviously wanted the spotlight. It was almost as if she, like Michael, could not breathe without it. But that spotlight was usually desired only for their work or public appearances, almost never for their personal lives. Her contradictory impulses, however, may have taken a toll on her that few would ever comprehend. Other divas also would have such inner conflicts. Janet's silence about family matters as well as her silence about her private life added an element of mystery to her public persona. No one was ever quite sure what to make of her. When she spoke in interviews, she surprisingly still had a soft, very girlish voice, not too different from the speaking voices of La Toya *and* Michael. Had she not really grown up? Had the years of working in show business robbed her, as it was said of Michael, of the fun and joy of childhood? Of maturation itself? Stories also circulated that she, like Michael and La Toya, had undergone cosmetic surgery to have her nose altered. But no comments came from Janet. Nor did complaints come from her. She remained a girl-like blank—except for one rather blatant fact. Even at this early stage in her adult career, Janet Jackson remained ferociously ambitious. Whether she was trying to prove herself as a talent within a very talented, competitive family was anyone's guess. But her ambition, drive, energy, and concentration would carry her into the next decade to become an even bigger star.

Before the Tumult: Whitney Houston

Before the era ended, another young performer with a soaring talent and, in time, a private life that would fascinate her generation, was well on her way to full-scale divadom. A larger-than-life heroine with a soaring talent, Whitney Houston was the star that the 1980s had been waiting for. Many within the entertainment industry had watched her grow up. Born in Newark in 1963, she had a musical pedigree (like Janet Jackson) that set her apart. Her mother, singer Cissy Houston, who was a founder of the pop-gospel group Sweet Inspirations, had done backup vocals for such big name performers as Aretha Franklin, Elvis Presley, Chaka Khan, Lou Rawls, and the Neville Brothers. Whitney's cousin was Dionne Warwick. As a girl, she had seen her mother at work in the studio and was entranced. Her favorite singer was Aretha. "When I heard Aretha, I could feel her emotional delivery so clearly. It came from down deep within," said Houston. "That's what I wanted to do." The church also ran in her blood. Her mother sang at the New Hope Baptist Church in Newark, New Jersey, where she also hosted radio broadcasts. Whitney performed in the choir.

During these years, she occasionally performed backups with her mother. Immediately, there was much talk about her voice. Once when Cissy Houston appeared at a New York nitery, she introduced young Whitney to the audience and asked her to sing. No one knew what to expect. She looked like an ordinary teenager, certainly not like an experienced performer with a commanding presence. Then she opened her mouth to sing "Tomorrow" from the Broadway show *Annie*. Hitting and holding the high notes, she held the room captive. Without makeup, without glamour grooming, without any hype, without much more than her extraordinary voice and the presence to support it, she was right then and there, star material.

When she was fifteen, Luther Vandross wanted to produce her debut album. Cissy Houston, however, believed her daughter was too young. But in 1980, when Whitney was spotted at Carnegie Hall by a photographer who urged her to pursue a modeling career, Cissy agreed to let her daughter

sign with a modeling agency. Eventually represented by the Wilhemina Agency, Houston appeared in such magazines as *Seventeen, Glamour,* and *Cosmopolitan.* Still, Cissy Houston wanted Whitney to put her professional aspirations on hold until her graduation from the parochial school Mount St. Dominic Academy in New Jersey. Houston then received her mother's blessings to pursue her career. She could just as easily have returned to simply singing in the church. Black churches around the nation were still known for having outstanding singers with the talent for big-time stardom, but perhaps without the drive or desire to go farther.

No one could say for sure what would become of the very young Whitney Houston. No one, that is, except Arista Records chief Clive Davis, who had not only worked with stars like Dionne Warwick and Barry Manilow, but had also revitalized the careers of Warwick and Aretha Franklin. He knew how to develop talent, highlight it, and pump it up for major stardom. Davis understood Houston's talent and realized the marketplace was now ready for her.

In the past, great divas had benefited from the guidance and devotion of men who saw themselves as Svengalis and who, more often than not, fell hard for the women, often finding themselves dumped once the women were determined to control their own destinies: Josephine Baker had her Pepito; Dandridge had arranger/composer Phil Moore; Diana Ross had Berry Gordy Jr. and because of him, the entire staff at Motown. Yet all these women knew that it was *their* talent—and not the men who wanted to see that talent shine—that made them stars. Unlike other Svengalis, Davis did not fall in love with his protégé. But he was convinced he had a star in the making. Reportedly, he spent two years and some $300,000 in the studio to produce her first album. With a sharp ear for pop sounds, he carefully selected middle-of-the-road-but-destined-to-be-popular songs. He used his clout to have Jermaine Jackson and Teddy Pendergrass perform duets with her.

Davis also oversaw her contact with the media. Perhaps he felt she was not ready for some of the talk shows. Perhaps he felt it was best that she not be seen too much. In short, he not only crafted an image for her on records but also in interviews and concerts. Davis deserved credit for giving her a platform, for providing her with the right type of advice, for insuring her the right type of promotion. Yet he could never take all the credit for her stardom. That credit would have to go to Houston herself, who, no matter what her later feelings, wanted

Whitney Houston appeared at the right time. In the mid-1980s, as Michael Jackson's album *Thriller* climbed the pop charts, he launched a new day for black pop stars and altered the musical landscape. Now black pop performers received more radio play on Top 40 stations. With the arrival of MTV and later VH1, Jackson, followed by such other African American

She was the lady that guys yearned to talk some trash to—and who young women saw as a modern heroine to emulate. On all the videos, she exuded the vitality and optimism of youth.

to perform enough to endure the endless rigors of rehearsing, recording, and being groomed, dressed, coifed, photographed, and interviewed. Much like the young women in the girl groups at Motown (or like those at the studios in Hollywood's glory days), she was focused and disciplined enough to make whatever personal sacrifices that were required; and compliant enough to endure whatever publicity demands she might not have felt comfortable with.

Released in 1985, her debut album *Whitney Houston* was a mix of pop, gospel, and romantic ballads. Because the critics had already heard all the industry buzz about Houston, most expected more from the album and many felt it was too slickly produced, too calculated, without material worthy of Houston's extraordinary talent. "Blessed with one of the most exciting new voices in years," wrote *Rolling Stone* in its June 6, 1985, issue, "Whitney Houston sings the hell out of the pleasant but undistinguished pop-soul tunes on her album." Record buyers, however, couldn't have cared less what the critics had to say.

stars as Prince and Lionel Richie, appeared in startlingly well-produced and well-directed music videos, which also helped them find crossover success. Houston joined the group. Her album's singles "How Will I Know," "Saving All My Love for You," and "The Greatest Love of All" quickly landed at the top of the charts. The sexy, bluesy "You Give Good Love" also scored well.

Her videos were also popular. Walking onstage in "The Greatest Love of All" video, she seemed a transcendent symbol: a new era young goddess who made the song an anthem for ordinary, everyday young working women and also issued a rousing call for independence and self-reliance. Never did her sexually charged pop/bluesy ballads like "Saving All My Love For You" and "You Give Good Love" (or the video conceptions for the music) appear tawdry or *too down*. Eventually, *Whitney Houston* would sell eight million copies domestically and 14 million internationally, at that time becoming the best-selling debut album by a female artist in the recording industry's history. The album broke new ground in an-

America's celebrated pop princess, Houston, performs with her celebrated cousin, Dionne Warwick.

other way. For the first time in the history of the recording industry—during the summer of 1986—the top-selling albums on the pop charts were by three African American women: *Whitney Houston*, Janet Jackson's *Control*, and Patti LaBelle's *Winner in You*. Other African American women also moved up the charts: Sade and Anita Baker, whose album *Rapture* was a smooth fusion of jazz, pop, and soul.

At the American Music Awards, Houston was a five-time winner, including awards for Best Female Vocalist as well as for Best Album and Video-style in the Soul/Rhythm and Blues category. At the Grammys, she was named top female pop vocalist. She also toured to sellout crowds. When she appeared at Carnegie Hall in 1985, such celebrities as Eddie Murphy, Daryl Hannah, Nick Ashford and Valerie Simpson, and the city's mayor, Edward Koch, were in attendance. Onstage that night, she had the glow of the supremely confident. When the audience booed the mayor, Whitney admonished them: she told the crowd that wasn't nice. The crowd loved it. No doubt, so did Koch. A *People* readers' poll voted her America's Top New Star in 1986. At the

time of that first album's release, she was twenty-two years old.

In 1987, a second album, simply called *Whitney*, drew mixed critical reactions, with complaints again that the material did not live up to the singer. "Everyone who's seen Whitney Houston in concert agrees: She's got a glorious voice, agile and assured, able to combine pop's clarity with gospel's embellishment," wrote Jon Pareles in the June 7, 1987, edition of *The New York Times*. Yet he believed that instead "of finding (or demanding) material to reveal her individuality . . . Ms. Houston submits to pop formulas designed for lesser singers—and she executes them with good grace and little heart." But again record buyers—young and older—snapped it up. Here she also had another first for a female vocalist: *Whitney* debuted on *Billboard*'s album charts in the number-one spot.

Everything looked as if it would always be smooth sailing for Houston. With her fashion model looks, her poised demeanor, and her undeniable talent, she grasped the imagination of the public. Glossy magazines like *People* and *Us* ran her on their covers. Most publications were happy to promote the image so carefully created for her: the good, wholesome, family-oriented star. Here was a young woman who liked to watch television, play tennis, eat pizza (she was so perfect that she didn't have to worry about her diet), and remained close to her family. One of her brothers sang backup for her; so did her cousin. Her brother also accompanied her on the road. So did her assistant and closest friend, Robyn Crawford. The highlight of one of Houston's concerts was the moment when Cissy appeared onstage to sing "You Are My Dream" to Whitney.

Aware of the importance of maintaining Whitney's image, her parents were eager to discuss their famous daughter with the press, again stressing how unaffected she was by her success, how at heart she was a simple young woman with simple tastes. Cissy enjoyed informing the media that she selected Whitney's clothes. "The clothes are stylish, but still youthful," she told *Us* magazine in its August 11, 1986, issue. "I'd like to keep her a nice, pure young lady, you know?" Her father, John Houston, also told *Us*: "We laugh and we talk—we do the same things we did all through the years—except she is away from home more. But her whole thing is always to get back home. Cissy was the same way, and so was Dionne." Speaking of herself, Whitney told the magazine: "Whitney Houston is usually at home, resting, on the phone. Listening to music. Maybe playing some tennis. I don't go out to clubs at all—that doesn't thrill me. I guess I'm a normal twenty-three-year-old kid, young woman. I go home, take showers, brush my teeth. I eat. I sleep. Just like a normal human being does. I drive a car—well, sometimes I don't drive normal!" Cissy also publicly breathed a sigh of relief when she said that the press had never linked her daughter with any men. "Not yet, thank God," she said. "I don't want her hurt. And I'd like to let her grow up gracefully." Little did any of the Houston family know what lay ahead for the young star in the years to come.

Occasionally, the press suggested that Houston, who neither wrote nor produced her music, was not making her own decisions. But her father dismissed such talk. "She picks the lights and sets that she wants," he said. "And her voice and manner

are so impressive that there are times when she's actually more of an influence on what happens in the studio than her producers are." But in truth, the big decisions were in the hands of Clive Davis. Other matters were left in the hands of her parents.

This may be the key to understanding what would happen to Houston in the following decade. Even though she was still at the point in her career where she clearly valued what others suggested, here was a young woman who may well have felt everything in her life was too arranged, too choreographed, too stage-managed by others; here was a young woman who may have longed to break free, not out of resentment, but simply in a quest for self-definition, self-fulfillment. Indeed it had happened to those past divas—again Baker, Dandridge, Ross—with their magical Svengalis. All the psychodrama of Houston's apparent decision-making process would be a subject that millions would discuss or dissect, examine or explore.

For the public, the young Whitney Houston achieved true diva status. Even then everyone knew she would not be a fly by night sensation, that indeed she was here to stay. Aside from the good girl ingenue image, she projected a youthful sophistication and elegance that was now rarely seen. Unlike Tina Turner, who was the wise survivor—still gritty, still earthy, still a star with tough-minded street smarts—and unlike Ross with her magnificent show-biz star glitz, Houston appeared ladylike in a non-showbiz way. Her style of dress was closer to haute couture for the cultivated women of Europe. Here she seemed closer to Lena Horne and Dorothy Dandridge. In the 1980s, few film or new music stars captivated the audience as Houston did—which simply meant that in the decades to come her changing image would shock and compel the public's attention all the more

And so the 1980s closed with new era divas—girlish, sweet, innocent, and endearing—like Houston and Janet Jackson finally taking center stage. At the same time, those divas from earlier times were still able to hold new audiences spellbound with their work, their revamped images, and their personal odysseys.

Million Dollar Babies
The 1990s

During this new decade, as the 20th century drew to a close, the nation found much to be optimistic about and much to be troubled by as well. Early in the 1990s, a historic event occurred in Virginia when Douglas Wilder was elected, at this late date, the country's first African American governor. Nelson Mandela, the leader of the African National Congress, imprisoned in hard labor because of his political activism in South Africa, was finally freed and arrived triumphantly in the United States where huge crowds greeted him in such cities as New York, Atlanta, and Los Angeles. When he addressed a joint session of Congress on June 27, 1990, many of those students who had rallied against apartheid in the previous decade believed they were witnessing the birth of a new era that, in some way or another, they had participated in.

But the nation remained plagued by its now often unspoken racial divisions and tensions. At no time was that more evident than in March 1991 when motorist Rodney King—following a high-speed chase by the police—had been brutally beaten by Los Angeles police officers, supposedly for resisting arrest. Captured on videotape and aired on television, the beating of King shocked viewers around the world. When the four policemen (seen on the tape) were acquitted in April 1992 of any wrongdoing by a superior court jury in the Los Angeles suburb of Simi Valley, widespread rioting erupted for four days in Los Angeles's Black South Central section. The National Guard and federal troops were mobilized to restore order. In the end, there were some 38 deaths, 4,000 arrests, 3,700 burned-out buildings, and an estimated $500 million worth of damage. Authorities declared it had been the largest urban disturbance since the Civil War. Demonstrations occurred in other cities as well. Another highly publicized racial uprising occurred in the Crown Heights section of Brooklyn. After a Hasidic Jewish driver accidentally hit and killed a seven-year-old African American child, several days of rioting followed.

Yet another uproar of another type occurred after Justice Thurgood Marshall—the first African American appointed to the Supreme Court—announced his retirement after twenty-four years. In his final judicial dissent, Marshall criticized the conservative majority of the court for recklessly overturning decisions that had protected the rights of blacks and other minorities. When President George Herbert Walker Bush

Lynn Whitfield and Debbi Morgan, two of the striking actresses in Kasi Lemmons's film *Eve's Bayou*.

Page 270: Whitney Houston.

nominated the conservative Clarence Thomas, who had served as the Chairman of the Equal Employment Opportunity Commission, to replace Marshall, liberal and African American groups vehemently opposed him, including members of the Congressional Black Caucus. Then Anita Hill, a former employee of Thomas who was then a law professor at the University of Oklahoma, stepped forward to accuse Thomas of sexual harassment in the workplace. When Hill and others testified during the televised hearings for Thomas's confirmation, Americans sat riveted to their TV sets. A national debate ensued over the issue of sexual harassment. Eventually, Thomas was confirmed as the second African American to serve on the Supreme Court.

By the time, William Jefferson Clinton was elected to the presidency in 1992, defeating the incumbent George Herbert Walker Bush, the nation seemed eager for a change. When Maya Angelou composed and then delivered a poem at Clinton's inauguration, it called to mind that historic inauguration of John F. Kennedy when poet Robert Frost had read a poem. The new president appointed more African Americans to his cabinet—in such positions as Secretary of Commerce, Secretary of

Halle Berry with Eddie Murphy in *Boomerang.*

Lonette McKee with Wesley Snipes in *Jungle Fever.*

Energy, and Secretary of Agriculture—than any president before him. But by the time of his second term, the president's administration would be rocked by scandals and cabinet resignations. Clinton himself would be impeached. Yet he would survive politically and would retain a remarkable rapport with his African American constituency. Some would even dub him America's first black president.

And so the divas of the 1990s found themselves—at the dawn of a new millennium—performing at a unique time in social/political history. They offered the nation diverse messages. Some divas came to prominence again as symbols of endurance. For some African American actresses, it was a promising period. For some others, the 1990s proved frustrating.

In popular music, stars like Whitney Houston and Janet Jackson, among others, signed multimillion-dollar record deals. This indeed was an era of Million Dollar Babies. Some stars from the world of rap glorified in over-the-top luxurious lifestyles and in high-end brand names: Gucci, Versace, Louis Vuitton, all signs once again of the diva having made it to the heights of success as well as signs of unbridled materialism. Other rap/hip-hop/rhythm-and-blues divas, such as newcomers Mary J. Blige and Faith Evans, provided confessional messages in their music about personal demons and tensions.

Love triangle: Joie Lee, Denzel Washington, and Cynda Williams in *Mo' Better Blues*.

Actresses: in Search of Roles

Early in the 1990s, various African American actresses were able to work with a degree of success in the movies. Though critics often assailed director Spike Lee for his images of black women, his film *Jungle Fever* nonetheless provided some splashy scenes for such actresses as that feisty veteran Ruby Dee; as well as Lonette McKee; Theresa Randle; the underappreciated Tyra Ferrell; and two newcomers who would be heard from in the next decade: Halle Berry and Queen Latifah. Lee's *Mo' Better Blues* showcased his sister Joie Lee and newcomer Cynda Williams while *Malcolm X* featured Lonette McKee and Angela Bassett. Another film that presented a striking array of African American actresses was Reginald Hudlin's *Boomerang*, in which Robin Givens, Lela Rochon, Grace Jones, Eartha Kitt, Tisha Campbell, and Halle Berry appeared.

At the same time, director Julie Dash became one of the first African American women to join the ranks of feature film directors with *Daughters of the Dust*, which spotlighted such African American actresses as Alva Rogers, Barbara-O, Cora Lee Day, Cheryl Lynn Bruce, Geraldine Dunston, Kaycee Moore, Eartha Robinson, and Vertamae Grosvenor, all in demanding, complex roles that challenged earlier con-

Nia Long with Mekhi Phifer in the family drama *Soul Food.*

ceptions of black women in the movies. Later, Kasi Lemmons's *Eve's Bayou* sought to examine familial tensions within an African American home with such actresses as Lynn Whitfield, the dazzling Debbi Morgan, Jurnee Smollette, Meagan Good, Ethel Ayler, Lisa Nicole Carson, and Diahann Carroll. Leslie Harris's *Just Another Girl on the I.R.T.* featured Ariyan Johnson as a seventeen-year-old Brooklyn girl whose dreams of college are altered when she discovers herself pregnant.

The fact that these films were directed by African Americans, especially African American women, was a statement unto itself of the importance of black filmmakers who could infuse and invigorate American cinema with themes and talent—and striking female characters—which otherwise might have gone unnoticed or unexplored. The actresses themselves gave alternately complicated and clever performances. Yet few were able to go beyond the film roles and reach audiences in another, more personalized way.

The underrated Tyra Ferrell with Wesley Snipes, Woody Harrelson, and Rosie Perez in *White Men Can't Jump.*

Angela Bassett: the Long Road to Stardom

In the early 1990s, however, one film actress emerged who captured the imagination of viewers onscreen and—at times—offscreen with a distinct image: that of a talented, serious African American actress in search of significant roles. Nothing *that* new about the image. In past eras, Fredi Washington, Dorothy Dandridge, and Cicely Tyson had faced the same problem. But Angela Bassett gave it a 1990s-style twist.

Born in New York in 1958, she had grown up in St. Petersburg, Florida, in a single-parent household, and for a time as a child, had lived on welfare. Her dream was

along on both the East and West Coasts in *The Cosby Show; Spenser: For Hire; 227; Tour of Duty;* and *thirtysomething*. Yet still unknown with an uncertain future, she moved to Los Angeles in 1988. Perhaps here she would find steady employment. Perhaps here she would get to work in films.

Bassett may have wondered how she could compete in Hollywood. She turned thirty the year she moved, which can be a difficult time for a film or television actress who has not yet found a career-defining role. By Hollywood's rigid gender standards, a woman who was thirty-five was practical-

Hardly an actress known for emotional restraint, Bassett nonetheless pulled back, delicately measuring each line of dialogue, each moment of screen time. In a supremely sweet moment of black sisterhood onscreen, she and Alfre Woodard meshed beautifully.

to be a pediatrician. Early on though, she was inspired by a recording of poems by Langston Hughes, read by Ossie Davis and Ruby Dee. Then in 1973, she sat mesmerized by a stage performance of James Earl Jones in *Of Mice and Men* in Washington, D.C. That persuaded her that she *had* to become an actress. In 1983, she acquired a Masters of Fine Arts from Yale's drama school.

Moving to a third floor walk-up on 105th Street and Central Park West in New York City, Bassett spent the next five years working in the theater. Off-Broadway she portrayed Antigone. On Broadway, she played roles in the August Wilson dramas *Ma Rainey's Black Bottom* and *Joe Turner's Come and Gone*. Occasionally, television work came

ly over the hill. Though she was striking with dark, almond shaped eyes, dramatic high cheekbones, a sensual month, and a lush deep brown color, it would take Hollywood some time before it fully recognized just how stunning she was. Her most distinguishing characteristic was her voice: melodious with the sounds of the cultivated Black South. Each syllable, vowel, and consonant seemed to be weighed; each phrase pronounced with a rhythmic flow. Highly charismatic, she was also able to draw attention in part because of her bearing and in part because of her inner fire. Even before she was a star, Angela Bassett was a *presence*. Yet despite her assets, she had to take odd jobs to support herself. A low point occurred when she worked in a beauty salon. "That was hell," she said. "I was like, I didn't go to Yale drama school to answer phones."

She may also have felt that she hadn't gone to Yale's drama school to play some of the roles she eventually found: on such TV programs as *Alien Nation, Perry Mason: The Case of the Silenced Singer*, and a string of forgettable programs such as *The Flash, Nightmare Cafe*, and *Family of Spies*. Her most important film credit was as a flight attendant in the Arnold Schwarzenegger comedy *Kindergarten Cop*. Yet very early, she won the respect of her colleagues in the industry. Budding directors knew they wanted someday to work with her. So too did young actors on the rise.

A break came when John Singleton, making his feature film directorial debut, cast her as the young divorced mother Reva Devereaux in the 1991 *Boyz N the Hood*. Portraying a mother who feels she cannot raise her son on her own and sends him to live with his father, she no doubt realized there were holes in the part. Many single African American women had successfully raised sons. Yet in all likelihood, Bassett also understood that Singleton was determined to make a film that expressed his belief that black men must live up to their responsibilities as fathers. Throughout she projected a contemporary sensibility: that of a professional African American woman, keenly aware of racial/social pressures. Thought vulnerable, she was also aware of the importance of maintaining her own strength. Throughout, she had the weighty presence that film demands of a star.

Director John Sayles also took note of her and cast her first in 1991 in *City of Hope* and then in 1992 in *Passion Fish*, which starred Alfre Woodard. A signal moment occurred in a scene that brought Woodard and Bassett together. Woodard was obviously nobody's slouch. Bassett could easily go unnoticed. If she tried too hard, it might look like a dramatic slugfest between the two women, which would throw the scene and perhaps the film off-balance. Both actresses played the scene perfectly, and the understated Bassett did not go unnoticed. She went on to play Katherine Jackson in

the 1992 TV drama on the Jackson Five titled *The Jacksons: An American Dream* and then portrayed Betty Shabazz opposite Denzel Washington in Spike Lee's *Malcolm X*.

Then came word of the forthcoming Tina Turner biopic *What's Love Got to Do with It*, to be directed by Brian Gibson. *What's Love Got to Do with It* looked as if it might feature Gibson's former wife Lynn Whitfield, who had starred in Gibson's television film *The Josephine Baker Story*. Within the film industry, many were surprised when Bassett won the role. For actor Laurence Fishburne, however, who was the director's first choice to play Ike Turner, an important reason to do the film was Bassett. "I couldn't pass up the opportunity to play the supporting male character for this black woman who's about to just blow up like crazy," he told the press. "It's very important that black actresses in particular have the best kind of support that they can get."

Bassett had her work cut out for her. It was one thing to play a famous star from the past who was no longer alive; a star like Billie Holiday or Josephine Baker who then-contemporary audiences didn't have vivid memories of when *Lady Sings the Blues* and *The Josephine Baker Story* appeared. It was another ball game altogether to play a woman like Tina Turner who was still very much alive. The comparisons could be brutal. Bassett also was a dramatic actress, not a singer who acted. Nor was she a dancer. But she threw herself into preparation for the film. She met with Turner to go over dance routines. Turner also pre-recorded songs which Bassett would lip-sync to. "I act it, I don't sing it," she later told the press. Here, her onscreen *star weightiness*—that ability to occupy space onscreen, not ever to slip into the background, not ever to be a soft presence even when she had to play softer moments—served her supremely well. Some of her most stirring work was in the dance scenes when she captured Turner's energy and stage persona, revealing the kind of emotional release that performing provided for a woman who otherwise had to camouflage her emotions out of fear of her abusive husband. You could believe the woman onscreen was indeed a star.

Bassett and Eddie Murphy in *A Vampire in Brooklyn*.

Word spread quickly of an exciting new black actress in the movies. At the Golden Globes, she won the award as Best Actress in a Musical or Comedy. Afterward, Bassett received an Oscar nomination as Best Actress. Though Holly Hunter took the Oscar home for her performance in *The Piano*, Angela Bassett was now an established actress. Of the Oscar nomination, Bassett thought, "This is great! This is the beginning of something big for me." But that excitement faded. "I didn't work again for another year and a half. I guess I was pretty naive to

think it would be different—that it was just about the talent—particularly for someone who looks like me. You forget that sometimes." She went on to co-star with Eddie Murphy in *A Vampire in Brooklyn* and opposite British actor Ralph Fiennes in director Kathryn Bigelow's ambitious but disappointing futuristic drama *Strange Days*. She also played Betty Shabazz again in the 1995 film *Panther*. The films kept her before the public. But otherwise they did little for her.

There followed a flashy role in *Waiting to Exhale*, a nothing part (almost a bit) in the

Jodie Foster film *Contact*, a supporting role in *Music of the Heart* with Meryl Streep, a quasi-lead in the science fiction bomb *Super Nova*, a lead opposite Danny Glover in the little-seen film version of the Athol Fugard drama *Boesman and Lena*, a likable part (and a winning performance) opposite Robert De Niro in *The Score*, and later, a decent role in John Sayles's *Sunshine State*. Her one showcase part was the lead in *How Stella Got Her Groove Back*, an old style "woman's picture" that appealed very much to female moviegoers and which had a longer shelf life than might have been expected. Back onstage in 1998, she played Lady Macbeth opposite Alec Baldwin at New York's Public Theater. Turning to television, she starred in *Ruby's Bucket of Blood* and the title role in *The Rosa Parks Story*, directed by Julie Dash. Though miscast in the latter TV drama, she played the part with an appropriate quiet authority. Later she had a recurring role in TV's *Alias* series and appeared in the films *Mr. 3000* (opposite Bernie Mac) and the disjointed Bob Dylan drama *Masked and Anonymous*.

Because black moviegoers as well as a segment of the intellectual community (black and white) yearned to see her in another knockout part, because it was repeatedly publicized that she was a *serious* actress with that degree from Yale's drama school, Bassett became the subject of much discussion: as a great actress wasted by the film industry. Actually, though not an actress of "interior power" like Tyson or like Gloria Foster in *Nothing but a Man*, she was best when *externalizing*: putting everything out front and center, not keeping things in. That worked splendidly in *Waiting to Exhale* when she lashed out at her philandering husband, walked outside her home, and set his car on fire. That was what worked so perfectly in those dance sequences in *What's Love Got to Do with It*. Like Joan Crawford, Bassett sometimes overused her eyes and mouth and frankly sometimes *overacted*. Surprisingly, a drawback was that beautiful Bassett voice, which could have worked well on radio; when disembodied,

it could have a vibrant life of its own. Onscreen, the voice could seem too studied, not natural enough, and occasionally, she fell into the trap of actors like Andre Braugher and James Earl Jones or an orator like Barbara Jordan, all of whom sounded at times as if they enjoyed hearing the sound of their own voices. Still, with all said and done, Bassett, like Crawford again, was undeniably a star in the movies; magnetic and convincing enough to make us believe in her as a rather regal Angela Bassett. She knew how to drive a scene to her advantage.

Nonetheless, the idea of Bassett as adrift (or underused) in a sea of Hollywood mediocrity really took hold in a segment of the movie-going audience, especially among academics; in turn it gave her a blazing off-screen identity. She was much admired by many college students, too, who idealistically identified with her plight: battling a world or an industry that did not understand or appreciate her. All of *that* helped bring her into the ranks of divadom.

What Angela Bassett, the woman, thought or felt was anybody's guess. Aware that a Hollywood actress must be seen around town, she occasionally turned up at important openings and industry events, dressed to the nines, and moving through the crowds with an imperial demeanor that simply added to her mystique. Glimmers of her frustration with the film industry, however, occurred early in the next millennium when she gave a very revealing interview to *Newsweek* in which she was critical of Halle Berry's role in *Monster's Ball*. That may not have helped her career. Industry leaders frowned on criticism of Hollywood by one of its own. Once she married the actor Courtney B. Vance, she lived a rather private life. In 2006, the couple became parents to twins (Bassett was then forty-seven) via a surrogate mother. She also appeared in the film *Akeelah and the Bee*. Nonetheless, for much of the 1990s, Angela Bassett was the best known, most admired, and most talked-about African American actress working in the movies.

Anna Deavere Smith.

Theater Lights

During the era, African American actresses rarely found the kind of acclaim or success in theater that in the past had made stars of Ethel Waters or her white dramatic counterparts like Katherine Cornell and Ethel Barrymore or musical stars like Mary Martin and Ethel Merman. Occasionally, a performer like Heather Headley made a name for herself on Broadway in such productions as *The Lion King* and the Elton John–Tim Rice pop version, *Aida*. But she realized theater alone was not enough to maintain her career. She also made albums. A mezzo-soprano like Audra McDonald came close to the Old Broadway kind of stardom. The critics praised her to the hilt, and she acquired a dedicated following—as well as three Tony Awards—for her performances in the Broadway shows *Carousel, Master Class*, and *Ragtime*. The production *Marie Christine*—the story of a Creole Medea who is obsessed with a man, in this instance, a white man—was created especially for her. It was also her first lead role. But the play met with mixed reviews. While McDonald continued working in theater, she too looked to other venues to keep her career on track. She recorded albums and played roles in such television specials as *Annie*. Later, she surprised even her most ardent followers when she walked off with another Tony Award for her dramatic performance in the revival of *A Raisin in the Sun*.

But the great exception in theater and possibly the greatest stage actress of her generation was Baltimore-born Anna Deavere Smith. Tall, with dark hair and expressive brown eyes, this graduate of the American Conservatory Theater in San Francisco had worked for years in New York, without much attention, as an actress and teacher. At times, it looked as if she might face the problem of previous light-skinned African American actresses whom producers didn't feel looked *black* enough. Yet, determined to make her own way in theater, no matter what the perceptions of others, Smith experimented with a new approach to character development and to narrative itself. Conducting revealing interviews with people from all walks of life who might unknowingly disclose deep secrets, sometimes with bruising and blistering comments on race or gender, Smith was a brilliant observer of America's cultural/racial landscape. She also had a sharp eye for the idiosyncrasies, or telling gestures and facial expressions, of her subjects. With her acting students, she staged presentations—beginning in 1983 in what she called *On the Road: A Search for American Character*—in which they would portray people who had been interviewed. Or, they would portray famous celebrities who had been interviewed on television. Always fascinating, the presentations were rich with insights. Yet these early free-wheeling performances did not yet have a controlling artistic vision or emotional center. Then Smith left New York, living for a time on the West Coast, still experimenting with *On the Road*. A performance at Los Angeles's Mark Taper theater—in which she played all the characters based on people she had interviewed—brought her attention.

In the early 1990s, she returned to New York to appear in her one-woman show, *Fires in the Mirror: Crown Heights, Brooklyn, and Other Identities,* based on transcripts of people who had lived through the Crown Heights riots of 1991. Playing all 29 roles, Smith brought to vivid, compelling life such well-known figures as the Reverend Al Sharpton and Rabbi Joseph Spielman as well as "ordinary" people—be it an Orthodox Jewish housewife named Roz or black kids on the block—connecting these disparate personalities and their stories with a searing artistic vision that brought light to a complex political/social/racial situation. Later, Smith appeared again at the Mark Taper in her second one-woman dramatic presentation, *Twilight: Los Angeles, 1992,* taking a look at the faces and voices of people who had lived through the Los Angeles uprisings of 1992. When the drama opened in New York, the critics fell over themselves in praising her. "The American gallery remains, as Whitman said, 'uncelebrated and expressed,' Odets wrote in 1937, defining a populist ambition that has had to wait more than half century for Anna Deavere Smith to fulfill it." So proclaimed critic John Lahr in the April 4, 1994, issue of *The New Yorker*.

Smith understood that she, too, would have to do film and television work. Both *Fires in the Mirror* and *Twilight: Los Angeles, 1992* were taped for PBS broadcasts. She also appeared in the movies *Philadelphia, Dave,* and *An American President* as well as in recurring roles on the television series *West Wing* and *The Practice*. She co-starred in the short-lived series *Presidio Med*. In 2003, she had her most important film role in *The Human Stain:* as the mother of a light-skinned young black man who crosses the color line. When *The Human Stain* was screened at the Toronto Film Festival, critic Lou Lumenick wrote that she had the "most powerful scene in the movie, when she accuses the young man of 'murdering' the family by passing as white and denying his heritage." Upon its New York opening, A. O. Scott wrote in the October 31, 2003, edition of *The New York Times:* "Ms. Smith, her face a mask of material stoicism, brings home the tragedy of Coleman's decision to pass for white with a speech so dryly and evenly enunciated that its lacerating insight only registers once the camera has turned away." Her performance should have been recognized by the Academy of Arts and Sciences with at least an Oscar nomination as Best Supporting Actress. But that did not happen. Nor did the various New York critics' associations honor her. Later, she returned to the theater in another one-woman show, *House Arrest*. For theatergoers, Smith was reminiscent of the stage actresses of the past: a master of technique yet spontaneous and larger than life.

Left: Macy Gray; top right, Erykah Badu; bottom, Cassandra Wilson.

Other Voices, Other Styles

Popular music was enlivened by the arrival of a new group of singers who became known as practitioners of neo-soul, a blend of soul music, jazz, blues, and even some hip-hop. Singer-songwriter Erykah Badu was considered the mother of the neo-soul movement with the release of her 1997 platinum-selling debut album, *Baduizm*. Born Ericka Wright in 1971, growing up in Dallas, and later a student at Louisiana's black university Grambling State, Badu's solemn voice, which could convey the heartache and pain of emotional wounds, was sometimes compared to Billie Holiday's. In concert, the serene Badu often appeared with her head wrapped high in African cloth. (Later in her career, she discarded the head wrap to reveal a short-cropped Afro.) Often speaking to her audience about "consciousness" and "spirituality," she also liked to begin her concerts by lighting a candle. She led the way for other neo-soul divas: India.Arie, Angie Stone, Bilal, Musiq, Me'Shell NdegeOcello, Dionne Farris, and the critically praised Jill Scott.

Then there was the most idiosyncratic, and perhaps most endearing of the neo-soul performers, Macy Gray, who arrived on the music scene with her debut album *On How Life Is*, which was followed in the next century by *The Id* and *The Trouble with Being Myself*. With her half-awake, "stoned" persona (you weren't sure if she knew exactly where she was when she performed), with her wardrobe of bell bottoms, flowing boas, and mismatched colors (the antithesis of ghetto fabulous), and with her mop-top hairdos (originally a towering Afro), the raspy-voiced Gray was in a category all her own. Sometimes affectionately referred to as "the nutcase," Gray had grown up in Canton, Ohio, and studied screenwriting at the University of Southern California. Sometimes in her music, she could be hilarious or be lighthearted. She also revealed the emotional highs and lows that could drive her to distraction. In her hit single "I Try," which won her a Best Female Pop Vocal Grammy, she told the tale of a woman trying to recover from a breakup. But Gray was not a shrinking violet. In a later single, "Gimme All Your Lovin' or I Will Kill You," she sang of pulling a pistol on her lover and demanding that he make love to her. "It's amazing," went the lyric, "what a gun to the head will do."

Other singers of more traditional pop or rhythm and blues rose up the ranks. Toni Braxton looked as if she was en route to major stardom with her hit, "Unbreak My Heart." But after problems with her record label drove her to declare bankruptcy, she was less visible. Still, she proved resilient and later appeared on Broadway in the Disney extravaganza *Beauty and the Beast*. Teen pop stars like Monica (Arnold) and Brandy (Norwood) appealed to younger audiences. Together they had a hit with the single "The Boy Is Mine." The star of the TV series *Moesha*, Brandy, for a time, worked nonstop. She starred in the huge TV ratings winner *Cinderella*, which featured a multicultural cast and was executive produced by Whitney Houston and Debra Chase. She also played Diana Ross's daughter in the TV musical drama *Double Platininum* and appeared in the horror flick *I Still Know What You Did Last Summer*. For a spell, Brandy's travails made good tabloid copy. There were breakups, a short-lived marriage, motherhood (her child was rumored to have been fathered not by her husband but singer/actor Tyrese), an eating disorder, and a reported breakdown. That was quite a bit for someone barely out of her teens.

Completely different from these stars were Cassandra Wilson and Tracy Chapman. Wilson was a daring jazz experimentalist and a critic's darling. Having begun her career in coffee houses and on the streets of Harvard Square, Chapman (like Lauryn Hill to follow) became a heroine for college students with her first hit, the 1988 folk ballad "Fast Car." Here was a tale of a woman trying to pull herself up from a life of shelters and jobs that led nowhere. Eschewing the glammed up look expected of her contemporaries, Chapman, a gratuate of Tufts University, wore dreadlocks and dressed almost as if she were about to go to class – in T-shirts and jeans. She also aligned herself with Amnesty International's Human Rights Tour. That made her seem (again like Hill to follow) to have sprung from old school Sixties-style social activism. After her second album *Crossroads* failed to click with critics and record buyers, Chapman surprised everyone in 1996 with her fourth album *Give Me One Reason*. On the title song, she announced: "Give me one reason to stay, and I'll turn right back arouund." Her career was back on track.

En Vogue.

Girl Grouping: 1990s Style

Early in the decade, girl groups came back into fashion, not that they had ever entirely disappeared, with the release of the debut album *Born to Sing* by the group En Vogue. Unlike the old days when groups like the Shirelles and the Supremes were composed of girls who were friends and hung out together (or who were family members like the Pointer Sisters), En Vogue had been created in 1988 by two recording entrepreneurs in the Bay Area, Denzil Foster and Thomas McElroy, who, so the story went, had auditioned some 3,000 singers to perform a song. The singers were narrowed down to four: Maxine Jones, Terry Ellis, Dawn Robinson, and Cindy Herron-Braggs, all of whom came from diverse backgrounds. Jones worked in a hair salon. Robinson had been a receptionist for a dentist. Herron-Braggs was a hotel clerk. Having majored in marketing at Prairie View A&M University in Texas, Ellis, then doing studio work in Houston, had used her rent money to fly to Oakland, California, for the audition. "A few weeks after the audition," she said, "I got a call telling me that they would take all four of us and that we were going to not just sing one song, but a whole album. I almost died."

With a battalion of arrangers, choreographers, publicists, and stylists, the women underwent training to create not only a sound for the pop market but an image: the idea was to make them a unit with interchangeable parts; to model them on the Supremes but with a contemporary edginess and a thumping beat. Much attention was focused on the group's visual effect on an audience. Daily, the young women worked out, and on those nights when they performed, En Vogue—soon to be dubbed the "queens of sybaritic soul"— might show up in tight, clinging gowns with stiletto heels. Or they might be glammed out in leopard jackets with slinky black skirts. Or they might wear tight, dark leather hot pants. Despite all the emphasis on the visual image, the music of En Vogue, a tribute to the Golden Age of Pop, proved appealing. The album *Born to Sing* was followed in 1992 by *Funky Divas*, which became a double platinum hit.

Young women clearly identified with them. And young men were willing to listen to what these knockout babes had to say. Songs like "Free Your Mind" and "My Lovin' (You're Never Gonna Get It)" saluted female control; these were not young women easily led astray by slick dudes with smooth lines. In their song "Lies," they spoke about honesty. In "You Don't Have to Worry," they sang of committed men with integrity. In "Hold On," they performed a cautionary tale about the dangers of suffocating a lover by demanding too much.

By 1993, En Vogue had sold nearly five million albums and had been nominated for five Grammys. The quartet also won lucrative endorsements for such products as Diet Coke, Maybelline, and Converse; appeared on such TV shows as *Roc;* and performed with presidential brother Roger Clinton at the MTV inaugural bash for William Jefferson Clinton.

With their success, the members of this manufactured girl group began to take their music and images more seriously and demanded more control. Sometimes, the young women had been uncomfortable with the messages in their videos. In the video for "Giving Him Something He Can Feel," a guy on the make removed his wedding ring. That image was followed by a quick cut of Cindy who nodded approvingly. The idea that they condoned one sister taking off with another's husband bothered the group. "We regret it now," said member Maxine Jones. "We should have made a bigger deal about it at the time." "I think for the first album we were pretty much going along with the game plan," said Terry Ellis, "meaning, we were all doing this for the first time. But as time went on, we felt the lyrics and the songs. You do that when you sing them so much."

The women also looked closely at the way they were being managed. Like so many girl-groups before (and after), En Vogue found themselves often overworked and underpaid. "With all the hits," Cindy Herron-Braggs said, "we never saw huge sums of money." When the women started asking questions, they were told that money was being spent on gowns, on video productions, onstage sets. By mid-1993, their problems—whether it was financial concerns or personal relationships—had intensified. En Vogue soon fell apart. When they reunited in 1997, their label, Elektra Records, asked them to sign a contract stating that each member would focus 100 percent on being part of the group for the next two years. Dawn Robinson, however, refused to sign the new deal and left the quartet. Now a trio, the women released an album, *EV3*. By then, popular tastes had changed. Unable to duplicate their earlier success, En Vogue's glory days had come to an end. But in the early 1990s, En Vogue had been one of the hottest acts in show business.

Queen Latifah.

Hip-hopping across the Nation

Appearing early in the decade and becoming even bigger stars by the end of the era were the women of hip-hop. By the 1990s, rap music was already a cultural phenomenon that had been around for almost twenty years, though the cultural mainstream did not seem aware of that fact.

Rap had reared its defiant head and proved its commercial viability in 1979 with the Sugar Hill Gang's "Rapper's Delight," generally considered to be the first big rap hit. Following were rappers such as Kurtis Blow, the group Run DMC, and the white group the Beastie Boys. Simply stated, rap itself was speaking in rhythmic musical raps or dialogue. Hip-hop was the musical interludes or "samples" in the background of the lyrics. Hip-hop also came to refer to the culture built around rap—the language, the clothes, the accessories, the attitudes—a culture that eventually influenced a wide spectrum of American (and world) society, crossing over from urban areas to the white suburbs, and altering the face or tone of literature, movies, fashion, advertising. When MTV, which in its early years was criticized for not playing videos by African American artists, aired the show *Yo! MTV Raps*, rap moved even more into the mainstream. Chuck D of Public Enemy said that "this grass-roots transformation of culture has spread over the planet like a worldwide religion for those 25 and under." Before the 1990s ended, hip-hop would outsell what had previously been the nation's best-selling format, country music. In 1997 alone, rap would sell some 81 million CDs, tapes, and albums. And rap moguls like Def Jam's Russell Simmons and Sean "Puffy" Combs (or "Puff Daddy" or later Sean "P. Diddy" Combs) became the Berry Gordys of their generation.

As hip-hop became more popular, its content came into sharp focus and was the topic of discussion and debate. A group like Public Enemy spoke of a system that had to be battled. "Fight the power," it said. The West Coast group N.W.A. was a proponent of what came to be known as "gangsta rap" as it sent out the message to "F... tha police." Rappers like Ice-T and Ice Cube (formerly of N.W.A.) spoke of rebellion. Later, rappers like DMX, Master P., Tupac Shakur, and Biggie Smalls appeared. The most powerful rap seemed influenced by the political upheaval of the 1960s and the images of blaxploitation cinema of the 1970s: anger, defiance, and a call to action against a violent dominant culture. Other messages could be disturbing as rappers glorified in their misogyny and their blatant materialism. Not only did they seem in rebellion against the system with its corrupt white cops and its oppressive power struggle, but they also seemed in a power struggle with their girlfriends or wives, who were often viewed but not always as little more than the rappers' "hoes" or "bitches": pretty young things that were there to be had. While some rappers were in awe of women—because of female sexuality—they also feared the power of that sexuality and sought to dominate it. The lyrics of male rappers, said *Billboard*'s R&B music editor Janine McAdams, could be "bigoted, degrading, violent, ignorant, pointless, inexcusable, and barely worth the trouble."

In such a misogynistic world, was there a place for female rappers who could become major stars?—or heroines for young female record-buyers? At first there didn't seem to be, even though the music of such women as Millie Jackson and Shirley Brown, who had recorded the talk record "Woman to Woman," clearly had been precursors of rap. Gradually, a rap star like MC Lyte reached an audience with her street-tough songs about drugs and relationships. Her breakthrough hit, "Paper Thin," was a tale of both female vulnerability *and* female assurance. In its first six months, "Paper Thin" sold 125,000 copies. "My mother keeps asking me why I have to swear in public," she told *Vanity Fair* in July 1990. "But sometimes you need a shock so that people pay attention." Also making a name for herself was rapper Shazzy with her rap-style take on family life and her domestic tales of incest and violence, and Roxanne Shante.

Then came Queen Latifah, who was credited with breaking through the walls of rap misogyny with her first album, *All Hail the Queen*, and her hit single, "Ladies First." A performer like Sister Souljah (born Lisa Williamson) used rap for political statements and later went from rap to a career as a successful novelist. Other women fused rap with rhythm and blues. That had been the case with Salt-n-Pepa and TLC.

Missy Elliott.

Rapping Divas

Popular in the early 1990s, Salt-n-Pepa's career stretched back to the late 1980s. Though thought of as a duo, the group was actually a trio: Cheryl "Salt" James, Sandra "Pepa" Denton, and Dee Dee "dj Spinderella" Roper, who replaced the original Spinderella LaToya Hanson. James, a Brooklyn native, and Denton, who had moved from Kingston, Jamaica, had met at Queensborough Community College. Both had studied nursing and also were employed as telephone representatives for Sears. Working with them at Sears in the mid-1980s were then unknown future stars Martin Lawrence and Christopher Reid and Christopher Lawrence who later formed the duo Kid 'N Play. At Queensborough Community College, the young women performed with the help of fellow student Hurby "The Lovebug" Azor, a budding producer/writer who was instrumental in establishing them. He even owned the copyrights to the group's names "Salt," "Pepa," and "Spinderella."

With their 1987 debut album *Hot, Cool & Vicious*, Salt-n-Pepa became the first female rappers to have an album that went gold. Their single "Tramp"—in which they dissected male/female courtship rituals and declared that men are the tramps—climbed the charts. Then their sexy "Push It" soared on both the rhythm and blues and the rap charts to sell over a million copies. It won the group its first Grammy nomination for best rap performance. On record, in videos, and in concert, they were a bold, raunchy, sexy group sometimes decked out in street garb that made them looked like ordinary hip-hop sisters. Later the look was streamlined and more glamorous. They were naughty street girls with provocative lyrics yet pulsating through their music was the idea that they were independent women, who made their own money and their own way in life. Perhaps the funniest girl group, they were also in interviews the most likable and spontaneous, unaffected by their success, not taking themselves too seriously as might be the case with some of the rap divas and girl groups to follow. Because all three members were later known as being single mothers, they embodied the lifestyle of many contemporary young women, who were able to take care of their families and themselves without relying on a man's help.

Salt-n-Pepa: fast-talking with plenty of energy and much humor.

TLC: New Style Girl Group

No girl group of the time, however, proved more successful than TLC. Here was a group that sought to stretch its talents with music and messages that were very much in sync with the youthful concerns of the new era. Here was a group whose personal tensions became well publicized. Here too was a group that had public battles with its record company that made the young women all the better known and perhaps all the more a potent symbol.

Its members had met in Atlanta. Like the women of En Vogue, none had known each other before talent scout Ian Burke set out to form a streetwise group that would be approachable to fans. There could be nothing aloof or high-falutin' about them. Nor could they be over-glamorized. "All the girl groups that were out at the time were model-like individuals," Burke once said. "You would think, 'I don't know if I'll ever be able to land one of these girls.'" Initially signed for the group were the young singer Crystal Jones and a sultry Iowa native named Tionne Watkins, who had studied at a beauty school and worked at a McDonald's. When a wide-eyed Philadelphia–born go-getter named Lisa Lopes moved to Atlanta and auditioned for Burke, she was signed to complete the trio, which originally was called Second Nature, then changed its name to TLC, after the initials of its members' first names. TLC could also be read as a group ready to provide some Tender Loving Care. When Crystal Jones left the group, she was replaced by Rozonda Thomas, who adopted the name Chilli, thereby enabling TLC to keep its name.

Early on, the three were spotted by Perri Reid, who was the wife of Antonio "L.A." Reid, a high-powered executive at LaFace Records. Making a very shrewd business move—that would later lead to much friction and legal woes—Perri Reid bought out Ian Burke's contract with TLC for the reported sum of $2,500. Thereafter the group—signed to record with LaFace—was managed by Reid's company Pebbitone, Inc. In the beginning, it was fairly smooth sailing. Their first album *Ooooooohhh . . . on the TLC Tip* sold four million copies. On their second album, *CrazySexyCool*, they reached a new level of maturity with songs in which they reversed gender roles and exhibited a new-found confidence.

Like the blues singers and girl groups of the past, they sang about love, men, sex, and the complicated kind of romantic hassles that could drive them mad. For them, love could be linked to danger—physical as well as emotional. The group would be at the vanguard in discussing in its music such topics or themes as AIDS, date rape, sexual harassment, and infidelity. While the women could be vulnerable, they could be tough and assertive—and they stood on guard against betrayal, revenge, and power plays. Their single "Creep" let it be known that they were not willing to sit back and abide by a guy's rules. Nor were they content to play it meek and submissive. Refusing to live up to *his* standards or assessments of them, they wanted him to live up to *theirs*. In "Kick Your Game," they informed a guy that if he hoped to win their affections, he had to say "something more clever than just your name." Nor were they content with inexperienced guys. "Take Your Time" gave advice about unhurried sex. And with a powerful lyrical song and video like "Waterfalls," TLC sang in a very open way about the dangers and communal destructiveness of AIDS. Many critics felt it was their masterwork.

Onstage and in videos, TLC dressed in clothes that celebrated hip-hop style: often baggy pants and sweats or colorful tops and sometimes, in this safe sex era, with condoms pinned to their outfits. The look worked perfectly for the time, and it was part of the way they helped reinvent and restyle the girl group. Like the Supremes, the personalities of TLC's members meshed together well. And again like the Supremes, TLC was something of a fairytale group that turned dark and disturbing. Tionne was known as T-Boz, a glorious, sometimes breathy, low-voiced blond sophisticate, the most womanly of the three and seemingly the most knowing and most experienced. Rozonda Thomas, now Chilli, projected vulnerability yet she was the most collected of the three. Lopes, the most energetic, wrote some of their material and could spin out her raps with the best of them. Known as "Left Eye," she said she had been given the nickname by an old boyfriend who commented that her left eye was larger than her right one. The name stuck, and she played it up to the hilt, painting a stripe under her left eye to better showcase it. Her fans would do the same. Girlish and cute, she was an impish sprite who in time became the most troubled and the most talked-about member.

Just as their music sold, so did their story. Or stories. First to make headlines was the ongoing saga of Left Eye. Curious fans followed her romance with professional football star Andre Rison. Just looking at the two could make you do a double take. Here were a big, hulking guy and a teeny-weeny, baby-faced, baby doll of a girl. Rumors spread that the two were set to marry. But while Lopes appeared mad for the guy, it looked as if Rison took their romance in stride. Apparently, in the mind of Lopes, the romance turned rancid. On June 9, 1994, Lopes, angered or distressed, or *who knows what*, set Rison's spectacular Atlanta home on fire. The whole incident sent shock waves through the music industry. This was not a case of a naughty diva playing with matches. Damages mounted to $1.3 million. Accustomed to stars who behaved badly, whether it was because of drugs, booze, divorce, or reckless love affairs, no one was quite prepared when Lopes later pleaded guilty to first degree arson. Placed on five-year probation, she was ordered to pay a fine of $10,000 and to enter an alcohol rehabilitation program. The incident, however, didn't affect TLC's popularity. Their music continued to sell.

But TLC was back in the news with a story that put them in the business section of *The New York Times*, as well as other newspapers around the country. In 1995, the group filed for bankruptcy, claiming in court that they were broke. How could this be true? Their album *CrazySexyCool* had gone platinum and eventually sold some 11 million copies. TLC announced, however, that because of the low royalty rate on their music, they were unable to meet their financial responsibilities. Their liabilities were in excess of $3.5 million, which included a claim of $1.3 million by Lloyd's of London for the

damages to Rison's home. Their record company LaFace—as well as their manager Perri Reid—said the bankruptcy suit was a ploy to break a contract that the young women now felt paid them too small a percentage of their earnings.

Here a dirty little secret of the music industry was being publicly exposed. Many young women (and men) of the past had been taken advantage of by music companies in shocking ways. Often, struggling newcomers signed contracts that required them to repay their record labels or management for expenses—such as promotion fees, tour fees, coaching fees. An artist like Little Richard had been one of the most outspoken about the music industry's exploitation. Motown's two Marys: Wells and Wilson (of the Supremes) as well as Gladys Knight, had battled with their label. En Vogue and Toni Braxton had similar problems. For years entertainers found themselves in hock to their record labels, or to their management companies.

Other record companies watched the drama, aware that if TLC pulled off its bankruptcy suit, other acts might use the same tactic to get out of those early contracts. The court upheld the bankruptcy suit. But TLC then settled out of court: the group was able to break the contract with its manager and renegotiated a record-company deal. They had triumphed in a way that surely earned them the respect of many other music groups that felt exploited by their labels or management. Here, too, was part of the way they redefined the girl group. At the height of their career, the young women of TLC had taken a risk that might have wrecked them. The suit had stalled their recording career. How can a recording artist, especially in popular music, survive without releasing an album for several years? Because the pop audience is constantly changing, a once-hot group can sound cold and dated in a very short time to a new generation. But after a five-year absence, TLC came back strong with the album *Fan Mail*. Some of the new material like "No Scrubs" and "Quickie" sent out familiar missives to the men in their lives. But a song like "Unpretty" ventured into new territory, focusing on the beauty myth that many young women fall prey to. *Fan Mail* sold six million copies. The trio also toured to sold-out arenas.

But the public drama had not ended. This trio seemed to have been formed and to have flourished in tabloid heaven. Events in the trio's lives, whether big or small, were subjects of public discussion. After Lopes had set Rison's home ablaze, the two ended up, for a time, engaged. Tionne Watkins later revealed that she suffered from sickle cell anemia. Not a scandalous, earth-shaking announcement, but newsworthy nonetheless. The music world was surprised when she married rapper Mack 10. She also authored a book of poetry titled *Thoughts* and started a clothing line, Grungy Glamorous. She was one of the music stars of the era who saw themselves as entrepreneurs—not only landing the big endorsements, but starting companies to sell clothes, perfume, whatever. Later, Chilli Thomas would have a hot and heavy romance with singing star Usher, but would dump him when it was publicly revealed that he had cheated on her. Often there was bickering—and battles within the group. At times, each of the women appeared fed up with one of the others; or both. "We thought about leaving each other, but we couldn't do it," T-Boz told the press. "It's like your own family. You can't choose the mom you have, you just accept who they are and live with them." "Our ridiculous fights are countless," Chilli announced. "We need to produce and direct a movie, like the one about the Temptations." Again like the Supremes, the pressures of fame and the business made them appear to be jittery, anxious, restless young women. But unlike the troubles of the Supremes, which were kept away from the public eye by Motown and not publicly revealed until after the fact, the conflicts of TLC were wide out in the open.

Lopes also recorded a solo album, *Supernova*, which was released abroad. "I'm Diana Ross, and not a Supreme," she sang. No matter what Ross's career problems, she remained for new generations *the* diva. (Aretha was considered *the* singer.) Among the younger generation, Ross's only rival for that title was Whitney Houston, who was considered both diva a*nd* singer. New drama hit the press when Lopes was reported missing for days in 2000. "She's fine," her agent said. "She's a grown-up and she doesn't have to tell everyone where she's going."

Putting their differences aside, TLC began work on a new album. But the world of these three young women turned tragic in April 2002. At that time, Lisa Lopes was in Honduras at a popular vacation spot on the Caribbean coast where she had a condominium in an area in which African healing was practiced. While at the wheel of a rented sport-utility vehicle, Lopes suddenly lost control of the vehicle, which ran off the road and turned over several times. Seven other passengers were in the van, including Lopes's sister and brother, three members of a rhythm and blues group, and two video producers, who were working on a video about Lopes's "spiritual journey." All survived save one: Lisa Lopes died at the scene. She was thirty years old. The fans and the music world grieved her. In an Atlanta suburb, thousands lined up early in the morning for her funeral, hoping to enter the 10,000-seat New Birth Missionary Baptist Church. "She was my heart," said football star Rison.

Six months after Lopes's death, TLC's album *3D* was successfully released. "The whole album is a tribute to Lisa and she's not a sad girl, she's a party girl," T-Boz announced. She and Chilli also said they could never record again without her. "You can't replace T-Boz, cannot replace Chilli, cannot replace Left Eye," Chilli told the press. Still, in the 1990s, TLC had become—for a time—the top best-selling girl group, having sold some 27 million albums worldwide.

Lauryn Hill: First Lady of Collegiate Hip-hop

With the arrival of Lauryn Hill, the rap scene saw another new brand of artistic heroine: not the kind of seemingly reckless free spirit of a Lisa Lopes, but a star with a social and political consciousness. Or so it seemed. In the world of images, audiences could not always tell what really lay at the heart of a star's public persona. But Hill stood apart from the sexy girl groups and the torchy singers and the all-around entertainers. Rising to fame with the Fugees, she sometimes looked like a throwback to the activism of the 1960s, which may explain why she became a darling of the intellectuals.

Unlike many past divas who had risen from tough urban childhoods, Hill had grown up in a middle-class home in South Orange, New Jersey. Her father, Mal, was a computer programmer/consultant; her mother Valerie, an English teacher. With their two children—Lauryn and her older brother Melaney—the Hills may have looked like the perfect nuclear family. In the stories that the media eventually promoted about Hill, she appeared to be a child sprung from the musical spirit of an earlier time. As a teenager, her mother had enjoyed listening to a variety of musical stars. But once she became a busy wife, mother, and professional woman, she put some of that musical past behind her. Valerie Hill recalled how she stacked her old 45 RPM records—everything from Motown to Stax, from Marvin to Aretha to Stevie to Donny Hathaway to Gladys Knight—in a corner of the basement of the family home. "One day little Lauryn found 'em," Valerie Hill later proudly told the press. "And thus began a journey. She started to play that music and loved it. One o'clock in the morning, you'd go in her room and you'd see her fast asleep with the earphones on. The Sixties soul that I'd collected just seeped into her veins." But she also responded to other music. Taken to see the movie version of the musical *Annie* on her seventh birthday, Little Lauryn "was mesmerized," her mother recalled. "Her eyes were glued to the screen. After that, she learned every single song. I heard that every day—'tomorrow, tomorrow.' I was sick of 'the sun will come out tomorrow.'" Such stories, of course, proved prophetic.

Hill's developing musical talents were apparent to everyone. So was her ambition. At age thirteen, she performed Smokey Robinson's "Who's Lovin' You" on the television program *Showtime at the Apollo*. During this first TV appearance, a nervous Hill had stood back from the microphone. The audience booed her—until her brother yelled to her, "Get close to the mike!" Thereupon, so the story went (according to her mother), Lauryn Hill

> grabbed the mike and sang that song with a vengeance, like, "How dare you boo me." She sang her heart out. At the end of the song, they were clapping and screaming for her. When we got home, she felt she had let herself down, and she started crying. I said, "Lauryn, they're gonna clap for you one day and maybe not the next, but you gotta take it all. This is part of the business that you say you want to be in. Now, if every time they don't scream and holler, you're gonna cry, then perhaps this isn't for you." And she looked at me like I had taken leave of my senses. To her, the mere suggestion that this wasn't for her was crazy.

Now off and running, a teenaged Hill juggled the demands of school with those of a budding career. "She would take a test, try out for a movie or a play, pass the test and get straight A's in school," a friend remembered. Winning a role as a runaway on the daytime soap opera, *As the World Turns*, she also played a rebellious student in the Whoopi Goldberg film, *Sister Act II*. In high school, she ran track, was a cheerleader, and formed the rap group The Fugees (short for the Refugees) with her classmate Prakazrel "Pras" Michel and his cousin Wyclef Jean. There didn't seem to be any bounds to her energy or her creativity. Accepted by six colleges upon graduation from high school, she chose to study history at Columbia University in New York. But after a year, she left to pursue her career with the Fugees. The three wrote and practiced in Wyclef Jean's basement. Signed to RuffHouse Records in 1993, the Fugees released their first album, *Blunted on Reality*. It bombed. At the time, Hill was eighteen.

But two years later, their second album, *The Score*—a fusion of hip-hop, reggae, and rhythm-and-blues—eventually sold 18 million copies, won two Grammys, and turned the trio into stars.

The Fugees were an inspiring sight to behold: three intense, intelligent, committed young artists. On *The Score*, they performed a re-styled version of Roberta Flack's hit "Killing Me Softly," which perhaps more than any other song, helped establish a persona for Hill as a controlled yet vulnerable, sensitive yet strong young woman. Clearly no backseat diva, she was the group's emotional core. There were always stories about her relationship with Wyclef Jean. In the mass imagination, the two belonged together: here were brave new artists clearing the way for a seemingly more thoughtful kind of hip-hop.

But whatever her relationship with Wyclef Jean, it did not last long. Nor did the Fugees. By 1998, Lauryn Hill—then twenty-three years old—had parted from the group and released a solo album, *The Miseducation of Lauryn Hill*, which sold 8 million copies in the United States and won her five Grammys, including Album of the Year. Here, her audience heard a sensual, spiritual, and revolutionary Hill—whose songs had references to the Bible and God. "Father, you saved me and showed me that life was much more than being some foolish man's wife," she sang in a duet with Mary J. Blige titled "I Used to Love Him." A spiritual Hill acknowledged the way religion had changed the course of her life and enabled her to walk away from a destructive path *and* a destructive man. Record buyers could play a guessing game. Was "I Used to Love Him" as well as such songs as "Lost Ones" and "Ex-Factor" about Wyclef Jean? By then, Hill had fallen in love with Rohan Marley. The son of the legendary reggae star Bob Marley and his wife Rita, Rohan had been a football player at the University of Michigan, and then with the Ottawa Rough Riders of the Canadian Football League. Though he and Hill did not marry, they had children and were viewed as a very hip couple.

For young college women, Hill was a heroine, perhaps partly because she didn't trade on a blatant sexual image, but also because of her comments on social/political issues as well as a strong race consciousness. In interviews, she might speak out about genocide in Rwanda or the ruthless tactics of the media. "There's always a constant spiritual war," she said, "but there's a battle for the souls of black folk and just folks in general, and the music has a lot to do with it." Hill's appeal could also be traced to her appreciation of popular music's history. Throughout that solo album, the influence of reggae was apparent on such songs as "Nothing Even Matters" and "Superstar." She also performed a duet with Carlos Santana. Her relationship with Bob Marley's son connected her to music world royalty. The title *The Miseducation of Lauryn Hill* itself referred to a book from the past, *The Miseducation of the Negro*. Hill also later wrote the song and directed the video, "A Rose Is a Rose" for Aretha Franklin. So much about Lauryn Hill seemed historically, musically, and culturally correct.

The media went haywire over Hill, fawning, celebrating, and hailing her with magazine cover portraits on *Rolling Stone* and then the most prized cover—on *Time*. Having one's face peering out from *Time* on newsstands around the country was no longer quite the power/success symbol it had been in past decades when Marian Anderson and Aretha Franklin had snagged the coveted cover. Still, it meant *something* and, in some respects, it elevated Hill to another league. Yet with all the attention and respect that Hill garnered, her image underwent a startling change within a short period of time. Rumors flew around about Rohan Marley's affairs with other women. So did stories about Hill's erratic behavior—and of a basic artistic inactivity. There were whispers of a breakdown. Four years passed before the release of a new album, *Lauryn Hill: MTV Unplugged No. 2.0*, in 2002. Fans and critics alike were eager to find out what she had been up to. And fans and critics alike found the album disappointing, disjointed, and bewildering. Accompanying herself on an acoustic guitar, she spent about thirty minutes—in what was termed "interludes"—between the music on this two-disc endeavor *talking* about God,

Though Hill withdrew from the spotlight, she kept writing. And she never lost the respect of her peers. Most understood the ties between her inner conflicts and the pressures of her career.

the Enemy, and life. "I had created this public persona, this public illusion," she said, "and it held me hostage." The critics were not kind. "Lauryn Hill has been to the edge, and lived to talk about it. And talk about it. And talk about it," wrote the critic for *Newsweek's* May 13, 2002, issue. The "most promising singer and songwriter of her generation" now sounded "not just unplugged but unhinged," and "should never have released this album," which was unedited with tunes that seemed "blurry, unfinished, rushed into being." In its May 10, 2002, issue, *Entertainment Weekly* called it "baffling on so many levels" and "the most bizarre follow-up in the history of pop."

Surely, Hill was attempting to be honest, to publicly sort out some of the messiness of her life. In sharing her "breakdown," Hill may, on one level, seem vaguely reminiscent of Billie Holiday. But for many, she appeared self-indulgent, affected, and publicly losing control. More significantly,

Holiday's tragedy could be viewed within the context of a racist culture. Though Hill obviously understood the problems of race and sexism within the music industry, she also struck some as having lived a far more privileged life than past divas who had to fight at every turn just to get to a door, let alone open it. Unlike past divas, she did not appear to have experienced much or to have lost much. Perhaps that was unfair to Hill. Yet that appeared to be the response of her public. Hill, however, never really disappeared from the entertainment scene. Though she withdrew from the spotlight, she kept writing. And she never lost the respect of her peers. Most understood the ties between her inner conflicts and the pressures of her career. Thus the Lauryn Hill story remained an ongoing one whose denouement had not yet come; whose meaning was not yet fully understood.

Lil' Kim.

Foxy Brown.

Battle of the Hip-hop Junior League Divas

Other young hip-hop performers showed up, rapaciously vying for attention. Two of hip-hop's young demi-goddesses of flash and trash, raunch and rowdiness, were the well-publicized rivals Foxy Brown and Lil' Kim. Known for being blatantly and sometimes outrageously sexy, Foxy Brown and Lil' Kim were not afraid to proclaim their sexual appetites or prowess in their music, doing so in a vein similar to that of male rappers. Without hesitation, they boldly spoke up about their demands, letting all in earshot know they could not be taken lightly and that men could not use and discard them. Some assumed that this kind of confident female power was entirely new. But, of course, the blues singers of the 1920s had never backed off from speaking up about sex or about putting a mean papa in his place. Although they might seem to be pining for a guy, the girl-groups of the 1960s also felt secure enough to make their feelings known. Such Supremes songs as "Come See about Me" and "Stop! In the Name of Love" were more assertive than one might have initially thought. And, of course, that underrated naughty girl Millie Jackson knew a thing or two about matters of the heart—as well as other parts of the human anatomy.

For a time, the media eagerly recorded the exploits of the diminutive Lil' Kim. In turn, Kim was eager to let the media know all she could about herself. Born Kimberly Jones in Brooklyn, she was a child of divorce who grew up fast while yearning for her father's approval. "It was like I could do nothing right," she said. "Everything about me was wrong—my hair, my clothes, just *me*." At fourteen, she left home and fell into the life of the streets. "I ran errands for drug dealers, lived with them—whatever it took to make ends meet," she once said. Some of her comments might have sounded like those of Ethel Waters, relating incidents in her early stormy life. Yet Lil' Kim's account never had the instructive mythic resonance of Waters's. It had the sound of youthful angst, perhaps simply youthful chatter without the deep emotional scars of Waters's early sorrows. "All my life men have told me I wasn't pretty enough—even

the men I was dating," she told the press. "And I'd be like 'Well, why are you with me, then? It's always been men putting me down just like dad. To this day, when someone says I'm cute, I can't see it. I don't see it no matter what *anybody* says." She seemed to be too consciously creating a public image with comments that had the ring of calculated self-promotion. Lil' Kim was far more knowing and intelligent than she may have appeared.

Music offered the young Kimberly Jones a chance to express herself and also bring some kind of structure to her wayward life. A pivotal period in her struggle to find herself occurred when she began rapping with one of rap's most popular performers, Biggie Smalls, sometimes known as the Notorious B.I.G., but born Christopher Wallace. During a mid-1990s appearance with Biggie in Brooklyn's Bedford-Stuyvesant, she performed "Player's Anthem." Fans took notice. Smalls took a liking to her. With his help, she recorded with his Junior M.A.F.I.A. posse. Then came her 1996 CD, *Hardcore*, which sold some two million copies. Now officially a hip-hop star, she delighted in the attention of her fans and glorified in being considered the woman in Biggie Smalls's life. Together the two, while perhaps not a striking pair, were an attention-drawing one, similar to Lisa Lopes and Andre Rison: Smalls, heavy, big boned, and broad shouldered, a bodacious sultan who dressed in suits and a white derby; Kim, a little girl of a rapper with big eyes and a big smile. Lil' Kim believed she had finally found a man who loved her. But then, along with the rest of the hip-hop world, she was stunned by the killings of two major hip-hop stars: Tupac Shakur, gunned down in Las Vegas in 1996; and then Smalls, in Los Angeles in 1997.

Though she and Biggie had never married, afterward she appeared to cast herself as something of a grieving widow, although she had to share that title with another star, Faith Evans, who actually *had* married Smalls and given birth to their son. Nonetheless, Kim had, if not an exalted place, then certainly some kind of special status in hip-hop. With production work by Sean Combs, she released the CD *Notorious*

FOXY FIRES HER GABBY ATT'Y

Revealed too much about her 'deaf' jam

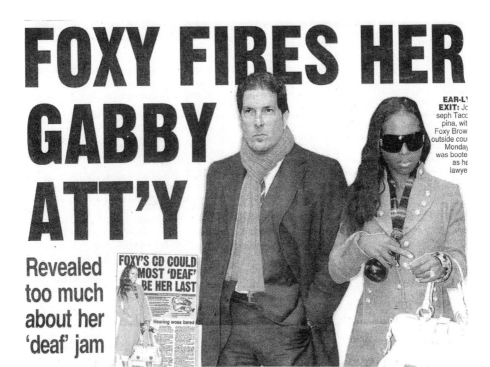

FOXY'S CD COULD MOST 'DEAF' BE HER LAST

Hearing woes bared

LIL' KIM'S MOVING TO THE BIG HOUSE

K.I.M. in 2000. On the single "Hold On," Kim performed an elegy to Biggie with Mary J. Blige. On other songs, she proudly proclaimed her sexual exploits. "When it comes to sex, call me Dr. Ruth / I ain't a prostitute, I just speak the truth," she sang. She also performed a little ditty called "Suck My D–K," which some critics considered a feminist anthem: Kim was surmising how the world might look if women hit on men the way men hit on them. Despite all the attention the album received, the critical reactions were mixed. "Unfortunately, behind the get-ups and the come-ons, the reality is grim: Lil' Kim's new rap album," wrote *Time*, "is a bomb."

But Lil' Kim hardly faded into the woodwork.

Though she stood under five feet, she was a tough little cookie, and for her fans, a deliciously trashy little tart. With her shorter than short dresses (often from top designers like Versace, Gucci, or Dolce and Gabbana), with her blonde wigs (or her pink or purple ones), with her fake eye lashes, with her fulsome bouncing breasts (the result of much-publicized implants), and her pert little potty mouth that could pout beautifully, she was reminiscent (in a coarser manner) of a number of stars, from Nina Mae McKinney to Betty Boop to Brigitte Bardot. Generally, she was credited with a shift in hip-hop diva images: By now, the hip-hop stars were discarding the baggy pants and sexy tops, the kind of street-gear that had been inspired by the way their fans dressed. Now hip-hop stars were known for being ghetto fabulous with their brand name items: Louis Vuitton and Cristal and their *bling* or *ice*—those sparkling jewels that bedecked their hands, arms, and necks. Always, Lil' Kim seemed eager to create a buzz. At an awards show, when Kim wore a pasty over her otherwise exposed left breast, a seemingly shocked Diana Ross, onstage with her, tried to adjust the pasty to make Kim look more dignified!; or perhaps just less trashy. Of course, Miss Ross realized *that* was impossible. Later the talk was not so much about *why* Kim dressed that way. Everyone knew *why*. Instead it was *why* Diana Ross had tried to get Kim to cover herself up. For a new generation, Lil' Kim was a wondrously overripe *it girl* with a wondrously over-the-top style. The same was true of singer Foxy Brown and other new music stars of this era. But few stars promoted themselves in the blatantly sexy way of Kim. Ice was one thing. A pasty was another.

The styles of diva aspirants like Kim and Foxy Brown seemed a replay or crude update of the attitudes and personas of the blues singers. Women like Ma Rainey and Bessie Smith—refusing to come across like woebegone ghetto girls—had reveled in their diamonds or horsehair wigs or the latest far-out fashions. But while the divas of the past had sought a kind of flashy grandeur, which they pulled off with an enjoyable flair, the new-age divas sometimes seemed hopelessly self-conscious about their bling, looking as if they were trying too hard, even desperate to prove (perhaps mainly to themselves) they could be glamorous; as if the clothes were camouflaging some of their deepest insecurities and doubts. Few could carry off the high-flung kind of glamour that Baker had exuded upon her ascension to stardom in France, when top designers dressed her, and when she looked as if she had been born for such elegant clothes. Nor did some of the new stars have the innate kind of glamour of a Diana Ross, who could be just as exciting in jeans and a sexy pullover as in her lush, full-skirted gowns. Baker and Ross were *naturals* who clearly enjoyed having the chance to look great in great clothes. The last thing on their minds was proving anything to anybody. As they grew older, Baker and, to a lesser extent, Ross, may have become campy. But no one could ever accuse them of being coarse or crude.

In 2000, Kim made headlines, following an incident—actually, a wild shoot-out—that occurred when she appeared as a guest disc jockey at New York's Hot 97 radio station. Outside the station, heated insults were exchanged among about twenty members of Kim's entourage and the entourage of a rival. Then there was gunfire. A man was shot in the back. Both groups, reported the *New York Post* in its July 7, 2001, edition, left the scene "before police arrived and no arrests have been made." The *Post* also reported that "Kim fled in a limo." The shoot-out was believed to have been the result of a heated feud between Lil' Kim and Foxy Brown. It was also believed that their feud had been fueled by their rival record labels. Foxy Brown was a star on Def Jam Records; Kim was with Bad Boy Entertainment. On an album recorded by the rap group Capone-N-Noreaga, Foxy had bashed Kim's relationship with Biggie Smalls. On her second album, Lil' Kim had sent word to Foxy: "You ain't a star." Divas of the past certainly had their rivalries. Baker and Ethel Waters were hardly friends. Waters also didn't care to give the time of day to poor newcomer Lena Horne. Usually, the rivalries were closely tied to the work of the women, and often the stars preferred to keep their feelings known only to people in show business. The rivalries had always seemed to be about *something*. But now that changed. Already, male rappers had made headlines because of their rivalries—and the violence that sometimes erupted because of that. Now such violence was associated with female stars.

Testifying before a grand jury, Lil' Kim denied any knowledge of having seen gun-toting members of her posse at the scene of the shoot-out. Later she accused prosecutors of launching a witch hunt against her. But on July 7, 2005, following a trial that kept her in the news, she was on the front page of the *New York Post* after a jury convicted her on three counts of perjury and a conspiracy charge. Even the august *New York Times* carried a front-page item on the case. Kim faced a maximum of twenty years in jail. Prosecutors had asked for a sentence of at least two years and nine months for lying to a grand jury. "You sat right there next to me and you looked in the eyes of the jury and you tried to trick them, to take them out. It was an insult to the [jurors] and to the system," the federal judge was reported to have told her. "Going to jail because you need to protect men with guns is not heroic. It's stupid and wrong."

"I testified falsely during the grand jury and trial," Kim admitted as her mother and supporters sat in the courtroom. "At the time, I thought it was the right thing to do, but now I know it was wrong." She added: "I am a God-fearing, good person." The federal judge sentenced her to a year and a day in prison. But Lil' Kim's problems did not end there. The Internal Revenue Service demanded payment of back taxes of $850,000, with an additional $50,000 in penalties.

Of course, the tabloid headlines and photographs helped make her more famous. Before serving her prison term, she filmed segments for a profanity-laden reality show, *Lil' Kim: Countdown to Lockdown* that became a ratings winner on Black Entertainment Television. Yet, whether the stories really drew interest from a broader audience in the way of Billie Holiday's headlines was doubtful. Again, Holiday's professional troubles—with the underlying theme of race and racism in America—had made her seem mythic and at times heroic. In some way, her story seemed representative of other Black Americans, who were also faced with racial discrimination. Kim's story, like those of some male rappers, seemed simply tawdry, and as the judge had said, "stupid." Even the fans watched the saga as an action-packed, but forgettable, soap opera.

Also landing in the pages of the tabloids—for other reasons—was Foxy Brown. Born Inga Marchand in Brooklyn, Brown had used such other names as Big Shorty and AKA earlier in her career. But when she signed with Def Jam Records, she renamed herself after the character played by Pam Grier in the 1974 movie *Foxy Brown*. Her debut album, *Ill Na Na*, which in street vernacular meant "excellent private parts," climbed the charts. In a short period of time, she was on the cover of *Vibe* magazine.

Offstage, she lived large and dressed small. She once giddily posed for the press behind the wheel of a 2005 GT Coupe, reportedly a $200,000 gift from rapper Jay-Z. Foxy was parked outside Chanel's posh boutique, where she had bought several handbags. In scanty, almost non-existent outfits that showcased her tight little bod with its bodacious curves—and with her long straight-haired wigs, her constantly widened large eyes, and her perpetual

Lil' Kim: as well-known for her outfits as her music.

come-ons—Foxy was petite and pushy enough to pass for Lil' Kim's sister. The two women had once been close friends. Foxy also was no stranger to violence. In 1998, reports surfaced of gunfire—directed at Foxy's boyfriend Kurupt—at a recording studio in Los Angeles. His bodyguard was killed. Two other rappers were injured. Many speculated that the shootout had grown out of a dispute between Kurupt and rapper DMX, who had reportedly made sexual overtures to Foxy. Two years later, there occurred the shooting incident that involved Lil' Kim.

In many respects, Foxy appeared to revel in the drama and disarray of her young life: its feuds, its torments. Her album *Broken Silence* commented on her personal experiences, from the car chases to the assaults. She also turned reflective in a number like "The Letter," on which she performed a suicide note addressed to her family. "I love you, Mom," she was saying. "I'm sorry." But that reflection was undercut on another number, when a more ribald Foxy announced that she wanted the guys, as well as everyone else, to know, "I taste like candy." Generally, fans were more familiar with the raunchy Foxy than the psychologically troubled one, and in the years to come, her real-life antics brought her more attention than her music. For a spell, the tabloids delighted in depicting her as a rather crude, out-of-control, little "witch" who had somehow stumbled into stardom. One day it would be a story about Foxy's wrath being directed at staffers at Louis Vuitton's flagship store in New York. Another day she might be reported cursing out a salesperson at the store David Z. On another occasion, when an employee at New York's fashionable Barney's couldn't find the size Foxy was looking for, she was said to have called the woman "a stupid bitch." On yet

sip in daily newspapers, so much was exposed about the two hip-hop performers, as well as any number of other stars, that their public may have felt it knew all there was to know about them. Or all that it cared to know.

Yet oddly enough, future generations might take an interest in these women as examples of the excess and narcissism of the era.

Other hip-hop divas were taken more seriously. Making music more than headlines was the ambitious and fiercely talent-

Of course, the tabloid headlines and photographers helped make Lil' Kim more famous.

another occasion, during an argument with two staff members at a nail salon over a $10 manicure, Foxy reportedly hit the women with her fists and cell phone. That little encounter landed her in court. All of these incidents at big-name stores led someone to comment: "Let's hope this hip-hop horror show discovers shopping at the Home Shopping Network." The nonstop fracas raised by Foxy made good copy and was fun to read. Then came reports that she suffered from a mysterious malady called *sensorineural hearing loss* and underwent surgery to repair the damage. Sadly, no one could quite figure out if Foxy, obviously troubled by something, was worthy of sympathy or contempt. Later she recovered her hearing.

Although both Foxy Brown and Lil' Kim drew media attention, there was only limited interest in them. In this age of the celebrity magazines; the nightly entertainment shows; the quasi-documentaries about celebrities on MTV, VH1, and E Entertainment; coverage of hip-hop in such publications as *Vibe* and *The Source*; and the steady stream of showbiz gos-

ed Missy "Misdemeanor" Elliott. Writing and/or producing for such stars as Christina Aguilera, Beyoncé, Mariah Carey, Justin Timberlake, and Whitney Houston, Elliott also released her own albums: *Supa Dupa Fly, Da Real World, This Is Not a Test,* and *The Cookbook*. Image-wise, she favored baggy street gear long after the fashion changed. But she would be the first to tell you that she loved her bling. Becoming more mainstream, she appeared in a highly touted Gap commercial with Madonna. Originally on the chunky side, she lost weight, not because she was dissatisfied with her body image but because of her battle with diabetes. Though she avoided controversy and rarely turned up in the tabloids like Foxy and Kim, she was by no means a hip-hop goody-two-shoes. Still, she was perhaps one of hip-hop's most understated image makers. Elliott seemed to feel her music—with its dancehall beats, dizzying rhythms, and sexy raps—had to speak for itself, which it did, most eloquently. She also starred in her own TV reality show, *The Road to Stardom with Missy Elliot.*

Faith Evans:
Hip-hop's First Lady

Then there was the resplendent, but often underrated, Faith Evans. Born in Lakeland, Florida, in 1973, Evans was the daughter of an aspiring singer who left her in the care of the child's grandparents in Newark, New Jersey. "I graduated from the school of hard knocks," Evans liked to say. As a girl, she sang wherever she could, at church as well as at "weddings, funerals, retirement parties, anything. Newark Airport family day," she once said. But Evans was also a serious student, who won a full academic scholarship to Fordham University. While studying there, she earned money as a backup singer for various performers, including future star Usher. After a year, she left Fordham to pursue a career. That enterprising future mogul of the rap age, Sean "Puffy" Combs, took her under wing. Signed to his company, Bad Boy Entertainment, she continued to do backup work. Then she became the first woman in the lineup of male stars at Bad Boy. Her 1995 debut album, *Faith*, went platinum with the hit singles "Soon As I Get Home" and "You Used to Love Me."

But she also became known in the hip-hop community because of her surprising marriage to Christopher Wallace, *The NOTORIOUS B.I.G.* The wedding had occurred nine days after they met. The couple had a son. But theirs proved to be a stormy relationship, with stories of physical abuse. "We were young, we fell in love, we were rebellious," she once said. "Yes, we certainly had our run-ins. And did it get physical every now and then? Yeah. But I wasn't the battered wife." Evans also had run-ins—some physical—with the ubiquitous Lil' Kim. "We both fell in love with the same man," Evans said rather stoically some years later. "It happens." Foxy Brown, however, had a different feeling about the friction between the two. "I respect Faith," Foxy said in defense of Evans. "When you're the wife, you needn't worry. Anyone can be a girlfriend or a baby's mommy. But there's only one wife." Enough said. At the time Wallace was murdered, he and Evans had separated. But his death appeared to leave her devastated.

What helped lift her out of her grief was a tribute record to Smalls that Combs put to-gether. Titled "I'll Be Missing You," it featured Evans with Combs and the group 112 in a hip-hop/gospel style version of the Police song, "Every Breath You Take." For the legions of hip-hop fans, Evans's rendition appeared heroic and stately: she was bravely continuing on in a world in which there was not as much light as before; she was a woman who knew her man as others hadn't; a woman who would never forget. For those with longer pop memories, the tribute recording might be considered the hip-hop equivalent of Judy Garland's character saluting her dead husband (a suicide) at the climax of *A Star Is Born*, announcing to an audience: "This is Mrs. Norman Maine." "I'll Be Missing You" won the 1998 Grammy for group rap performance as well as the MTV Video Music Award for Best Rhythm and Blues Video.

Perhaps the most restless and searching of these new era divas, Evans—nine months after Smalls's death—remarried, moved to Atlanta, and had two more children. Obviously, she wanted a different kind of life. Two more platinum-selling albums were released: *Keep the Faith*—in which her strength as a writer was apparent as she mastered slow songs along with numbers with club beats; and the 2001 Grammy winner, *Faithfully*. She also appeared in the film *The Fighting Temptations*.

But her troubles were not behind her. In 2004, there was a drug arrest. After she and her new husband, Todd Russaw, who also managed her career, pled guilty to possession of small amounts of cocaine and marijuana, the two entered pretrial intervention programs. Once again she set out to pull her life together. Asking Combs for a release from her contract with Bad Boy Entertainment, she never fully explained her reasons for that decision. Apparently, it wasn't easy. Eventually, she signed with Capitol Records. At the same time, she worked with a trainer to get herself back in physical shape. The new Faith Evans was leaner but not meaner. Her vulnerabilities would always show. In 2004, she pulled up stakes again and moved to Los Angeles. By 2005, she had a new album. With her rhythm and blues style and her hip-hop flavor, Evans's *The First Lady* would be her dec-

Evans had a deep and moving sadness, which suggested a kind of emotional depletion. That in turn signaled to her audience the idea that she had suffered and walked down many troubling paths.

laration of independence. In a confessional mood, she addressed her drug arrest in the single "Again."

"I'm really an inner spirit that only makes itself known through the music," Evans once said. "A lot of people think I'm an introvert or quiet and moody. I've even heard some people say that there's a certain mystery or darkness about me. I'm not that way. I'm just really into what I do." Actually, there *was* a great mystery about her. Evans had a deep and moving sadness, which suggested a kind of emotional depletion. That in turn signaled to her audience the idea that she had suffered and walked down many troubling paths. Watching, as much as listening to Faith Evans, you felt somehow she might never find whatever it was she

was searching for. Was the source of her angst a fundamental loneliness? Was it a feeling of basic alienation? Was it an acute sensitivity that might always make her feel like an outsider? You could never fully understand what she was all about, just as audiences of the 1930s and 1940s had never understood what Billie Holiday was really about. The *Los Angeles Times* once referred to Evans and another troubled singer, Mary J. Blige, as "women's women, artists whom female fans don't regard as otherworldly superstars but as wise older sisters." That might be true. Yet Evans and Blige certainly did seem otherworldly, indeed they were perhaps the two genuinely mysterious goddesses in the world of hip-hop and new style rhythm and blues.

Mary J. Blige.

The Enigmatic Queen of Hip-hop Soul

The other diva with sadness in her eyes and pain in her voice, who rose to be known as the Queen of Hip-hop Soul—just as Bessie Smith had been the Empress of the Blues—was Mary J. Blige. With the exception of Faith Evans, no other hip-hop diva ever expressed or channeled such emotional pain into her music and persona with as much drama and telling honesty. Blige perfected confessional, bluesy songs that charted her bumpy passages through life. *That* drew audiences to her, along, of course, with her powerful voice. Her persona made her one of the most interesting stars of the era and into the next millennium. Though eventually known to the mainstream, Blige would always have a greater impact on African American audiences, especially black women.

By now it almost seemed a hip-hop or diva cliché to say that Blige had come from tough beginnings. One of four children—with an older sister and two younger brothers—she was the daughter of a nurse and a musician. As she would tell it, her father "was never really around." "I had a tight relationship with my dad when I was a kid, and I wondered if I had done something wrong to make him leave." She grew up in the Schlobohm housing projects—dubbed the Slow Bomb by its residents—in Yonkers, New York. "There was always some shit going on," she once said. "Every day I would be getting into fights over *whatever*. You always had to prove yourself to keep from getting robbed or jumped." The family was "poor, but it never seemed that there was anything we wanted that we didn't get."

Like Lil' Kim, she was conscious of her looks. "I started listening to kids in my class who said I looked like a camel. I couldn't see myself being good at anything really. No one had ever really told me I could sing or do anything good." She found solace performing in the junior choir of the House of Prayer Church. "I felt so much better going to church every Sunday, just being there testifying and just being kids," she once said. "It seems all my problems started after I stopped going there." Dropping out of high school, Blige took odd jobs, styled hair for kids in her mother's apartment, and spent time getting high. Then at seventeen,

her friends talked her into recording a Karaoke–style rendition of Anita Baker's song, "Rapture." Her mother thought she had talent and, through a friend, was able to get a copy of the recording into the hands of Andre Harrell, then the CEO of Uptown Records. Impressed, he signed her to Uptown in 1990. Soon the company's ambitious young executive, Sean Combs, began working with her. Already a wunderkind who rose quickly at Uptown from intern to vice president of artists and repertoire (A & R), Combs worked with some of black music's most successful new stars—whether it be hip-hop performers or rhythm-and-blues stars, from Heavy D to Biggie Smalls to the group Jodeci. Combs had Blige sing *over* rhymes rather than sing over melodies. Her sound ultimately became a blend of neo-funk, rhythm and blues, and hip-hop. In 1992 her first album, *What's the 411?*, sold 2.2 million copies.

Shrewdly, Uptown set out to create a specific look, tied in to a specific image, for this "girl with doe eyes" and an almond-shaped face. That, of course, was important in establishing a professional identity for her that connected all the more to record-buyers and concert-goers. Often, she was seen wearing her signature applejack caps. Uptown's director of artist development, Sybil Pennix, wanted to retain Blige's basic style, which she believed was "the everyday girl look for girls from Mount Vernon, White Plains, and Yonkers," a look that partly obscured the face. "If you see black kids in the street, they have their hats pulled way down on their eyes to look mysterious," said Pennix. "Black people always had to obscure the way they look in some way. That goes back to not letting the white man know where we're coming from. We've gotten a lot of flack for pulling her hat down too far, but that's her." Paying attention to such details was Combs. "Everything, from your clothes, shoes, and make-up, he was in on," said Blige.

Despite the success of *What's the 411?* Blige appeared uneasy and acquired a reputation for being difficult. For many in show business, she was a "girl" with rough edges, an attitude, and bad manners. You could take the girl out of the ghetto. But could you take the ghetto out of the girl? During an early interview, she argued with a reporter. Then she asked the reporter to step outside to set the record straight. Other times, as *Newsweek* reported in its May 5, 1997, issue, it was rumored "she showed up at interviews drunk or high or not at all." Bad press followed an incident in London in 1992. Arriving late for a performance, she

out to be just the opposite, something very special. But she's still a victim because she doesn't know it yet.

Uptown enrolled Blige in a twenty-four-week program to teach her how to behave like a celebrity. "A lot of times in this industry, artists are pimped," said one of Blige's groomers. "It's like if you have a prostitute just going out there to bring in the money

No one could figure out why a young woman with so much success behaved so badly or recklessly.

sang three songs, and then abruptly left the stage. When she returned about forty minutes later, she was booed by the audience. It's a wonder anyone had stayed. No one could figure out why a young woman with so much success behaved so badly or recklessly. Was she uncomfortable with her sudden fame? Did all the attention from the media and fans make her feel insecure and doubtful of her talents? Was she trying to throw her career away? Was it a familiar case of a star who believed she didn't deserve success?

Andre Harrell was philosophical. "You're talking about taking an inner-city girl and delivering her to public opinion," he once said. "It's a tremendous responsibility being famous. Every now and then she might get grumpy. I guess with greatness there comes a little luggage." Referring to her background, Harrell offered a telling comment:

You can't get rid of all that pain and all those horrors overnight. She lacks the self-confidence of someone of her stature because she grew up with someone telling her, "You ain't nothing, and you're never going to be anything." In the end, she turned

and no one's catering to her well-being, then what happens? She just falls apart. If you don't put back into this person, if you don't educate them, stimulate them and motivate them it's a path to destruction." Blige may not have liked the reference to prostitution, but certainly the pimp analogy was appropriate for certain entertainment executives. "I believe that everyone is merely an actor, and you must be able to play your role for each particular situation," the representative also said. "Mary has to be able to talk to rap magazines and talk to Diane Sawyer. You must be able to fit into every particular realm of this business and of life." So the grooming began. But Blige hardly appeared pleased.

"Hell, I already knew how to sit right and talk right," said Blige. "I just didn't want to be Ms. Prissy or any of that other bulls–t. And even if I didn't know how to set my fork down right, f–k it—this is the way I want to eat, so screw whoever doesn't like it."

Yet Blige's attitude simply enhanced the image. Her fans liked the idea that she carried her past with her, that she had not forgotten all the pain she had endured, indeed that she remembered where she came from. And fans liked her recklessness. Stories still made the rounds about Mary, the drinker, the druggie, and the carouser; the Mary who got herself entangled in a reportedly abusive relationship with the singer K-Ci of the group Jodeci.

Later she tried to explain herself—and her actions. "I really didn't care about me or my career in the least bit," Blige said of her early years of fame. "I know it sounds weird, but it was one of the lowest points of my life. I didn't like myself and had a whole lot of people telling me there was something wrong with me." She also felt artistically stranded after Sean Combs was fired from Uptown by Andre Harrell in 1993. When Combs formed his own Bad Boy Entertainment, Blige couldn't go with him because of her contractual obligations. Of her con-

Preserving her personal identity? A partially obscured Mary J. Blige in one of her apple-jack hats.

temporaries, like the singers Brandy and later Beyoncé, Blige noted that "they always have their parents around them. I never had that. I was always alone, looking out for myself. So when Puff got his own company and started looking for singers just like me, it really hurt me."

Like TLC, she learned the hard way about the financial realities of the music industry. "You have to pay back every dime that the record company invested in you before you see a penny," she told *Essence* magazine in March 1995. "As hard as I worked, I wasn't making *any money* sometimes. And I wasn't happy about that at all. But I guess you could say I've become more of a businesswoman than I was before. I have more creative control over my vision because you can't trust anyone with your money, your life, your image."

Her only recourse seemed to be to let her music tell some of her story. Whether intended or not, in time her songs played on the troubled, hard-edged, inner city girl image. That certainly was the case with the 1994 release of Blige's album *My Life*. Saying she had been too insecure to write music for her first album, here she had songwriter credits for every song except her remake of the bluesy "I'm Going Down." "*My Life* is a dark, suicidal testimony," she later said. "I thought I was the only person that needed help, but there were so many other people ready to kill themselves too. So I saw how I moved people."

The same was true of her third album, *Share My World* in 1997, followed by *Mary* in 1999. Her first single from the latter, "All I Can Say" was written by Lauryn Hill, and she had a duet with former beau K-Ci on the song "Not Lookin'," in which she commented on gender politics (and perhaps their relationship): a man was out for pleasure; a woman wanted affection. Another duet, "Don't Waste Your Time," featured her with idol Aretha. Blige herself was now sometimes referred to as a new generation's Aretha. Of course, no one would ever be Aretha. But she was clearly an important artist and symbol for a new era. With her hair either red or blond, with her gold lame skirts, with her tight leather or leopard pants, and with her large, forbidding sunglasses, which covered part of her face much as the apple-jack caps once had done, she became a style-setter: a *fashionista* for the round-the-way girls. In its September 1998 issue, *Vogue* celebrated her style, as well as that of such other rappers as Lil' Kim and Missy Elliott, in an article "Rappers Deluxe," which featured them in furs and announced that rappers had traded "baggy for Bulgari" and were now "less ghetto, more Gucci."

Then came *No More Drama* in 2001, which made Mary J. Blige a mainstream star. Here she had a huge hit, "Family Affair," a sexy, pulsating dance number in which she exhorted her followers to leave conflicts and *attitude* behind—to join in a cathartic celebration of sound and movement. "Don't need no hateration/holleration," she sang. "Let's get it percolating / while you're waiting / so just dance for me," she called out. "Mary J. is in the spot tonight / And I'm going to make you feel all right." On another song, she began by saying: "I want to talk to the ladies tonight / about the situation I'm pretty sure you all can be able relate to." Then she let everyone know, especially the guys, that "today I'm not feeling pretty / See I'm feeling quite ugly. Having one of those days when I can't make up my mind / So don't even look at me." The song's title: "PMS." "The worst part of being a woman is PMS," she said. Many women found the song hard to resist. But mainly, on *No More Drama*, a confessional yet more mature Mary came into focus. On the title song "No More Drama," Blige—examining her life and its pain and problems—proclaimed that she was putting all of that drama behind her to start anew with a different point of view.

As her vulnerabilities became even more apparent, there were new accents for the rough-edged Mary that many identified with: now she could be tough yet sweet; hard yet warm; guarded yet willing to open the door to her softer side. But the greatest image shift came in the new millennium at the time of her sixth album, *Love and Life*, in 2003, which marked a return—after nine years—to working full-scale with Sean Combs, who shaped the songs around soul records of the

1970s. Still in a confessional mood, she informed her followers that the old Mary was a *new* Mary, liberated from excess drama. Mary J. Blige was supposedly happy, following her marriage to Kendu Isaacs. Her fans may have been skeptical about the happiness bit. All you had to do was take one look at Mary and you saw—behind her eyes—the face of a woman who you might feel still struggled with life's discontents. "Spend any time with Mary J. Blige and a certain sadness inevitably oozes into the atmosphere," *Entertainment Weekly* commented in its September 5, 2003, issue. "She's probably the greatest soul singer of her generation—a voice streaked with hard-living grit, a repertoire littered with tales of bad times and heavy hearts." In the imagination of her public, Mary J. Blige plowed on through life—and her music—with personal tensions that were real, not manufactured, and which might not ever go away entirely. A professional triumph came with her album *The Breakthrough*, which earned her eight Grammy nomination's. She won three.

The true source of her pain perhaps would never really be known. Yes, the childhood had been tough. But the details would always seem sketchy. Yes, bad love affairs had drained her. But exactly what went wrong in those relationships would never be fully discussed—or what made her feel the need to escape in alcohol and drugs. Her most (publicly) explicit problems were those of her career and the callousness and exploitation of the music industry. Most of the other facets seemed under wraps, unexplained, all kept by Mary to herself. That reticence to discuss *everything*—or perhaps even her own ability to yet sort out her deep-rooted sorrows—enabled her to maintain her mystery in a tell-all era. And that mystery endowed her with a glorious aura that made her an even more powerful artist—and an even more compelling metaphysical hip-hop/rhythm and blues goddess.

Mariah Carey:
Biracial Blues

During the 1990s, Mariah Carey climbed to the top tier of the music industry to become a best-selling recording artist and a multiple Grammy winner. Yet audiences seldom thought of her as an African American star. When Carey appeared on television, or when her music played on radios, black audiences at first had a feeling that there was something "ethnic" about her. Yet her racial/ethnic identity seemed undefined. Some even suggested it was hidden. Actually, Mariah Carey was biracial: the daughter of Patricia Carey, a white former opera singer and Alfred Roy Carey, a black aeronautics engineer from Venezuela. When she was three years old, her parents divorced. Afterward, it was tough going for the little girl living in Long Island, New York. There were always money problems as her mother anxiously searched for work. "We moved around thirteen times," she said of those early years. "We lived with 'boyfriends' or whomever. Sometimes it was 'You guys have to move tomorrow' type of thing. Maybe we didn't pay our rent. My entire childhood and adolescence were in some ways real great and in others a total mess. By the time I was six, I was my family's caretaker."

Growing up biracial was also difficult for Carey, who felt "separate from everybody." "My struggles began when I was five," she said. At school when she drew a picture of her father with a brown crayon, two white teacher's assistants laughed. As a girl, about all she knew for sure was that she wanted to sing. Her life took a storybook turn in 1988. By then the eighteen-year-old Carey was performing backups for the then-hot star Brenda K. Starr. That same year she met Sony entertainment executive Tommy Mottola at a party. He was given a copy of a Carey demo. After leaving the party, Mottola listened to it in his limousine, was so impressed that he headed back to speak to the girl with the five-octave voice, but could not find her. Of course, Mottola eventually caught up with her and was instrumental in her career.

Signed to a contract with Columbia Records, her success came quickly with the release of her debut album, *Mariah Carey*, that brought her two Grammys and hit singles: "Vision of Love," "I Don't Wanna Cry," "Someday," and "Love Takes Time." Her vocals were breathtaking. She could soar with the high notes of a soprano and dip to the low of an alto. She also mastered a soaring melisma, that vocal technique (popularized by Whitney Houston) of holding one syllable over several notes. With her later releases—she would sell 150 million albums—Carey tied with Elvis Presley in having more number one hits than anyone since the Beatles, who had twenty. Carey and Elvis each had seventeen. She also wrote or co-wrote almost all of her number one hits, and created what rapidly became a holiday standard, "All I Want for Christmas Is You."

No diva of the era quite exuded sex the way Carey did; in some respects, her personal style seemed to be *all* come-on with her big broad smile, her dreamy inviting eyes, her revealing low-cut dresses, and her delirious (and sometimes touching) eagerness to please. To watch her at the awards shows was a sight to behold. Whenever Carey had to step onstage, she rose from her seat like Aphrodite en route to Mount Olympus. She looked as if she was being transported to another world, and that smile seemed to offer the promise that she might take you along with her. No goddess ever accepted an award as blissfully and sensually as Ms. Carey. Yet oddly enough, aside from the pleasing perpetual come-on, there was something bland about this gorgeous babe.

Marketed as a pop star, not rhythm and blues and certainly not hip-hop, although rhythm and blues and hip-hop proved important to her sound and appeal, her racial background did not seem to be a topic for discussion. Carey never denied who she was or where she was from. But that background was kept *in* the background by her handlers. Instead, much media attention was focused on her relationship with Mottola, who became the CEO of Sony, parent company of Columbia Records. After twenty years of marriage, he left his wife to wed Carey in an elaborate ceremony, in which the bride wore a $25,000 gown that had a twenty-seven-foot train. Afterward, the couple moved into a palatial $10 mil-

No other star could rise from her seat to go onstage to accept an award like Mariah Carey.

Carey's career was in full swing until the film *Glitter*. But she surprised her critics by returning to the top of the charts with *The Emancipation of Mimi*.

lion home in Bedford, New York, which had two swimming pools, a recording studio, and specially built pizza ovens, just to name a few of the amenities. It looked like a match made in music heaven. Instead of a happy ending, now her problems, so she was later to say, were just beginning. Carey found Mottola over-bearing and over-controlling. Perhaps she should have known that was what happens when you marry the boss.

In time, the two fought about everything: about her choice of music, her choice of clothes, her choice of hairstyles. So dominating was Mottola that Carey felt she couldn't even leave the house for a hamburger without him tracking her down and telling her to get back home. It became "an emotionally abusive relationship," she said.

Feeling imprisoned, she called her Bedford mansion "Sing Sing." Later, she said the marriage almost killed her. From the start, though, Carey insisted on splitting all the bills. "I never wanted to be in a situation where someone could tell me to get out of my own house. Maybe it was because I didn't want people to say I was being taken care of. Of course, they said it anyway."

After four years of marriage, Carey left Mottola in 1997. For a time, she stayed at Sony. Yet she felt the company no longer had her best interests. Finally, she left to sign an $80 million deal with Virgin Records in 2000. But her career ran into trouble. Hoping to make the transition to movies, she appeared with Terrence Howard, Eric Benet, Dorian Harewood, and singer Da

Brat in the film *Glitter*, the tale of a backup singer discovered by a club DJ who is determined to make her a star. Blasted by the critics, *Glitter* backfired on Carey and drew howls from audiences. Known as one long excruciating embarrassment, *Glitter*'s soundtrack had also been released on September 11, 2001.

At the time of this career failure, stories popped up about Carey's weight gain, then her "nervous breakdown," and a possible suicide attempt. Collapsing at her mother's home in Long Island, Carey was hospitalized because of "exhaustion," so the media was informed. Virgin Records reportedly paid her $28 million to leave the label.

star Derek Jeter, who was also biracial. "I used to think that 90 percent of the reason my life was messed up was because I was mixed," she said. "It was important for me that he was from a loving interracial family. He was a catalyst for my transition from my life with Tommy. And I'm so grateful for that."

But Mariah Carey had other problems. Now in her thirties, she had to deal with the issue of age. The history of popular culture already was littered with pop stars, some of whom had been great artists, whose careers lost steam or just collapsed as they hit their mid- and late-thirties—and as a new generation of record buyers comes of age, on the

Female music and movie stars always know the clock is ticking. For a star like Carey, her appeal, aside from the incredible voice, was very much tied to her looks and sexuality.

Afterward her album for Island Records—*Charmbracelet*—failed to put her back on top.

By now, race had come into the story, as it looked as if Carey were trying to reclaim, or hold onto, her career by aligning herself with African Americans. In her 1998 one-woman show, *I'm Still Here . . . Damn It!*, comedienne Sandra Bernhard had particularly harsh words for Carey: "Now she's trying to backtrack on our asses, gettin' real niggerish up there at the Royalton Hotel suite, with Puff Daddy and all the greasy chain-wearing black men. 'Oooh, Daddy . . . I got a little bit of black in me, too. I didn't tell you that?'" Despite such harsh criticism, Carey believed she was coming to terms with her racial background, thanks in part to her well-publicized relationship with baseball

lookout for its own stars, not those of a previous era. Some, like Ethel Waters, were able to make the transition by establishing a new identity for themselves. Would Mariah Carey ever be able to do that? Or was Mariah Carey finished?

Somehow against the odds, Carey released a new album in 2005 titled *The Emancipation of Mimi*. Mimi had been her childhood nickname. Critics, who had not expected much, did a double take. Her voice was as strong as ever and her sound was part soul, part rhythm and blues, part gospel, part pop, part hip-hop. Of course, her sound had always been that (guest rappers had appeared on her records as early as 1995). But now it was recognized as such. The fans loved it. *The Emancipation*

Two great voices, two great stars: Mariah Carey and Whitney Houston.

of Mimi became the best-selling album of 2005 and the winner of three Grammys. Though she had backed off from discussing race in the past, now she appeared more eager to do so, or perhaps now a segment of the media pushed her to do so. When she appeared on the cover of *Essence* in April 2005, the headline read: *"Mariah Carey: America's Most Misunderstood Black Woman."* Still, Carey never had the intense following among African Americans that other divas did. And at times, perhaps because of her statements about the difficulty of growing up biracial, true as they no doubt were, for some she seemed something of a tragic mulatto figure. But *that* seemed to be changing: African American perceptions of her. To her credit, Carey survived at a time when most had predicted her career was over.

Oprah, the Supreme

During the Clinton years, Oprah Winfrey became even more prominent on the national landscape: she was indeed the most powerful, the most watched, and the wealthiest woman on television. Her Midas touch even extended to projects and personalities in some way *related* to her. Sales of her personal chef's cookbook, *In the Kitchen with Rosie*, stunned the publishing industry when it then became the fastest-selling hardcover book in publishing history. Later, a frequent guest on her program, Dr. Phil, emerged as the star of his own hugely successful talk show, produced by Oprah herself.

Were there ever any chinks in her armor? Actually; briefly, *yes*. Midway in the 1990s, even the almighty Oprah was at the center of stories that were not always flattering. Word spread, and eventually hit the press, of off-camera tensions at her television program. A portrait was painted of an all-controlling Oprah who, behind the scenes, was perhaps not what she appeared to be in front of the camera. The July 23, 1994, issue of *TV Guide* commented that at Oprah's Harpo Studios, the style and atmosphere in the building "could not be more decorous: muted colors; open, glass offices; noise-muffling carpeting. But beneath the exquisitely maintained surface, there is—as with so many of her guests—turmoil." The publication reported that in the past two years, her show had lost nine producers. "Though the myth of Winfrey's extended working family is in one sense true—people *are* cared for and coddled—in another sense, as with so many families, there is also dysfunction." "People adore her," said a former Winfrey associate. "They give their lives to her. People who work there get divorced, put off having kids, having no outside lives. Because everything, all your time and energy is given to Oprah." The cause of the tensions was attributed to an executive producer at the show, who had been a friend and professional associate of Winfrey's since they both had worked together in Baltimore. Some staffers found the executive producer too demanding and at times too humiliating of those around her. "What was unusual at *Oprah* was the level of anxiety—bordering on terror." Said one staffer: "You walked on eggshells every moment."

But most baffling was the fact that Winfrey appeared—to some staffers—at a loss in handling the situation. "Oprah knew for years how awful it was to work there. We all complained to her. But she was afraid to do anything," a longtime producer later said. "It was just so disturbing and sad. Oprah would do these shows about raising your self-esteem, but she had terrible problems with it herself. She never felt as if she were responsible for her own success, so she let Harpo just run out of control."

Among staffers, there was a belief that Winfrey was "not good at confrontation—a condition to which she herself will admit." "She just wants to be loved," said a then-current employee. "She's a [Southern-style] matriarch," another associate added. "From the time a new producer joins the show, in fact, Winfrey becomes and remains intimately involved with his or her life, handing out advice on things like boyfriends or finances, buying jewelry and new cars, offering employees free, professional therapy sessions." "She is everybody's mother," said a former employee, "which is lovely, except that it can become smothering."

At the same time, despite the fact that *The Oprah Winfrey Show* had won two Emmys in May 1994—for best show and best host—*TV Guide* pointed out, as did other media outlets, that the ratings "fell to their lowest point in three years. Not dramatically. Not enough to cause panic in TV-station executives' ranks. But noticeably. 'Everyone in the industry has been talking about it,' a spokesperson for a rival talk show says. 'We've been wondering when people outside would start to sit up and take notice.'"

With competition from such other talk shows as those hosted by Jenny Jones, Ricki Lake, and Jerry Springer, all known for their bluntness, their political incorrectness, and some might say their unfiltered trashiness, *The Oprah Winfrey Show* had to somehow stay ahead of the pack, yet without lowering its standards. Eventually, the executive producer who had proven so difficult left the show. Winfrey began doing lighter fare. Often, there were celebrity stories. Often, there were shows about self-help and spirituality. Later down the road,

Oprah Winfrey – so prominent on the national landscape.

she turned her eye to make-overs, not only for women who wanted to shed their dowdy selves, but also for people who wanted different living spaces, different decors. With the help of experts, homes and apartments were transformed.

But Oprah never entirely abandoned her focus on shows about American lives, families, and relationships in tatters. Uncovering some of the nation's dirty little secrets, she again brought on experts to advise the troubled guests on her programs. But in some respects, Oprah herself became America's grand therapist.

Of course, with her steady weight concerns, Oprah was a living example of the way one could make herself over time and again. At one point, she lost eighty pounds (going down from a high of 220). Almost religiously, she did sit-ups, lifted weights, and daily ran five-to-eight miles. In 1994, she even completed the Marine Corps Marathon. With the zeal and discipline for which she was famous, Winfrey made it through the slump and rose to be an even more appealing public figure.

In 1997, she made headlines because of a remark on her April 16, 1996, broadcast, which had discussed mad cow disease: a debilitating and ultimately fatal illness caused by eating beef from contaminated livestock. So stunned was Winfrey by much of what she heard about the disease that she commented: "It has just stopped me cold from eating another burger." For any other talk-show personality, the remark would have prompted laughter and then been forgotten by the next day. But a Texas rancher complained, saying that because of her comment, cattle prices actually fell and that he lost almost $7 million. Afterward, Winfrey was sued in federal court by the Texas cattle industry, which accused her of defaming beef on her talk show. A trial in Amarillo, Texas, followed. When the talk show queen arrived in the city, reporters, photographers, and television crews were in pursuit. In February 1998, headlines announced that Oprah had been cleared of the liability charges. If anything, Winfrey's determination to stand up for herself won her even more admirers.

Otherwise, her nonstop schedule and productivity continued. She produced such TV movies as *Before Women Had Wings* (in which she starred), *The Wedding*, and later the adaptation of Zora Neale Hurston's *Their Eyes Were Watching God*, under the banner of *Oprah Winfrey Presents*. All were ratings hits. Less successful was the film adaptation of Toni Morrison's novel *Beloved*, in which she starred. The movie's failure at the box-office may have been one of Winfrey's greatest disappointments. But she remained undaunted. Believing Americans were not reading enough, she established her own book club. Her stamp of approval just about guaranteed huge book sales. That included the reissue of a classic like John Steinbeck's *East of Eden*, or later, Tolstoy's *Anna Karenina*. Then she turned the publishing industry on its head when she launched her own magazine, *O*, which monthly featured her on the cover and became another instant hit. She also became a partner in a new cable station, Oxygen, which was devoted to women's issues. In 2001, she donated $10 million to a Nelson Mandela school for girls in South Africa. In the next millennium, she also embarked on

a series of four daylong seminars entitled "Live Your Best Life Tour." Tickets in Raleigh, North Carolina, were priced at $185 and sold out in just two hours. The proceeds went to a local charity. In 2004, she surprised her studio audience when she announced that each one of the 276 in attendance would receive a new Pontiac. The automobile company picked up the taxes, registration, and title licensing fees. Winners simply had to pay the insurance.

She also bought herself a $51 million estate in Montecito that sat on forty-two acres. Not long afterward, she gave herself a star-studded fiftieth birthday party in Santa Barbara with a who's who list of guests: everyone from Tina Turner, Stevie Wonder, John Travolta, and Diane Sawyer to Brad Pitt, Jennifer Aniston, and Maya Angelou. Later, she threw another star-studded bash to honor African American women of prominence: everyone from Cicely Tyson (who, Oprah said, was the inspiration for the event), Coretta Scott King, Dorothy Height, Melba Moore, Halle Berry, Janet Jackson, Patti LaBelle, and gospel star Shirley Caesar, to Maya Angelou, Terry McMillan, and Diahann Carroll. Of course, the press let it be known who was *not* on the guest list, none other than Winfrey's *Color Purple* co-star, Whoopi Goldberg.

Was there nothing this woman could not do? Well, apparently, there was. In 1992, it was reported that Winfrey had approached a Manhattan shop, which, though opened for business, kept its doors locked for security reasons. She was turned away. "It happened to me twice. I went to ring the doorbell in a store, and the people inside gestured us to go away," said Winfrey. Locating a pay phone, she called the store to see if it was open. She was told it was. "We walked back across to the store and saw two white ladies coming out," said Winfrey. "We rang the buzzer again, and they wouldn't let us in. I thought, 'I think this is a racist moment I'm experiencing here.' Andre [her hairdresser who was with her] was saying, 'Yeah, this is racist.' I couldn't believe it was happening." Back in Chicago, Winfrey called the store again, explained the situation, and was told that the store

"We walked back across to the store and saw two white ladies coming out. We rang the buzzer again, and they wouldn't let us in. I thought, 'I think this is a racist moment I'm experienceing here.' "

had been doing inventory. "Oh, no you weren't because I saw other women coming out of the store," Winfrey said. Later she spoke to the company's president who apologized and offered her a complimentary spending spree. "No, thanks, I won't be coming to your store again," Winfrey was quoted as saying.

In 2005, a similar incident occurred when Winfrey arrived at a posh store in Paris to do a little shopping. Again, she was refused admittance. The incident made headlines. The *New York Post*'s June 23 issue reported the store had refused to let her in because it had been "having a problem with North Africans." Representatives for the store, however, later apologized, saying that staffers were preparing for a special event. During her new TV season in the fall, Winfrey discussed the incident with the president of the store's United States division. Though there remained a discussion about what had actually been the cause, Winfrey wanted it known that even as powerful and productive a woman as herself could be discriminated against.

As the years moved on, other aspects of the Winfrey story remained the same as before. She and longtime beau Stedman Graham still had not married. But Winfrey didn't seem fazed by that fact. In a sense, she had refused (for whatever reasons) to settle into the type of bourgeois domestic arrangement that would have been expected of her. Yet no one questioned it. She still waged a war with her weight problems. Yet in the mid-1990s, she made a surprising confession. "I remember the last time I lost weight," she said in 1995. "Some woman said to me, 'Well, at least we still have Barbara Bush,' and I thought, 'Oh, no, they don't like me anymore.' I didn't deliberately go out and put the weight back on for that reason, but that concern was certainly embedded in my subconscious." One of the rare occasions on which Winfrey looked exasperated occurred when rumors swirled about her relationship with her best friend, Gayle King. Winfrey announced on June 3, 1997, "I am not a lesbian." In 2006, she again denied that she and King were lovers.

But basically, Winfrey could do what she pleased without fear of public censure or rejection. She remained an untouchable figure who was hardly scrutinized nor criticized in the way that another famous woman of the time, Martha Stewart, had been, even before her legal problems. Of course, the deeper forces at work within Oprah Winfrey, once again what drove her to nonstop productivity, and what indeed was left of the "private" non-public Oprah, remained as elusive as before. So too was the basis of her unprecedented appeal to so broad an audience—and the different ways in which whites and African Americans viewed her. Nonetheless, Winfrey herself recalled the comment that Quincy Jones had made to her so many years earlier: "Your future's so bright, it burns my eyes." Even in Hollywood, the town of perpetual hype, truer words had never been spoken.

**Ms. Jackson:
Dandridge Fever**

Though the shadow of her brother may still have loomed over her, Janet Jackson, in the 1990s, still appeared willing, indeed insistent, on ambitiously going the full distance with everything she pursued. In concert and on her videos, she was a magnetic dancer, perhaps over-choreographed and perhaps never as free-spirited as one might have hoped, but still enjoyably stylized and determined to put on a good show. But the real goal appeared to be to replace the ingenue image with a more adult Janet. Working with Jimmy Jam and Terry Lewis, her 1989 album, *Rhythm Nation: 1814,* which sold briskly in the new decade, presented her as a socially conscious heroine, with comments on racism, poverty, and social injustices.

But during the Clinton era, as that rapaciously sexual chameleon Madonna dominated the charts and also the coverage of the media, Jackson appeared hell-bent—with the release of the album titled, *Janet.* (her name followed by a period)—on creating a sexually bolder persona. On the single "If," a hot and assured Janet announced, "Close your eyes and imagine my body undressed." Later there came the album *The Velvet Rope.* Here on the single "Rope Burn," she commanded: "Tie me up, tie me down / make me moan real loud / take off my clothes, no one wants to know / I wanna feel a rope burn." Yet no matter how hard she tried to be womanly and sexually aggressive, she looked to many like a good girl playing bad—and an entertainer incapable of spontaneity. Referring to her as a public cipher, *The New York Times* critic Jon Pareles commented that she did not "come across as a natural performer; there's effort behind every dance move, nervousness in every high note. On *Janet.,* she hides her voice less than before, challenging herself with long phrases and using her lack of vocal power to signal intimacy and vulnerability. Yet her stardom has less to do with self-expression than with discipline and technological manipulation, just getting the job done." The one occasion when she projected a relaxed natural sensuality was in the black-and-white Herb Ritts–directed video, "Love Will Never Do," in which she loos-

ened up in a simplified setting: just a pretty young woman flirting and playfully taunting a couple of guys. Still, her music career soared. In the early 1990s, she had snagged a three-album contract with Virgin Records that reportedly earned her between $32 and $50 million. The albums did well. So did her concert performances when she filled stadiums and brought in viewers for her HBO production, *Janet Live.*

Yet Jackson may have felt that the height of stardom—as well as the key to reaching an even broader audience—would come only with a successful acting career. Shortly after director John Singleton scored with his film *Boyz N the Hood,* Jackson won a leading role in his second feature, *Poetic Justice,* opposite Tupac Shakur. Though able to hold the screen, she still looked like she was struggling to be grown-up; she was not quite a leading lady, especially when compared with her co-stars, the assured Tyra Ferrell and the rambunctiously overwrought Regina King. Her speaking voice also proved problematic: hers was the voice of a girl; she didn't sound like a fully formed person with varied life experi-

The transition to adult movie roles: Jackson with Tupac Shakur in *Poetic Justice.*

The women of the Jackson family: Katherine Jackson, at top, with her daughters Janet, Rebbie, and La Toya.

ences. The same was true of her brother Michael. Other singers faced similar problems when they tried to make the switch to films. Hollywood producers—and moviegoers—had shown little interest in her.

Yet determined to become a movie star, she proved prescient when she publicly expressed her admiration for Dorothy Dandridge—and her desire to portray Dandridge on the screen. When word spread through the film capital of a forthcoming biography of Dandridge, to be published in 1997, other black actresses became caught up in Dandridge fever. So did a significant segment of Black America. For this new generation, Dandridge's life and career encapsulated the inner conflicts, frustrations, and mighty dreams of African American women in Hollywood. She remained the one great complicated, larger than life, tragic black film actress of the 20th century. Many actresses of the 1990s realized that

Dandridge's struggles within a white-male-dominated movie industry were not too different from their own.

On rare occasions in the past, there had been a search for a black actress to play an important movie role. That had been the case with the role of Peola in the original 1934 version of *Imitation of Life* and then for the lead in *Carmen Jones* in 1954. Now the famous as well as the unknowns yearned to portray Dandridge: such actresses as Vanessa Williams, Lela Rochon, Lynn Whitfield, Whitney Houston, and Halle Berry seemed ready and willing to play her at the drop of a hat. When that biography of Dandridge was finally published, *Ebony*, which in the past had celebrated Dandridge with major stories, ran an excerpt from the book with a cover portrait of Dandridge and such actresses as Berry, Houston, Williams, and Jackson. And the question: "Who Will Play Dorothy Dandridge."

Janet Jackson may have felt the role was hers: after all, she had spoken up about it. But the most famous of the era's divas, Whitney Houston, won the rights to the book and was initially set to play the leading role. Eager to do anything to please Houston, Disney Studios was ready to mount a lavish production around her. But due to a number of factors, the Houston project did not materialize. In the end, Halle Berry starred as Dandridge, not in a feature film but in an HBO presentation, *Introducing Dorothy Dandridge*. Jackson did pay tribute to Dandridge in her black-and-white music video, "Twenty Fourplay." But otherwise for Janet Jackson, the experience of losing the role of a lifetime must have been disheartening and perhaps depressing.

Throughout the 1990s, Jackson sought hard to keep her private life private. Though stories surfaced of a feud with her brother Michael, she came to his defense when he was accused of the molestation of an underage boy in 1993. She said she was convinced of his innocence. But she did not seem able to hold back in commenting on her sister La Toya, especially after La Toya appeared to betray Michael by saying she believed he was guilty of the molestation charges. "That's when people feel it's true, when it comes from your own flesh and blood. To me, it's just her way of jumping on something to get attention. Maybe it's because she never had the success she wanted," said Jackson. "I feel like I have only one sister, Rebbie. What's going on in La Toya's life, I don't even know. I haven't spoken to her in I don't know how long. The person I see on the news and these infomercials is not the person I grew up [with]." She also denied La Toya's claims that the Jackson children had been physically abused. For many, Jackson, in what was repeatedly called a dysfunctional family, was considered the Normal One.

Throughout the decade, rumors swirled about additional cosmetic surgery. Indeed, Jackson looked terrific, but with a nose that

A new look for Jackson, who was known for her discipline and focus — and her determination to change with the times. Perhaps no one else worked harder to be a star.

Ready for her close-up, La Toya, the family rebel.

clearly was different from that of those earlier years. The press also reported on supposed romances with Bobby Brown (before Whitney) and Robert De Niro. But Janet said close to nothing. Even her relationship with Rene Elizondo, whom she had dated since 1988, was rarely discussed. La Toya, however, broke the news that the two had secretly married. Jackson's publicist denied the story. But in 2001, details of the marriage were made public when the two fought it out in court over their divorce. Elizondo wanted their prenuptial agree-

ment nullified. At the time of the signing, he had suffered from low self-esteem, so he said. After all, Janet Jackson was a huge star, and he was a lowly whatever. He also said he had helped shape her new image. He asked for a $25 million settlement. Perhaps it was now clear why Jackson had always looked as if she trusted few people.

Still, Janet Jackson remained focused on her career. At times, she looked almost desperate to stay current by continuing to exploit her sexuality. That seemed to be the case in 2004, shortly before the release of her CD *Damita Jo*. At the conclusion of a duet between Jackson and Justin Timberlake at the Super Bowl telecast, Timberlake—as he later said he had been instructed—pulled down the top of Jackson's costume. Suddenly, there on national television, Janet Jackson's breast was exposed! A countrywide outcry followed. Critics complained that this family show had turned crude and vulgar, thanks to Ms. Jackson. Others said it was merely a tawdry, but feeble, attempt by Jackson to promote her forthcoming album. The National Football League was also indignant. So, too, was the network that had broadcast the game, CBS, which feared fines from the Federal Communications Commission. Letting it be known that he had no idea she would be bare breasted, Timberlake said it was a "wardrobe malfunction." It had been his understanding that only the top layer of her costume would come off. Jackson concurred and appeared surprised and stung by the criticism. Possibly from Jackson's perspective, the cruelest blow was a comment by *The New York Times* television critic Alessandra Stanley: "Perhaps the one moment of honesty in that coldly choreographed tableau was when the cup came off and out tumbled what looked like the normal middle-aged woman's breast instead of an idealized Playboy bunny implant."

But most damaging to her career were the tepid sales of *Damita Jo*. *Entertainment Weekly*, in its April 9, 2004, issue, lamented that the album was the same one she had been making since 1993's *Janet*. "By now, though, her endless wanna-bump-all-night emoting sounds one-dimensional and juvenile, a far cry from the serious-adult-artist image she likes to present. These days, Michael discloses more in his angry, paranoid musical hissy fits than his sister does in her own songs." Was Jackson's heyday about to come to an end? That question lingered even after a new album, *20 Y.O.*, appeared in 2006.

Regardless, Janet Jackson had made a place for herself in pop history. She was one of the great performers. Despite her reticence to discuss her private life (and her later relationship with music mastermind Jermaine Dupri), an ongoing story had enveloped her nonetheless. When in the year 2005 her brother Michael was on trial on new charges of child molestation, members of the entire Jackson family rallied around him and appeared in the courtroom on various occasions. The day that family members dressed in white was particularly memorable for media hounds. Were they trying to look innocent and pure of heart? Were they hoping to be stunningly stylish amidst such woes—like demi-gods and goddesses who stood above the puny tribulations of the rest of humankind? Was it one more performance for this family of performers? Returning to the family fold was La Toya, standing near Janet. It was an iconic image planted indelibly into the collective consciousness of an entire nation: La Toya, the bad sister, and Janet, the good one, united in a common cause with the other Jacksons.

A more sexualized image for Jackson.

Whitney:
Troubling Times for
the Pop Princess

The other diva who had risen to dream girl status in the 1980s, but whose career and image were now undergoing a disturbing transition, was the troubled Whitney Houston. Perhaps no star's public persona was as ruthlessly dissected, analyzed, and ultimately trashed as was Houston's in the 1990s and the decade that followed. Public perceptions of her changed dramatically.

At the start of the decade, Houston remained an all-American pop princess. Her career soared to even greater heights. What took her in a wholly new professional direction was the 1992 film, *The Bodyguard.* Writer–director Lawrence Kasdan's screenplay had been floating around for well over a decade. Its story was that of a pop star who, after receiving death threats, hires a loner bodyguard to protect her. A relationship develops between the two. At one time, *The Bodyguard* was a vehicle for Steve McQueen. This was also the same project that had once been envisioned for Diana Ross and Ryan O'Neal. In the 1990s, however, there was no chance that such a film would star Ross. The studios now turned their eyes toward Houston. Here was a gorgeous woman with movie-star attributes and a built-in fan base. Not only was she selling in record stores, but she was drawing in huge crowds at her concerts. Few stars received as much media coverage. Then at the height of his stardom, actor Kevin Costner wanted to work with Houston. No one seemed to have any particular concerns as to whether or not Houston could act. The feeling no doubt was that Houston, so dramatically and emotionally charged in her music, might be just as compelling as an actress. Besides, any film starring Houston would also have a soundtrack with Houston singing. That alone should ensure profits for a film. Now was the time to do *The Bodyguard*—with Houston and Costner as the stars and Mick Jackson as its director.

Onscreen, Houston and Costner had a cautious kind of chemistry. Neither seemed ready to jump into the other's arms. Each always seemed on guard. But that proved perfect. *The Bodyguard* was often a drama about two people afraid to feel or fall in love.

It also touched on issues of class (the high-flying diva and the lowly protector). Not since Ross's performance in *Lady Sings the Blues* had an African American female performer had so strong, or so discussed, a screen debut. Though not as critically successful as Ross's work, Houston's performance was far better than some of the critics gave her credit for. Haughty as all get-out, Houston gave a tough, shrewd, assured star performance: her pop star heroine could be imperial, demanding, abrasive, dismissive yet vulnerable and sensitive. Most importantly, she had an electric, glamorous movie star presence, big enough to fill the big screen. *The Bodyguard* ended up being a smash hit in the domestic market *and* abroad. Generally, it was assumed that the films of black stars did not do as well in Europe (with the exception, for a time, of the films of Wesley Snipes). Houston clearly had international appeal. All the studios took notice.

And indeed, the soundtrack was a hit with the sweeping romantic ballads "I Will Always Love You" (written by Dolly Parton) and "I Have Nothing" going to the top of the charts. In other hands, both songs might have been sappy, each a tale of a woman hopelessly lost without her man. But in "I Have Nothing," Houston turned lyrics like "Don't make me close one more door / I don't want to hurt any more" and "Stay in my arms if you dare / Must I imagine you there / Don't walk away from me" into queenly demands. Hers was the sound of authority; a woman aware of her vulnerabilities in a primal struggle with a man she loves; yet a woman not willing to relinquish control. With her big powerful voice, and her ability to reach and sustain those high notes, Houston transformed it into a triumphant anthem.

Appearing to have reached a new level of emotional maturity, and having acquired a type of romantic wisdom, Houston was now at the peak of her career and was elevated to a vaulted and much envied position. She had managed to do something that the rap stars hadn't. Nor had Janet Jackson. In households throughout the nation, both the younger generation and that generation's parents were listening to

Houston. Still crossing over lines of age, class, and race, her music appealed to a vast audience that felt a true emotional connection to her.

Then came the film version of Terry McMillan's best-selling novel, *Waiting to Exhale*, which had surprised the publishing industry. Previously, the fiction of black female writers such as Toni Morrison and Alice Walker had had commercial success. Indeed, at one point in the 1990s, Morrison, Walker, and McMillan were all on *The New York Times'* bestseller list at the same time. But while the novels of Morrison and Walker were considered "literary" and "serious," McMillan reached a previously ignored and largely untapped audience: mainly African American women eager for popular fiction with readily identifiable contemporary characters and situations. *Waiting to Exhale* was a new kind of black pop novel, which would be imitated by scores of other young black writers, male and female, in the years to come.

Still, the film industry didn't have high hopes for the movie. Was there really an audience for a drama about four young African American women dealing with their relationships (with men and their families) while maintaining their friendships with one another? The critics were mixed about the movie. But *Waiting to Exhale*—an ensemble piece that co-starred Houston with Angela Bassett, Lela Rochon, and Loretta Devine under Forest Whitaker's direction—opened as the country's number one film and became something of a cultural phenomenon. African American women went to see it more than once, sometimes in groups. Here was a classic case of a film (a post-feminist tale) that touched on, if it did not answer, the needs of an audience for some comment on issues and conflicts confronting black women in the 1990s. The film also crossed over, reaching African American men and also white female moviegoers. Rightly or wrongly, much of the film's commercial success, in the eyes of the movie moguls, was due to Whitney Houston. Again there was a hit soundtrack, produced by Babyface, which featured, along with Houston, a lineup of glittering divas: Aretha Franklin, Patti LaBelle, Chaka Khan, Cece Winans, Mary J. Blige, Faith Evans, the group TLC, Toni Braxton, Brandy, For Real, Shanna, and Sonja Marie.

Among African American stars, Houston was clearly Hollywood's golden girl. Hotly pursued by the studios, Houston set up her own production company and struck a deal to do films for Disney. In 1996, she starred opposite the era's most acclaimed African American leading man, Denzel Washington, in *The Preacher's Wife*, a remake of the 1947 *The Bishop's Wife* with Loretta Young, Cary Grant, and David Niven. Though a box-office disappointment, *The Preacher's Wife* had a fine gospel-style soundtrack, and Houston's career remained in high gear. Showbiz trade papers like *Daily Variety* carried front-page stories that she had won the rights to the big Dandridge biography and would play the role that just about every other young black actress in Hollywood had hoped for. Then there was a sad turn of events. Houston became pregnant, but suffered a miscarriage. Eventually, she elected not to play Dandridge, a role ironically that might have worked well for her.

But precisely at this time, the Houston image, so skillfully cultivated by Clive Davis and her handlers as well as Houston herself, began to unravel. In the mind of the public, Houston had made a terrible lapse of judgment (to put it mildly) when she married the singer Bobby Brown in 1992. The wedding had been a grand affair on the grounds of Houston's five-acre $11 million mansion in New Jersey. Eight hundred guests were in attendance as a stunning Houston walked down the aisle in a $40,000 Marc Bouwer wedding gown.

Right away there were concerns about this match. Could any two stars have been any more different? She had come of age in a middle-class family and community. He had grown up outside Boston in Roxbury's sometimes-violent Orchard Park Projects. She seemed the embodiment of youthful ladylike sophistication and elegance. He appeared to be all homeboy and *street*. She was controlled sensuality. He was out of control raw sexuality. She was demure. He was explosive. Her career was flying high with an income of $34 million in 1993–94

The different faces of Whitney Houston, whose film *The Bodyguard,* with Kevin Costner, became a huge international hit.

that placed her 23rd on *Forbes's* list of the world's top-earning entertainers. His career had gone *Kaputt*. Having once been a member of the teen idol group New Edition, he had great success as a solo performer with a hit song like "My Prerogative," in which he generated a fierce, sexy energy and defiance. But the hits had stopped coming. Most importantly, her private life was precisely that, *private*. His was in constant motion that was constant fodder for the tabloids. Offstage, he was considered a "bad boy," in and out of trouble with the law and known to have had any number of women in and out of his life. He reportedly had three children by two former girlfriends. Following the marriage, he was almost killed in a 1995 shootout in Roxbury. That same year, he was treated for alcohol abuse at the Betty Ford Center. And often it appeared as if she had to come to his rescue. When he was about to lose his $1.5 million Tudor-style home in Atlanta, which the IRS had put tax liens on, her management company Nippy, Inc. bought the house at a public auction. But apparently, to little avail. *People* later reported that the "once-stylish home now lies abandoned, with doors hanging off their hinges, toilets overflowing and snakes slithering across the bottom of the swimming pool." No one could figure out why they had married. No one believed it would last. No one probably wanted it to last. But the couple had a daughter, Bobbi Kristina, and remained together longer than anyone had imagined.

Yet during the mid- and late 1990s into the next century, scandalous stories and ugly gossip surfaced about Houston: about reported separations between Brown and her; about missed concert dates; about her use of drugs. The stories were not new to show business insiders; they had been around for several years. But now the stories went public. The media, once so adoring of Houston, now appeared eager to dismantle the old image. Houston still commanded star treatment with cover articles in such publications as *Harper's Bazaar* and *Premiere*. But just about everything else, from the *National Enquirer* to *Star* to *People* to *Us Weekly* ran features on a frazzled and seemingly out-of-control Whitney, who reck-lessly disregarded advice of family and friends as she rushed down a path of seeming self-destructiveness. The press reported that Houston had begun missing performances around 1994. Drawing much attention was a scheduled concert at the 12,500-seat Chronicle Pavilion in Concord, California, which she canceled just before curtain time. Then there was a performance at a White House state dinner for South African President Nelson Mandela: Houston arrived two hours late. By 1996, a book chronicling her problems, *Bad Girl, Good Girl: An Insider's Biography of Whitney Houston*, was published.

Of course, most stories centered on her marriage. "Whitney Houston: With a new movie and obsessed fans to worry about, she doesn't need husband troubles. So why is she back with bad boy Bobby Brown?" was the headline of the December 18, 1995, *People* cover story. Houston was also one of the first African American female stars who had to deal with published reports that she was gay. In the past, insider stories or "whispers" had made the rounds about the same-sex relationships of stars like Ma Rainey, Bessie Smith, Ethel Waters, and Billie Holiday. But while the women were alive, never did such stories make it to print. "I'm not gay, I'm not lesbian," *People* quoted Houston as saying in its April 17, 2000, issue. When asked by the *Los Angeles Times* to cite the biggest misconception about her, Houston replied: "That I'm gay, that my husband is a womanizer, that he's a wife-beater." Houston's comments on the same-sex issue appeared before Oprah's.

For a time, Whitney remained above the gossip. Within the industry, no one cared about the headlines as long as they didn't affect business; as long as Houston kept selling records. Her album, *My Love Is Your Love*, sold 9 million copies. It was also assumed that, despite the stumble with *The Preacher's Wife*, she would continue making hit movies. At the Grammy telecast in 2000, she gave a rousing performance and walked off with a Grammy for her song "It's Not Right, but It's Okay." That had been her sixth Grammy, but the first since 1993. "Honey, this one is for you, the original R&B king. I love you," she said to husband Brown from the podium.

One of the entertainment world's most publicized marriages: Houston and Bobby Brown.

But the rest of 2000 was not as illustrious, and matters took a turn for the worst. At Hawai`i's Keahole-Kona International Airport, she was stopped by security guards, who reportedly spotted 15.2 grams of marijuana in her pocketbook. Houston simply left the bag with the guards, boarded the plane, and by the time police arrived, was airborne. At a photo shoot for the cover of *Jane* magazine, she kept staffers waiting for hours. Once Houston arrived, so the magazine's editor Jane Pratt later said, "She was acting really strange. She was singing to herself. Then she would pretend to play the piano, like an air piano. Her eyes were very heavy-lidded." Though Houston said she had a cracked tooth, Pratt felt that "Novocain doesn't make you act that way. Everyone there thought she was on something."

But the most publicized event occurred during a rehearsal 48 hours before her scheduled performance—a medley to be done with Garth Brooks, Ray Charles, Isaac Hayes, Queen Latifah, and Dionne Warwick—on the Oscar broadcast of 2000.

Appearing unfocused and disoriented, she flubbed the lyrics to "Over the Rainbow." Finally, Burt Bacharach, the event's music director, told her to go home. "She just kind of moved her mouth a little bit," reported an observer. Said singer Garth Brooks: "Um, I can only say this about Whitney: she came in, she rehearsed, she tried her best, but she was so sick, and we'll just leave it at that." Said Bacharach: "Whitney's chronic condition is very sad." On the Oscar broadcast, Faith Hill was brought in as the last minute replacement. Within the industry, this incident may have hurt Houston more than anything else. To be unprepared for Hollywood's biggest night was a violation of industry codes and decorum, and was tantamount to blatantly insulting the industry.

Afterward, the stories about her became even more widespread, and even more a part of the public record. *People* ran a cover story that many within show business considered damaging: *"Whitney's Troubled Times: Her Oscar Fiasco Caps Months of Bizarre Behavior"* read the cover headline of the April 17, 2000, edition. "It's like watching a car accident in slow motion and not being able to stop it," an unidentified star said. In the midst of the negative press, Houston showed she still had clout and power when she signed a $100 million, multi-album deal with Arista. She received $5 million as a "signing bonus." But this was one of the few bright spots as new articles appeared. A month later, there was a rumor that she had died from an overdose. At a 2001 televised performance of a Michael Jackson concert at which she was a guest performer, she was rail thin. Again there were drug stories, especially when she missed an important party for Clive Davis. During a 2002 television interview with Diane Sawyer, Houston responded to a question about her possible drug usage by saying: "Crack is wack." The television program *Dateline* covered her 2003 visit with husband Brown to Israel, spotlighting occasions when she appeared disoriented. Houston was also estranged from her father, whose company filed a lawsuit against her. Then John Houston died.

Houston herself let her critics and the media know what she thought of them with the single "Whatchulookinat" on her album, *Just Whitney*. The song was lively and clever. But sales for the album were tepid. Was the public weary of her? When her husband starred in the reality TV show *Being Bobby Brown*, Houston also appeared

Glossy and glamorous, Houston, no matter what, remained a larger-than-life star with a larger-than-life talent.

but, to put it delicately, hardly at her best. Yet, ironically, on that reality show, Houston still held onto some of her privacy. When seen, she was usually in public spaces: hotel lobbies, restaurants, or the outer rooms of her hotel suites. Always, she was seen with her wigs in place. Later, Houston entered a drug-rehab facility. But the drug stories did not go away.

Perhaps most disturbing—and for her fans, heartbreaking—was the story that later appeared in the April 10, 2006, issue of the *National Enquirer*. *"Inside Whitney's DRUG DEN"* was the cover headline of an article that reported (along with photographs of drug paraphernalia in Houston's home) of her drug binges. Partly told by Bobby Brown's sister, supposedly to get help for Houston, the story read more like a tale of betrayal, not by Houston but her sister-in-law, who was reportedly paid $200,000 for the article. The following week, the tale continued on the cover and in the pages of the *National Enquirer*. Weeks later, the tabloid ran a cover story with the headline, *"Whitney Diagnosed with Deadly Brain Tumor."*

Despite Houston's seemingly erratic behavior, frankly, some of the coverage was unfair, malicious, and cruel. A word that then came into the public lexicon might best describe what was happening with Houston, *Schadenfreude:* the delight in seeing a once admirable figure in decline; the delight in joining in the fray to tear that person down. That had happened with many great stars in the past. Just weeks before her death, Marilyn Monroe's career was considered finished; in one of her last interviews with *Life* magazine, she had poignantly asked the interviewer not to make her a joke. And no star had ever been repeatedly more maligned by the press than Elizabeth Taylor, who for years— decades, really—was criticized for everything from her marriages, to her movies, to her weight, to her clothes. Taylor had the last laugh because she somehow survived it. One could only hope that Houston would do the same.

None of the media stories about Houston attempted to understand the source of her troubles. Houston had an emotional depth that many of her contemporaries, as well as those who wrote about her, lacked. Rarely did the stories deal with a fundamental fact about Houston that was well known to those around her: yes, she could be as imperial as any diva, but at heart she was never mean-spirited or petty, never abusive, and was basically a generous, very likable woman. "She was really polite, a really nice customer," recalled a waitress at a West Hollywood restaurant who had once served Houston and her party of twenty. That night, Houston had surprised and pleased diners with an impromptu karaoke performance. Even Jane Pratt at that *Jane* magazine photo shoot was quick to tell the press that regardless of any problems, Houston "gave one of the best cover shoots ever. She's a consummate performer." But obviously stories about the *bad* Whitney sold magazines and newspapers. It reminded one of Billie Holiday's comment that they didn't come to see her perform—they came to see her fall down.

Still, in the mind of the public, she was the diva goddess of the age. Even though she was not in concert or the recording studio as much in those later years, she remained at the forefront of the popular imagination: perhaps a tragic diva yet one whose talent and personal story compelled attention. And just when the media predicted the worst for her, Houston, in late 2006, filed for a divorce from husband Brown. Looking radiant and aglow, she also arrived with Clive Davis at an event honoring Johnny Mathis. Davis also let the public know: there were but two great singers: Aretha and Whitney. Her story yet continues.

Mavens of the
New Millennium
The 2000s

As one century ended and another began, so did a new millennium. Despite dire predictions about catastrophes and upheavals that would occur around the world at the strike of midnight, January 1, 2000, revelers joyously brought in the new age without such a crisis. But the optimistic mood of the nation rapidly evaporated after the horrific events that occurred on September 11, 2001. Two jetliners, filled with passengers, were hijacked by Al Qaeda terrorists and then crashed into New York City's World Trade Center buildings. Another hijacked jetliner crashed into the Pentagon. And a fourth plunged into an open field in Pennsylvania. America had experienced a homeland terrorist attack that left more than three thousand dead and others severely injured. With the country stunned and in mourning, the administration of President George W. Bush declared a war on terrorism. One war followed in Afghanistan. Then another came in Iraq. The world now seemed a smaller place and certainly a different and dangerous one.

Much like the aftermath of the attack on Pearl Harbor on December 7, 1941, a jittery nation looked for signs and symbols of survival and endurance. In the 1940s, the divas had emerged as social symbols and cultural signs that promoted America as indeed, despite its racial history, a land of the free and home of the brave. In this new era, one might have expected grim or solemn diva images. But that was hardly the case. Along with other entertainment stars, many divas aligned themselves with social or political causes, attempting to show, like the divas of the 1940s, that they were part of a united front; an integral part of the fabric of a country that was determined to face its problems head-on. Many divas were eager to have it known that they were troubled by world events. Within show business circles, there also remained important charitable events—in which the divas participated—devoted to the fight against AIDS, now a global problem.

Yet, though audiences were aware of the involvement of their dark divas in various causes, those same audiences did not seem as much in search of divas that were patriotic, social, or political symbols as they had during the Second World War, nor did the new generation of divas appear to touch on a nation's fears about future terrorist attacks. The divas now coming to prominence offered dreamy escapist images that drew in crowds. They also appeared to be figures on a national landscape where opportunities still abounded. In their world, the nation's domestic problems often didn't exist. The theme of the diva who pulled herself up from a humble background still elicited attention and admiration; and still was a part of a generic diva narrative. Yet now, as in the 1990s, the idea of racial struggle was more a part of diva subtext rather than a bold, upfront declarative diva statement. The images that the public still appeared most responsive to were those of glamour and grit. Personal messages about personal relationships still proved captivating. Yet, curiously in the early part of this new millennium, there didn't seem to be new stars with *big stories*, the stuff of which larger than life myths and legends were made.

Page 338: Halle Berry.

Halle Berry:
Stardom at Last

The first of the era's goddesses to ascend to a new level of stardom was an actress who had been on the scene for over a decade, Halle Berry. Admired and relatively well-known, she was a delicate young beauty who had been born in Cleveland, Ohio, the second daughter of an interracial couple. Her mother, Judith Ann Hawkins Berry, was a white psychiatric nurse who worked at Cleveland's Veterans Administration hospital for thirty-five years; her father, Jerome Berry, was an attendant at the same hospital. By the time Halle was four and her sister Heidi was six, their father had left the family. Though there was later an attempt at reconciliation between her parents, Berry said that her father physically abused her mother; the couple then parted for good.

Moving Halle and Heidi to Oakwood Village outside Cleveland, the strong-willed Judith Berry was determined that her children have as "normal" a childhood as possible. "Mom's family turned their backs on her," said Berry. "And the black side of my family turned their backs on her too. She was alone." But her mother, said Berry, "was tough" and explained the hard facts of racial life in America. "She taught me when I was little that I'm her daughter, I'm half white," Berry said, "but when you leave this house people will assume you're black and you'll be discriminated against. So accept being black, embrace it. She said if I fight it, I will have a battle with them and a battle inside myself."

At school, her classmates, both black and white, sometimes teased her, calling her zebra. But she excelled: she was a member of the honor society, editor of her school paper, a cheerleader, and prom queen. Of her high school experiences, she said, "I felt like I was accepted there until it came to being prom queen." After she beat a blue-eyed blond for the title, Berry and her friends were accused of having stuffed the ballot box. A coin was tossed to decide the winner. Nonetheless, that was the first of several beauty crowns. Standing five-feet, six-inches tall, she was Miss Teen Ohio at age eighteen, then Miss Teen All-American, then in 1986, as Miss Ohio, the first runner-up in the Miss USA pageant, and afterward

the first African American to represent America in the Miss World contest.

During this time, she briefly enrolled in college but dropped out to move to Chicago to become a model. Spotted by a talent manager who encouraged her to try acting, she relocated to New York in 1989. Three months later she won a role in the short-lived TV sitcom *Living Dolls*, a recurring role on the nighttime TV soap *Knots Landing*, and in 1990, the part of a crack head in Spike Lee's feature *Jungle Fever*. From then on, she never stopped working, going from one movie to another: *Strictly Business*, *B.A.P.s*, *Losing Isaiah*, *Executive Decision*. Yet the results were mixed. In a film like *Bulworth*, as Warren Beatty's love interest, she garnered media attention mainly because the film was controversial—and shockingly misguided. In a lousy film like the melodrama *The Rich Man's Wife*, a sudsy tale of murder and blackmail, she had the opportunity nonetheless to prove her mettle like past stars Bette Davis and Joan Crawford, who managed to elevate the bad films in which they sometimes appeared. But Berry didn't seem able to really hold the screen; there didn't seem to be layers to her screen persona.

Other times, in ensemble features like *The Flintstones*, as a Stone Age secretary, she was surprisingly engaging. In *Boomerang*, she was absolutely right as the lovely young school teacher—the good girl ingenue—whom Eddie Murphy must prove he is worthy of. And in a film like *Why Do Fools Fall in Love*, ostensibly the story of rock and rock singer Frankie Lymon, but actually a melodrama about the three women who each claimed to be his wife, Berry was sharp and confidently commanding. On occasion, she also appeared in important television dramas: the lead role in CBS's mini-series *Queen*, based on Alex Haley's follow up to *Roots*; the lead opposite actor Jimmy Smits in Showtime's *Solomon and Sheba*; another lead in the Oprah Winfrey-produced, Charles Burnett-directed adaptation of Dorothy West's novel, *The Wedding*. Highly touted as these presentations were, Berry herself did not carry them. The success of *Queen* and *The Wedding* could be attributed (both were quite successful in the ratings) to their hype and to the top-notch actors who surrounded Berry. In *Queen*, she had a sequence in which she was berated by an angry Lonette McKee, who looked as if she took it *personally* that Berry's dramatics could in no way match hers. Like Janet Jackson, Berry's problem was partly her voice; a girl's sound, without the womanly tones that her roles called for.

say, 'Oh, we love Halle, we just don't want to go black with this part.' What enrages me is that those are such racist statements, but the people saying them don't think they are. I've had it said right to my face." Yet Berry could be philosophical. "I always had to rise above it," she said, "I can't go off like a raving lunatic even though my heart wants me to say, 'OK, take a deep breath,'

Berry worked for years in all types of films before finally reaching stardom.

To her credit, she could be more candid about the problems she faced as a black actress and the industry's longstanding racial attitudes than were other African American performers. She had lost a role as a park ranger in the John Woo directed *Broken Arrow* because a studio executive believed there was no such thing as a *black* park ranger. "What's hardest for me to swallow," she once said, "is when there is a love story, say, with a really high-profile male star and there's no reason I can't play the part. They

and I realize that's the insidiousness of racism. People don't even know when they're being racist." Nonetheless, she was determined "to be an actress of color who can make a difference and go down a path that no woman has gone before. To make a way out of *no way*."

During these years, her looks and her style carried her. Slim with curves and the face of an angel, she had the demeanor and grace of an Audrey Hepburn which made her unique, especially among the new generation of African American movie actresses. And one yearned to see her in some role that might bring out her delicate, sexy charms. Her performances in *Boomerang* and *The Flintstones* came closet. Otherwise it just wasn't happening.

Her private life drew some attention. Linked to actor Wesley Snipes and basketball player Charles Oakley, she was engaged to actor Christopher Williams. One relationship with a prominent man (whom she refused to identify) turned violent: he hit Berry so hard across her face that her eardrum was punctured. She lost eighty percent of her hearing in her left ear. Then she fell in love with Atlanta Braves star David Justice, whom she had first seen while watching a baseball game on television. When she met a reporter who told her that Justice was a fan and wanted a signed picture, she signed the photograph and sent along her phone number. Eleven months after the two met, they married on New Year's Day, 1993. For the media, it was a perfect match: not exactly Marilyn Monroe and Joe DiMaggio nor Hazel Scott and Adam Clayton Powell, but still two attractive accomplished African Americans in the world of popular culture.

Still, beneath the poised and placid Berry that the public was beginning to feel it knew, there were signs of a restless, perhaps calculating, young woman. In 1993, a Chicago dentist sued her for $80,000. When they had dated between 1989 and 1991, he said he had loaned her money to move to Los Angeles, set her up in an apartment, and provided a car rental for her. Berry said the money had been a gift. The case was dismissed by the judge. By 1996, her marriage to Justice was officially over. "She wasn't the same person I was with before we got married," Justice said. "She carried a lot of baggage from her previous relationships. I've never known a girl who could throw a tantrum like she does."

Her breakup with Justice landed her on the May 13, 1996, cover of *People*. That kind of coverage—in *People*, which did not frequently run full-cover stories on African American stars—could not hurt an actress's career; nor could the other media coverage. Her arrival at openings or charity events was reported by such television shows as *Entertainment Tonight*. Perhaps better than her contemporaries, including Angela Bassett, Berry understood how important it was for a Hollywood actress, black or white, to be visible, to be seen at the right place, and to be seen in the right clothes with the right attitude. She was fortunate that because of her looks, the media enjoyed running her picture in the celebrity pages. The truth was that while Halle Berry was by no means a real star onscreen, in a strange way, at those openings, she seemed lit from within, far more glowing, charismatic, and glamorous than in her movie roles. On the red carpet, her ambition showed, and she responded to the newsreel camera as if it were her consort, more alive and charming with it than with her co-stars. At public events, she was clearly a star.

Yet, there was no big career-defining movie role. When she saw her opportunity to strike at big stardom, she seized it; that came with the plum part of Dandridge. Though Whitney Houston still had the movie rights, it was said that one evening when she saw Berry, Houston casually remarked that Berry should play Dandridge. It was an unwritten Hollywood law that usually when one star is announced for a biopic, everyone else backs off. But now Berry apparently believed she had been given the go-ahead sign. Working with her long time manager, who appeared as devoted to her as Dandridge's manager Earl Mills had been, Berry was able to negotiate a deal to star in a TV movie on HBO, titled *Introducing Dorothy Dandridge*. If Halle Berry deserved credit for nothing else, she had to be credited for getting the drama into production. Clearly identifying with Dandridge, she learned that they both had been born at the same hospital in Cleveland; both had grown up without their fathers; both battled the industry's attitudes about African Americans, African American women in particular. Once when she tried on a gown of Dandridge's, given to her by Dandridge's manager, she was stunned to see that it fit perfectly. Both were about the same size.

The highly publicized *Introducing Dorothy Dandridge* had a wide viewership, especially among African Americans. Yet, as *The New*

York Times critic Caryn James pointed out, the drama simplified the actress (she was stripped of her complexity, including the type of self-absorption she sometimes manifested and which proved essential to her rise to stardom as it is to any star's rise). The TV movie was also more eager to focus on the racism of the nightclub experiences Dandridge endured rather than the racism of Hollywood. Nor did it ever fully examine the complicated nature of Dandridge's relationships with her mother, sister, and her first husband Harold Nicholas. Berry's identification with Dandridge, as well as her affection for the actress, was apparent and touching. In some scenes, she was more involved, more *alive*, and more energetic than she had ever before been onscreen. In the end, her heartfelt performance won her a Golden Globe Award and then, the real prize, an Emmy. Some felt that those awards were also the industry's way of absolving its own guilt feelings about not having fully recognized Dandridge with an Oscar and the big roles. Halle Berry was now in a different league. Still, as everyone in the industry knew, Berry had succeeded on television, not in a feature film.

Then came an event that looked as if it might mark the end of her career altogether. In Los Angeles on February 23, 2000, Berry reportedly drove through a red light and crashed into another car driven by a young woman. An eyewitness told *People* (for its April 17, 2000, edition) that the young woman's car had been sent airborne: "It was a brutal, brutal car accident. That girl would have been dead," said the witness. Berry, however, left the scene. "To drive away with blatant disregard? I'm extremely outraged," said the eyewitness. The other driver was left trapped inside her car. "I really was petrified when that smoke was going up in my car and I could not get out," the young woman said. Later taken to Cedars-Sinai Medical Center, she had multiple fractures in her right wrist, which caused constant pain. She also endured pain in her neck and back. At the hospital, she noticed that Berry came in, dressed in jeans and a tank top with a bandage on her forehead. At that time, she didn't know Berry had been the driver of the car that had hit her. Berry had a forehead wound that required twenty-two stitches.

On March 31, Berry was indicted on charges of leaving the scene of an accident, which was a misdemeanor with a possible penalty of a $10,000 fine and up to a year in jail. Why not felony charges for hit-and-run? According to law-enforcement investigators, the felony charge wasn't pursued because Berry had reported the accident at the hospital when she went there for treatment.

Rumors circulated of previous hit-and-run accidents involving Berry. The only con-

Winning the plum role *and* an Emmy: Halle Berry in *Introducing Dorothy Dandridge.*

firmed accident—reported by *People* in its April 17, 2000, issue—had occurred in February 1997. The driver of the other vehicle had sued Berry, but later requested that the suit be dropped. That Chicago dentist who had sued her for an unpaid loan now claimed, so reported the *New York Post* on March 21, 2000, that in 1991 Berry had called in a panic and begged him for money, $20,000 of which was to cover an accident, in which she had struck a boy on a bicycle. "What did the police do?" he asked. "Nothing." He said she told him, "I left." Also reported was that Berry's neighbors referred to her as "Halle on wheels."

Stars had usually endured scandals about the pain they had inflicted on themselves whether through reckless love affairs and marriages or drugs or alcohol. Or pain that had been inflicted on them, often by people they had trusted. But here was a star charged with causing physical and emotional harm to someone else. Berry's PR representatives went into overdrive to salvage her career. On the television program *20/20*, Berry said that all she really remembered about the accident was approaching an LA intersection. The next thing she recalled was waking up in the driveway of her home. Her publicist also told *People* that Berry's fiancé at that time, singer Eric Benet, "has been with her an awful lot. I know she feels there's no way she could have gotten through this without him." The comments were obviously meant to elicit sympathy for Berry.

On May 10, 2000, she stood before the judge in Los Angeles's Superior Court. As she pleaded no contest to the misdemeanor charge, a bandage still covered her forehead with its 22 stitches. Although a no-contest plea carried the same weight as a conviction, it permitted the accused to avoid admitting any wrongdoing. Sentenced to three years probation and a $13,000 fine, Berry later appeared on *The Today Show* where she said: "I feel like I have a very defensible reason for leaving, because of my head injury, which put me in a state of mind that did not make me responsible in that moment." What was being stressed always was Berry's emotional pain and the fact that she had been unfairly judged; in essence, Berry was made to look like a victim. Of what, it is hard to say. But the strategy succeeded in rehabilitating her image. That same year, she appeared as Storm in the big hit *X-Men*, a sci-fi saga inspired by characters from Marvel Comics.

That next year, Berry married singer Eric Benet and wanted it known that she had a new stability in her life. She also starred opposite John Travolta and Hugh Jackman in the film *Swordfish*. She had succeeded in being cast in a lead opposite white actors. Actually, the same had been true of her film *The Rich Man's Wife*. But this time it was a *big*

picture with A-list stars. Critics and audiences, however, were surprised by a sexually gratuitous and exploitative scene in which, while reading a book, she lowered the book and was shown bare-breasted. Much to-do was made over the fact (so stated in the *New York Post*, June 8, 2001) that she reportedly was paid an extra $500,000 for the scene. She denied the story. But now Berry, once the most ladylike of leading ladies, had a new highly sexualized image.

By the end of 2001, her feature film *Monster's Ball* was released. Here was a little independent picture, directed by Marc Foster, in which Berry played the morose Leticia, the widow of a convict (Sean Combs) who is executed. Left alone to raise her overweight young son, she is numbed and at emotional loose ends when the boy is suddenly killed. Evicted from her home, adrift in a small town where she appears to have no friends, she meets the prison guard (Billy Bob Thornton) who had led her husband to his execution. In a very graphic scene, Leticia implores him to make love to her. But *make love* was the not the term she used to express her hot desire for the guy. Protected and shielded by him, she ends up living in his home. He knows his role in her husband's death; she remains unaware until the end of the picture.

Often moody and sometimes moving, *Monster's Ball* was also puzzling. Never did the film explain how Leticia ended up in this community, why she has no family or black friends who might comfort her at her moments of great distress. Nor did the script ever have the character confront the man with whom she ultimately lives. Everything about Leticia was vague and undefined: except, of course, the portrait of her as a highly sexed African American woman who sees this white man as her knight in shining armor—who accepts him without questions. On most levels, *Monster's Ball* was a white male fantasy: less the story of Leticia and more the tale of a guilt-ridden white man who finds redemption in an African American woman's arms.

Within the African American community, *Monster's Ball* was strongly criticized, leading audiences to question how Berry

Making history: Oscar–winner Berry with Oscar–winner Denzel Washington.

could have accepted the role. Other actresses, notably Angela Bassett, announced that they had turned the part down. "It's about character," Bassett. "I wasn't going to be a prostitute on film. I couldn't do that because it's such a stereotype about black women and sexuality. It's about putting something out there you can be proud of ten years later. I mean, Meryl Streep won Oscars without all that." Of course, Leticia was not a prostitute. But some felt, given the sex scene, she might as well have been.

Within the restricted world of the film, Berry nonetheless managed to create a vul-

nerable and fragile character. Sensitive and at times poignant, she was far more moving and powerful in her melancholic (and sometimes mopey) moments than she had been in her previous screen roles. The performance brought out a heretofore unseen quality in Berry: she seemed lost, struggling to hold onto herself and to find some kind of moorings in a lonely life. In most respects, it was a disturbing but fine performance. When she was nominated for the Oscar as Best Actress of 2001, many within the Black Community had hoped she would not win, not so much because they didn't feel she had given a worthy performance but because they felt she had not been given a worthy role.

Still, Berry became the first African American to win the Academy Award in the Best Actress category, thereby becoming a part of motion picture history. Though criticized for her highly emotional Oscar acceptance speech, which indeed was a tad long, she was earnest, and when she stated that the award was bigger than herself, when she spoke of the women who had come before her, such as Dandridge, Lena Horne, and Diahann Carroll as well as her contemporaries—Bassett, Vivica A. Fox, and Jada Pinkett Smith—she really rose to the occasion in a meaningful and triumphant way. That was an altogether extraordinary Academy Award night as Denzel Washington also walked off with a Best Actor Oscar for his performance in *Training Day* (another controversial film and role) and Sidney Poitier was honored with a special Oscar.

But the roles and movies that immediately followed were either disappointing (at best) or flatout disasters. In the 2002 James Bond feature, *Die Another Day* (which she had signed to do before her Oscar win), she played the sexy Jinx, an NSA agent who first appears in a bikini as she comes ashore from the sea. Basically, the role was perfect for a young starlet eager to make a name for herself rather than for an established screen star. It did little for Berry other than to keep her name out there. The same was true of her repeat appearance as Storm in the 2003 sequel *X2: X-Men United* and then the psychological thriller, *Gothika*.

Hoping for a franchise role in the movie *Cat Woman*, which might spawn sequels as did movies featuring such other comic book heroes as Batman and Spider Man, Berry enthusiastically promoted it. On *The Oprah Winfrey Show*, she not only discussed the film but also her private life: such topics as breakdowns, fidelity, healing, and her decision by then to divorce Eric Benet. "I'll never get married again," she told Winfrey. But even her candor could not help *Cat Woman*, which the critics pounced on it. "The feline attribute she most lacks," wrote A. O. Scott in *The New York Times*, "is the one the movie is most desperate to manufacture, which is elegant graceful cool." Worse, Berry had put herself in the unenviable position of being compared to Eartha Kitt's Cat Woman from the old *Batman* TV series and Michelle Pfeiffer's inventive turn as Cat Woman in the feature, *Batman. Cat Woman* was an unqualified bomb. Though various projects were announced, nothing immediately came to fruition.

Finally, Berry appeared in a television movie (something most Oscar–winning actresses avoided): the Oprah Winfrey produced adaptation of Zora Neale Hurston's *Their Eyes Were Watching God*, which, despite mixed reviews, was a ratings winner. Most attributed the success of the drama to Oprah Winfrey's imprimatur. Despite an Emmy nomination, Berry's performance seemed vague and unformed, similar at times to her Leticia character yet without the strong direction it sorely needed. She also lent her voice to the film *Robots*, served as the executive producer for the HBO drama *Lackawanna Blues*, appeared again as Storm in *X-Men: The Last Stand*, and then opposite Bruce Willis in *Perfect Stranger*.

Continuing her iconic red carpet appearances, Berry remained on the scene: still closely watched by the fashionistas, still widely covered by the paparazzi, still something of an industry darling because no matter what, she looked, moved, glowed, and behaved like a star. Appearing in print and television commercials as a spokeswoman for the cosmetics company Revlon, she also became in 2005 "the face" in ads for the Italian design company Versace.

Though her contemporaries were not always kind in privately discussing her talents, and though many believed that on-screen she lacked the presence of a movie star, Berry nonetheless had made a place for herself in Hollywood history. Future generations might be intrigued by her vagueness, trying to figure her out; using their own ingenious imaginations to explain who she was. Future generations might also be drawn to her unique position as a black woman in the industry in the late 20th century and the early 21st.

Top left: the stars of TV's *Girlfriends*. Top right: the stars of *Living Single*. Bottom left: Kimberly Elise. Bottom right: Thandie Newton.

Other Actresses

Other actresses worked in movies, television, and theater with varying degrees of success. Often criticized for its depiction of a basically lily white New York City, the sitcom *Friends* made news when actresses Gabrielle Union and Aisha Tyler were cast—at different times—as possible love interests. Later, Tyler appeared on such series as *CSI* and *The Ghost Whisperer*. Union also worked in such films as *Deliver Us from Eva* and the short-lived TV series *Night Stalker*. The rather passive Gloria

Reuben found important roles in such series as *ER* (in which her passivity actually deepened her character, who was suffering from AIDS), *The Agency*, and *1-800-Missing*. Victoria Rowell worked successfully on daytime TV. Lorraine Toussaint appeared on *Any Day Now*. For some years after her role as Olivia on *The Cosby Show*, former child star Raven-Symone disappeared only to resurface as the star of the hit tweens sitcom *That's So Raven*. Whoever could have predicted that

Symone would develop into such an enjoyably chatty, klutzy actress?

Whoever could have predicted the ambition of singer Eve who starred successfully in her own sitcom, called, what else but, *Eve*? The actresses of the television series *Girlfriends*—Tracee Ellis Ross (daughter of Diana Ross), Golden Brooks, Jill Marie Jones, and Persia White—also won fans, as did Mo'Nique and Countess Vaughan, stars of everyone's favorite guilty pleasure TV series, *The Parkers*. Penny Johnson Jerald gave a riveting performance as the manipulative wife of the first African American president n the series *24*. Among the other actresses working successfully in movies were British star Thandie Newton, who won important roles in *Beloved, Where's Charlie* (a remake of *Charade*, the Cary Grant–Audrey Hepburn caper in which she played the Hepburn role), *Mission Impossible II* (as Tom Cruise's leading lady), and *Crash;* Kerry Washington in *Ray;* T'Keyah "Crystal" Keymah; Nia Long (whose career stretched from *Boyz N the Hood* to the remake of *Alfie*); the fiercely talented Regina King (compelling in *Ray*); and Sanaa Lathan, daughter of director Stan Lathan, who played lead roles in such films as *Love and Basketball, Out of Time,* and *Something New* as well as the TV movie *Disappearing Acts,* and the series *Nip/Tuck*.

In theater, Sarah Jones scored with her one-woman show *Bridge and Tunnel.* Tonya Pinkins (a soap opera veteran) and Anika Noni Rose won raves (and a Tony) for *Caroline, or Change.* And LaChanze won a Tony for her performance in the Broadway musical *The Color Purple.* Another theater veteran, S. Epatha Merkerson appeared on the long-running television series *Law & Order.* One might have felt grateful that the actress was finally working steadily. But then, Merkerson surprised everyone by finally landing a role in *Lackawanna Blues* that won her attention, plus a Golden Globe and an Emmy.

Of the new actresses, surely the most promising was Kimberly Elise. If one judged her by her seemingly spacey performance as the young mother in *Set It Off,* you might think she didn't know what she was doing. But Elise, perhaps following in the tradition of the great Beah Richards, was a highly serious, complicated actress who gave highly unusual interpretations. When she appeared as the daughter Denver in *Beloved,* she, along with Beah Richards, was spellbinding. Later, Elise was Denzel Washington's leading lady in the 2002 *John Q* and the remake of *The Manchurian Candidate.* Then came the surprise hits *Woman Thou Art Loosed* and *Diary of a Mad Black Woman,* in which she starred as an emotionally battered woman in each.

But if ever there was an actress unfairly overlooked, it was surely Khandi Alexander. For years, she found employment in such television shows as *ER.* But audiences probably had no idea how deep her talents were—until she starred, along with T. K. Carter, in the HBO drama *The Corner.* As a drugged out mother, she created a character both moving and at times so pathetic that viewers may have wanted to turn away from her. She was achingly real, like the kind of lost souls you see (and avoid) every day on the streets of the big cities. Her performance was deserving of the big awards—or at least an Emmy nomination. It may well have been the best TV performance by an actress that year. But she, like her co-star Carter, was overlooked. Alexander later appeared in the series *CSI: Miami.* Always you pulled for this actress, hoping the elusive powerhouse roles she was worthy of would come her way.

Of the models, the spectacular Naomi Campbell remained the most talked about—but not as much for her stunner walks down the runway as for the tabloid headlines. Campbell made the front pages of the New York papers when, in the midst of a harangue, she reportedly struck one of her maids and then another. The other model who kept herself visible on and off the runway was Tyra Banks. Like singer Eve, she had a drive no one could have foreseen. In 1995, she appeared in John Singleton's *Higher Learning.* She also worked on television. And she remained a successful Victoria's Secret model. Then she turned up on episodes of *The Oprah Winfrey Show,* dispensing consumer advice. You may have wondered what she was trying to do. And at times, you may have been turned off by her patently false attempts to be down home and girlfriend-friendly. But the calculating and clever Banks was preparing for a career shift which came about when she starred on the reality show, *America's Next Top Model,* and then her own talk program, *The Tyra Banks Show.*

Her Royal Highness of Badness: Queen Latifah

Also rising to new heights in the new century was a woman who had first made her reputation in hip-hop, but now reached a broader audience: Queen Latifah. Born Dana Owens in 1970, she had grown up in Newark and East Orange, New Jersey, the daughter of a police officer. When her parents separated (she was eight years old), her mother Rita Owens—then working two jobs while completing her education—moved to the projects with Dana and Dana's older brother Lance (called Winki). The going was tough. But Rita Owens later became a high school art teacher. Standing five-feet, ten inches tall at age fourteen, Dana was a dancer and a star basketball player, who led her high school team to two New Jersey championships. Her senior year, she was voted Best Dancer, Best All-Around Student, and Most Popular Student. In her neighborhood, she became known to the kids as Latifah, which in Arabic meant "sensitive," "delicate," and "kind." By then, she was also performing rap.

At age eighteen, in 1988, she signed with Tommy Boy Records. Professionally, she added Queen to the Latifah, inspired perhaps by the words of her mother who had always taught her to think highly of herself. The next year her debut album, *All Hail the Queen*, sold 450,000 copies. Not much in the pop market, but very good for a debut album that proved influential—as did other albums such as *Black Reign* and *Nature of a Sista*. The "Queen" moniker made her appear wise beyond her years, and was reminiscent of Ma Rainey's image as *Ma*, the mother figure of a community. For Latifah, it was the male-dominated community of rap in which she presented herself as a powerful young woman in control with goals, ideals, and standards; a young woman who stood up, spoke for herself, and challenged many of rap's prevailing attitudes about women.

That idea certainly came across in Latifah's first hit single "Ladies First." "Who said that the ladies couldn't make it?" she rapped. "You must be blind / If you don't believe / well here listen to this rhyme / Ladies First there's no time to rehearse / I'm divine and my mind expands through the universe / A female rapper with a mes-sage to send." Featured on the video for the song were images of such strong, pioneering women as Sojourner Truth, Angela Davis, and Winnie Mandela. "You ain't a bitch or a ho," she informed her sistas in her later song, "U.N.I.T.Y." In "Nuff of the Ruff Stuff," she rapped: "As a black woman me want equality / Equality and the freedom to be me." Young women applauded the arrival of Latifah. But Latifah was also aware of how to boost something as fragile as the male ego. In her song "Superstar," she let insecure guys know that "money ain't gonna make me love you" and "You ain't gotta be no superman / So if you want to talk to me you can." Other times Latifah conformed to the type of street credentials that male rappers liked to boast of. On her album *Black Reign*, she rapped about keeping guns in songs like "No Work" and "Just Another Day."

In the Afrocentric 1990s, the youthful Latifah performed in ensembles made of African fabric and wore queenly hats that enhanced her empowerment image. Dubbed the "Queen of Royal Badness" and the "Royal Female of Hip-Hop," here was a large woman with breasts and full hips who was proud of her body and not trying to be svelte to conform to someone else's definition of beauty or femininity.

Yet, ironically, in this post-feminist age when rappers' lyrics were being viewed as "significant" or weighty political statements, Latifah resisted being called a feminist. "I don't use music for politics," she once said. "I do not preach. I don't really take on sexism—but racism, yeah. I do. I experience racism every day." Of course, like other young women of a new generation, she lived by feminist codes. Never did she doubt that a woman was anything but equal to a man. And one might have been told off in no uncertain terms if he ever suggested that a woman should not receive the same pay for the same work as a man.

Of the young rap divas, she clearly had a thought-out master plan. Rap served as a springboard to move to another level of stardom. She formed the company Flavor Unit, which handled music management, film–video production, real-estate invest-

A breakthrough role: Latifah as the defiant Cleo in *Set It Off*, with (top, left to right) Vivica A. Fox, Kimberly Elise, and Jada Pinkett-Smith.

ments, and recording deals. She also pulled off image changes.

The first shift came with her appearance on the television sitcom *Living Single*, which premiered in 1993 and featured four young women, coping with careers and their love lives. There was the sharp-tongued divorce attorney Max (Erika Alexander); the money-and-man-hungry Regine (Kim Fields); the ditzy Synclaire (Kim Coles); and Latifah as Khadijah James, the founder/editor of *Flavor* magazine and a den mother of sorts to the other women. Also on the show were two male neighbors in their apartment building. Though the critics were not excited by the series, which had been created by a young African American woman, Yvette Lee Bowser, *Living Single* caught on with young African American viewers, and quiet as it was kept, was a precursor to *Friends*, which also examined the relationships of a group of young friends. Latifah's Khadijah possessed a clear-eyed maturity that proved essential in the way the women dealt with their "issues" and their daily dilemmas. As an actress, she was feeling her way around and developing her comic technique while relying on her instincts and

Latifah in her controversial hit *Bringing down the House,* with Steve Martin (left) and Eugene Levy.

common sense to create a character. Perhaps most appealing was her relaxed self-assurance.

Then in 1996, she surprised moviegoers with her fierce performance in the feature film, *Set It Off.* Here was another story about a quartet of young black women—played by Vivica A. Fox, Jada Pinkett-Smith, Kimberly Elise, and Latifah as the lesbian character Cleo. Beset by financial and personal problems, the quartet became bank robbers. Some young actresses might have had second thoughts about playing a lesbian character so early in their careers for fear of being type cast. But preparing for her role, Latifah worked with a coach and pulled out all stops to dig deep inside herself to understand what made this woman tick. After this performance, her most daring and accomplished, she would never be thought of exclusively as a rap star. Nor as just a television star. Still exploring herself, she accepted supporting roles in the films *Hoodlum; Sphere; Living Out Loud,* in which as a nightclub performer, she did a fine rendition of that jazz standard "Lush Life"; and *Bone Collector,* as a nurse to a quadriplegic played by Denzel Washington. She also hosted *The Queen Latifah Show* and authored the 1999 book *Ladies First: Revelations of a Strong Woman.*

A coup came when she beat out such contenders as Whoopi Goldberg, Rosie O'Donnell, and Kathy Bates for the role of the prison Matron Mama Morton in the hit movie musical, *Chicago.* Not by any stretch of the imagination a great performance, it was a case of likable play-acting rather than acting, Latifah nonetheless won an Oscar nomination as Best Supporting Actress of 2002. Then came a starring role in the 2003 feature film, *Bringing down the House.* Many of her followers were surprised and disappointed to see her cast as an ex-convict who ends up as a nurturing figure to a white family. How could the Queen let herself fall into the trap of portraying a mammy-like character? At times, one felt embarrassed for her, especially since she was also listed as an executive producer of the film. But *Bringing down the House* reaped in a hefty profit, and the film capital—captivated by the dollar signs at the box office—looked at Latifah in a yet another new way: as a viable box-office star.

Roles followed in *Scary Movie 3; The Cookout; Barbershop 2: Back in Business; Taxi; Beauty Shop;* and *Last Holiday.* Endorsements came. As a spokeswoman for Cover Girl makeup, she appeared in full-page magazine ads. Her red carpet entrances at awards shows and other industry events were covered on the tube by *Entertainment Tonight* and *Access Hollywood*. In a flashy color layout, *Vogue* celebrated her *look*: a full-figured woman who was helping to change ideas about beauty and body definition. Frequently, the media seemed to be congratulating itself on being able to appreciate her.

Energetic in interviews, Latifah was a consummate professional, always about the business of promoting a film or her music or some other endeavor. Always too, she was the perfectly coifed *down-home* Latifah, who never adopted a grand manner or an overly glamorous pose. Yet, never was the down-home Latifah *overplayed*: she never let herself become a caricature. Growing older and aware that her fan base was changing, she also released *The Dana Owens Album*, her first album since 1998. Here she performed such standards as "Hello Stranger" and "I Put a Spell on You." Hip-hop was part of her public record. But it no longer defined her. In some ways, her self-reinventions were reminiscent of those of Ethel Waters, who left her early blues-singing days behind her and never looked back.

With all the attention and fanfare, Latifah managed somehow to keep her private life private. Unlike other divas, Latifah appeared to have neither great scandals nor stormy love affairs; at least none that the public knew of. Nor did she exhibit the kind of mystery or emotional pain that had made Mary J. Blige and Faith Evans both so compelling. In all likelihood, emotional pain and mystery were not what Queen Latifah saw herself as being about. In this respect, she resembled women like Sarah Vaughan, Ella Fitzgerald, and Carmen McRae who, for all their talent, were without a compelling story that ignited the public's imagination. Yet there remained a public curiosity about Latifah, as if that public were waiting for a fascinating story to unfold.

Other performers arrived on scene, winning large followings and sometimes the praise of the critics. Singer Aaliyah showed great promise. Born Aaliyah Dana Haughton in New York, and bred in Detroit, she began performing as a little girl and by age eleven, appeared on television's *Star Search*. Though she lost in the competition, afterward she performed for five nights in a Las Vegas engagement that starred Gladys Knight. In 1994, she released her debut album, *Age Ain't Nothing' but a Number*, which was produced by rhythm and blues star R. Kelly. When word leaked out of a marriage between Aaliyah and Kelly, it looked as if a scandal might erupt. He was then twenty-seven. She was fifteen. But Aaliyah told the press, "I'm not married. That's all I really want to say about it." Later it was rumored that the marriage was annulled. With her next albums—*One in a Million* in 1996 (when she was a senior in high school) and *Aaliyah* in 2001—she became known for her sultry music about love and relationships. The single "Are You That Somebody" dealt with chastity and waiting for the right fellow. "Try Again" looked at a long courtship. And, of course, the title song from her album *Age Ain't Nothing' But a Number* was about loving an older man.

Slender with long, flowing hair and dark eyes, she had a youthful elegance reminiscent of Whitney Houston and totally different from the style of other young women singing at this time. When she was linked with Roc-a-Fella Records CEO Damon Dash, it looked like the perfect hip-hop romance. Early on, Aaliyah branched out and won plum film roles: as the lead in *Romeo Must Die* with martial arts star Jet Li, and as a vampire in the adaptation of Anne Rice's *Queen of the Damned*. When she was signed to appear in the two sequels to the highly successful film *The Matrix*, it looked as if she might become an important screen actress. But Aaliyah never lived to do those films.

After spending three days on and around the Bahamian island of Abaco, where she shot a video for her song "Rock the Boat," Aaliyah boarded, along with eight others, a small twin-engine Cessna bound for Opa-locka, Florida. The plane rose little more than forty feet when it suddenly veered left and plummeted into a marsh in a fiery crash.

Later, reports revealed that the plane had been overloaded with the nine passengers and their luggage as well as camera and sound equipment. Its engine had failed. Three passengers survived the crash but later died. "I've been on some gruesome ones," said a mortician, "but this one was bad." An emergency team discovered Aaliyah's body twenty feet from the fuselage. It was believed that she and five others died instantly. Aaliyah was dead at age twenty-two.

A performer like singer-pianist Alicia Keys was a darling of the intellectual community. So much about her seemed just right: like Lauryn Hill, Keys projected a seriousness, a focus, a desire to do music that was popular yet never down and dirty, never *bootylicious*. Born in 1981 and growing up in New York's Hell's Kitchen and Harlem, the daughter of a couple that separated when Alicia was two, she started playing the piano as a child. By seven, she was studying classical music. By fourteen, after she had been told by her classical music teacher that there was nothing more he could teach her, she studied jazz. At fifteen, she signed with Columbia Records. At sixteen, Keys, a straight A student who by then had been exposed to the work of the masters—Beethoven, Ellington, Miles Davis, Carole King, and Marvin Gaye—graduated from high school and accepted a scholarship to Columbia. But after four weeks, Keys, again like Hill and also Faith Evans, left university life to pursue her career.

When Columbia Records showed no enthusiasm for the music she was working on, she got out of her contract to sign with Arista. When its founder and president, Clive Davis, was forced out of the label, he started J Records and took Keys with him. Her 2001 debut album, *Songs in A Minor*, sold ten-million copies. From it, there came the smash single "Fallin'," which helped create an image for Keys as a young, passionate woman, here caught in the grip of a searing romance. In her single "Troubles," she spoke of sadness and fears. With a sound that was mainly rhythm and blues but also jazzy with a bit of gospel, Keys's music conveyed the conflicting drives of womanly identity. Never did she project simply raw emotion. Always there was an overriding intelligence that struck a cord with young women her age. *Songs in A Minor* earned her five Grammys, including the awards for Best Rhythm & Blues Album, Best New Artist, Best Female Rhythm & Blues Vocalist as well as—for "Fallin'"—Best Rhythm & Blues Song and Song of the Year. Her follow-up album *The Diary of Alicia Keys* also sold well and won big awards.

Perhaps the most appealing aspect of Keys was her refusal to promote herself in an overly sexual manner. True, she never downplayed her great looks, and, true, she performed a sexy duet with that dashing Lothario of the music world, Usher. But her sensuality seemed natural, never pumped up, simply a part of her identity.

Also on the scene was the performer Ashanti, whose record label dubbed her "The Princess of Hip-Hop and Rhythm and Blues." Still a teenager, she hit the charts with her song "Foolish," the story of a woman who loves a man too much to leave him.

Of course, no one could really predict what the future would bring for stars such as Keys and Ashanti. But for a new generation, the glam star of the first part of the era was a stunning young woman who first drew attention as a member of a hugely successful girl group and became known simply by her first name: Beyoncé.

The Great A's. Clockwise from the top left: Aaliyah; Ashanti, who was dubbed "The Princess of Hip-hop and Rhythm and Blues"; Aaliyah and music mogul Damon Dash; Alicia Keys: projecting a serious image.

Destiny's Child: Kelly, Michelle, and of Course, Beyoncé

Of the new century's early girl groups, none was more popular or publicized than Destiny's Child. At its center was the glossy and golden-haired Beyoncé Knowles, who was also at the heart of a *supposed* controversy. Simply stated, the controversy was that Destiny's Child was *never* really a group; instead other singers were being used as background fodder and flavor for the launching of Beyoncé's solo career. It was a *supposed* controversy because some observers believed it was, in some respects, a manufactured one that helped give Destiny's Child an image.

Born in 1981, Beyoncé looked as if she had been groomed for show business from day one by two very driven parents. Her father, Mathew Knowles, was a one-time sales executive with Xerox. Her mother, Tina, owned a hair salon. By age seven, Beyoncé was either prepping herself for stardom or being relentlessly prepped by her parents: she was already singing, dancing, rehearsing, performing to a karaoke machine, and entering talent contests. Under Mathew Knowles's guidance, she was teamed in 1991 with three other girls: Kelly Rowland, LeToya Luckett, and LaTavia Roberson. Rowland, who was Beyoncé's cousin, moved in with the Knowles family when she was eleven. "We were always rehearsing and doing shows. But I see my mom every day," Rowland told the press. The quartet—which was once called Girls Tyme—had a great break when they appeared on television's *Star Search*. But Beyoncé (then nine) and company lost. The group was also signed, but then dropped, by Elektra Records. But that didn't dampen Beyoncé's enthusiasm. Nor did it affect her ambition *or* that of her father, who clearly believed his baby was going to be a star.

Having attended private school, Beyoncé—after eighth grade—was homeschooled. Of course, this gave her more time to rehearse and also prevented any outside distractions that might take her off focus—such as extracurricular activities or friends with other interests. Like many stage parents who looked as if they had pushed their child to stardom, Mathew and Tina Knowles dismissed such an idea by saying a career was what their daughter had wanted. They had a point, of course. No stage parent can ever make a star out of a child who in some way does not want it— or does not believe he or she wants it. Even those former child stars who became resentful and angry with their parents for having lost their childhoods knew at heart that it was they who had to succeed at the auditions; it was they who had to maintain the concentration and discipline required to reach stardom. So it was with Beyoncé.

Years later she would defend both her parents. "People expect me to be a certain way, like a Diana Ross—and they expect my father to be like Joe Jackson because that's been the pattern when parents manage children. People think that he just controls everything and does everything, but I actually control everything. People think I have the same story as the Jackson 5, and I have a completely different story. I had a very healthy, happy childhood—my mother made sure of it and I love her for it." Obviously close to her mother, Beyoncé also said: "My mother is the balance. She's very strong and will say whatever she feels and protects me always, but she always kept me a normal kid." Her father, she observed, "was more focused. He wanted it for me and did everything because he's my father and wanted me to be happy but he's a workaholic." She also admitted that working with her father wasn't "an easy thing." "We bump heads, we have arguments."

Beyoncé also wanted it known that for her family, show business was not a way out of the ghetto, as had been the case with many other African American child stars. "I didn't grow up poor," she told the press. "We had a very nice house, cars, a housekeeper. I wasn't doing this because I didn't have a choice, or to support the family, or because I had to get out of a bad situation. I just was determined; that is what I wanted to do so bad."

Signed by Columbia Records in 1996, Beyoncé and the other three members of the group saw the rehearsals, the workouts, the discipline come to fruition two years later with the release of their first album, called *Destiny's Child*, which was also the

Earlier days when there were four in Destiny's Child: top, LaTavia Roberson and Kelly Rowland; bottom, Beyoncé Knowles and LeToya Luckett.

new name for the quartet. A second album, *The Writing's on the Wall*—with the hit single "Say My Name"—followed in 1999. But behind the scenes, things were hardly rosy and sweet. Instead there was open dissension. Fed up with the management of Mathew Knowles and believing that Knowles had favored his daughter, Luckett and Roberson left the group, charged Knowles with nepotism, and sued for financial mismanagement. Beyoncé was also accused of having "a Diana Ross complex." The case was settled. Its terms were kept confidential. Kelly Rowland, however, had no complaints.

Afterward, Beyoncé and Kelly found two new members—Michelle Williams and Farrah Franklin—to appear in the video for their hit, "Say My Name." Was the group now back on track? Not really. After five months, Franklin left Destiny's Child. She likened the set-up "to a cult." Destiny's Child then became a trio—and an even bigger success. For new audiences, it didn't matter that two of the original members were no longer there. It was almost as if those earlier members hadn't existed.

Amid much fanfare, the trio released the album *Survivor* in 2001. For a month, MTV aired a daily two-hour retrospective of the group's videos. Their recording for the soundtrack of the movie *Charlie's Angels* was also a hit. So were their tours, during which the girls reportedly were forbidden to drink or cuss. And, of course, tight reins were kept to prevent all those horny male groupies from getting too close. The Knowles's other daughter, Solange, was a backup dancer on the tours. The costumes were designed by Tina Knowles. On recordings like "Independent Women, Part II," in videos, in concert, and in interviews, the three women worked hard to project the idea that they were self-reliant, that they could take care of themselves and handle the guys. On their big hit "Bootylicious" as well as in their fierce body-shaking video for it, Destiny's Child also proclaimed their sexual power and sent out the word that they were three fabulous babes who enjoyed being sexy. "I don't think you're ready for this jelly / My body's too bootylicious for you, baby," they sang. The word *bootylicious*, apparently first coined by rapper Snoop Dogg, eventually made its way into the national lexicon.

Critics often liked them, especially Beyoncé. Whatever flaws were spotted also were dismissed. Praising Beyoncé in concert for having "the voice that defines Destiny's Child: velvety yet tart, with an insistent flutter and reserves of soul belting," critic Jon Pareles commented:

> The other sound that defines Destiny's Child is the way its melodies jump in and out of double-time. Above brittle, syncopated rhythm tracks, quickly articulated verses alternate with smoother choruses. The secret hidden by studio production is that Beyoncé can't keep up with the complex rhythms: On stage, she kept falling behind. But given a wordless moan or a chance to sweep through a phrase, she was enough.

For other critics there seemed to be disparity between the image and the reality of Destiny's Child. "The mystery of Destiny's Child," wrote *Newsweek*, "is that it's nearly impossible to pin down who they are or what they really believe in. The new CD features a paean to 'Independent Women,' yet the girls' everyday actions seem to be controlled by manager Mathew Knowles. . . . And while they sing about 'nasty girls' who should 'put some clothes on,' they never

seem to be wearing more than a washcloth's worth of material between them. As a cultural riddle, Destiny's Child are intriguing. As a marketing phenomenon, they are as cynical as the record biz itself."

Though no one really cared, rumors wouldn't die that this group really wasn't a group; that all along, the plan had been to use other singers simply to prop up Beyoncé on her route to stardom. One story insisted that the other members were sent to tanning salons to keep them browner so that Beyoncé would be the "fairest" of them all. Still, attempts were made to quell the rumors. On some songs, Kelly Rowland sang leads. The girls themselves informed the press always that they were good friends. No one could say for sure what their feelings were. Yet, from Beyoncé's point of view, all the talk helped the group. "I think in order for your group to be successful your story has to be interesting," Beyoncé said. "Our story was very squeaky clean, so I thank God for the controversy. I'm happy because it helps me sell records."

For a spell, the young women went their separate ways, though each member was quick to say that Destiny's Child had not broken up. Kelly Rowland appeared in the slasher film *Freddy vs. Jason* and also had a hit CD, *Simply Deep*. Michelle Williams recorded a solo gospel album, *Heart to Yours*, and appeared on Broadway in the Elton John/Tim Rice version of *Aida*. But as a solo performer, Beyoncé had the greatest success. She starred in the MTV Hip-Hopera *Carmen*, which was in some respects an update of *Carmen Jones*. Her album, *Dangerously in Love*, won her five Grammys and sold seven million copies. She also appeared in the movies *Austin Powers: Goldmember*, *The Fighting Temptations*, and later *The Pink Panther* remake with Steve Martin. Lucrative endorsements were lined up with AT&T and L'Oreal. Her face graced the covers of such magazines as *Elle*, *Harper's Bazaar*, *People*, and *Newsweek*. The trio reunited for what they said was their final album, *Destiny Fulfilled*, and also launched a farewell tour. Destiny's Child's members looked determined to do things, even when it came to dissolving the group, with the appearance of harmony.

Then Beyoncé took off full-steam. At the 2004 Grammys, she held her own as she performed with Prince. At the 2004 Academy Awards show, she sang no less than three songs in three different outfits. At the 2005 Kennedy Center Honors, in which such American artists as Tony Bennett, Suzanne Farrell, Julie Harris, Robert Redford, and the indestructible Tina Turner were celebrated, Beyoncé—dressed like the Turner of old—sang and shook her way through "Proud Mary" in homage to Turner. Everyone knew Beyoncé could never be Tina Turner. But Turner looked on approvingly at Beyoncé's energetic, stylish tribute. In its 2005 music issue, *Vanity Fair* ran her on its cover with luscious sexy color portraits inside. In the entertainment world, a *Vanity Fair* cover had the status significance of a *Life* magazine cover in the 1940s and 1950s, or a Barbara Walters interview; especially for African American stars who rarely saw their faces on the full cover of *Vanity Fair*.

Beyoncé also turned up on *Vanity Fair*'s cover, along with Eddie Murphy and Jamie Foxx, when she starred in the movie version of *Dreamgirls*, playing the Diana Ross–inspired role of Deena. The highly publicized film was generally praised by the critics and won the Golden Globe for Best Picture of the year in the Musical or Comedy category. Beyoncé also earned a Globe nomination. But most of the attention — and the critical acclaim — went to newcomer Jennifer Hudson in the role of Effie, the heavyset member of the singing group who is pushed aside to make way for Deena as the group's lead singer. Hudson had originally been a contestant on the hit TV show *American Idol*. The prize that year went to another talented African American singer Fantasia Barrino. But Hudson had been voted off the show much too early. Many viewers remembered that season very well. Later beating out almost 800 other young women vying for the role of Effie, Hudson won a Golden Globe, a Screen Actors Guild Award, and also an Oscar as Best Supporting Actress. For Beyoncé, it had to be difficult to watch another performer walk off with all the accolades. Yet, whatever her feelings, Beyoncé gave an assured performance. Unfortunately, the character was underwrit-

ten and softened without real drive or tough ambition. (The same had been true of the character in the Broadway version.) How could a basically passive person ever become a star? That was the question left in the minds of audiences. But in her later scenes in *Dreamgirls*, Beyoncé communicates what the script refused to acknowledge: there was a hardness in her character's face and voice; there was a disillusionment as well. Had the script matched Beyoncé's insights, she would have had the ammunition to give an even stronger performance. Regardless, *Dreamgirls* proved important in Beyoncé's ongoing career.

With her honey-blond hair, her well-stacked curves, and her clinging gowns, she was touted as a great style-setter who made light of those stars who felt they had to be bone thin to look good. Letting her public know that she enjoyed eating french fries, she wanted it known that she refused to starve herself for physical perfection. Beyoncé also had a skilled publicist who informed the media where this gorgeous young woman would be at key times. New York's daily papers were full of pictures of her at some event or opening or just strolling through some part of the world.

Her ongoing romance with performer Jay-Z was well publicized. Here was a great hip-hop-style power couple: he was rapper, music executive, entrepreneur, and stylish man about town with his own popular Manhattan club, 40/40; she, of course, the reigning glamorous female star in the music industry's galaxy. Smooth as Jay-Z was, he also had the rough and ready persona of a brother who knew his way around the hood. When the two vacationed in St. Tropez, the press went wild. "What I gave her was a street credibility, a different edge," Jay-Z said.

No matter where or when, Beyoncé, like Halle Berry, was a media sweetheart that the reporters, photographers, and videographers were always in hot pursuit of. Some might wonder if America's long-held color fixation explained some of this media fascination: after all, both women were lighter with keener features. One thinks back to Angela Bassett's comment about the lack of opportunities after her Oscar

Dreamgirls on the Big Screen: Beyoncé, Anika Noni Rose, and that young powerhouse and Oscar–winner, Jennifer Hudson.

nomination: "But I didn't work again for another year and a half. I guess I was pretty naive to think it would be different—that it was just about the talent—particularly for someone who looks like me. You forget that sometimes." Regardless, their offscreen or offstage appearances not only were a sign of their stardom, but those appearances also helped affirm that stardom.

Some questioned if Beyoncé was really the kind of potent star that past divas had been. Talented, she was, without a doubt. And splendidly ambitious. Yet in some respects, she may have been a woman used by the media and the public to fill a void, that left by Whitney Houston after her career had taken such a dramatic turn. Despite her glamour and her extravagant lifestyle, at heart Beyoncé did not yet possess a haugh-

ty, high-and-mighty *attitude*. Beyoncé seemed nice and perhaps too disciplined. Her public sweetness was clearly appealing—and counter to what many expected. Nor did she have that underside of mega-stardom, that compelling self-destructive underlayer that had to be kept in check. She did not seem to walk the tightrope on which a diva could lose her balance, fall, and then struggle to pick herself back up; the tightrope walk of Waters, Baker, Holiday, Dandridge, Aretha, Miss Ross, and Houston, which had kept the public fascinated. In the mid-years of the new decade, her public persona was not yet complex enough. And audiences still didn't know the *other* Beyoncé hidden from public view. But, of course, one could never predict her future—and the inevitable changes that would come to pass.

And So What Goes
Around Comes Around

Nonetheless, Beyoncé continued a tradition that reaches back to the days of Ma Rainey and Bessie Smith. From the early years of the 20th century, to today, America's dark divas have kept us dazzled with their energy, their control, their haughtiness, and their optimism. The early divas began their careers knowing they were thought of as the Other, the Dark Mysterious Side of Experience. And they knew, too, that they were considered the sexiest of forbidden fruit. Like her predecessors, Beyoncé played on such notions and used her style to become an international star. But she also used her sounds and sexy image to make personal statements to her followers. She stood as one of them, basically a good-natured urban girl who had grown up with the same problems they had. She was ready to lead them on a journey of fun. Having started off as a little girl pleasing her mother and father, she ended up as an entertainer who had contributed much to the flavor of American popular culture, and who had answered specific needs of her age.

Decade after decade, America's dark divas were always able to go beneath the misconceptions their culture had about them as black women. They came up with personal visions of what life could—and did—mean. Ethel Waters's early raunchy ghetto heroine said life was damn tough, but that she was determined to get through it anyway, even if it did mean she had a chip on her shoulder. Josephine Baker and Diana Ross, who had grown up on ghetto streets just as mean and hard as Ethel's, always had such unreal energy and drive that we knew immediately here were women who could never be kept in their place. We admired their guts and determination to fulfill themselves, no matter what, and to have some fun, too. Cicely Tyson, in her early television roles and in films, was so rigid in her refusal to compromise or play herself cheap that we saw the beauty of having convictions and of holding on to ideals. Marian Anderson showed us that even under the most difficult situation, grace and poise could see us through. Lena Horne let us see the long road that can lead to self-liberation. Aretha Franklin lets us know that

life was richer and fuller if we learned to feel, to go all the way with our emotions. Tina Turner informed us that you could always create a new chapter in your life—even when everyone else was ready to write you off. Whitney Houston let us know that an extraordinary voice could transform any kind of material, giving it emotional power and beauty. The talents of these women kept us entertained. Their personal styles kept us informed of who they were.

Many like Joyce Bryant, Holiday, and Houston had troubled lives. Several like Holiday and Dandridge ended up tragically. When we looked at their experiences—their joys as well as their heartaches—we were forced to ask fundamental questions about the society and country in which they—and we—lived. When she was not permitted to sing at Constitution Hall, Marian Anderson made us realize it was not just her problem; it concerned every one of us. Through socially troubled times, the divas were always around, ready to whisper secrets to us. No matter what their personal problems, they made us forget ours. Or they made us think our problems could be worked out. Whether they served as pop myths, social symbols, sex symbols, political symbols, survivors, new school ingenues, or mavens of a new millennium, they enriched our lives and became cultural icons for various eras. Most important, because they were indeed black beauties, they were an uncanny source of inspiration.

And so, when the houselights dimmed and it was time for the blues sister or the colored chorus girl or the girl singer or the member of a girl group to take her place and do her bit or when the movie house went dark and the screen flickered with an image of a goddess up there or when the lights in our living rooms were turned low and the image of a homegrown actress sprang to life on that tiny box in our homes, each woman went forward. City, country, continent, it never mattered. We were always by her side. And as we swayed and hummed or moved to the beat, or had private dreams of our own, we were glad we were there. For through her magic, she made her story ours.

Notes

For the reader's convenience, and not to disrupt the narrative with many parenthetic references in the text, notes to quotes and facts from newspapers, periodicals, and books consulted for this updated and expanded edition follow. When the source for consecutive quotes within a paragraph is the same, the source is listed only once.

Notes for Chapter 8, *Old Style Goddesses of Glitz, New School Ingenues*

214:   He kept hitting me: Tina Turner with Kurt Loder, *I, Tina* (New York, William Morrow and Company, Inc., 1986).

215:   I moved from place: Ibid.

215:   good will of the: Ibid.

216:   beyond the basic fact: Ibid.

217:   just thought it was: Ibid.

219:   acquired European politesse." In: Judith Thurman, "Architectural Digest Visits Tina Turner," *Architectural Digest*, March 2000.

219:   Above all other women: Carl Arrington, "Thunder Dame," *People*, July 15, 1985.

221:   She and my dad: "A Boomin' *Zoomin'* Helps Aretha Franklin Past Her Dad's Death and A Career Threatening Phobia," *People*, October 14, 1985.

221:   spent over a half: Ibid.

221:   on minimum voltage: John O'Connor, No Title, *The New York Times*, July 17, 1986.

222:   was inaccurate and completely: "Letters: Aretha Franklin," *People*, March 30, 1981.

222:   How dare you be: Liz Smith, "Liz Smith," *New York Newsday*, May 11, 1993.

223:   When I saw Tina: Cathleen McGuigan with Linda Buckley, "The New First Ladies of Soul," *Newsweek*, July 21, 1986.

223:   I realized I wasn't: Allison Samuels, "Health: Smooth Operations," *Newsweek*, July 5, 2004.

224:   I looked at the: Donna Summer with March Eliot, *Donna Summer: The Journey* (New York: Villard Books, 2003).

224:   one of the most: "Song: Donna Summer," *People*, September 6,1982.

224:   I didn't know who: "Endless Summer," *People*, June 28, 1999.

224:   a divine ruling,": Liz Smith, "Liz Smith," *New York Newsday*, October 2, 1992.

224:   persistence about prying more: Ibid.

225:   Donna Summer, empress of: "Endless Summer," *People*, June 28,1999.

226:   Not only have we: Frank Rich, "Theater: 'Lena Horne: The Lady and Her Music,'" *The New York Times*, May 13, 1981.

226:   It's like looking at: Michiko Kakutani, "Lena Horne: Aloofness Hid the Pain, Until Time Cooled Her Anger," *The New York Times*, May 3, 1981.

226:   He didn't see me: Ibid.

226:   I left myself feel: Ibid.

228:   I felt as if: Diana Ross, *Diana Ross: Memoirs* (New York: Villard Books, 1993).

228:   I was cold, shaken: Ibid.

229:   That was the only: J. Randy Taraborrelli, *Call Her Miss Ross* (New York: Birch Lane Press, 1989).

229:   Diana Ross doesn't want: Ibid.

229:   How could anyone think: Ibid.

231:   Call her Miss Ross: Ibid.

232:   Wilson and Birdsong balked: Geoff Boucher, "All Over but the Shouting," *Los Angeles Times*, July 12, 2000.

232:   a black leather jacket: Tracy Connor and Alex Divine, "Diana Ross Is 'Bust-Ed' In Britain," *New York Post*, September 23, 1999.

232:   as she bungled her: Todd Venezia, "DIANA'S ALFABET," *New York Post*, January 1, 2003.

233:   was one big joke: Bill Hoffman, "Ross can't hurry jail, judge says," *New York Post*. March 11, 2004.

237:   The audience went bananas: "Whoopi Goldberg," *People*, December 23-30, 1985.

237: a still developing fringe: Frank Rich, "Stage: 'Whoopi Goldberg' Opens," *The New York Times*, October 15, 1984.

238: The name came out: "Whoopi Goldberg," *People*, December 23-30, 1985.

239: I'd like you to: Ibid.

240: Whoopi Goldberg in *Clara's*: "Lows in Acting for '88," *People*, January 9, 1989.

240: Does Hollywood Think Whoopi: Roger Ebert, "Weekend Movies: Fun's burgled from Whoopi," *New York Post*, March 20, 1987.

240: To me, it's justifying: Spike Lee Interview, "Whoopi's Blues Eyes," *Harpers*, January, 1987.

242: I was very nervous: Richard Johnson, "Makin' Whoopi howl at the Hilton," *New York Post*, October 9, 1993.

242: The jokes today were: Bill Hoffman, "Goldberg is gored Friars Club lunch," *New York Post*, October 9, 1993.

242: was confused as to: Montel Williams, "Bye, it's been on pleasure, says Montel," *Daily News*, October 9, 1993.

243: Ted Danson is not: Marsha Kranes, "HE'S A LOVER, NOT A HATER!" *New York Post*, October 11, 1993.

246: a one-day fling: Alan Richman, "OPRAH," *People*, January 12, 1987.

246: starving to be pretty: Lisa DePaulo, "Oprah's Private Life: The Inside Story," *TV Guide*, June 3, 1989.

248: vicious, malicious lie and: Richard Johnson, "Page Six: Columnist axed over Oprah rumor," *New York Post*, May 31, 1989.

252: to avoid potential harm: Michael Sauter, "Encore: There She Goes, Miss America," *Entertainment Weekly*, July 26, 1996.

252: When I was Miss: Elizabeth Kaye, "Miss America's Crown of Thorns," *Rolling Stone*, January 31, 1985.

252: inappropriate person: Jack Kroll, "Success is the Best Revenge," *Newsweek*, August 15, 1994.

252: I know when everything: Ibid.

255: I wasn't thinking about: Patrice Miles, "Phylicia and Ahmad: Off-Camera and Personal," *Essence*, July 1986.

255: She ain't no Goody: Roderick Townley, "Phylicia Ayers-Allen: She'll Show You the Serenity – but Not the Strife," *TV Guide*, September 7, 1985.

260: first black bitch: Edmund Newton, "Diahann!" *Essence*, October 1984.

262: The House of Fears: J. Randy Taraborrelli, *Michael Jackson: The Magic and the Madness* (New York: Birch Lane Press, 1991).

263: There was an added: "Jackson's Heights," *US*, March 5, 1990.

264: Lie. Lie. Lie.: "LaToya's Still Unwelcomed," *New York Newsday*, November 18,1993.

266: When I heard Aretha: Mary Shaughnessy, "Whitney Houston's A Chip Off the Old Pop Diva," *People*, December 9, 1985.

269: She picks the lights: Merle Ginsberg, "Whitney Houston," *US*, August 11, 1986.

Notes for Chapter 9, *Million Dollar Babies*

278: That was hell: Stephan Talty, "Angela's Assets," *Time Out*, February 19-26, 1998.

278: I couldn't pass up: Martha Southgate, "Soul Survivor," *Premiere*, July, 1993.

278: I act it, I: Ibid.

279: This is great! This: Allison Samuels, "Angela's Fire," *Newsweek*, July 1, 2002.

282: most powerful scene in: Lou Lumenick, "The Talk of Toronto," *New York Post*, September 8, 2003.

286: A few weeks after: Ken Parish Perkins, "En Vogue: Funky Divas," *Blackbook*, 1993.

286: queens of sybaritic soul: Wayne Robbins, "Soul Queens and Gritty Rappers," *New York Newsday*, September 17, 1992.

286: We regret it now: Ken Parish Perkins, "En Vogue: Funky Divas," *Blackbook*, 1993.

286: With all the hits: Allison Samuels and Karen Schoemer, "And Then There Were Three. . ." *Newsweek*, June 23, 1997.

288: this grass roots transformation: Chuck D, "Essay: The Sound of Our Young World," *Time*, February 8, 1999.

288: bigoted, degrading, violent, ignorant: Dinitia Smith, "The Queen of Rap: Latifah Sells 'Womanism,'" *New York*, December 3, 1990.

292: All the girl groups: Jon Pareles, "Lisa Lopes, Rapper, Dies in Honduras Crash at 30," *The New York Times*, April 27, 2002.

294: We thought about leaving: Lorraine Ali, "Songs in the Key of TLC," *Newsweek*, November 18, 2002.

294: She's fine: Richard Johnson, "Page Six," *New York Post*, September 12, 2002.

294: She was my heart: "Thousands say goodbye to 'Left Eye,'" *New York Post*, May 3, 2002.

294: The whole album is: Lorraine Ali, "Music: Songs in the Key of TLC," *Newsweek*, November 18, 2002.

296: One day little Lauryn: Toure, "Lady Soul," *Rolling Stone*, February 18, 1999.

296: was mesmerized: "Hip Hop Hooray!" *People*, April 19, 1999.

296: Get close to the: Toure, "Lady Soul," *Rolling Stone*, February 18, 1999.

296: She would take a: "Hip Hop Hooray!" *People*, April 19, 1999.

297: There's always a constant: Toure, "Lady Soul," *Rolling Stone*, February 18, 1999.

300: It was like I: Allison Samuels, "A Whole Lotta Lil' Kim," *Newsweek*, June 26, 2000.

302: Unfortunately, behind the get-ups: Christopher John Farley, "Sex Bomb," *Time*, July 3, 2000.

303: You sat right there: Kati Cornell Smith, "Lil' Liar Gets A Year," *New York Post*, July 7, 2005.

303: I testified falsely during: Ibid.

305: a stupid bitch: Richard Johnson, "Page Six: And now. . . it's the annual," *New York Post*, January 3, 2005.

307: I graduated from the: Baz Dreisinger, "Faith in a comfort zone," *Los Angeles Times*, April 6, 2005.

307: We were young, we: Ibid.

307: I respect Faith: Danyel Smith, "She got game foxy brown is the illest," *Vibe*, December 1998–January 1999.

308: I'm really an inner: Faith Hill biography, Online, http://www.askmen.com/women/singer_150/1640_faith_evans.htm'.

308: women's women, artists whom: Baz Dreisinger, "Faith in a comfort zone," *Los Angeles Times*, April 6, 2005.

310: was never really around: Deborah Gregory, "Proud Mary," *Essence*, March/1995.

310: I had a tight: Allison Samuels, "Muchobliged," *Newsweek*, August 25, 2003.

310: There was always some: Deborah Gregory, "Proud Mary," *Essence*, March, 1995.

310: I started listening to: Allison Samuels, "Muchobliged," *Newsweek*, August 25, 2003.

310: I felt so much: Deborah Gregory, "Proud Mary," *Essence*, March, 1995.

310: the everyday girl look: Toure, "Stardom Shaped By the Street And the Makers of Image," *The New York Times*, August 6, 1995,

310: Everything from your clothes: Allison Samuels, "Muchobliged," *Newsweek*, August 25, 2003.

311: You're talking about taking: Toure, "Stardom Shaped by the Street And the Makers of Image," *The New York Times*, August 6, 1995.

311: You can't get rid: Ibid.

311: A lot of times: Ibid.

311: Hell, I already knew: Allison Samuels, "Music: A Diva Does It Her Way," *Newsweek*, May 5, 1997.

312: I really didn't care: Ibid.

312: *My Life* is a: Rob Brunner, "Merry J. Blige," *Entertainment Weekly*, September 5, 2003.

315: We moved around thirteen: Joan Morgan, "Free at Last," *Essence*, April 2005.

315: separate from everybody: "To Have, And Have A Lot," *People*, January 18, 1999.

315: My struggles began when: Joan Morgan, "Free at Last," *Essence*, April, 2005.

316: an emotionally abusive relationship: Ibid.

317: Now she's trying to: Ibid.

320: Oprah knew for years: Gretchen Reynolds, "A Year to Remember: Oprah Grows Up," *TV Guide*, January 7, 1995.

320: not good at confrontation: Gretchen Reynolds, "The Oprah Myth," *TV Guide*, July 23, 1994.

320: fell to their lowest: Ibid.

322: It has just stopped: Sam Howe Verhovek, "Talk of the Town: Burgers v. Oprah," *The New York Times*, January 21, 1998.

323: It happened to me: "Angry Oprah: Snooty store turned me away because they thought I was a black thief," *Star*, June 2, 1992.

323: I remember the last: Gretchen Reynolds, "A Year to Remember: Oprah Grows Up," *TV Guide*, January 7, 1995.

323: I am not a: Richard Johnson, "Page Six: Rumblings behind the Oprah rumor," *New York Post*, June 18, 1997.

323: Your future's so bright: WABC, *The Oprah Winfrey Show*, November 10, 2005.

325: come across as a: Jon Pareles, "Recordings View: A Sex Object By the Name of Jackson," *The New York Times*, May 23, 1993.

327: That's when people feel: Edna Gundersen, "All About Janet," *USA Today*, February 18, 1994.

329: Perhaps the one moment: Alessandra Stanley, "The TV Watch: A Flash of Flesh: CBS Again Is in Denial," *The New York Times*, February 3, 2004.

334: once-stylish home now: "Not Who You Think She Is," *People*, December 18, 1995.

334: That I'm gay, that: "Star Blight," *People*, April 17, 2000.

335: She was acting really: Ibid.

335: She just kind of: Ibid.

336: Crack is wack: ABC, *Primetime*, December 4, 2002.

337: Whitney Diagnosed with Deadly: *The National Enquirer*, May 22, 2006.

337: She was really polite: "Star Blight," *People*, April 17, 2000.

Notes for Chapter 10, *Mavens of the New Millennium*

342: Mom's family turned their: Jane Ciabattari, "I Know I Will Survive," *Parade*, August 22, 1999.

342: was tough: Dana Kennedy, "Halle Berry, Bruised and Beautiful, Is on a Mission," *The New York Times*, March 10, 2002.

342: I felt like I: "Hurts So Bad," *People*, May 13, 1996.

343: What's hardest for me: Dana Kennedy, "Halle Berry, Bruised and Beautiful, Is on a Mission," *The New York Times*, March 10, 2002.

344: She wasn't the same: "Hurts So Bad," *People*, May 13, 1996.

346: has been with her: "Collision Course," *People*, April 17, 2000.

346: I feel like I: "Question of Blame," *People*, May 29, 2000.

347: Its about character: Allison Samuels, "Angela's Fire," *Newsweek*, July 1, 2002.

348: I'll never get married: Liz Smith, "Liz Smith," *New York Post*, May 24, 2004.

348: The feline attribute she: A. O. Scott, "Review: Not-So-Cuddly Cat: This One Cracks a Mean Whip," *The New York Times*, July 22, 2004.

352: I don't use music: Peter Watrous, "When the Queen Speaks, People Listen," *The New York Times*, August 25, 1991.

355: I'm not married. That's: "The Saddest Song," *People*, September 10, 2001.

356: I've been on some: Ibid.

359: We were always rehearsing: Lorraine Ali, "A Date With Destiny," *Newsweek*, May 21, 2001.

359: People expect me to: Lisa Robinson, "Above and Beyoncé," *Vanity Fair*, November/2005.

359: I didn't grow up: Ibid.

360: a Diana Ross complex: Allison Samuels, "What Beyoncé Wants," *Newsweek*, July 29, 2002.

360: to a cult: Lorraine Ali, "A Date With Destiny," *Newsweek*, May 21, 2001.

361: the voice that defines: Jon Pareles, "Pop Review: Empowerment, Allure And a Runway's Flair," *The New York Times*, August 1, 2005.

361: The mystery of Destiny's: Lorraine Ali, "A Date With Destiny," *Newsweek*, May 21, 2001.

361: I think in order: Ibid.

362: What I gave her: Lisa Robinson, "Above and Beyoncé," *Vanity Fair*, November/2005.

363: But I didn't work: Allison Samuels, "Angela's Fire," *Newsweek*, July 1, 2002.

Select Bibliography

Additional sources can be found in the Notes.

Albertson, Chris. *Bessie.* New York: Stein and Day, 1974.

Anger, Kenneth. *Hollywood Babylon.* San Francisco: Straight Arrow, 1975.

American Business Consultants. *Red Channels: The Report of Communist Influence in Radio and Television.* New York: Counterattack, 1950.

Bailey, Pearl, *The Raw Pearl.* New York: Harcourt, Brace & World, 1968.

Baker, Jean-Claude, and Chris Chase. *Josephine: The Hungry Heart.* New York: Random House, 1993.

Basie, Count as told to Albert Murray. *Good Morning Blues: The Autobiography of Count Basie.* New York: Random House, 1985.

Bass, Charlotta. *Forty Years: Memoirs From The Pages of A Newspaper.* Los Angeles: self-published, 1960.

Black, Gregory D., and Clayton R. Koppes. *Hollywood Goes To War: How Politics, Profits and Propaganda Shaped World War II Movies.* Berkeley: University of California, 1987.

Bogle, Donald. *Blacks in American Films and Television: An Illustrated Encyclopedia.* New York: Fireside, 1990.

——————. *Bright Boulevards, Bold Dreams: The Story of Black Hollywood.* New York: Ballantine, 2006.

——————. *Dorothy Dandridge: A Biography.* New York: Amistad, 1998.

——————. *Primetime Blues: African Americans on Network Television.* New York: Farrar, Straus, and Giroux, 2002.

——————. *Toms, Coons, Mulattoes, Mammies, and Bucks: An Interpretive History of Blacks in American Films,* Fourth Edition. New York: Continuum, 2001.

Bond, J. Max. *The Negro in Los Angeles: A Dissertation.* Los Angeles: University of Southern California, 1936.

Bricktop with James Haskins. *Bricktop.* New York: Atheneum, 1983.

Brown, Ruth, with Andrew Yule. *Miss Rhythm: The Autobiography of Ruth Brown, Rhythm & Blues Legend.* New York: Donald I. Fine Books, 1996.

Bryant, Clora, Buddy Collette, William Green, Steven Isoardi, Jack Kelson, Horace Tapscott, Gerald Wilson, and Marl Young, editors. *Central Avenue Sounds: Jazz in Los Angeles.* Berkeley, Los Angeles: University of California, 1999.

Buckley, Gail Lument. *The Hornes: An American Family.* New York: Alfred A. Knopf, 1986.

Calloway, Cab, and Bryant Rollins. *Of Minnie the Moocher and Me.* New York: Thomas Y. Crowell, 1976.

Carroll, Diahann, and Ross Firestone. *Diahann!* Boston: Little, Brown and Company, 1986.

Ceplair, Larry, and Steven Englund. *The Inquisition In Hollywood: Politics in the Film Community, 1930-1960.* Garden City: Anchor, 1980.

Chilton, John. *Billie's Blues: The Billie Holiday Story, 1933-1959.* New York: Stein and Day, 1975.

Cook, Bruce. *Listen to the Blues.* New York: Charles Scribner's Sons, 1973.

Cooper, Ralph, and Steve Dougherty, *Amateur Night At The Apollo: Ralph Cooper Presents Five Decades of Great Entertainment.* New York: HaperCollins Publishers, 1990.

Dandridge, Dorothy, and Earl Conrad. *Everything and Nothing: The Dorothy Dandridge Story.* New York: Abelard-Schumann, 1970.

Davis, Ossie, and Ruby Dee. *With Ossie & Ruby: In This Life Together.* New York: William Morrow Company, Inc., 1998.

Davis, Sammy, *Hollywood in a Suitcase.* New York: William Morrow, 1980.

Dunham, Katherine. *Journey to Accompong.* New York: Henry Holt, 1946.

———. *A Touch of Innocence.* New York: Harcourt Brace and World, 1959.

Ellington, Duke. *Music Is My Mistress.* Garden City: Doubleday, 1973.

Flanner, Janet, edited by Irving Drutman. *Paris Was Yesterday.* New York: Viking, 1972.

Franklin, Aretha, with David Ritz. *Aretha: From These Roots.* New York: Villard Books, 1999.

Gillespie, Dizzy, with Al Fraser. *To Be Or Not To Bop: Memoirs--Dizzy Gillespie.* Garden City: Doubleday, 1979.

Gleason, Ralph J. *Celebrating the Duke and Louis, Bessie, Billie, Bird, Carmen, Miles, Dizzy and Other Heroes.* New York: Delta, 1976.

Goldberg, Whoopi. *Book.* New York: Bob Weisbach Books/William Morrow, 1997.

Hajdu, David. *Lush Life: A Biography of Billy Strayhorn.* New York: Farrar, Straus and Giroux, 1996.

Hammond, John. *On Record.* New York: Ridge, 1977

Haney, Lynn. *Naked at the Feast: A Biography of Josephine Baker.* New York: Dodd, Mead, 1981.

Holiday, Billie, and William Dufty. *Lady Sings the Blues.* New York: Doubleday, 1956.

Horne, Lena, and Richard Schickel. *Lena.* Garden City: Doubleday, 1965.

Houseman, John. *Run-Through. New York: Simon and Schuster, 1972.*

Hughes, Langston, and Milton Metzer. *Black Magic: A Pictorial History of the Negro in American Entertainment.* Englewood Cliffs, New Jersey: Prentice-Hall, 1967.

Jablonski, Edward. *Harold Arlen: Happy with the Blues.* Garden City: Doubleday, 1961.

Jackson, Carlton. *Hattie: The Life of Hattie McDaniel.* Lanham, New York, and London: Madison Books, 1990.

Jackson, La Toya with Patricia Romanowski. *La Toya: Growing Up in the Jackson Family.* New York: Dutton, 1991.

Jackson, Mahalia, and Evan McLeod Wylie. *Movin' on Up.* New York: Hawthorn, 1966.

James, Etta, and David Ritz. *Rage to Survive.* New York: Villard Books, 1995.

Johnson, James Weldon. *Black Manhattan.* New York: Atheneum, 1968.

Jones, LeRoi. *Blues People.* New York: William Morrow and Company, 1963.

Katz, Ephraim. *The Film Encyclopedia.* New York: HarperPerennial, 1994.

Kimball, Robert, and William Bolcum. *Reminiscing With Sissle and Blake.* New York: Viking, 1963.

Kitt, Eartha. *Alone with Me.* Chicago: Henry Regnery, 1976.

———. *Confessions of A Sex Kitten.* London: Sidgwick & Jackson Limited, 1989.

———. *Thursday's Child.* New York: Duell, Sloan, and Pearce, 1956

Latifah, Queen, with Karen Hunter. *Ladies First: Revelations of a Strong Woman.* New York: William Morrow and Company, 1999.

Lawrence, A.H. *Duke Ellington and His World.* New York: Routledge, 2001.

Mapp, Edward. *Blacks in the Performing Arts*. Metuchen: Scarecow, 1978.

Morse, David. *Motown*. New York: Collier, 1971.

Murray, Albert. *Stomping the Blues*. New York: McGraw-Hill, 1976.

Navasky, Victor. *Naming Names*. New York: Viking, 1980.

Nicolas, A. X. *The Poetry of Soul*. New York: Bantam, 1971.

Placksin, Sally. *American Women in Jazz*. New York: Wideview, 1982.

Reeves, Martha, and Mark Bego. *Dancing in the Street: Confessions of a Motown Diva*. New York: Hyperion, 1994.

Rose, Phyllis. *Jazz Cleopatra: Josephine Baker in Her Time*. New York: Doubleday, 1989.

Rose, Tricia. *Black Noise: Rap Music and Black Culture in Contemporary America*. Middletown, Connecticut: Wesleyan University, 1994.

Ross, Diana. *Secrets of a Sparrow: Memoirs*. New York: Villard Books, 1993.

Shaw, Arnold, *Honkers and Shouters*. New York: Macmillan, 1978.

Short, Bobby. *Black and White Baby*. New York: Dodd, Mead, 1971.

Short, Bobby, with Robert MacKintosh. *The Life and Times of A Saloon Singer*. New York: Clarkson Potter Publishers, 1995.

Simone, Nina, with Stephen Cleary. *The Autobiography of Nina Simone*. New York: Pantheon, 1991.

Stewart-Baxter, Derrick. *Ma Rainey and the Classic Blues Singers*. New York: Stein and Day, 1970.

Summer, Donna, with Mark Eliot. *Ordinary Girl: The Journey*. New York: Villard Books, 2003.

Taraborrelli, J. Randy. *Call Her Miss Ross*. New York: Birch Lane, 1989.

—————. *Michael Jackson: The Magic and the Madness*. New York: Birch Lane, 1991.

Taylor, Frank C, with Gerald Cook. *Alberta Hunter*. New York: McGraw-Hill, 1988.

Waters, Ethel, with Charles Samuel. *His Eye Is on the Sparrow*. Garden City: Doubleday, 1950.

White, Walter. *How Far the Promised Land?* New York: Viking, 1955.

Wilson, Mary, with Patricia Romanowski and Ahrgus Juilliard. *Dreamgirl: My Life as a Supreme*. New York: St. Martin's, 1986.

Wilson, Mary, and Patricia Romanowski. *Supreme Faith: Someday We'll Be Together*. New York: HarperCollins, 1990.

Woll, Allen. *Black Musical Theatre: From Coontown to Dreamgirls*. New York: De Capo, 1991.

Index of Names

A

Aaliyah, 355–56, *357*
Abatino, Giuseppe "Pepito," *46*, 50, 266
Alexander, Erika, 256, 353
Alexander, Khandi, 350
Alice, Mary, 203, *257, 259*
Alix, May, 63, 65
Allen, Debbie, 203, *254,* 255, 257–58
Anderson, Ivie, 14, 19, 60, *64,* 65, *66,* 68, 75, 89, 148
Anderson, Marian, 89, 92, *107–10,* 111, 113, 144–45, 158–59, 173, 202–3, 297, 365
Angelou, Maya, 186, 246, 273, 322
Arlen, Harold, 86
Armstrong, Lil Hardin, 30, 63, 104
Armstrong, Louis, 30, 63, 68, *71,* 75, 113, 165, *364*
Arnold, Monica, 284
Arroyo, Martina, 158
Arthur, Jean, 60
Ashanti, 356, *357*
Atkinson, Brooks, 52, 88
Avery, Margaret, 237
Ayler, Ethel, 202, 256, 275

B

Babyface, 332
Bacharach, Burt, 171, 335
Badu, Erykah, *283,* 284
Bailey, Pearl, 113, 117, 120, *121,* 122, *123–24,* 134, 136, 201, 237
Baker, Anita, 260, 268, 310
Baker, Josephine, 14, 16, *18,* 19, 24, *26,* 28, 36, 40, 42, 43, 44, *45–48,* 49, *50–51,* 52, 54, 56–57, 87, 89, 109, 113, 128, 131, 143–44, 152, 182, 184, 189, *196,* 197–98, *199,* 201, 203, 208, 218, 226, 229, 232, 254, 266, 269, 278, 302–3, 363, *364,* 365
Baker, LaVern, 68–69, *141,* 165
Balanchine, George, 100, 202
Ballard, Florence, 169, *170,* 231
Banks, Tyra, 350
Barbara-O, 275
Basie, Count, 62, 69–70, 113
Bassett, Angela, 19, 192, 218, 275, 276, 277–78, *279,* 280, 332, 344, 347–48, 362
Battle, Kathleen, 158
Beals, Jennifer, *234,* 235
Beavers, Louise, 72, 73–75, 79, 81, 89
Belafonte, Harry, 136, 138, 154, 250
Belafonte, Shari, 250
Bellson, Louis, *123,* 124
Berlin, Irving, 86
Berry, Halle, 14, 19, 56, 218, *273,* 275, 280, 322, 326–27, *338, 341,* 342, *343,* 344, *345,* 346, *347,* 348, 362
Bethune, Mary McLeod, 60
Beverley, Trazana, 203
Birdsong, Cindy, *170,* 232
Bledsoe, Tempestt, *256*
Blige, Mary J., 19, *273,* 297, 302, *309,* 310–11, *312,* 313, 332, 355
Bogart, Neil, 224
Bonet, Lisa, *256,* 257, 259
Bouillon, Jo, 50, 197
Boyd, Stephen, *137*
Brando, Marlon, 100, 120
Braxton, Toni, 284, 293, 332
Broderick, Helen, 86–87
Brooks, Golden, 350
Brown, Anne, 113

Brown, Bobby, 328, 332, 334, *335,* 336–37
Brown, Charnele, 257, *259*
Brown, Foxy, *299,* 300, *301,* 302–5, 307
Brown, Ruth, 140, 165, 173–74
Brown, Shirley, 288
Bruce, Cheryl Lynn, 275
Bryant, Clora, 113
Bryant, Joyce, 120, *130,* 131–32, 134, 145, 201, 365
Bumbry, Grace, 158, 203
Burrows, Vinnie, 203

C

Caesar, Shirley, 143, 322
Calloway, Cab, 79, *96,* 113
Cambridge, Godfrey, 162, 186
Campbell, Naomi, 350
Campbell, Tisha, 275
Capers, Virginia, 203
Carey, Mariah, 222, 235, 305, *314,* 315, *316,* 317, *318*
Carlos, Laurie, 203
Carroll, Diahann, 83, 134, 140, *149, 150–52,* 201–2, 218, *260,* 275, 348, 362
Carroll, Vinnette, 203
Carson, Lisa Nicole, 275
Carter, Betty, 113, 201
Carter, Jimmy, 203, 212
Carter, Rosalind, 203
Carter, Nell, 203, *250*
Carter, T.K., 350
Cash, Rosalind, 154, *191–92*
Chapman, Tracy, 284
Charles, Ray, 173–74, 335
Charles, Suzette, 251–52
Chase, Debra, 284
Childress, Alice, 154
Chinn, Alva, 143
Churchill, Savannah, 140
Cleveland, Pat, 143
Clifford, Linda, 206
Clift, Montgomery, 120
Clough, Inez, 38
Cocteau, Jean, 48
Colbert, Claudette, 60, 79
Cole, Nat "King," *126,* 165, 216, 218
Cole, Natalie, 203, 242
Cole, Olivia, 74, 192, *247,* 248
Coles, Kim, 353
Colette, 48
Collins, Janet, 140
Collins, Joan, *137*
Combs, Sean "Puff Daddy," 288, 302, 307, 310, 312–13, 346
Cosby, Bill, 155, 254–55, *256,* 257–58, 277, 349
Costner, Kevin, 331, *333*
Coward, Noël, 31
Cox, Ida, 30–31, 104
Cruise, Tom, 350

D

Dale, Clamma, 203
Dandridge, Dorothy, 14, *19,* 56, 66, 73, 75, 102, 113, 117, *118, 120, 133,* 134, *135,* 136, *137,* 138, 140, 145, 150, 216, 218, 235, 245, 248, 259, 266, 269, 277, 326–27, 332, 344–45, 348, 363, *364,* 365
Dandridge, Ruby, 73, 134
Dandridge, Vivian, 75, 113, 134, *137,* 138
Danson, Ted, *240–41,* 242–43
Darden, Norma Jean, 143

Daṣh, Damon, 355, 357
Dash, Julie, 275, 280
Dash, Sarah, *204,* 205
Davis, Bette, 60, 94, 342
Davis, Clifton, 201, *258*
Davis, Clive, 221, 266–67, 269, 332, 336–37
Davis, Ossie, 154, 277
Davis, Sammy, Jr., 136, *168,* 198, 218, 233, 242
Day, Cora Lee, 275
Day, Doris, 120
Dean, James, 100, 120
Dee, Ruby, 113, 140, 154, *155, 156,* 275, 277
De Lavallade, Carmen, 140
Del Rio, Dolores, 120
De Niro, Robert, 216, 242, 280, 328
Denison, Jack, *137,* 138
Denton, Sandra "Pepa," *290*
Denny, Jack, 87
Destiny's Child, *358,* 359, *360,* 361
Devine, Loretta, 231, 259, 332
Dietrich, Marlene, 60, 135, 201
Dion, Celine, 222
Dobbs, Mattiwilda, 140
Dobson, Tamara, *193,* 194, 195
Donegan, Dorothy, 113, 140, 174, 201
Dorsey, Jimmy, *63*
Dowd, Tom, 174
Duncan, Isadora, 50
Dunham, Katherine, 14, 75, 92, *99,* 100–102, 127, 202, 259
Dunston, Geraldine, 275

E

Eckstine, Billy, 68, 165
Einstein, Albert, 48, 127
Elise, Kimberly, *349,* 350, *353,* 354
Elizondo, Rene, 328
Ellington, Duke, 62, *64,* 65–66, 68, 71, 75, 79, 89, 113, 356
Elliott, Missy, *289,* 305, 312
Ellis, Terry, *285,* 286
En Vogue, *285,* 286, 292–93
Estefan, Gloria, 222
Evans, Faith, 19, 273, 300, *306,* 307–8, 310, 332, 355
Eve, 350

F

Falana, Lola, 203
Fales, Susan, 258
Ferrell, Tyra, *275,* 325
Fields, Kim, 353
Fitzgerald, Ella, *61, 62,* 63, 69, *113,* 141, 355
Flack, Roberta, *148,* 171, 202, 297
Flanner, Janet, 47–48
Ford, Betty (Center), 334
For Real, 332
Foster, Gloria, 154–56, 192, 280
Fox, Vivica A., 348, *353,* 354
Foxx, Redd, 122, 161
Franklin, Aretha, 14, 19, 24, *172,* 173, *174, 175,* 180, 202–3, 209, *220,* 221–23, 225–26, 259, 266, 297, 312, 332, 337, 363, 365
Franklin, Farrah, 360
Freeman, Bee, 75
Freeman, Morgan, 260

G

Garbo, Greta, 120, 248
Gaynor, Gloria, 206
Geffen, David, 224,

Gershwin, George, 97, 106, 135, 252
Gershwin, Ira, 252
Gibbs, Marla, 162, 192, 259
Giovanni, Nikki, 156
Givens, Robin, *247*, 248, 250, 251, 252, 275
Glover, Danny, 280
Godfrey, Lynnie, 203
Goldberg, Whoopi, 74, *236*, 237, *238–41*, 243, 255, 296, 322, 354
Good, Meagan, 275
Goodman, Benny, 63, 68
Gordy, Berry, 167, 169, 180, 182, 184, 228, 231, 233, 266, 288
Gossett, Lou, Jr., 186
Grant, Cary, 332, 350
Grant, Micki, 203
Graves, Teresa, 192
Gray, Macy, *283*, 284
Greenfield, Elizabeth Taylor, 21
Grier, Pam, *193*, 194, *195*, 303
Grist, Reri, 158
Grosvenor, Vertamae, 275
Guy, Jasmine, *257*, 259–60

H

Haley, Alex, 342
Hall, Adelaide, *39*, 40, 52, 143
Hall, Juanita, 122, 140, 150
Hansberry, Lorraine, 74, 154
Hardison, Kadeem, *257*
Harlow, Jean, 60, 73–74, 96
Harrell, Andre, 310, 311, 312
Harrelson, Woody, 275
Harris, Edna Mae, 75
Harris, Leslie, *275*
Harris, Sam, 86
Harris, Theresa, 73, 75
Harry, Jackée, *247*, 248, 259–60
Hart, Moss, 86
Harvey, Georgette, 38, 88
Hayton, Lennie, *97*, 98, 226
Headley, Heather, 281
Hegamin, Lucille, 30
Hemsley, Sherman, *258*, 259
Hendryx, Nona, *204*, 205
Hepburn, Audrey, 343, 350
Hepburn, Katharine, 60, 74, 201
Herron-Braggs, Cindy, 285–86
Heyward, Dorothy, 87
Heyward, DuBose, 87
Hill, Faith, 335
Hill, Lauryn, 284, 294, *295*, 296–98, 312, 356
Hinderas, Natalie, 140
Holiday, Billie, *2*, 14, *15*, 19, 36, 56, 60, 62–63, 65, *67–68*, 69–70, *71*, 75, 85, 87, 89, 98, 113, 115, *116*, 117, 134, *140*, 145, 148, 173, 175, 180, *181*, 182, 201–2, 218, 251, 278, 284, 298, 303, 308, 334, 337, 363, *364*, 365
Holliday, Jennifer, 231
Holly, Ellen, 192
Hopkins, Linda, 202
Hopkins, Telma, 250
Horne, Lena, 14, *17*, 19, 24, 56, 62, 69, 75, 89, *90*, 92, *93–97*, 98, 101–2, 104, 106, 116–17, 120, 128, 134–36, *141*, 143, 152, 186, 201, 216, 218, *225*, 226, 245, 259, 269, 303, 348, *364*, 365
Horsford, Anna Maria, *258*, 259–60
Houseman, John, 39

Houston, Cissy, 221, 266
Houston, John, 269, 326, 336
Houston, Whitney, 14, 16, 19, *265*, 266–67, *268*, 269, *270*, 273, 284, 294, 305, 315, *318*, 326–27, *330*, 331–32, *333*, 334, *335–36*, 337, 344, 355, 363, *364*, 365
Hudlin, Reginald, 275
Hudson, Jennifer, 362, *363*
Humes, Helen, 62, *200*, 201
Hunter, Alberta, 24, *29*, 30–31, 54, 88, *202*, 203
Hyman, Phyllis, 203

I

Iman, 143

J

Jabara, Paul, 224
Jackson, Ernestine, 203
Jackson, Janet, 19, *210*, *261*, 262, *263*, 264, 266, 268–69, 273, 322–23, *324–27*, 328, *329*, 331, 343
Jackson, La Toya, 262, 264, *326*, 327, *328*, 329
Jackson, Mahalia, 143, *173*, 174, 202, 221
Jackson, Michael, 217, 228, 231, 233, 239, 262, 264, 267, 326–27, 329, 336
Jackson, Millie, 203, 260, 288, 300
Jackson, Rebbie, 262, 264, *326*, 327
Jackson Five, 262, 278
Jagger, Mick, 216, 218
James, Cheryl "Salt," *290*
James, Etta, 166
James, Olga, 136
Jamison, Judith, 203
Jay-Z, 303, 362
Jerald, Penny Johnson, 350
Johnson, Ariyan, 275
Johnson, Beverly, 143
Johnson, Lyndon, 124, 129, 243
Jones, Crystal, 292
Jones, Etta, 75, 113, 134, *137*
Jones, Grace, *206*, 235, 275
Jones, James Earl, 186, 277, 280
Jones, Jill Marie, 350
Jones, Maggie, 30
Jones, Maxine, 285–86
Jones, Quincy, 224, 239, 245, 323
Jones, Sarah, 350
Jones, Sissieretta "Black Patti," 22, 23
Justice, David, 344

K

Kelly, Grace, 120
Kelly, Paula, 191, *247*, 248
Kennedy, John, 148, 219, 273
Keymah, T'Keyah "Crystal," 350
Keys, Alicia, 356, 357
Khan, Chaka, *178*, 203, 266, 332
Kimball, Florence Page, 158
King, Evelyn "Champagne," 206
King, Mabel, 192, 203
King, Regina, 259, 325, 350
Kitt, Eartha, 19, 77, 92, 100, 102, 120, *125–26*, *127*, *128*, 129, 131, 134, 145, 186, 201, 219, 243, 251, 275, 348
Knight, Gladys, *164*, 203, 293, 296, 355
Knowles, Beyoncé, 16, *19*, 305, 312, 356, *358*, 359, *360*, 361–62, *363–64*, 365
Knowles, Mathew, 359–61
Knowles, Solange, 361
Knowles, Tina, 359, 361
Koch, Edward, 268

L

Labelle, *204*, 205
LaBelle, Patti, 166, 170, *204*, 205, 223–25, 258, 268, 322, 332
LaChanze, 350
La Guardia, Fiorello, *80*, *108*
Lamarr, Heddy, 94, 120
La Rue, Florence, 203
Lathan, Sanaa, 350
Lathan, Stan, 350
Laurence, Lynda, 232
Le Beauf, Sabrina, *256*
Le Corbusier, 48
Lee, Canada, *81*, 82, 88, 106
Lee, Joie, *274*, 275
Lee, Spike, 240, 275, 278, 342
Lemmons, Kasi, 272, 275
Lennox, Annie, 221
LeNoire, Rosetta, 203, 250
Lewis, Barbara, 166
Lewis, Dawnn, *257*, 259
Lil' Kim, 19, *299*, 300, *301*, 302–3, *304*, 305, 307, 310, 312
Lillie, Beatrice, *88*
Lincoln, Abbey, 154
Lion, Jean, 50
Little Eva, 166
Little Richard, 165, 293
Long, Nia, *275*, 350
Lopes, Lisa "Left Eye," *291*, 292–94, 296, 300
Louis, Joe, 60, 92, 111, 140, 162
Luckett, LeToya, 359, *360*
Luna, Donyale, 143
Lyles, Aubrey, 40
Lynn, Gloria, 141
Lyte, MC, 288

M

McCarthy, Joseph, 120
McClendon, Rose, 38–39, 79, 89
McCoo, Marilyn, 203
McDaniel, Hattie, *72*, 73–75, 81, 89, 122, 194, 241
McDonald, Audra, 281
McDonald, Michael, 223
McGee, Vonetta, *190*, 191
McKee, Lonette, 192, *247*, 248, *273*, 275, 343
McKinney, Nina Mae, *55*, 56, *57*, 65, 94, 115, 302
McMillan, Terry, 322, 332
McNair, Barbara, 152
McNeil, Claudia, 154, *155*, 202
McQueen, Butterfly, 73, *75*, 100, 201
McRae, Carmen, 69, 141, *144*, 355
Mabley, Jackie "Moms," 24, 68, 122, *160*, 161–62, *192*, 237
Makeba, Miriam, 171
Marie, Sonja, 332
Martha and the Vandellas, *166*, 167
Martin, Barbara, 169, *170*
Martin, Helen, 259
Martin, Sara, 30
Marvelettes, The, *163*, 167
Maynor, Dorothy, *81*, 89, 113
Mbulu, Letta, 203
Mercer, Mabel, 201
Merkerson, S. Epatha, 350
Merritt, Theresa, 192
Middleton, Velma, 63
Miller, Flournoy, 40
Miller, Marilyn, 86

Mills, Florence, 28, 30, 40, *41*, 42, 46, 52, 264
Mills, Stephanie, 203
Mingus, Charles, 100
Mo' Nique, 350
Monroe, Marilyn, 120, 131, 134, 209, 259, 337, 344
Montez, Maria, 194
Montgomery, Barbara, 203, 259
Moore, Kaycee, 275
Moore, Juanita, 140
Moore, Melba, 155, 203, 322
Moore, Phil, *66*, 134–35, 266
Morgan, Debbi, *272*, 275
Moroder, Giorgio, 224
Morrison, Toni, 212, 237, 246, 322, 332
Morrow, Ethel, 202
Moses, Ethel, 75
Moten, Etta, 73
Mowry, Tia and Tamera, 259
Murphy, Eddie, 251, 268, *273*, *279*, 326, 342, 362

N
Naylor, Gloria, 248
Newton, Thandie, *349*, 350
Nicholas, Denise, 154, 192
Nicholas, Fayard, 134
Nicholas, Harold, 134, 345
Nicholas Brothers, 122, 134
Nichols, Nichelle, 192
Niven, David, 332
Nixon, Richard M., 124, 162, 205
Norman, Jessye, 158
Norwood, Brandy, 284, 312, 332

O
O'Connor, John, 221–22
O'Neal, Ryan, 229, 331
O'Neill, Eugene, 38
O'Neill, Gail, 143
Odetta, *164*, 171
Onassis, Jacqueline Kennedy, 219
Owens, Jesse, 60

P
Pagnol, Marcel, 48
Payne, Freda, 203
Payne, Scherrie, 232
Payton, Jo Marie, 250
Perez, Rosie, *275*
Peters Sisters, 52, *75*
Phifer, Mekhi, *275*
Pinkett-Smith, Jada, 259, 348, *353*, 354
Pinkins, Tonya, 350
Pirandello, Luigi, 48
Pointer Sisters, The, 203, 239, *259*, 260, 285
Poitier, Sidney, 82, 136, 140, 154, 246, 348
Porter, Cole, 31, 97, 198
Powell, Adam Clayton, Jr., *76*, *80*, 82–83, 92, *103*, 106, 138, 144, 344
Powell, Eleanor, *88*
Premice, Josephine, 201, 203, 258
Preminger, Otto, 135–36, 138, 150
Price, Leontyne, 140, *157*, 158–59
Prince, 217, 267, 362
Pryor, Richard, 122, 181, 189, 237, 254
Pulliam, Keshia Knight, *255*, *256*

Q
Queen Latifah, 14, 275, *287*, 288, 335, *351*, 352, *353–54*, 355

R
Rainey, Ma, 14, 19, *20*, 21–22, 24, *25*, 28, 30, 33, 42, 62, 86, 165, 173, 217, 277, 302, 334, 352, 365
Ralph, Sheryl Lee, 231, *233*, 254
Randle, Theresa, 275
Randolph, Amanda and Lillian, 73
Rashad, Phylicia Ayers-Allen, *253*, 254–55, *256*, 258, 264
Raven-Symone, 257, 349–50
Rawls, Lou, 174, 266
Reed, Alaina, 203, 259
Reed, Tracy, 192
Reed, Vivian, 203
Reese, Della, 141, 171, *173*
Reeves, Martha, 167
Reinhardt, Max, 48
Remarque, Erich Maria, 48
Reuben, Gloria, 349
Reynolds, Debbie, 120
Rich, Frank, 226, 237
Richards, Beah, 154, 192, 350
Richie, Lionel, 228, 267
Richmond, June, *63*
Riperton, Minnie, 203
Roberson, LaTavia, 359, *360*
Robeson, Paul, 31, 38, 40, 78, 81, 92, 98, 106
Robinson, Bill "Bojangles," 76, 85, *96*
Robinson, Dawn, 285–86
Robinson, Eartha, 275
Robinson, Fannie, *76*
Robinson (Peete), Holly, 260
Robinson, Jackie, 92, *109*, 136, 154, *156*
Robinson, Smokey, 165, 167, 231, 296
Robinson, Vicki Sue, 206
Rochon, Lela, 275, 326, 332
Rogers, Alva, 275
Roker, Roxie, 192, 257
Rolle, Esther, 154, 192
Roosevelt, Eleanor, 88, 109, 162
Roosevelt, Franklin D., 111
Roper, Dee Dee "dj Spinderella," *290*
Rose, Anika Noni, 350, *363*
Ross, Diana, 14, 16, 19, 92, 169, *170–71*, 173, 178, *179*, 180, *181*, 182, *183*, 184, 188–89, 191, 208, 216, 218, 221, 223, *227*, 228–29, *230*, 231–33, 235, 266, 269, 284, 294, 302, 331, 350, 359–60, 362–63, 365
Ross, Tracee Ellis, 350
Rowell, Victoria, 349
Rowland, Kelly, *358*, 359, *360*, 361
Ryan, Roz, 259

S
Salt-n-Pepa, 260, 288, *290*
Sanchez, Sonia, 156
Sands, Diana, 151, *153*, 154, 162, 186
Sanford, Isabel, 192
Saunders, Gertrude, 30, 36, 40, 42
Schuyler, Philippa, 113, 140
Scott, Hazel, 19, 75, 83, 92, *94*, *103*, *104-5*, 106, 117, 120, 138, 144, 201, 344
Scott, Seret, 203
Shakur, Tupac, 288, 300, *325*
Shange, Ntozake, 203

Shanna, 332
Shante, Roxanne, 288
Sharpe, Dee Dee, 166
Shazzy, 288
Sherrill, Joya, 113
Shirelles, The, *164*, 165–66, 285
Short, Bobby, 66, 83, 135
Sidney, Sylvia, 60
Silverstein, Robert, 11
Simmons, Russell, 288
Simms, Hilda, 113, 140
Simone, Nina, *148*, 171
Simpson, Valerie, 203
Sims, Naomi, 143
Sinclair, Madge, 192
Singleton, John, 278, 325, 350
Sissle, Noble, 40, 46, 62, 96, 98
Sister Sledge, 206
Sister Soulijah, 288
Smalls, Biggie, 288, 300, 302–3, 307, 310
Smith, Anna Deavere, 19, *281*, 282
Smith, Bessie, *12*, 14, 16, 19, 24–25, 28, 30–31, *32*, 33–34, *35–36*, 42, 44, 47, 56, 62–63, 65, 68, 86, 161, 165, 173, 175, 182, 186, 202, 205, 221, 302, 310, 334, 365
Smith, Clara, 30–31
Smith, Liz, 222, 224, 242
Smith, Mamie, 30–31
Smith, Mildred, 140
Smith, Trixie, 30
Smollette, Jurnee, 275
Snipes, Wesley, *273*, 275, 331, 344
Snow, Phoebe, 259
Snow, Valaida, 40, 62
Spielberg, Steven, 237, 239–40, 245, 258
Spivey, Victoria, 30–31, 56
Stanton, Dakota, 141
Staples Singers, 203
Starr, Brenda K., 315
Stewart, Amii, 206
Stickney, Phyllis Yvonne, *247*
Sudano, Bruce, 224
Sullivan, Ed, *120*, 124, 169
Sullivan, Maxine, 62–63, 201
Sul-Te-Wan, Madame, 73
Summer, Cree, *257*, 259
Summer, Donna, 14, 19, *176*, *207*, 208, *209*, *222*, 224–25
Supremes, The, *146*, *168*, 169, *170–71*, 180, 186, 231–32, 285–86, 292–94, 300
Sweet Honey in the Rock, 260

T
Taylor, Clarice, 154, 203, 256
Taylor, Elizabeth, 21, 120, 198, 231, 337
Teer, Barbara Ann, 154
Temptations, The, 169, 294
Terrell, Jean, 170
Tharpe, Sister Rosetta, *112*, 113
Thomas, Carla, 166
Thomas, Edna, *38*, 79, 89
Thomas, Rozonda "Chilli," *291*, 292–94
Thomson, Virgil, 158
Thornton, Big Mama Willie Mae, 141
Tierney, Gene, 120
TLC, 288, *291*, 292–94, 312, 332
Toussaint, Lorraine, 349
Truman, Harry S., 111, 140
Turner, Ike, 205, 215, 218, 278

Turner, Tina, 19, 166, *205*, 212, *213*, 214, *215*, 216–19, 223, 225, 232, 235, 255, 269, 278, 322, 362, 365
Twain, Shania, 222
Tyler, Aisha, 349
Tyson, Cicely, 14, 19, 143, 154, 156, 178, *185*, 186, *187–88*, 189, 191, 235, 238, *247*, 248, 277, 280, 322, 365

U
Uggams, Leslie, 140, *145*, 192
Union, Gabrielle, 349
V
Vance, Courtney B., 280
Vanderbilt, Consuelo, 50
Vandross, Luther, 221, 266
Vaughan, Countess, 350
Vaughan, Sarah, 68–69, 113, 141, *142*, *225*, 355
Verrett, Shirley, 158
Vreeland, Diana, 50

W
Walker, Ada Overton, *14*, 22
Walker, Alice, 212, 237, 332
Wallace, Babe, *61*
Wallace, Sippie, 30
Ward, Ada, 40
Ward, Clara, *139*, 143, *173*, 174
Warwick, Dionne, 171, *225*, 266, *268*, 269, 335

Washington, Baby, 166
Washington, Denzel, *274*, 278, 332, *347*, 348, 350, 354
Washington, Dinah, 24, 113, *141*, 143, 173–74, 260
Washington, Fredi, 14, *38*, 40, 44, 56, 60, *72*, 75, *76*, 77, *78*, 79, 80, *81–82*, 83, 88–89, 94, 148, 235, 277
Washington, Isabel, *60*, *76*, 77, *80*, 82–83
Washington, Kerry, 350
Waters, Ethel, 14, *16*, 19, 21, 24, 28, 30–31, 35–36, 40, 46–47, *53*, 54, 56, *58*, 69–70, 74–75, 81, *84–86*, 87, *88*, 89, 92, 100, *114*, 115–17, 128, 145, 148, 151–52, 156, 175, 182, 189, 197, 202, 218, 233, 281, 300, 303, 317, 334, 355, 363, 365
Watkins, Tionne "T-Boz," *291*, 292–94
Webb, Clifton, 86
Webb, Elida, 40, 77
Welch, Elisabeth, 52
Welles, Orson, 79, 127
Wells, Mary, *164*, 167, 169, 293
Whitaker, Forest, 332
White, Jane, 140
White, Karen Malina, 259
White, Persia, 350
White, Slappy, 124, 161
Whitfield, Lynn, 232, *247*, 248, *272*, 275, 278, 326
Whitman, Stuart, *137*

Williams, Billy Dee, 181, *260*
Williams, Camilla, 140
Williams, Cynda, *274*, 275
Williams, Helen, 143
Williams, Herb, *88*
Williams, Kellie Shanygne, 250
Williams, Mary Lou, 24, 63, 113, 201
Williams, Michelle, *358*, 360–61
Williams, Robin, 240, 242
Williams, Vanessa, *249*, 251–52, 326
Wilson, Cassandra, *283*, 284
Wilson, Dooley, 100
Wilson, Edith, 30–31
Wilson, Julie, 134
Wilson, Mary, 169, *170*, 231–32, 293
Winans, Cece, 332
Winfrey, Oprah, 19, 237, *244*, 245–46, *247*, 248, 255, *319*, 320, *321*, 322–23, 334, 342, 348, 350
Woodard, Alfre, *235*, 277, 278
Woodard, Charlaine, 203

Y
Young, Lester, 69, 175
Young, Loretta, 60, 332

Z
Ziegfeld, Florenz, 40, 52, 83

About the Author

Donald Bogle is one of the foremost authorities on African Americans in film and the arts. He is the author of the classic *Toms, Coons, Mulattoes, Mammies, and Bucks: An Interpretive History of Blacks in American Films,* which is published by Continuum. His best-selling *Bright Boulevards, Bold Dreams: The Story of Black Hollywood* received the Hurston/Wright Finalist Legacy Award in Non-fiction. His other books include the critically acclaimed *Dorothy Dandridge: A Biography; Blacks in American Films and Television: An Illustrated Encyclopedia;* and *Primetime Blues: African Americans on Network Television.* He has appeared on such television programs as *Entertainment Tonight; Today; Good Morning, America;* and *Nightline;* and has served as a commentator on such documentaries as Spike Lee's *Jim Brown: All-American,* American Movie Classics Channel's *Small Steps . . . Big Strides,* and TV Land's three-part series on African Americans on television. He also co-hosted Turner Classic Movies' award-winning series *Race and Hollywood.* The first edition of the present book, *Brown Sugar,* covered eighty years of America's black female superstars, and was turned into the highly successful four-part PBS documentary series by Mr. Bogle.